Public Archives of Nova Scotia
Publication No. 4

# LOYALISTS AND LAND SETTLEMENT

IN

# NOVA SCOTIA

A List compiled by
MARION GILROY

Under the direction of
D. C. HARVEY
Archivist

Published by authority of the Board of Trustees of the
Public Archives of Nova Scotia

CLEARFIELD

Originally published
1937

Reprinted for
Clearfield Company, Inc. by
Genealogical Publishing Co., Inc.
Baltimore, Maryland
1990, 1995, 2002

International Standard Book Number: 0-8063-4598-5

*Made in the United States of America*

# PREFACE

THE accompanying list of Loyalists was compiled by Miss Marion Gilroy, M.A., from the land papers in the Public Archives of Nova Scotia and checked with the land papers in the Department of Lands and Forests of the province. The records in the Archives comprise petitions, surveyors' warrants, descriptions and certificates and draft grants; but in few instances are all these papers found complete. This is particularly true of draft grants and for that reason it was necessary to use the files of the Department of Lands and Forests to supplement our sources of information.

The records in the Archives frequently give personal information as to the origin and status of the Loyalists, while the papers in the Department of Lands and Forests are official as to warrants and escheats; but in many instances it has not been possible from both sources to discover more than the name, general location, date of grant and number of acres granted.

Though these names have been compared with those in census returns of Pre-Loyalists and other records, it is not possible to assert that every Loyalist has been located or every Pre-Loyalist eliminated; but the list of Loyalists is as complete and as accurate as it could be made from available material. Broadly speaking, Loyalist grants are assumed to have ceased by 1800 but in a few instances after this date, such as that of the regranting of Digby township in 1801, grants of considerable proportion were made and have been included in this list. No notice has been taken of individual claimants who petitioned during the first quarter of the nineteenth century; and the most diligent search has not been able to discover the names of the second battalion of the 84th Regiment, Royal Highland Emigrants, for which Col. John Small received in trust 105,000 acres in Hants County; but those who were still there in 1816 and received a grant of the lands then occupied by them have been included. Moreover the Island of Cape Breton, because of the lack of available records, has been reserved for a separate study.

The list has been arranged under three headings: grants, warrants and escheats. Those in the first group are shown by the records to have received legal title to the lands specified. Those listed under *warrants* applied for land, and survey of that land was authorized, but no evidence could be found that they completed the transaction, although there is reason to believe that many of them remained in Nova Scotia. Those listed under *escheats*—the legal process by which lands granted were forfeited to the Crown for non-fulfilment of conditions specified in the grant—were included to throw light upon the number of Loyalists who received grants of land and either chose to forfeit them or to accept other grants in exchange.

It should be noted also that there were only nine counties in the peninsula of Nova Scotia at this time, Annapolis, Cumberland, Halifax, Hants, Kings, Lunenburg, Queens, Shelburne and Sydney, the last two having been organized in 1784, after the Loyalists had arrived. Though some grants had been made out before these two counties were marked off and are located in Queens and Halifax they are shown in this list in the new counties of Shelburne and Sydney (Antigonish and Guysborough). No attempt was made to revise the list in accordance with later revisions of the boundaries of Annapolis, Cumberland, Hants and Kings, but the general location of these Loyalists will be sufficiently clear to anyone who has a working knowledge of the geography of Nova Scotia.

The general purpose of this publication is to collect in as compact a form as possible all the information that has survived on Loyalist settlements in Nova Scotia and to make this accessible to the descendants who are interested. No attempt has been made to discuss the merits or demerits of the Loyalists as such; but two petitions, one of which is well-known, have been added as an appendix to show that even in 1783 the Loyalists themselves differed as to character and temper. Appendix B has been inserted because it tells something of the fate of Colonel Small's followers.

D. C. HARVEY.

Halifax, April 10th, 1937.

# CONTENTS

| | Page |
|---|---|
| ANNAPOLIS COUNTY | |
| 1. Grants | 7 |
| 2. Warrants | 26 |
| 3. Escheats | 30 |
| CUMBERLAND COUNTY | |
| 1. Grants | 38 |
| 2. Warrants | 42 |
| HALIFAX COUNTY | |
| 1. Grants | 43 |
| 2. Warrants | 54 |
| 3. Escheats | 55 |
| HANTS COUNTY | |
| 1. Grants | 60 |
| 2. Warrants | 62 |
| 3. Escheats | 62 |
| KINGS COUNTY | |
| 1. Grants | 63 |
| 2. Warrants | 65 |
| 3. Escheats | 65 |
| LUNENBURG COUNTY | |
| 1. Grants | 67 |
| 2. Warrants | 69 |
| 3. Escheats | 69 |
| QUEENS COUNTY | |
| 1. Grants | 72 |
| 2. Warrants | 74 |
| SHELBURNE COUNTY | |
| 1. Grants | 76 |
| 2. Warrants | 106 |
| 3. Escheats | 115 |
| SYDNEY COUNTY | |
| 1. Grants | 119 |
| 2. Warrants | 144 |
| 3. Escheats | 145 |
| APPENDIX A | |
| Petition of the Fifty-five Gentlemen | 146 |
| Counter-Petition of other Loyalists | 147 |
| APPENDIX B | |
| Petition from certain members of the 2d Battalion, 84th Regiment | 153 |

# ABBREVIATIONS

Am. – American.
Anna. – Annapolis

Batt. – Battalion.

Capt. – Captain.
Co. – Company, County.
Corp'l – Corporal.

Dep'y – Deputy.
Dr. – Doctor, Drummer.
Duke Cumb.'s Reg't – Duke of Cumberland's Regiment.

E. – East.

Hlf'x – Halifax.
Har. – Harbour.

Indep. – Independent.

K.C. Rangers – King's Carolina Rangers.

Lieut. – Lieutenant.
Lt.-Col. – Lieutenant-Colonel.

Nav. Offi. – Naval Officer.
N.J. Vol's – New Jersey Volunteers.
N.Y. – New York.
N.C.O. – Non-commissioned Officer.
N. – North.
N.C. Vol's – North Carolina Volunteers.
Not reg'd – This grant is not marked registered.

Reg't – Regiment.
R.I. – Rhode Island.
R. – River.
Rd. – Road.
Rds. – Rods.
R.F. Am. Reg't – Royal Fencible American Regiment.
R.G. Batt. – Royal Garrison Battalion.
R.N. – Royal Navy.
R.N.C. Reg't – Royal North Carolina Regiment.
R. Reg't of Artillery – Royal Regiment of Artillery.

Serj't – Serjeant.
Shel. – Shelburne.
S. – South.
S.C. Reg't – South Carolina Regiment.
St. – Street.

T'n – Town.
T.L. – Town Lot.
Tp. – Township.

W.H.L. – Ware-house Lot.
W.L. – Water Lot.
W. – West.
Wharf L. – Wharf Lot.

## Annapolis County
### (a) GRANTS

| Name | Date | Situation | Acres | Origin or Rank |
|---|---|---|---|---|
| Ackerman, Abraham | 1784 | Wilmot Township | 200 | |
| Ackerson[Akerson]Garret | 1787 | " " | 200 | |
| Adams, Charles | 1784 | Clements " | 100 | |
| Adams, John | 1784 | Wilmot " | 150 | |
| Adams, Philip | 1784 | Clements " | 300 | |
| Addington, William | 1801 | Digby " | 150 | |
| Aikens, James | 1784 | Bryer Island | 100 | |
| Aikins, John | 1801 | Digby Township | 750 | |
| Allair, Peter Alex'r | 1784 | Clements " | 150 | |
| Allaire, Peter Alexander | 1784 | Digby " | 100 | |
| Allen, Robert | 1784 | Wilmot Township | 100 | |
| Amberman, Paul | 1801 | Digby " | 350 | |
| Anderson, Isaac | 1798 | Granville " | 3½ | |
| Anderson, Jonathan | 1784 | Clements " | 350 | |
| Anderson, Jonathan | 1798 | Granville " | 39 | |
| Anderson, Joseph | 1799 | " " | 11½ | |
| Ardell, William | 1784 | Wilmot " | 100 | |
| Armstrong, Francis | 1796 | Digby | T. L. | |
| Armstrong, Francis | 1801 | Digby Township | 419 | |
| Armstrong, William | 1786 | " " | 172 | |
| Armstrong, William | 1801 | " " | 125 | |
| Arnold, Stephen | 1801 | " " | 144 | |
| Astman, Jacob | 1784 | Clements " | 150 | |
| Austen, Stephen | 1784 | " " | 100 | |
| Austin, Benjamin | 1788 | Wilmot " | 100 | |
| Austin, James | 1785 | Digby " | 1 | Negro |
| Aymer, James | 1784 | Clements " | 500 | |
| Babis, John | 1785 | Digby " | 1 | Negro |
| Bailey, Jacob (Rev.) | 1784 | Clements " | 350 | |
| Bailey, Jacob (Rev.) | 1785 | Cape Grant | 200 | |
| Bain [Baine] George | 1801 | Digby Township | 150 | |
| Baker, Christian | 1784 | Clements " | 100 | |
| Baker, Samuel | 1784 | " " | 400 | |
| Balmer, Benedict | 1784 | " " | 300 | |
| Balne, Christopher | 1784 | " " | 100 | |
| Barclay, Thomas | 1784 | Wilmot " | 200 | Major |
| Barclay, Thomas | 1785 | " " | 800 | " |
| Barclay, Thomas | 1797 | " " | 470 | |
| Barclay, Thomas | 1797 | " " | 470 | |
| Barton,—(Heirs) | 1801 | Digby " | 1250 | |
| Barton, Joseph | 1784 | Digby | T. L. | Colonel |
| Barton, Joseph | 1786 | Digby Township | 100 | |
| *Barton, Joseph | 1787 | " " | 800 | Colonel |
| Bartrum, David | 1784 | Wilmot Township | 100 | |
| Baseley, Abraham | 1784 | Digby | T. L. | |
| Basely, James | 1784 | " | T. L. | |
| Bateman, Peter | 1786 | Digby Township | 82 | |
| Bates, James | 1785 | " " | 1 | Negro |
| Bawl, John Adam | 1784 | Clements " | 100 | |
| Baxter,—(Heirs) | 1801 | Digby " | 239 | |
| Baxter, Isaac | 1784 | Wilmot " | 350 | |
| Baxter, Isaac | 1784 | " " | 350 | |
| Baxter, James | 1786 | Digby " | 150 | |
| Baxter, James | 1796 | Annapolis Basin | 20 | |

* In 1834, 329 acres were escheated from heirs.

# PUBLIC ARCHIVES OF NOVA SCOTIA

| Name | Date | Situation | Acres | Origin or Rank |
|---|---|---|---|---|
| Baxter, James | 1801 | Digby Township | 496 | |
| †Bayard, Samuel | 1791 | Hfx-Annapolis Rd.(part possibly in Lunen. Co.) | 640 | |
| Bayeaux, Thomas | 1801 | Digby Township | 345 | |
| Bazely, Abraham | 1784 | Clements " | 200 | |
| Bazely, William | 1784 | " " | 250 | |
| Bean, John | 1784 | Clements Township | 100 | |
| Beardman, Andrew | 1796 | Digby | W. L. | |
| Beardsley, Robinson | 1785 | Wilmot Township | 100 | |
| Beaverhout, Henry | 1785 | Digby " | 1 | Negro |
| Beeman—(Widow) | 1801 | Digby Township | 200 | |
| Beeman, Andrew | 1784 | Digby | T. L. | |
| Beeman, Andrew | 1784 | " | T. L. | |
| Beeman, Joseph | 1801 | Digby Township | 100 | |
| Benjamin, Pompey | 1785 | " " | 1 | Negro |
| Bennett, David | 1784 | Clements " | 100 | |
| Bennett, Isaac | 1784 | " " | 100 | |
| Benson, Christopher | 1784 | " " | 550 | |
| *Benson, Christopher | 1787 | " " | 700 | Capt. N. Y. Rangers |
| Benson, Christopher, Jr. | 1784 | " " | 100 | |
| Benson, Christopher, Jr. | 1787 | " " | 500 | 1st. Lieut. Refugee Co. |
| Benson, William | 1787 | " " | 500 | 2nd. " " " |
| Benson, Yaf | 1785 | Digby " | 1 | Negro |
| Betner, Henry | 1784 | Clements " | 200 | |
| Betner, Henry | 1784 | Digby | T. L. | |
| Betts, Hiram | 1801 | Digby Township | 100 | |
| Bice, Jacob | 1787 | Clements Township | 139 | |
| Bierdman[Beardman] Andrew | 1786 | " " | 100 | |
| Bing, Thomas | 1785 | Digby " | 1 | Negro |
| Bird, Thomas | 1785 | " " | 1 | " |
| Bishoff, George | 1785 | Clements " | 100 | |
| Bishop, John | 1784 | " " | 150 | |
| Bishop, Jonathan | 1784 | Bryer Island | 100 | |
| Bishop, Leverill | 1801 | Digby Township | 292 | |
| Bixon, Demeis | 1785 | " " | 1 | Negro |
| Black, George | 1801 | " " | 200 | |
| Blackford, Martin | 1787 | Sandy Cove | 199 | |
| Blackford (Blashford) Martin | 1801 | Digby Township | 200 | |
| Bloss, Conrad & 2 others | 1784 | Annapolis (Vicinity) | 1000 | |
| Boaker, Andres | 1798 | Granville Township | 4¾ | |
| Bochme (Bochine) Fred. | 1784 | Clements " | 100 | |
| Bogart, Cornelius | 1784 | " " | 400 | |
| Bogart, Cornelius | 1798 | Granville " | 15½ | |
| Bogart, Luke | 1798 | " " | 6½ | |
| Bogart, Thewness | 1798 | " " | 51 | |
| Boggart, Tunis | 1784 | Clements Township | 100 | |
| Bogua, John | 1787 | Digby " | 100 | |
| ⎰Bohaker, Andrew ⎱Bohaker, Daniel ⎱Bohaker, John | 1798 | Granville Township | 82¾ | |
| Boice, Jacob | 1801 | Digby " | 300 | |
| Boltenhouse, Bedford | 1785 | Wilmot " | 100 | |
| Bonnell, Isaac | 1784 | Digby | T. L. | |
| Bonnell, Isaac | 1796 | " | W. L. | |
| Bonnell, Isaac | 1800 | " | W. L. | |
| Bonnell, Isaac | 1801 | Digby Township | 801 | |
| Bothwick, William | 1784 | Clements Township | 100 | |
| Botner, Elisha | 1786 | Digby " | 150 | |
| Botsford, Amos | 1784 | Clements " | 200 | |

† Grant could not be found among the Land Papers in the Dept. of Lands and Forests; but a Council Minute of Oct. 10, 1791, maps and escheats show it was granted.

* 600 acres were escheated in 1827. Benson had been dead since 1805.

# LOYALISTS AND LAND SETTLEMENT IN NOVA SCOTIA 9

| Name | Date | Situation | Acres | Origin or Rank |
|---|---|---|---|---|
| Botsford, Amos | 1784 | Digby | T. L. | |
| Boukler[Brickler]Andrew | 1784 | Clements Township | 300 | |
| Bowdon, Thomas | 1784 | " " | 300 | |
| Bowlsby[Bowlsly]Abram | 1801 | Digby " | 100 | |
| Bowlsby[Bowlsly] Rich'd | 1801 | " " | 400 | |
| Bowly, Charles | 1788 | Wilmot " | 150 | New Jersey |
| Bowly, John | 1788 | " " | 150 | " " |
| Brailey, John | 1784 | Clements " | 100 | |
| Brainsmuid[Brinsmaid] Samuel | 1786 | " " | 100 | |
| Brandon, Conrad | 1784 | Clements Township | 100 | |
| Brannon, Patrick | 1784 | " " | 100 | |
| Bray, James | 1798 | Granville " | 25 | |
| Breher, Jacob | 1784 | Clements " | 100 | |
| Brevart, Elias | 1784 | " " | 100 | |
| Brewen, Henry | 1785 | Digby " | 1 | Negro |
| Brewer, Cornelius | 1785 | " " | 1 | " |
| Brewer, Jacob | 1787 | Sandy Cove | 100 | |
| Brewer, Jacob | 1796 | Digby | T. L. | |
| Brewer, Jacob | 1800 | " | W. L. | |
| Brewer, Jacob | 1801 | Digby Township | 100 | |
| Brinley, Francis | 1784 | River Sisabou | 52 | |
| Brinsmade, Samuel | 1784 | Clements Township | 100 | |
| Brooks, Abram | 1801 | Digby " | 200 | |
| Brown, Charles | 1784 | Clements " | 100 | |
| Brown, Eleanor | 1801 | Digby " | 113 | |
| Brown, James | 1784 | Clements " | 100 | |
| Brown, Samuel | 1784 | " " | 100 | |
| Brudnell, Edward (Rev.) | 1786 | {Petit Passage {St. Mary's Bay, N. | {146 {154 | |
| Brudnell, Edward (Rev.) | 1786 | Digby Township | 110 | |
| Bruen [Brain] Andrew | 1784 | Clements Township | 450 | |
| Bruen, Jacob | 1784 | " " | 100 | |
| Bruen, Jacob | 1784 | " " | 100 | |
| Brumel, Jacob | 1785 | Digby " | 1 | Negro |
| Brundige, Marcus | 1796 | Clements Township | 9 | |
| Buckler, Jacob | 1784 | " " | 300 | |
| Bucks, Edward | 1784 | Wilmot " | 100 | |
| Budd, Betsy | 1801 | Digby " | 250 | (Am. Reg't. |
| Budd, Elisha | 1788 | " " | 200 | Subaltern. King's |
| Budd, Elisha | 1801 | " " | 800 | |
| Budd, Joseph | 1784 | Digby | T. L. | |
| Budd, Joseph | 1786 | Clements Township | 100 | |
| Budd, Tamar | 1801 | Digby " | 250 | |
| Bull, Benjamin | 1784 | Clements " | 100 | |
| Bull, Elizabeth | 1801 | Digby " | 100 | |
| Burket, John | 1796 | Clements " | 54 | |
| Burket, John | 1796 | Digby | T. L. | |
| Burket, John | 1796 | " | W. L. | |
| Burkett, John | 1784 | " | T. L. | |
| Burkett, John | 1789 | Digby Township | 200 | |
| Burkett, John | 1801 | " " | 541 | |
| Burns, John | 1784 | Clements " | 100 | |
| Burns, William | 1801 | Digby " | 200 | |
| Burrell, Josiah | 1787 | Sandy Cove | 100 | |
| Buskirk, Thomas | 1784 | Digby | T. L. | |
| Butler, John | 1784 | Clements Township | 100 | |
| Butler, William | 1784 | " " | 250 | |
| Cagney, John | 1784 | " " | 200 | |
| Caldwell, James | 1784 | " " | 100 | |
| Caldwell, John | 1788 | Long Island, E. | 190 | |
| Callahan,—(Widow) | 1784 | Clements Township | 200 | |
| Callahan, Rebecca | 1786 | Lower Annapolis | 200 | |

| Name | Date | Situation | | Acres | Origin or Rank |
|---|---|---|---|---|---|
| Calner, John | 1784 | Clements Township | | 400 | |
| Calvert, John | 1784 | " | " | 200 | |
| Campbell, John | 1784 | " | " | 100 | |
| Campbell, Malcom | 1784 | " | " | 100 | |
| Campbell, Malcom | 1784 | " | " | 100 | |
| Carter, Frederick | 1785 | Wilmot | " | 100 | |
| Carty, James | 1784 | " | " | 150 | |
| Catern, Henry | 1784 | Clements | " | 100 | |
| Chan, John | 1784 | " | " | 100 | |
| Chandler, John | 1787 | Wilmot | " | 1000 | Massachusetts Bay |
| Chandler, Joshua | 1784 | Clements | " | 300 | |
| Chryst, Jacob | 1785 | Digby | " | 100 | |
| Chryst, Jacob | 1801 | " | " | 200 | |
| Clark,—(Mrs.) | 1784 | Clements | " | 250 | |
| Clark, Scott L. | 1784 | " | " | 150 | |
| Clark, William, Jr. | 1801 | Digby | " | 230 | |
| Clarke, [Carle] Phebee | 1784 | Clements Township | | 100 | |
| Clayton, Joseph | 1785 | Digby | " | 1 | Negro |
| Clayton, Joseph | 1785 | " | " | 5 | |
| Club, James | 1786 | " | " | 94 | |
| Cobas, John | 1785 | " | " | 1 | Negro |
| Cobb, Nicholas | 1786 | " | " | 192 | |
| Coffman, Michael | 1784 | Clements | " | 100 | |
| Colbourn, Charles | 1787 | Digby | " | 300 | |
| Colbourn, Charles | 1801 | " | " | 815 | |
| Colbourne, Charles | 1786 | " | " | 315 | |
| Coleburn, Charles | 1796 | Digby | | T. L. | |
| Colville, John | 1801 | Digby Township | | 160 | |
| Comfort,— | 1784 | Clements | " | 200 | Corporal |
| Commindinger,Lodowick | 1784 | " | " | 350 | |
| Conihane, Francis | 1784 | Digby | | T. L. | |
| Conihane, Francis | 1796 | " | | T. L. | |
| Connelly, Michael | 1784 | Clements Township | | 100 | |
| Conolly, Joseph | 1801 | Digby | " | 200 | |
| Corfet, Charles | 1784 | Clements | " | 200 | |
| Cornwall, George | 1784 | " | " | 400 | |
| Cornwall, George | 1799 | Granville | " | 30 | |
| Cornwall, Jacob | 1801 | Digby | " | 380 | |
| Cornwall, Thomas | 1801 | " | " | 178 | |
| Cosman, James | 1801 | " | " | 500 | |
| Cosman, John | 1784 | River Sisabou, E. | | 200 | |
| Cosman, John | 1801 | Digby Township | | 700 | |
| Cossaboom, David | 1801 | " | " | 278 | |
| Cossaboom, James | 1801 | " | " | 145 | |
| Cossaboom, Samuel | 1801 | " | " | 201 | |
| Cossins, Thomas | 1801 | " | " | 100 | |
| Coughtry, John | 1784 | Clements | " | 250 | |
| Covert, Abraham | 1784 | Wilmot | " | 100 | |
| Covert, John | 1801 | Digby | " | 100 | |
| Covert, John, Jr. | 1801 | " | " | 100 | |
| Covert, William | 1784 | Wilmot | " | 100 | |
| Cox, Thomas | 1784 | Clements | " | 300 | |
| Crabb, Jonathan | 1784 | Bryer Island | | 100 | |
| Craig, James | 1787 | Digby Township | | 50 | |
| Craig, James | 1796 | Digby | | W. L. | |
| Craig, James | 1801 | Digby Township | | 509 | |
| Craige, James | 1795 | " | " | 84 | |
| Craige, John | 1801 | " | " | 100 | |
| Cronck, Joseph | 1801 | " | " | 300 | |
| Croscup, John | 1798 | Granville | " | 22 | |
| Cross, William | 1801 | Digby | " | 100 | |
| Cunningham, Elizabeth | 1801 | " | " | 252 | |
| Cunningham, Thomas | 1784 | Clements | " | 100 | |
| Curley, Lewis | 1785 | Digby | " | 1 | Negro |

LOYALISTS AND LAND SETTLEMENT IN NOVA SCOTIA 11

| Name | Date | Situation | Acres | Origin or Rank |
|---|---|---|---|---|
| Custard, John | 1785 | Digby Township | 1 | Negro |
| Cutler, Ebenezer | 1801 | " " | 1442 | |
| Dakin, Thomas | 1787 | " " | 200 | |
| Dakin, Thomas | 1801 | " " | 216 | |
| Dalher, John | 1784 | Clements " | 100 | |
| Davenport, Thomas | 1784 | " " | 200 | |
| Davenport, Thomas | 1784 | Digby | T. L. | |
| Davids, Hugh | 1784 | Wilmot Township | 500 | Lieutenant |
| Davis, Benjamin | 1785 | Digby " | 1 | Negro |
| Davoue, Frederick | 1784 | Clements " | 400 | |
| Dawkins, Edward | 1786 | Digby " | 128 | |
| DeCoudre, Louis | 1784 | Clements " | 400 | |
| Degan, William | 1784 | Digby | T. L. | |
| DeLancey, Stephen | 1785 | Clements Township | 370 | Lieut.-Colonel |
| DeLancey, Stephen | 1801 | Digby " | 1200 | |
| DeLong, Simon | 1784 | Wilmot " | 100 | |
| Dement, Mary | 1784 | Clements " | 200 | |
| Demerd, Thomas | 1785 | Digby " | 1 | Negro |
| DeMolithe, Christian | 1784 | Clements " | 700 | Captain |
| Denniston, Patrick | 1801 | Digby " | 63 | |
| Denton, Joseph | 1801 | " " | 210 | |
| Depeu, Peter | 1786 | " " | 188 | |
| De St. Croix, Joshua | 1784 | Wilmot Township | 450 | Captain |
| De St. Croix, Thomas | 1784 | " " | 100 | |
| De Coudres—(Heirs) | 1801 | Digby " | 119 | |
| Dewey, Joseph | 1784 | Clements " | 100 | |
| Dickson, Robert | 1784 | Digby | T. L. | |
| *Dickson, Robert | 1791 | Hfx-Annapolis Rd. Part possibly in Lunen. Co. | 640 | |
| Dickson, Robert | 1801 | Digby Township | 400 | |
| Diorisky, Cardell | 1784 | Clements " | 100 | |
| Ditmars, Dowie | 1784 | " " | 200 | Captain |
| Ditmars, Dowie | 1786 | " " | 495 | |
| Ditmars, Dowie, Jr. | 1787 | " " | 120 | |
| Ditmars, Dowie, Sr. | 1787 | " " | 72 | |
| Ditmars, Dowie, 3rd. | 1787 | " " | 128 | |
| Ditmars, John | 1787 | " " | 145 | |
| Ditmars, John | 1801 | Digby " | 500 | |
| Dixon, James | 1787 | Sandy Cove | 50 | |
| Dixon, Jane | 1787 | " " | 50 | |
| Dixon, John | 1787 | " " | 50 | |
| Dixon, Margaret | 1787 | " " | 50 | |
| Dixon, Robert | 1787 | Clements Township | 200 | |
| Dixon,. Walter | 1785 | Digby " | 1 | Negro |
| Dobbs, John | 1784 | Clements " | 550 | |
| Dominick, Francis | 1796 | Digby | W. L. | |
| Donaldson, Samuel | 1784 | " | T. L. | |
| Donaldson, Samuel | 1784 | " | T. L. | |
| Dowling, Dennis | 1801 | Digby Township | 144 | |
| Drake, William | 1801 | " " | 230 | |
| Driskill, Dennis | 1786 | " " | 96 | |
| Duck, Peter | 1801 | " " | 230 | |
| Dunbar, Jabez Woodroffe | 1801 | " " | 167 | |
| Dunbar, Joseph | 1801 | " " | 687 | |
| Dunn, John | 1797 | Wilmot " | 138 | |
| Dunn, Stephen | 1784 | Clements " | 100 | |
| Durling, Daniel | 1784 | Wilmot " | 300 | |
| Durling, Daniel | 1784 | " " | 250 | |
| Durling, Daniel | 1801 | Digby " | 450 | |
| Duryee, John | 1784 | Clements " | 250 | |
| Duryee, Samuel | 1784 | " " | 100 | |

\* Grant could not be found in the Department of Lands and Forests; but a Council Minute of October 10, 1791, escheats and maps show that it was granted.

# PUBLIC ARCHIVES OF NOVA SCOTIA

| Name | Date | Situation | Acres | Origin or Rank |
|---|---|---|---|---|
| Eager,—(Widow) | 1784 | Clements Township | 100 | |
| Eberhard, Christian | 1784 | " " | 100 | |
| Edson [Edison] John | 1801 | Digby " | 500 | |
| Edmun, David | 1785 | " " | 1 | Negro |
| Ellis, Thomas | 1796 | " | W. L. | |
| Engstropp, Peter | 1784 | Clements Township | 100 | |
| Ensenberg, Frederick | 1784 | " " | 150 | |
| Etter,Thos.&Thomson,J. | 1796 | Annapolis Basin | 21 | |
| Ettinger,Lewis & 2 others | 1784 | Annapolis (Vicinity) | 1000 | |
| Ettridge, James | 1784 | Clements Township | 350 | (N. Y. Rangers |
| Ettridge, James | 1787 | " " | 500 | 3rd. Lieut. Indep. Co. |
| Etzner, Nicholas | 1784 | " " | 100 | |
| Euler, Conrad | 1784 | " " | 150 | |
| Evans, Lemuel | 1801 | Digby " | 200 | |
| Everitt, Catherine | 1801 | " " | 100 | |
| Everitt, Jacob | 1784 | Clements " | 150 | |
| Everitt, James | 1801 | Digby " | 262 | |
| Exellious, Ignatius | 1784 | Clements " | 150 | |
| | | | | |
| Fairweather, Benjamin | 1798 | Granville " | 13½ | |
| Fales, Benjamin | 1786 | Wilmot " | 420 | |
| Fales, Benjamin (Heirs) | 1787 | " " | 500 | |
| Fales, Ebenezer | 1786 | " " | 180 | |
| Farmer, Samuel | 1785 | Digby " | 1 | Negro |
| Farrington, Anthony | 1783 | Wilmot " | 5000 | Major |
| Ferguson, Charles | 1801 | Digby " | 100 | |
| Ferret, James | 1784 | Clements " | 100 | |
| Fillis, John | 1785 | Digby " | 1 | Negro |
| | | | | |
| Finder, James | 1786 | Digby Township | 132 | |
| Fink, Barnabas | 1784 | Wilmot " | 350 | |
| Fitzgerald, Daniel | 1801 | Digby " | 119 | |
| Fitzgerald, James | 1801 | " " | 68 | |
| Fitzgerald, William | 1784 | Digby | T. L. | |
| Fitzgerald, William | 1784 | " | T. L. | |
| Fitzgerald, William | 1786 | Digby Township | 100 | |
| Fitzgerald, William | 1801 | " " | 394 | |
| Fitz Randolph, David | 1784 | " " | 250 | |
| Fitz Randolph, Robert | 1784 | Wilmot " | 400 | |
| Fitzrandolph, Robert | 1801 | Digby " | 158 | |
| Flack, John | 1784 | Clements " | 100 | |
| Fleet, James | 1784 | " " | 100 | |
| Fleet, James | 1798 | Granville " | 36 | |
| Florentine, Abraham | 1784 | Clements " | 250 | |
| Florentine, Abraham | 1784 | Digby | T. L. | |
| Florentine, Anna | 1784 | Digby | T. L. | |
| Florentine, Thomas | 1784 | Clements Township | 100 | |
| Floyd, Henry | 1785 | Digby " | 1 | Negro |
| Foreman, James | 1787 | " " | 103 | |
| Fountain, Stephen | 1787 | Sandy Cove | 152½ | |
| Fowler, Gilbert | 1786 | Digby Township | 133 | |
| Fowler, Henry (Heirs) | 1798 | Granville " | 15½ | |
| Fowler, John | 1796 | Digby | W. L. | |
| Fowler, Jonathan | 1784 | Clements Township | 150 | |
| Fowler, Jonathan | 1784 | Digby | T. L. | |
| Fowler, Jonathan | 1786 | Digby Township | 112 | |
| Fowler, Jonathan | 1796 | Annapolis Basin | 19 | |
| Fowler, Jonathan | 1800 | Digby | W. L. | |
| Fowler, Jonathan | 1801 | Digby Township | 735 | |
| Francis, Charles | 1785 | " " | 1 | Negro |
| Fraser, Francis | 1784 | Clements " | 200 | |
| Frazer, Daniel | 1784 | " " | 200 | |
| Freeman, Stephen | 1784 | Digby | T. L. | |
| Freeman, Stephen | 1786 | Digby Township | 100 | |
| Fryer, Samuel | 1785 | " " | 1 | Negro |

## LOYALISTS AND LAND SETTLEMENT IN NOVA SCOTIA 13

| Name | Date | Situation | Acres | Origin or Rank |
|---|---|---|---|---|
| Gallaghart, Andrew | 1784 | Clements Township | 350 | |
| Garnet, Peter | 1784 | " " | 100 | |
| Germain, Hugh | 1801 | Digby " | 178 | |
| Gidney, John | 1801 | " " | 300 | |
| Gidney, Joseph | 1801 | " " | 985 | |
| Giesler, Joseph | 1784 | Clements " | 200 | |
| Gilbert, Perez | 1801 | Digby " | 400 | |
| Gilbert, Thomas | 1787 | " " | 1000 | Colonel |
| Gilbert, Thomas | 1801 | " " | 200 | Major |
| Gilbert, Thomas (Heirs) | 1801 | " " | 1400 | Colonel |
| Gilleland, Joseph | 1801 | " " | 95 | |
| Gillespie, Hugh | 1784 | Clements " | 400 | Sergeant |
| Gimpel, Henrick | 1784 | " " | 100 | |
| Godfrey, Bristen | 1785 | Digby " | 1 | Negro |
| Godfrey, Edward | 1785 | " " | 1 | " |
| Godfrey, John | 1785 | " " | 1 | " |
| Goety, Christian | 1784 | Clements " | 100 | |
| Gorbe, John | 1784 | " " | 400 | |
| Gouger, Edward | 1788 | Wilmot " | 200 | Corp'l. N. Jersey Vol's |
| Gouger, Stephen | 1788 | " " | 250 | " 1st. Batt. N. |
| Grant, David | 1801 | Digby " | 200 | (Jersey Vol's |
| Grant, John | 1801 | " " | 125 | |
| Grant, Sarah (Heirs) | 1801 | " " | 600 | |
| Grant, William | 1784 | Bryer Island | 100 | |
| Gray, William | 1784 | Clements Township | 100 | |
| *Gray, William | 1786 | Halifax-Annapolis Road | 200 | |
| Greiser, August | 1784 | Clements Township | 100 | |
| Griffin, Obadiah | 1801 | Digby Township | 100 | |
| Griffin, Obadiah, Jr. | 1801 | " " | 100 | |
| Griffin, William | 1801 | " " | 46 | |
| Griffin, William | 1801 | Digby Township | 46 | |
| Griffith, Francis | 1785 | " " | 1 | Negro |
| Grigg, John | 1801 | " " | 500 | |
| Groates, Christopher | 1784 | Clements " | 200 | |
| Gunn, George | 1784 | " " | 250 | |
| Gunn, George | 1786 | Bear River | 450 | |
| Gunn, George | 1786 | Digby Township | 100 | |
| Gunnell, Thomas | 1787 | " " | 200 | |
| Haggerty, Patrick | 1784 | Digby | T. L. | |
| Haggerty, Patrick | 1784 | Wilmot Township | 200 | Captain |
| Haggerty, Patrick | 1786 | Digby " | 133 | |
| Haggerty, Patrick | 1788 | " " | 345 | |
| Haggerty, Patrick | 1800 | Digby | W. L. | |
| Haight, Ambose | 1786 | Clements Township | 300 | |
| Haight, Ambrose | 1784 | Digby | T. L. | |
| Hains, Alexander | 1801 | Digby Township | 700 | |
| Hall, John | 1784 | Clements " | 100 | |
| Hall, John | 1788 | Granville " | 500 | |
| Halliburton,—[John] | 1786 | Wilmot " | 1000 | |
| Halls, John | 1784 | Annapolis (Vicinity) | 200 | |
| Halls, Robert | 1784 | " " | 200 | |
| Halstead, Christopher | 1785 | Digby Township | 1 | Negro |
| Ham, Peter | 1784 | Clements " | 100 | |
| Hamilton, Archibald | 1784 | Digby | T. L. | |
| Hamilton, Archibald | 1786 | Digby Township | 100 | |
| Hamilton, Arch. (Heirs) | 1801 | " " | 100 | |
| Hamilton, Archibald | 1801 | " " | 100 | |
| Hamilton, George | 1784 | Clements " | 100 | |
| Hamilton, Henry | 1801 | Digby " | 100 | |
| Hamilton, John | 1801 | " " | 100 | |
| Hammill, Daniel | 1784 | Clements " | 550 | |

* Grant could not be found in Department of Lands and Forests; but escheats and maps show it was granted

# PUBLIC ARCHIVES OF NOVA SCOTIA

| Name | Date | Situation | Acres | Origin or Rank |
|---|---|---|---|---|
| Hanselspiker, William | 1801 | Digby Township | 100 | |
| Hardenbrook, Abel | 1784 | Clements " | 400 | Captain |
| Hardenbrook, Catherine | 1784 | "      " | 250 | |
| Hardenbrook, John | 1784 | "      " | 100 | |
| Hardenbrook, Nicholas A | 1784 | "      " | 100 | |
| Hardy, Elias | 1784 | Cape St. Mary's | 700 | |
| Hare, Thomas | 1786 | Digby Township | 205 | |
| Hare, Thomas (Heirs) | 1796 | Digby | W. L. | |
| Hare, Thomas (Widow) | 1796 | " | W. L. | |
| Harris, Francis | 1787 | Sandy Cove | 100 | |
| Harris, Francis | 1801 | Digby Township | 100 | |
| Harris, Mendart | 1784 | Clements " | 450 | |
| Harrison, Thomas | 1784 | "   .   " | 500 | |
| Harrison, Thomas | 1786 | Digby " | 138 | |
| Hart, Henrick | 1784 | Clements " | 100 | |
| Hartman, Anton | 1784 | "      " | 100 | |
| Hatfield, Isaac | 1786 | Digby " | 100 | |
| Hatfield, Isaac | 1796 | Digby | T. L. | |
| Hatfield, Isaac | 1796 | " | T. L. | |
| Hatfield, Isaac | 1796 | " | W. L. | |
| Hatfield, Isaac | 1801 | Digby Township | 600 | |
| Hatze, Andrew | 1784 | Clements " | 200 | |
| Hayes, John | 1784 | Wilmot " | 100 | |
| Hayes, Joseph | 1784 | "      " | 300 | |
| Heaton, Peter | 1784 | Clements " | 250 | |
| Hecht, Frederick Wm. | 1796 | Digby | T. L. | |
| Height, Ambois | 1796 | " | W. L. | |
| Henderson, Andrew | 1784 | Clements Township | 200 | |
| Henderson, Joseph | 1801 | Digby " | 382 | |
| Hendry, William | 1784 | Clements " | 200 | (Rangers |
| Henning, Thomas | 1787 | "      " | 100 | Indep. Co., of N. Y. |
| Heron, Christian Fred. | 1784 | "      " | 100 | |
| Hertrick, John Conrad | 1784 | "      " | 100 | |
| Hewett, John | 1801 | Digby " | 300 | |
| Hicks, Charles | 1784 | Clements " | 250 | |
| Hicks, John | 1784 | "      " | 400 | |
| Hicks, John | 1784 | Wilmot " | 500 | |
| Hicks, Thomas | 1797 | "      " | 300 | |
| Hicks, Thomas | 1797 | "      " | 334 | |
| Higgins, Joseph | 1784 | Clements Township | 100 | |
| Hill, John | 1784 | Digby | T. L. | |
| Hill, John | 1784 | " | W. L. | |
| Hill, John | 1796 | " | W. L. | |
| Hill, John | 1800 | " | W. L. | |
| Hill, John | 1801 | Digby Township | 188 | |
| Hill, Richard | 1786 | "      " | 100 | |
| Hill, Richard | 1796 | Digby | W. L. | |
| Hill, Richard | 1801 | Digby Township | 280 | |
| Hill, Robert | 1801 | "      " | 60 | |
| Hilliard, Gersham | 1784 | Digby | T. L. | |
| Hines, Richard | 1801 | Digby Township | 100 | |
| Hinxman, Charles | 1801 | "      " | 67 | |
| Hisenbrook, Andrew | 1784 | Clements " | 100 | |
| Hislop, William | 1786 | Digby " | 44 | |
| Hitchcock, John | 1786 | "      " | 184 | |
| Hitchcock, Samuel | 1787 | "      " | 200 | |
| Hockenhull, John | 1801 | "      " | 119 | |
| Hodger, John | 1788 | Long Island, E. | 100 | |
| Hoffmann, Jacob | 1784 | Wilmot Township | 300 | |
| Holdsworth, James | 1796 | Digby | T. L. | |
| Holdsworth, James A. | 1796 | Annapolis Basin | 12 | |
| Holdsworth, James A. | 1796 | Digby | W. L. | |
| Holdsworth, James A. | 1801 | Digby Township | 1294 | |
| Holdsworth, James H. | 1784 | Clements " | 100 | |

LOYALISTS AND LAND SETTLEMENT IN NOVA SCOTIA 15

| Name | Date | Situation | Acres | Origin or Rank |
|---|---|---|---|---|
| Holdsworth, James H. | 1784 | Digby | T. L. | |
| Holdsworth, John | 1796 | " | W. L. | |
| Holdsworth, John | 1800 | " | W. L. | |
| Holdsworth, John | 1801 | Digby Township | 400 | |
| Holdsworth, Thomas | 1784 | Digby | T. L. | |
| Holland, John | 1785 | Digby Township | 1 | Negro |
| Holland, William | 1784 | Clements " | 100 | |
| Hollingshead, George | 1801 | Digby " | 200 | |
| Hollinshead, George | 1788 | " " | 100 | |
| Holmes, Cornelius | 1784 | Clements " | 250 | |
| Holmes, Joel | 1786 | Digby " | 185 | |
| Hornoesser, Andreas | 1784 | Clements " | 100 | |
| Houseman, John | 1784 | Digby | T. L. | |
| Hovey, John | 1784 | Clements Township | 100 | |
| Hoyt, Jesse | 1784 | River Sisabou, E. | 200 | |
| Hoyt, Jesse | 1801 | Digby Township | 300 | |
| Huggeford, Peter | 1784 | Cape St. Mary's | 700 | |
| Huggeford, Thomas | 1784 | Bryer Island | 500 | Major |
| Huggeford, Thomas | 1784 | Digby | T. L. | |
| Huggeford, Thomas | 1801 | Digby Township | 100 | |
| Hughston, James | 1801 | " " | 600 | |
| Huntly, Joshua | 1784 | Bryer Island | 100 | |
| Hupenden, Philip | 1784 | Clements Township | 200 | |
| Hustead, Jonathan | 1784 | " " | 150 | |
| Hutchins, James | 1784 | " " | 100 | |
| Hutchinson, Francis | 1785 | Wilmot " | 100 | |
| Hutchinson, Margaret | 1785 | " " | 100 | |
| Hutchinson, Margaret, Jr | 1785 | " " | 100 | |
| Hutchinson, Nancy | 1785 | " " | 100 | |
| Hutchinson, Thomas | 1801 | Digby " | 200 | |
| Hutson, William | 1784 | Clements " | 200 | |
| Irvin, James | 1786 | Digby " | 168 | |
| Irwin, John | 1785 | " " | 1 | Negro |
| Irwin, Thomas | 1784 | Digby | T. L. | |
| Ivereau, Joshua | 1784 | Clements Township | 300 | |
| Jackson, James | 1785 | Digby " | 1 | Negro |
| Jacob, John | 1784 | Clements " | 100 | |
| James, Benjamin | 1784 | " " | 1000 | |
| James, Francis | 1784 | Digby | T. L. | |
| James, Francis | 1784 | " | T. L. | |
| James, Robert | 1785 | Digby Township | 1 | Negro |
| Jeger, John | 1784 | Clements " | 150 | |
| Jeroleman, Jacob | 1788 | Digby " | 300 | |
| Jingo, John | 1785 | " " | 1 | Negro |
| John, Peter | 1801 | " " | 310 | |
| Johnson (Johnston), Martin | 1801 | " " | 300 | |
| Johnson, Peter | 1784 | Wilmot " | 100 | |
| Johnston, Robert | 1785 | Digby " | 1 | Negro |
| Johnstone, Adam | 1784 | Clements Township | 100 | |
| Jones, Benjamin | 1801 | Digby " | 200 | |
| Jones, Cereno M. | 1801 | " " | 562 | |
| Jones, Edward | 1787 | Clements " | 90 | |
| Jones, Elisha | 1784 | Digby " | 100 | |
| Jones, James | 1789 | " " | 250 | |
| Jones, James | 1796 | Digby | T. L. | |
| Jones, James | 1801 | Digby Township | 250 | |
| Jones, John | 1787 | Sandy Cove | 100 | |
| Jones, Josiah | 1801 | Digby Township | 950 | |
| Jones, Mechitabel | 1784 | River Sisabou, E. | 200 | |
| Jones, Nathaniel | 1801 | Digby Township | 200 | |
| Jones, Phineas | 1784 | River Sisabou, E. | 200 | |

| Name | Date | Situation | Acres | Orign or Rank |
|---|---|---|---|---|
| Jones, Simeon | 1784 | Digby Township | 100 | |
| Jones, Simeon | 1801 | " | 625 | |
| Jones, Stephen | 1784 | River Sisabou, E. | 200 | |
| Jones, Stephen | 1801 | Digby Township | 700 | |
| Jones, Stephen, 2nd. | 1801 | " | 200 | |
| Jones, William | 1787 | Clements " | 55 | |
| Jordan, John | 1785 | Digby " | 1 | Negro |
| Jordan, Miles | 1785 | " " | 1 | " |
| Jordan, Mungo | 1785 | " " | 1 | " |
| Journay, John | 1784 | " " | 200 | |
| Jugler, Frants | 1784 | Clements " | 100 | |
| | | | | |
| Kam, John | 1784 | " " | 550 | |
| Kearin, Terence | 1786 | Digby " | 100 | |
| Keating, Garret | 1784 | Wilmot " | 100 | |
| Keen, Jesse | 1796 | Digby | T. L. | |
| Keen, Jesse | 1796 | " | W. L. | |
| Keene, Jesse | 1786 | Digby Township | 137 | |
| Keine, Jesse | 1801 | " " | 367 | |
| Kelly, John | 1784 | Clements " | 100 | |
| Kelly, Mathias | 1801 | Digby " | 100 | |
| Kenning, Thomas | 1784 | Clements " | 200 | |
| Kerin, Terence | 1784 | " " | 400 | |
| Kerin, Terence | 1787 | Digby " | 415 | |
| Kerm, Nicholaus | 1784 | Clements " | 150 | |
| Kerr, William | 1787 | Sandy Cove | 54 | |
| Kerr, William | 1801 | Digby Township | 50 | |
| Ketchum, Jehiel | 1801 | " " | 300 | |
| Kidston, James | 1796 | Digby | T. L. | |
| King, George | 1784 | Wilmot Township | 200 | |
| Kip, Thomas | 1786 | Digby " | 132 | |
| Klahold, Casper | 1784 | Clements " | 100 | |
| Klapper, Jacob | 1784 | " " | 100 | |
| Klingsocher, Christian | 1784 | " " | 200 | |
| Klingsocher, Julices | 1784 | " " | 400 | |
| Knipchild, Henry | 1786 | Digby " | 285 | |
| Knischild, Henry | 1784 | Clements " | 350 | |
| Kopp, George Keirn | 1784 | " " | 100 | |
| Krait [Krair] George | 1784 | " " | 100 | |
| Kuhn, John | 1784 | " " | 100 | |
| Kysh, Anthony Geo. | 1784 | Digby | T. L. | |
| Kysh, Anthony George | 1788 | Long Island, E. | 100 | |
| | | | | |
| Lamb, Owen | 1784 | Clements Township | 100 | |
| Lamb, Peter | 1784 | " " | 100 | |
| Lambertson, John | 1801 | Digby " | 162 | |
| Lambertson, Tunis | 1801 | " " | 146 | |
| Lawrence, Benjamin | 1796 | Digby | T. L. | |
| Lawrence, Benjamin | 1796 | " | W. L. | |
| Lawrence, Benjamin | 1801 | Digby Township | 270 | |
| Lawrence, John | 1784 | Clements " | 200 | |
| Lawson, John | 1784 | " " | 100 | |
| Lawson, John | 1786 | Digby " | 132 | |
| Lawson, John . | 1801 | " " | 125 | |
| Lee, John | 1784 | Clements " | 200 | (Rangers |
| Lee, John | 1787 | " " | 100 | Indep. Co. N. Y. |
| Lent, Abraham | 1784 | " " | 100 | |
| Leonard, Daniel | 1786 | Digby Township | 201 | |
| Leonard, James | 1786 | " " | 148 | |
| Leonard, Joseph | 1785 | " " | 1 | Negro |
| Leonard, Robert | 1786 | " " | 142 | |
| Leonard, Robert | 1796 | Digby | W. L. | |
| Leonard, Robert | 1800 | " . | W. L. | |
| LeRoy, Francis P. | 1801 | Digby Township | 294 | |

# LOYALISTS AND LAND SETTLEMENT IN NOVA SCOTIA 17

| Name | Date | Situation | Acres | Origin or Rank |
|---|---|---|---|---|
| Leslie, Abraham | 1785 | Digby Township | 1 | Negro |
| Lewis, John | 1796 | Digby | W. L. | |
| Lewis, Thomas | 1801 | Digby Township | 200 | |
| Lideker, Thomas | 1785 | " " | 1 | Negro |
| Lincoln, Michael | 1784 | Bryer Island | 100 | |
| Littany, William H. | 1801 | Digby Township | 150 | |
| Liverpole, James | 1785 | " " | 1 | Negro |
| Livesay, Ebenezer | 1784 | Clements " | 100 | |
| Logree, Liberty | 1785 | Digby " | 1 | Negro |
| Long, Alexander | 1784 | Clements " | 100 | |
| Long, Alexander | 1786 | Digby " | 150 | |
| Long, Alexander | 1801 | " " | 144 | |
| Long, Peter | 1787 | " " | 200 | |
| Long, Peter | 1801 | " " | 70 | |
| Longworth, Isaac | 1786 | " " | 150 | |
| Longworth, Isaac | 1796 | Digby | T. L. | |
| Longworth, Isaac | 1801 | Digby Township | 200 | |
| Loutitt, William | 1784 | Bryer Island | 100 | |
| Lowe, John | 1801 | Digby Township | 462 | |
| Lowe, William | 1801 | " " | 421 | |
| Lower,—see Sower | 1784 | | | |
| Lower, George | 1784 | Clements " | 100 | |
| Lownds, James | 1784 | " " | 250 | |
| Lownds, James, Jr. | 1784 | " " | 100 | |
| Lownds, Matthew | 1784 | " " | 100 | |
| Lownds, Thomas | 1784 | " " | 100 | |
| Loyal, James | 1784 | " " | 100 | |
| McAllister, David | 1784 | " " | 100 | |
| McAslin, Dougald | ·1789 | Digby " | 200 | |
| McChean, James | 1786 | " " | 220 | |
| McCollough, Allan | 1784 | Clements " | 100 | |
| McConnell, Benj'n | 1801 | Digby " | 825 | |
| McDonald, David | 1784 | Clements " | 100 | |
| MacDonald, William | 1786 | Digby " | 156 | |
| McDonald, William | 1801 | " " | 135 | |
| McDougal, John | 1787 | " " | 96 | |
| McDougald, Duncan | 1786 | Clements " | 125 | |
| McFarrin, James | 1784 | " " | 150 | |
| McGregor, Alexander | 1784 | " " | 100 | |
| McGrigor, Alexander | 1788 | Long Island, E. | 66 | |
| McGuire, John | 1784 | Clements Township | 100 | |
| McIntire, James | 1788 | Long Island | 95 | |
| McKay, John | 1788 | Long Island, E. | 71 | |
| McKenzie, Alexander | 1784 | Wilmot Township | 150 | |
| McKoun, John | 1784 | River Sisabou, E. | 200 | |
| McLaron, Neil | 1784 | Clements Township | 100 | |
| McMaster, John | 1784 | Wilmot " | 150 | |
| McMullen, Peter | 1796 | Digby | T. L. | |
| McMullen, Peter | 1796 | " | W. L. | |
| McMullen, Peter | 1801 | Digby Township | 400 | |
| McNamara, John | 1786 | Lower Annapolis | 100 | |
| McNaughton, Alexander and 2 others | 1784 | Annapolis (Vicinity) | 1000 | |
| McNeil, John | 1795 | Wilmot Township | 400 | |
| McNeil, Neil | 1784 | Digby | T. L. | |
| McNemara, John | 1784 | Clements Township | 100 | |
| McNight, William | 1785 | Digby " | 1 | Negro |
| McQuean, John | 1786 | " " | 164 | |
| Majoribanks, Thomas | 1801 | " " | 150 | |
| Martin, Joseph | 1785 | " " | 1 | Negro |
| Marvin, Joseph | 1786 | " " | 194 | |
| Mathews, David | 1784 | Cape St. Mary's | 700 | |
| May, Elias | 1784 | Wilmot Township | 100 | |

## PUBLIC ARCHIVES OF NOVA SCOTIA

| Name | Date | Situation | Acres | Origin or Rank |
|---|---|---|---|---|
| Mead, Isaac | 1785 | Digby Township | 1 | Negro |
| Mead, Jonas | 1796 | Digby | T. L. | |
| Mead, Jonas | 1801 | Digby Township | 200 | |
| Mear, William | 1796 | Digby | T. L. | |
| Megher [Magher] James | 1801 | Digby Township | 200 | |
| Melvin, Michael | 1784 | Clements " | 100 | |
| Merrit, Nehemiah | 1799 | Digby | 14½ | |
| Messelre, Frederick | 1784 | Clements Township | 150 | |
| Middleton, Henry | 1785 | Digby " | 1 | Negro |
| Middleton, William | 1784 | Clements " | 100 | |
| Migman [Myman] Chris. | 1784 | " " | 100 | |
| Miller, Abraham | 1801 | Digby " | 100 | |
| Miller, Peter | 1784 | Clements " | 100 | |
| Miller, Thomas | 1784 | Cape St. Mary's | 700 | (N. J. Vol's |
| Millidge, Phineas | 1785 | Digby Township | 200 | Ensign. 1st. Batt. |
| Millidge, Phineas | 1797 | Wilmot " | 300 | " N. J. Vol's |
| Millidge, Phineas | 1797 | " " | 300 | |
| Millidge, Phineas | 1801 | Digby " | 200 | |
| Millidge, Thomas | 1784 | Wilmot " | 500 | Major |
| Millidge, Thomas | 1788 | Digby " | 245 | |
| Millidge, Thomas | 1801 | " " | 400 | Major |
| Mills, Hope | 1801 | " " | 400 | |
| Mitchell,— | 1784 | Clements " | 200 | Sergeant |
| Mitchell, Henry | 1785 | Digby " | 1 | Negro |
| Monro, Alexander | 1788 | Long Island | 183 | |
| Montgomery, Joseph | 1784 | Clements Township | 300 | |
| Moody, James | 1801 | Digby " | 2258 | |
| Moody, John | 1801 | " " | 500 | |
| Moore, Jeremiah | 1801 | " " | 200 | |
| Moore, Samuel | 1784 | Wilmot " | 550 | |
| Moore, Samuel | 1797 | " " | 198 | |
| Moore, Samuel | 1797 | " " | 198 | |
| Moore, William | 1801 | Digby " | 200 | |
| More, John | 1801 | " " | 121 | |
| Morehous, John | 1784 | Clements " | 200 | |
| Morehouse, James | 1787 | Digby " | 200 | |
| Morehouse, John | 1787 | Sandy Cove | 263 | |
| Morehouse, John | 1801 | Digby Township | 130 | |
| Morehouse, Jonathan | 1801 | " " | 330 | |
| Morford, John | 1801 | " " | 200 | |
| Morford, Margaret, see Stennigar, Jane and Morford, M. | 1801 | | | |
| Morrison, John | 1784 | Clements " | 250 | |
| Morrison, Samuel | 1785 | Digby " | 1 | Negro |
| *Muir, William | 1786 | Halifax-Annapolis Road | 200 | |
| Muir William | 1801 | Digby Township | 250 | |
| Munro, George | 1784 | Clements " | 100 | |
| Mussels, William | 1784 | Bryer Island | 300 | |
| Mussels, William | 1784 | Digby | T. L. | |
| Mussels, William | 1801 | Digby Township | 250 | |
| Myers, John | 1784 | Clements " | 100 | |
| Nelis, Benjamin | 1785 | Digby " | 1 | Negro |
| Nichols, David | 1788 | Wilmot " | 108 | |
| Nichols, George | 1788 | " " | 108 | |
| Nichollas, John | 1801 | Digby " | 200 | |
| Northrop[Northup]Josh. | 1801 | " " | 200 | |
| Northup, Joseph | 1784 | " " | 100 | |
| Northup, Joshua | 1784 | " " | 100 | |
| Nugent, Michael | 1784 | Clements " | 200 | |
| Nugent, Michael | 1786 | Digby " | 214 | |

\* Grant not shown in Department of Lands and Forests; but maps and escheats show it was granted.

LOYALISTS AND LAND SETTLEMENT IN NOVA SCOTIA 19

| Name | Date | Situation | Acres | Origin or Rank |
|---|---|---|---|---|
| Oakes, Jessee | 1801 | Digby Township | 270 | |
| Oakes, Phineas | 1801 | " " | 100 | |
| Oaks, Jesse | 1784 | St. Mary's Bay, S. | 500 | |
| Odell, Daniel | 1796 | Clements Township | 24 | |
| Offeny, William | 1784 | " " | 150 | |
| Orchard, George | 1784 | " " | 100 | |
| Outhaus, Nicholas | 1788 | Long Island, E. | 167 | |
| Outhaus,[Cuthaus],Rob't | 1788 | " " " | 112 | |
| Outhit, Thomas | 1785 | Wilmot Township | 200 | |
| Owing, Francis | 1784 | Clements " | 150 | |
| | | | | |
| Parks, James | 1788 | Wilmot Township | 100 | |
| Parr, John | 1784 | Clements " | 200 | |
| Patterson, Alexander | 1786 | Digby " | 174 | |
| Patterson, Alexander | 1801 | " " | 144 | |
| Paul, John | 1786 | " " | 118 | |
| Peak, James, Jr. | 1784 | Clements " | 100 | |
| Peak, Samuel | 1784 | " " | 300 | |
| Pemberton, Jeremiah | 1784 | Wilmot " | 500 | Lieutenant |
| Pemberton, Sarah | 1784 | " " | 100 | |
| Perreau, Peter D. | 1784 | Clements " | 200 | |
| Peters, Maurice | 1787 | Sandy Cove | 250 | |
| Peters, Thomas | 1785 | Digby Township | 1 | Negro |
| Pfitzer, Michael | 1784 | Clements " | 100 | |
| Phillips, Martha | 1787 | Wilmot " | 500 | (er H.M. Navy |
| Phipps, David | 1783 | " " | 5000 | Master and Command- |
| Pickell, Casper | 1784 | Clements " | 150 | |
| Pickup, Samuel | 1784 | " " | 200 | |
| Pickup, Samuel | 1786 | " " | 300 | |
| Polhamus, John | 1784 | " " | 450 | |
| Pope, Thomas | 1784 | " " | 200 | |
| Pope, Thomas | 1786 | Bear River | 166 | |
| Porteous, John | 1784 | Clements Township | 200 | |
| Porteous, John | 1786 | Bear River | 325 | |
| Post, David | 1801 | Digby Township | 294 | |
| Post, Gilbert | 1787 | " " | 70 | |
| Post, Gilbert | 1789 | " " | 69 | |
| Post, Gilbert | 1801 | " " | 400 | |
| Potter, Joseph | 1784 | Clements " | 500 | |
| Prettyman, John | 1785 | Wilmot " | 100 | |
| Prince, John | 1785 | Digby " | 1 | Negro |
| Pritchard, Gaius | 1801 | " " | 200 | |
| Pundt, Catherine | 1786 | " " | 95 | |
| Purdy, Anthony | 1784 | Clements " | 300 | |
| Purdy, Daniel | 1801 | Digby " | 200 | |
| Purdy, Gabriel | 1786 | Clements " | 334 | |
| Purdy, Gabriel | 1787 | " " | 334 | |
| Purdy, Gilbert | 1784 | " " | 400 | |
| Purdy, Joseph | 1801 | Digby " | 400 | |
| Purdy, Josiah | 1784 | Clements " | 100 | |
| Purdy, Nathaniel | 1801 | Digby " | 200 | |
| Pye, Roger | 1784 | Bryer Island | 300 | Captain |
| Pyne, Daniel | 1788 | Digby Township | 111 | |
| | | | | |
| Quereau, John | 1798 | Granville " | 21 | |
| | | | | |
| Ramsay, James | 1784 | Wilmot " | 300 | |
| Rapalje, J— | 1784 | Clements " | 100 | |
| Rappelly, Daniel | 1787 | " " | 35 | |
| Rappelly, John | 1787 | " " | 68 | |
| Ray, Robert | 1784 | Digby | T. L. | |
| Ray, Robert | 1784 | " | T. L. | |
| Ray, Robert | 1785 | " | W. L. | |
| Ray, Robert | 1786 | Digby Township | 154 | |

# PUBLIC ARCHIVES OF NOVA SCOTIA

| Name | Date | Situation | Acres | Origin or Rank |
|---|---|---|---|---|
| Ray, Robert | 1796 | Digby | T. L. | |
| Ray, Robert | 1796 | " | W. L. | |
| Ray, Robert | 1801 | Digby Township | 200 | |
| Raymond, Simeon | 1787 | Sandy Cove | 492 | |
| Reddick, Henry | 1785 | Digby Township | 1 | Negro |
| Reed, James | 1788 | " | 400 | |
| Reid, James | 1784 | Digby | T. L. | |
| Reid, James | 1796 | " | W. L. | |
| Reid (Read) James | 1801 | Digby Township | 665 | |
| *Reid, John | 1791 | Hfx-Annapolis Rd. (May be partly in Lunen. Co.) | 640 | |
| Remsen, Isaac | 1784 | Clements Township | 100 | |
| Remson, Jacob, see Remson, John | 1787 | | | |
| Remson, Johannes | 1801 | Digby " | 100 | |
| Remson, John and Remson, Jacob | 1787 | Clements Township | 244 | |
| Remson, Rem | 1801 | Digby " | 400 | |
| Rhinedollar, Emanuel | 1784 | Digby | T. L. | |
| Rhoades, Abraham | 1784 | Clements Township | 100 | |
| Rice, Ashbill | 1801 | Digby " | 250 | |
| Richards, Charles | 1787 | " " | 200 | |
| Ritchie, Andrew, Jr. | 1801 | " " | 100 | |
| Ritchie, James | 1786 | Clements " | 100 | |
| Ritchie, John | 1801 | Digby " | 100 | |
| Ritchie, Mathew | 1786 | Clements " | 100 | |
| Ritchie, Thomas | 1801 | Digby " | 166 | |
| Roberts, Francis | 1785 | " " | 1 | Negro |
| Robertson, John | 1784 | Annapolis (Vicinity) | 400 | |
| Robertson, Robert | 1796 | Digby | T. L. | |
| Robertson, William | 1784 | " | T. L. | |
| Robertson, William | 1801 | Digby Township | 275 | |
| Robinson, Beverley | 1784 | Wilmot " | 300 | Lieut.-Colonel |
| Robinson, Beverley | 1785 | " " | 700 | " " |
| Robinson, James | 1801 | Digby " | 90 | |
| Robinson, John | 1784 | Annapolis (Vicinity) | 200 | |
| Robinson, John | 1801 | Digby Township | 162 | |
| Robinson, Robert | 1784 | Wilmot " | 500 | Lieutenant |
| Robinson, Robert | 1787 | " " | 400 | |
| Robinson, Robert | 1801 | Digby " | 114 | |
| Roblee, Thomas | 1784 | Clements " | 300 | |
| Rockling, Philip | 1784 | " " | 100 | |
| Rollo,— | 1784 | " " | 250 | Captain |
| Rollo, Robert | 1801 | Digby " | 350 | |
| Rome (Roome) John | 1788 | " " | 150 | |
| Roop, Isaac | 1787 | " " | 64 | |
| Roop, Jacob | 1787 | " " | 200 | |
| Roop, John | 1787 | " " | 187 | |
| Roop, John | 1801 | " " | 100 | |
| Rope, Christian | 1784 | Wilmot " | 150 | |
| Rosenerantz, Johann | 1784 | C.ements " | 100 | |
| Ross, Alexander | 1784 | " " | 150 | |
| Ross, Alexander | 1788 | Long Island, E | 70 | |
| Ross, Isabella | 1801 | Digby Township | 100 | |
| Ross, John | 1784 | Bryer Island | 150 | |
| Roup, Isaac | 1784 | Digby | T. L. | |
| Roup, Isaac | 1788 | Digby Township | 200 | |
| Roup, Isaac | 1796 | Digby | W. L. | |
| Rowe, John P. | 1784 | " | T. L. | |
| Rowe, John Peter | 1796 | " | W. L. | |
| Rowe, John Peter | 1801 | Digby Township | 400 | |
| Rubee, John | 1784 | Clements " | 100 | |

\* Grant not shown in Department of Lands and Forests; but a Council Minute, October 10, 1791, maps and escheats show it was granted.

# LOYALISTS AND LAND SETTLEMENT IN NOVA SCOTIA 21

| Name | Date | Situation | Acres | Origin or Rank |
|---|---|---|---|---|
| Ruen, Ischs | 1784 | Clements Township | 100 | |
| Ruggles, John | 1785 | Wilmot " | 800 | |
| Ruggles, Joseph | 1797 | "      " | 454 | |
| Ruggles, Joseph | 1797 | "      " | 454 | |
| Ruggles, Richard | 1785 | "      " | 800 | |
| Ruggles, Timothy | 1784 | "      " | 1000 | General |
| Ruscall, James | 1784 | Clements " | 100 | |
| Rutherford, Henry | 1784 | Digby | | T. L. |
| Rutherford, Henry | 1786 | Digby Township | 92 | |
| Rutherford, Henry | 1796 | Digby | | T. L. |
| Rutherford, Henry | 1800 | " | | W. L. |
| Rutherford, Henry | 1801 | Digby Township | 2782 | |
| Ryerson, Francis | 1784 | Clements " | 250 | |
| Ryerson, Francis, Jr. | 1784 | "      " | 100 | |
| Ryerson, George | 1784 | "      " | 150 | |
| Ryerson, John F. | 1784 | "      " | 200 | |
| Ryerson, Mott | 1784 | "      " | 100 | |
| | | | | |
| Salvage, John | 1784 | "      " | 100 | |
| Sampson, John | 1785 | Digby " | 1 | Negro |
| Saunders, Abraham | 1785 | "      " | 1 | " |
| Saxton, George | 1801 | "      " | 200 | |
| Saxton, John | 1801 | "      " | 300 | |
| Scarbury, George | 1785 | "      " | 1 | Negro |
| Scarbury, William | 1785 | "      " | 1 | " |
| Schade, Johannes | 1784 | Clements Township | 150 | |
| Scheiber, Andreas | 1784 | "      " | 100 | |
| Schlagbaum, Frant | 1784 | "      " | 100 | |
| Schlauderbeck, Michael | 1784 | "      " | 150 | |
| Schmid, James | 1788 | Long Island | 200 | |
| Schmild, Gottlieb | 1784 | Clements Township | 100 | |
| Schooner, John | 1785 | Digby " | 1 | Negro |
| Schufer, Casper | 1784 | Clements " | 100 | |
| Schultze, Gottlieb | 1784 | "      " | 100 | |
| Scok, Frederick | 1784 | "      " | 100 | |
| Seaban [Seaman] Benj. | 1801 | Digby " | 125 | |
| Seaban, Jeremiah | 1801 | "      " | 325 | |
| Seaban, Willoughby | 1801 | "      " | 125 | |
| Seabury, David | 1801 | "      " | 284 | |
| Seaman, Thomas | 1786 | Clements " | 100 | |
| Seidler, Andreas | 1784 | "      " | 200 | |
| Shaver, Detman | 1784 | "      " | 150 | |
| Shaw, Moses | 1799 | Granville " | 34½ | |
| Shephard, John | 1785 | Digby " | 1 | Negro |
| Shephard, York | 1785 | "      " | 1 | " |
| Shook, David | 1801 | "      " | 125 | |
| Shriver, George | 1787 | "      " | 200 | |
| Shuter, Niles | 1784 | Clements " | 100 | |
| Sibly, David | 1801 | Digby " | 100 | |
| Simpson, Agnes | 1801 | "      " | 100 | |
| Sinclair, Arthur | 1801 | "      " | 100 | |
| Sizeland, Solomon | 1786 | "      " | 231 | |
| Sizely, Solomon | 1796 | Digby | | T. L. |
| Skenhauser, Frant Anton | 1784 | Clements Township | 100 | (Land Forces. |
| Skinner, John | 1783 | Wilmot " | 3000 | Reduced Capt. H.M. |
| Slocum [Slocombe] John | 1801 | Digby " | 310 | |
| Slocumb, John | 1784 | Wilmot " | 300 | |
| Slocumb, Jonathan | 1784 | "      " | 200 | |
| Small, J. Christian | 1801 | Digby " | 240 | |
| Small, John Christian | 1796 | Digby | | T. L. |
| Smith, Austin | 1784 | Wilmot Township | 100 | |
| Smith, Austin | 1784 | "      " | 300 | |
| Smith, Jacob | 1801 | Digby " | 230 | |
| Smith, James | 1784 | Clements " | 100 | |

| Name | Date | Situation | Acres | Origin or Rank |
|---|---|---|---|---|
| Smith, James | 1784 | Clements Township | 100 | |
| Smith, James | 1784 | Wilmot " | 200 | |
| Smith, James | 1784 | " " | 300 | |
| Smith, James C. | 1784 | Digby | T. L. | |
| Smith, Jasper | 1801 | Digby Township | 100 | |
| Smith, Jeremiah | 1784 | Clements " | 200 | |
| Smith, John | 1784 | " " | 400 | |
| Smith, John | 1784 | Wilmot " | 500 | |
| Smith, John (Heirs) | 1796 | Digby | W. L. | |
| Smith, Jonathan | 1787 | Wilmot Township | 100 | |
| Smith, Joseph | 1784 | Clements " | 350 | |
| Smith, Joseph and Warwick, John | 1796 | Annapolis Basin | 30 | |
| Smith, Joseph | 1796 | Digby | T. L. | |
| Smith, Joshua | 1784 | Clements Township | 200 | |
| Smith, Joshua | 1796 | Digby | T. L. | |
| Smith, Joshua | 1796 | " | W. L. | |
| Smith, Joshua | 1801 | Digby Township | 523 | |
| Smith, Peter | 1784 | Clements " | 200 | |
| Smith, Samuel | 1784 | Wilmot " | 300 | |
| Sneeden, Stephen | 1801 | Digby " | 450 | |
| Snieder, Thomas | 1784 | Clements " | 100 | |
| Snodgrass, Andrew | 1784 | Digby | T. L. | |
| Snodgrass, Andrew | 1786 | Digby Township | 122 | |
| Snodgrass, Andrew | 1801 | " " | 320 | |
| Snodgrass, Eunice | 1801 | " " | 182 | |
| Snow, Josiah | 1796 | Clements " | 7 | |
| Soulis, Daniel | 1787 | Sandy Cove | 100 | |
| Sower [Lower] George | 1784 | Clements Township | 100 | |
| Sproach, Samuel | 1784 | " " | 100 | |
| Sproal, William | 1784 | " " | 100 | |
| Stanton, James | 1787 | Sandy Cove | 151 | |
| Steele, Murphy | 1785 | Digby Township | 1 | Negro |
| Stennegar, Henry | 1801 | " " | 100 | |
| Stennigar, Jane and Morford, M. | 1801 | " " | 212 | |
| Sterns, Benjamin | 1787 | " " | 257 | |
| *Sterns, Jonathan | 1791 | Hfx-Annapolis Rd. (May be partly in Lunen. Co. | 640 | |
| Stevens, Enos | 1784 | River Sisabou, E. | 200 | |
| Stevens, Phineas | 1784 | " " " | 200 | |
| Stewart, John | 1784 | Clements Township | 200 | |
| Stewart, John | 1787 | Sandy Cove | 108 | |
| Stewart, Mathew | 1787 | " " | 170 | |
| Stocking, Federick | 1784 | Clements Township | 100 | |
| Street, Ebernezer | 1784 | " " | 200 | |
| Street, Ebenezer | 1784 | Digby | T. L. | |
| Street, Samuel | 1784 | Clements Township | 150 | |
| Street, Samuel | 1801 | Digby " | 113 | |
| Stretch, John | 1784 | Digby | T. L. | |
| Strickland, Amos | 1784 | Clements Township | 250 | |
| Stuart, John | 1784 | Digby | T. L. | |
| Stump, John | 1784 | " | T. L. | |
| Stump, John | 1785 | Digby Township | 400 | |
| Sutherland, George | 1784 | Clements " | 500 | |
| Sutherland, George | 1786 | Bear River | 500 | |
| Sutherland, O'Sullivan | 1784 | Clements Township | 450 | |
| Swim, Matthias | 1785 | Wilmot " | 100 | |
| Sypher [Syphar] Jacob | 1801 | Digby " | 250 | |
| Tarbol, Samuel | 1784 | " " | 150 | |
| Tarrant, Leonard | 1784 | Clements " | 250 | |

\* Grant not in Department of Lands and Forests; but Council Minute of October 10, 1791, maps and escheats show it was granted.

# LOYALISTS AND LAND SETTLEMENT IN NOVA SCOTIA 23

| Name | Date | Situation | Acres | Origin or Rank |
|---|---|---|---|---|
| Tate, William | 1784 | Clements Township | 200 | |
| Taylor, Edward, see Taylor, William | 1786 | | | |
| Taylor, Edward | 1796 | Digby | W. L. | |
| Taylor, Edward & Wm. | 1796 | " | T. L. | |
| Taylor, Edward & Wm. | 1801 | Digby Township | 397 | |
| Taylor, Elijah | 1784 | Clements " | 150 | |
| Taylor, John | 1784 | Digby " | 200 | |
| Taylor, John | 1784 | River Sisabou, E. | 200 | Captain |
| Taylor, John | 1784 | "   "   " | 180 | |
| Taylor, John | 1799 | Clare Township | 1000 | |
| Taylor, John | 1801 | Digby " | 300 | |
| Taylor, John | 1801 | "    " | 686 | |
| Taylor, Nicholas | 1784 | Clements " | 100 | |
| Taylor, Wm. & Taylor E. | 1786 | Digby " | 197 | |
| Taylor, William | 1796 | Digby | W. L. | |
| Taylor, William, see Taylor, Edward | 1801 | | | |
| Thomas, Joseph | 1786 | Digby Township | 96 | |
| Thomas, Joseph | 1789 | "    " | 118 | |
| Thomas, Joseph | 1798 | Granville " | 16¾ | |
| Thomas, William | 1796 | Digby | T. L. | |
| Thomas, William | 1796 | " | W. L. | |
| Thomas, William | 1801 | Digby Township | 750 | |
| Thompson, Alexander | 1786 | "    " | 150 | |
| Thompson, Alexander | 1796 | Digby | W. L. | |
| Thompson, Alexander | 1801 | Digby Township | 144 | |
| Thomson, John | 1796 | Digby | W. L. | |
| Thomson, John, see Etter, Thomas | 1796 | | | |
| Thorn, Richard | 1798 | Granville Township | 56½ | |
| Thorn, Stephen | 1784 | Clements " | 350 | |
| Thorne, Edward | 1796 | "    " | 9 | |
| Thorne, Edward | 1798 | Granville " | 150¾ | |
| Thorne, Edward | 1801 | Digby " | 734 | |
| Thorne, Edward, Jr. | 1799 | Granville " | 9¾ | |
| Thorne, Stephen | 1798 | "    " | 39¼ | |
| Thursdon, Ann | 1784 | Digby | T. L. | |
| Tidd, Samuel (Heirs) | 1801 | Digby Township | 550 | |
| Timpany, Robert | 1800 | Digby | W. L. | |
| Timpany, Thomas | 1785 | Digby Township | 1 | Negro |
| Tippet, Gilbert | 1784 | Clements " | 400 | |
| Titus, Daniel and Titus, Jacob | 1787 | Digby " | 200 | |
| Titus, Edmund | 1787 | "    " | 200 | |
| Titus, Isaac | 1784 | Digby | T. L. | |
| Titus, Isaac | 1787 | Digby Township | 200 | |
| Titus, Isaac | 1801 | "    " | 180 | |
| Titus, Jacob, see Titus, Daniel | 1787 | | | |
| Titus, James | 1800 | Digby | W. L. | |
| Titus, James | 1801 | Digby Township | 200 | |
| Tobias, Christian | 1789 | "    " | 273 | |
| Tobias, Christian | 1796 | Digby | T. L. | |
| Tobias, Christian | 1801 | Digby Township | 290 | |
| Tompkins, Samuel | 1785 | "    " | 1 | Negro |
| Totten, Ann | 1792 | Annapolis | W. L. | |
| Totten, Gilbert | 1792 | " | W. L. | |
| Totten, Isaac | 1792 | " | W. L. | |
| Totten, Jane | 1792 | " | W. L. | |
| Totten, Joseph | 1784 | Clements Township | 300 | |
| Totten, Joseph | 1784 | "    " | 300 | |
| Totten, Peter | 1784 | "    " | 300 | |
| Totten, Peter | 1784 | Digby | T. L. | |

24 PUBLIC ARCHIVES OF NOVA SCOTIA

| Name | Date | Situation | Acres | Origin or Rank |
|---|---|---|---|---|
| Totten, Peter | 1792 | Annapolis | W. L. | |
| Totten, Susannah | 1792 | " | W. L. | |
| Totten, William | 1789 | Digby Township | 85 | |
| Traves, Caleb | 1798 | Granville " | 3½ | |
| Trinder, James | 1784 | Digby | T. L. | |
| Tromper, Hendrick | 1784 | Clements Township | 100 | |
| Trusdell, James | 1784 | Wilmot " | 100 | |
| Trusdell, John | 1784 | " " | 200 | |
| Trusdell, John | 1784 | " " | 300 | |
| Tucker, Reuben | 1797 | Digby " | 450 | |
| Tucker, Reuben | 1797 | " " | 200 | |
| Tucker, Reuben | 1801 | " " | 1218 | |
| Tucker, Robert | 1785 | Wilmot " | 300 | Doctor |
| Tucker, Robert | 1786 | Clements " | 387 | |
| Tucker, Thomas | 1785 | Digby " | 1 | Negro |
| Turnbull, George, Robert and William | 1801 | " " | 225 | |
| Turner, Florian | 1784 | Clements " | 100 | |
| Turner, John | 1784 | " " | 100 | |
| Turner, John | 1801 | Digby " | 130 | |
| Turner, Serjeant | 1786 | " " | 100 | |
| Tuscheher, George | 1784 | Clements " | 100 | |
| Tympany, Robert | 1801 | Digby " | 853 | |
| Van Buren, James | 1784 | Clements " | 350 | |
| Van Buren, James, Jr. | 1784 | " " | 100 | |
| Van Buren, Kamann | 1784 | " " | 100 | |
| Van Buskirk, Abraham | 1787 | Wilmot " | 200 | |
| Van Buskirk, Garret | 1787 | " " | 200 | |
| Van Buskirk, Henry | 1787 | " " | 200 | |
| Van Buskirk, John | 1787 | " " | 200 | |
| Van Buskirk, Laurence | 1787 | " " | 200 | |
| Van Emburgh, Gilbert | 1801 | Digby " | 200 | |
| [Van] Horn, Laurence | 1784 | Clements " | 400 | |
| Van Horn, Laurence | 1787 | " " | 82 | |
| Van Horn, Laurence, Jr. | 1784 | " " | 100 | |
| Vankirk, John | 1787 | " " | 52 | |
| Vankirk, John | 1787 | Digby " | 200 | |
| Van Tassel, William | 1801 | " " | 200 | |
| Van Tassel, William | 1801 | " " | 100 | |
| Veitch, John | 1788 | " " | 100 | |
| Veitch, William | 1788 | " " | 100 | |
| Verilum, Anthony V. | 1784 | Clements " | 100 | |
| Viets [Veits] Roger | 1796 | Digby | T. L. | |
| Viets, Roger | 1800 | " | W. L. | |
| Viets, Roger | 1801 | Digby Township | 237 | |
| Vroom, George | 1787 | " " | 200 | |
| Vroom, John | 1787 | Clements " | 78 | |
| Vroom, John | 1801 | Digby " | 200 | |
| Vroom, Peter | 1787 | Clements " | 55 | |
| Vroom, Peter | 1787 | Digby " | 200 | |
| Wagener, Richard | 1786 | Clements " | 100 | |
| Wagner, John Chris. | 1784 | " " | 400 | |
| Wagner, Nicholas | 1784 | " " | 100 | |
| Walk, John | 1785 | Digby " | 1 | Negro |
| Walker, Adam | 1789 | " " | 200 | |
| Walker, Adam | 1796 | Digby | T. L. | |
| Walker, Adam | 1796 | " | W. L. | |
| Walker, Adam | 1801 | Digby Township | 200 | |
| Walker, Thomas | 1788 | Clements " | 265 | Lieut. N. Y. Vol's |
| Walker, Thomas | 1792 | Annapolis | W. L. | |
| Walter [Waller] Conrad | 1784 | Wilmot Township | 100 | |
| Ward, James | 1787 | Digby " | 200 | |

# LOYALISTS AND LAND SETTLEMENT IN NOVA SCOTIA

| Name | Date | Situation | Acres | Origin or Rank |
|---|---|---|---|---|
| Warne, Samuel | 1787 | Digby Township | 200 | |
| Warne, Thomas | 1787 | " " | 100 | |
| Warren, John | 1785 | " " | 1 | Negro |
| Warwick, John | 1784 | Digby | T. L. | |
| Warwick, John | 1786 | Digby Township | 172 | |
| Warwick John & Smith J | 1796 | Annapolis Basin | 30 | |
| Warwick, John | 1796 | Digby | T. L. | |
| Warwick, John | 1801 | Digby Township | 302 | |
| Watt, Charles | 1801 | " " | 121 | |
| Watt, Thomas | 1784 | Clements " | 200 | |
| Watt, Thomas | 1784 | Digby | T. L. | |
| Watt, Thomas | 1786 | Digby Township | 74 | |
| Watt, Thomas | 1796 | Annapolis Basin | 8 | |
| Watt, Thomas | 1801 | Digby Township | 150 | |
| Weeks, Elijah | 1786 | Clements " | 340 | |
| Weidman, Valentine | 1784 | " " | 150 | |
| Weipenborn, John | 1784 | " " | 100 | |
| Welling, Charles | 1784 | " " | 450 | |
| Welsh, Morris | 1801 | Digby " | 250 | |
| Wendell, Withelm | 1784 | Clements " | 200 | |
| White, Samuel | 1789 | St. Mary's Bay Road | 79 | |
| Wight, Henry | 1785 | Digby Township | 1 | Negro |
| Wight, Lary | 1785 | " " | 1 | " |
| Willet, Cornet | 1784 | Wilmot " | 500 | |
| Willett, Walter | 1784 | " " | 500 | Lieutenant |
| Williams, Elijah | 1784 | River Sisabou, E. | 200 | |
| Williams, Frederick | 1789 | Digby Township | 390 | |
| Williams, Frederick | 1801 | " " | 1119 | |
| Williams, Henry | 1785 | " " | 1 | Negro |
| Williams, Isaac | 1785 | " " | 1 | " |
| Williams, John | 1784 | Clements " | 100 | |
| Williams, John | 1785 | Digby " | 1 | Negro |
| Williams, John, Jr. | 1785 | " " | 1 | " |
| Williams, Richard | 1784 | Digby | T. L. | |
| Williams, Richard | 1796 | " | W. L. | |
| Williams, Thomas | 1801 | Digby Township | 709 | |
| Williams, William | 1785 | " " | 1 | Negro |
| Wilmot, James | 1784 | " " | 100 | |
| Wilmot, James | 1796 | Digby | W. L. | |
| Wilmot, James | 1784 | Clements Township | 200 | |
| Wilmot, James | 1801 | Digby " | 150 | |
| Wilson,— | 1784 | Digby | T. L. | Captain |
| Wilson, Abraham | 1801 | Digby Township | 200 | |
| Wilson, Abraham, Jr. | 1789 | " " | 200 | |
| Wilson, Christopher | 1784 | Wilmot " | 150 | |
| Wilson, Mary | 1784 | " " | 200 | |
| Winner, Jacob | 1784 | " " | 100 | |
| Winslow, Edward | 1784 | " " | 1000 | |
| Wiswell, John | 1785 | " " | 100 | |
| Wiswell, John (Rev.) | 1786 | Wilmot Township | 500 | |
| Wiswell, John (Rev.) | 1788 | " " | 500 | |
| Wiswell, Peleg | 1785 | " " | 100 | |
| Wiswell, Peleg | 1801 | Digby " | 597 | |
| Wortman, Philip | 1801 | " " | 190 | |
| Wright, D— | 1784 | Clements " | 400 | |
| Wright, John | 1800 | Digby | W. L. | |
| Wright, John | 1801 | Digby Township | 100 | |
| Youman, Peter | 1785 | " " | 1 | Negro |
| Young, Timothy | 1800 | Digby | W. L. | |
| Zeneva, Edmund | 1784 | Clements Township | 200 | |

## Annapolis County
### (b) WARRANTS

| Name | Date | Situation | Acres | Origin or Rank |
|---|---|---|---|---|
| Akins, Benjamin | 1789 | Clements Township | 50 | Negro |
| Albertie,— | 1787 | Long Island | 600 | Captain |
| Atsop, John | 1789 | Clements Township | 50 | Negro |
| Austin, James | 1789 | " " | 50 | " |
| Babis, John | 1789 | " " | 50 | " |
| Banks, James | 1789 | " " | 50 | " |
| Barnes, Samuel | 1789 | " " | 50 | " |
| Barton, William | 1789 | " " | 50 | " |
| Bayeux, Thomas | 1787 | Long Island | 100 | |
| Beaverhout, Henry | 1789 | Clements Township | 50 | Negro |
| Benjamin, Pompey | 1789 | " " | 50 | " |
| Benson, Jaf | 1789 | " " | 50 | " |
| Biggs, Adam | 1789 | " " | 50 | " |
| Bird, Thomas | 1789 | " " | 50 | " |
| Black, George | 1789 | " " | 50 | " |
| Bonnel, Isaac | 1787 | Long Island | 100 | |
| Borres, Jeffery | 1789 | Clements Township | 50 | Negro |
| Bradley, March | 1789 | " " | 50 | " |
| Brenton, James | 1785 | Wilmot " | 1000 | |
| Brothers, Samuel | 1789 | Clements " | 50 | Negro |
| Brown, Eli | 1789 | " " | 50 | " |
| Brown, Henry | 1789 | " " | 50 | " |
| Brown, James | 1789 | " " | 50 | " |
| Brown, Samuel | 1789 | " " | 50 | " |
| Brudenell, Edward | 1787 | Long Island | 100 | |
| Brumel, Jacob | 1789 | Clements Township | 50 | Negro |
| Bush, Cuffe | 1789 | " " | 50 | " |
| Bush, William | 1789 | " " | 50 | " |
| Butler, Anthony | 1789 | " " | 50 | " |
| Buxton, Demps | 1789 | " " | 50 | " |
| Bying, Thomas | 1789 | " " | 50 | " |
| Caldwell, John | 1787 | Long Island | 250 | |
| Carrol, George | 1789 | Clements Township | 50 | Negro |
| Cattopoll, William | 1789 | " " | 50 | " |
| Clements, Frances | 1789 | " " | 50 | " |
| Cleton, Joseph | 1789 | " " | 50 | " |
| Clingsher, Christian | 1787 | Long Island | 250 | |
| Cobus, John | 1789 | Clements Township | 50 | Negro |
| Conner, Peter | 1789 | " " | 50 | " |
| Cromwell, Joseph | 1789 | " " | 50 | " |
| Curby, Lewis | 1789 | " " | 50 | " |
| Custos, John | 1789 | " " | 50 | " |
| Demary, Thomas | 1789 | " " | 50 | " |
| Douglas, Thomas | 1789 | " " | 50 | " |
| Downer, Jeremiah | 1787 | Long Island | 100 | |
| Du Bois, Peter | 1789 | Clements Township | 50 | Negro |
| Edmund, David | 1789 | " " | 50 | " |
| Edmund, James | 1789 | " " | 50 | " |
| Eldridge, Titus | 1789 | " " | 50 | " |
| Farmer Samuel | 1789 | " " | 50 | " |
| Fisher, Moses | 1789 | " " | 50 | " |

LOYALISTS AND LAND SETTLEMENT IN NOVA SCOTIA 27

| Name | Date | Situation | Acres | Origin or Rank |
|---|---|---|---|---|
| Floid [Floyd] Henry | 1789 | Clements Township | 50 | Negro |
| Fowler, Caleb | 1790 | Wilmot " | 100 | |
| Francis, Charles | 1789 | Clements " | 50 | Negro |
| Francis, Thomas | 1789 | " " | 50 | " |
| Francklin, Benjamin | 1789 | " " | 50 | " |
| Fryer, Samuel | 1789 | " " | 50 | " |
| Garvis, Samuel | 1789 | " " | 50 | " |
| Gordon, John | 1789 | " " | 50 | " |
| Gordon, William | 1789 | " " | 50 | " |
| Gotfrey, Bristol | 1789 | " " | 50 | " |
| Gotfrey, John | 1789 | " " | 50 | " |
| Gotfrey, Robert | 1789 | " " | 50 | " |
| Grant, Michael | 1787 | Long Island | 100 | |
| Greegs, Glasgow | 1789 | Clements Township | 50 | Negro |
| Green, Adam | 1789 | " " | 50 | " |
| Griffith, Francis | 1789 | " " | 50 | " |
| Haines, Bartholemy | 1787 | Long Island | 450 | |
| Harris, Christopher | 1789 | Clements Township | 50 | Negro |
| Harris, Robert | 1789 | " " | 50 | " |
| Hendorf, Frederick | 1787 | Long Island | 400 | |
| Heywood, Robert | 1785 | Digby Township | 100 | |
| Hill, John | 1790 | " " | 200 | |
| Hill, Richard | 1787 | Long Island | 100 | |
| Holland, John | 1789 | Clements Township | 50 | Negro |
| Holstead, Richard | 1789 | " " | 50 | " |
| Irvin, John | 1789 | " " | 50 | " |
| Israel, Balteus | 1787 | Long Island | 150 | |
| Jackson, Henry | 1789 | Clements Township | 50 | Negro |
| Jackson, James | 1789 | " " | 50 | " |
| Jackson, London | 1789 | " " | 50 | " |
| James, Aron | 1789 | " " | 50 | " |
| James, Robert | 1789 | " " | 50 | " |
| Johnston, Luke | 1789 | " " | 50 | " |
| Johnston, Robert | 1789 | " " | 50 | " |
| Jones, Benjamin | 1787 | Long Island | 100 | |
| Jones, Eben'r | 1787 | " " | 250 | |
| Jones, Elijah | 1787 | " " | 100 | |
| Jones, Elisha | 1787 | " " | 150 | |
| Jones, Nathaniel | 1787 | " " | 50 | |
| Jordon, Abednego | 1789 | Clements Township | 50 | Negro |
| Jordon, Miles | 1789 | " " | 50 | " |
| Jordon, Mings | 1789 | " " | 50 | " |
| Kelsey, James | 1789 | " " | 50 | " |
| Kiess, Sarah | 1789 | " " | 50 | " |
| Legnee, Liberty | 1789 | " " | 50 | " |
| Leonard, Isaac | 1789 | " " | 50 | " |
| Leonard, Joseph | 1789 | " " | 100 | " |
| Leslie, Abraham | 1789 | " " | 50 | " |
| Leslie, Prince | 1789 | " " | 50 | " |
| Lowing, Ceasar | 1789 | " " | 50 | " |
| Lymen, Jacob, Jr. | 1789 | " " | 50 | " |
| Lynus, Cato | 1789 | " " | 50 | " |
| Lynch, Jacob, Sr. | 1789 | " " | 50 | " |
| McGregor, Alexander | 1787 | Long Island | 100 | |
| McNeil, Charles | 1787 | " " | 300 | |
| McNeil, John | 1793 | Wilmot Township | 400 | |
| McNeil, Neil | 1787 | Long Island | 500 | |

## PUBLIC ARCHIVES OF NOVA SCOTIA

| Name | Date | Situation | Acres | Origin or Rank |
|---|---|---|---|---|
| McNight, William | 1789 | Clements Township | 50 | Negro |
| Marriel, Philip | 1789 | " " | 50 | " |
| Martin, William | 1789 | " " | 50 | " |
| Meed, Larry | 1789 | " " | 50 | " |
| Millidge, Thomas | 1787 | Long Island | 100 | |
| Mitchell, Henry | 1789 | Clements Township | 50 | Negro |
| Mitleton, Henry, Jr. | 1789 | " " | 50 | " |
| Mitleton, Henry, Sr. | 1789 | " " | 50 | " |
| Moeser, Joseph | 1789 | " " | 50 | " |
| Moor [e], Henry | 1789 | " " | 50 | " |
| Morrison, Samuel | 1789 | " " | 50 | " |
| Nelis, Benjamin | 1789 | " " | 50 | " |
| Nugent, Richard | 1789 | " " | 50 | " |
| O'Brian, William | 1787 | Long Island | 100 | |
| Peters, John | 1789 | Clements Township | 50 | Negro |
| Philipho, George | 1789 | " " | 50 | " |
| Philipps, Deman | 1789 | " " | 50 | " |
| Pioneer, Quaske | 1789 | " " | 50 | " |
| Plato, Robert | 1789 | " " | 50 | " |
| Pomp, John | 1789 | Clements Township | 50 | Negro |
| Prime, Michael | 1787 | Long Island | 200 | |
| Ransom, Prince | 1789 | Clements Township | 50 | Negro |
| Ransom, York | 1789 | " " | 50 | " |
| Reddick, Anthony | 1789 | " " | 50 | " |
| Reddick, Henry | 1789 | " " | 50 | " |
| Reddick, Joseph | 1789 | " " | 50 | " |
| Ringwood, Isaac | 1789 | " " | 50 | " |
| Roberts, Anthony | 1789 | " " | 50 | " |
| Roberts, Francis | 1789 | " " | 50 | " |
| Salter, John | 1789 | " " | 50 | " |
| Salter, Prince | 1789 | " " | 50 | " |
| Saunders, Abraham | 1789 | " " | 50 | " |
| Saxton, Thomas | 1787 | Long Island | 100 | |
| Seabury, George | 1789 | Clements Township | 50 | Negro |
| Seabury, William | 1789 | " " | 50 | " |
| Seymour, Francis | 1789 | " " | 50 | " |
| Sheppard, John | 1789 | " " | 50 | " |
| Sheppard, York | 1789 | " " | 50 | " |
| Sim, Joseph | 1789 | " " | 50 | " |
| Smith, Isaac | 1789 | " " | 50 | " |
| Smith, Mary | 1789 | Wilmot " (?) | 50 | |
| Spinner, Luke | 1789 | Clements " | 50 | Negro |
| Street, Samuel | 1785 | Digby " | 100 | |
| Striphor, John | 1789 | Clements " | 50 | Negro |
| Tate, Thomas | 1789 | " " | 50 | " |
| Theld, Gilbert | 1787 | Long Island | 100 | |
| Thomas, Abigal | 1789 | Clements Township | 50 | Negro |
| Tompkins, Samuel | 1789 | " " | 50 | " |
| Tong, Pamelia | 1789 | " " | 50 | " |
| Turker, Thomas | 1789 | " " | 50 | " |
| Turner, Aberdeen | 1789 | " " | 50 | " |
| Turner, John | 1789 | " " | 50 | " |
| Van Davis, Ben. | 1789 | " " | 50 | " |
| Walk, John | 1789 | " " | 50 | " |
| Wall, Thomas | 1787 | Long Island | 200 | |
| Ward, John | 1793 | Wilmot Township | 150 | |

LOYALISTS AND LAND SETTLEMENT IN NOVA SCOTIA 29

| Name | Date | Situation | Acres | Origin or Rank |
|---|---|---|---|---|
| Warmar, Ceasar | 1789 | Clements Township | 50 | Negro |
| Warner, Henry | 1789 | " " | 50 | " |
| Warner, John | 1789 | " " | 50 | " |
| Welton, Elizabeth | 1789 | Wilmot " (?) | 50 | |
| Wight, Augustus | 1789 | Clements " | 50 | Negro |
| Wight, Henry | 1789 | " " | 50 | " |
| Wight, Larry | 1789 | " " | 50 | " |
| Wilkeson, Jacob | 1789 | " " | 50 | " |
| Williams, Isaac | 1789 | " " | 50 | " |
| Williams, John | 1789 | " " | 50 | " |
| Williams, John, Jr. | 1789 | " " | 50 | " |
| Williams, Thomas | 1789 | " " | 50 | " |
| Wills, Francis | 1789 | " " | 50 | " |
| Withers, Timothy | 1789 | " " | 50 | " |
| Witing, Pompey | 1789 | " " | 50 | " |
| Woodroff, Philip | 1789 | " " | 50 | " |
| Worthly, Philip | 1787 | Long Island | 300 | |
| Wragg, Thomas | 1789 | Clements Township | 50 | Negro |
| Wright, James | 1789 | " " | 50 | " |
| Wright, John | 1787 | Long Island | 100 | |
| Young, James | 1787 | " " | 100 | |
| Youghman, Peter | 1789 | Clements Township | 50 | Negro |

## Annapolis County

### (c) ESCHEATS

◻ Names marked with this sign were included in the new grant of Digby Township, 1801.

▲ Those marked with this sign are included in the grants to (a) John Perrot and others, 1786, Halifax-Annapolis Road, 16,782 acres, and (b) William Brinley and others, 1791, Halifax-Annapolis Road, 25,600 acres. Neither of these grants is in the records of the Department of Lands and Forests, yet evidence from the Records of the Court of Escheats, maps and in the case of Brinley a Council Minute of Oct. 10, 1791, seems to show they were granted, supplying the very date the grants were issued.

| Name | Date | Situation | Acres | Esch'd | Origin or Rank |
|---|---|---|---|---|---|
| ▲Addington, William | 1786 | Halifax-Annapolis Rd. | 200 | 1819 | |
| ◻Aikins, John | 1784 | Digby Township | 250 | 1800 | |
| ▲Airs, John | 1786 | Halifax-Annapolis Rd. | 200 | 1819 | |
| Allair, Peter Alexander | 1784 | Digby Township | 200 | 1800 | |
| ◻Amberman, Paul | 1784 | " " | 350 | 1800 | |
| ▲Anderson, Jonathan | 1786 | Halifax-Annapolis Rd. | 100 | 1819 | |
| ▲Ankhony, Joseph | 1786 | " " | 200 | 1819 | |
| ▲Ankhony, Joseph | 1786 | " " " | 200 | 1819 | |
| Aplin, Joseph | 1785 | Wilmot Township | 1000 | 1811 | |
| Babcock, Benjamin | 1784 | Digby " | 100 | 1800 | |
| ◻Baine, George | 1784 | " " | 250 | 1800 | |
| Bannister, Thomas | 1785 | St. Mary's Bay | 1000 | 1796 | |
| Bantrum, Thomas | 1784 | Digby Township | 100 | 1800 | |
| ▲Barclay, Henry | 1791 | Halifax-Annapolis Rd., part possibly in Lunen. Co. | 640 | 1819 | |
| Barry, Mary | 1784 | Digby Township | 100 | 1800 | |
| Beasley, Joseph | 1784 | " " | 250 | 1800 | |

# 30 PUBLIC ARCHIVES OF NOVA SCOTIA

| Name | Date | Situation | Acres | Esch'd | Origin or Rank |
|---|---|---|---|---|---|
| ⊡Beeman, (Widow) | 1784 | Digby Township | 200 | 1800 | |
| Beeman, Ebenezer | 1784 | " " | 100 | 1800 | |
| Beeman, Thomas | 1784 | " " | 100 | 1800 | |
| Belcher, Adam | 1784 | " " | 100 | 1800 | |
| Bennett, David | 1784 | " " | 250 | 1800 | |
| ▲Benson, William | 1786 | Halifax-Annapolis Rd. | 200 | 1819 | |
| Betts, Richard | 1784 | Digby Township | 300 | 1800 | |
| Betts, Richard, Jr. | 1784 | " " | 150 | 1800 | |
| Billop, Christopher | 1785 | St. Mary's Bay | 1000 | 1796 | |
| Birdsell, Jeremiah | 1784 | Digby Township | 200 | 1800 | |
| ▲Black, John | 1786 | Halifax-Annapolis Rd. | 100 | 1819 | |
| ⊡Blashford [Blackford], Martin | 1784 | Digby Township | 200 | 1800 | |
| ▲Boaker, Andrews | 1786 | Halifax-Annapolis Rd. | 200 | 1819 | |
| ▲Boaker, Andrews | 1786 | " " " | 200 | 1819 | |
| ▲Boaker, Ardews | 1786 | " " " | 100 | 1819 | |
| Bonham, Malachi | 1784 | Digby Township | 100 | 1800 | |
| ⊡Bonnell, Isaac | 1784 | " " | 200 | 1800 | |
| ▲Bonnett, David | 1791 | Halifax-Annapolis Rd., part possibly in Lunen. Co. | 640 | 1819 | |
| ▲Bonnett, Isaac* | 1791 | (Same) | 640 | 1819 | |
| ▲Borthwick, William | 1786 | Halifax-Annapolis Rd. | 50 | 1819 | |
| Botsford, Amos | 1784 | Digby Township | 250 | 1800 | |
| Bouchier, John | 1784 | " " | 150 | 1800 | |
| ⊡Bowlsly, Abraham | 1784 | " " | 100 | 1800 | |
| ⊡Bowlsly, Richard | 1784 | " " | 400 | 1800 | |
| Bowser, John | 1784 | " " | 350 | 1800 | |
| ▲Boyce, George | 1786 | Halifax-Annapolis Rd. | 50 | 1819 | |
| ▲Boyce, George | 1786 | " " " | 200 | 1819 | |
| Bragg, John | 1784 | Digby Township | 150 | 1800 | |
| Branson, David | 1784 | " " | 100 | 1800 | |
| Bray, James | 1784 | " " | 200 | 1800 | |
| Brickett, John | 1784 | " " | 200 | 1800 | |
| Bridgewater, John | 1784 | " " | 300 | 1800 | Captain |
| ▲Brinley, William | 1791 | Halifax-Annapolis Rd., part possibly in Lunen. Co. | 640 | 1819 | |
| ▲Brower, Isaac | 1786 | Halifax-Annapolis Rd. | 100 | 1819 | |
| Brown, Daniel I. | 1784 | Digby Township | 500 | 1800 | Major |
| Brown, David | 1784 | " " | 100 | 1800 | |
| Brown, Geo., John & Jos. | 1784 | " " | 350 | 1800 | |
| Brown, John, see Brown, George | 1784 | | | | |
| Brown, Joseph see Brown, George | 1784 | | | | |
| Brown, M. (Rev.) | 1784 | " " | 250 | 1800 | |
| Brown, Peter | 1784 | " " | 200 | 1800 | Doctor |
| ▲Browne, Daniel Isaac | 1791 | Halifax-Annapolis Rd., part possibly in Lunen. Co. | 640 | 1819 | |
| ▲Brymer, A., Jr. | 1791 | (Same) | 640 | 1819 | |
| ▲Brymer, Alexander, Sr. | 1791 | " | 640 | 1819 | |
| Buce, Jacob | 1784 | Digby Township | 300 | 1800 | |
| Buffington, Richard | 1784 | " " | 100 | 1800 | |
| Bull, William | 1784 | " " | 250 | 1800 | |
| ▲Bull, William | 1786 | Halifax-Annapolis Rd. | 100 | 1819 | |
| Bunell, Solomon | 1784 | Digby Township | 400 | 1800 | |
| Burkit, John | 1784 | " " | 300 | 1800 | |
| ▲Burns, Charles | 1786 | Halifax-Annapolis Rd. | 100 | 1819 | |
| Burns, Michael | 1784 | Digby Township | 200 | 1800 | |
| Cain, John | 1784 | " " | 100 | 1800 | |
| Campbell, Robert | 1784 | " " | 200 | 1800 | |
| Campbell, William | 1785 | St. Mary's Bay | 1000 | 1796 | |

* Called James Bonnett in the escheat.

# LOYALISTS AND LAND SETTLEMENT IN NOVA SCOTIA    31

| Name | Date | Situation | Acres | Esch'd | Origin or Rank |
|---|---|---|---|---|---|
| Caniff, Daniel | 1784 | Digby Township | 200 | 1800 | |
| Carrier, Green | 1784 | " " | 250 | 1800 | |
| ▲Cattern, Henry | 1786 | Halifax-Annapolis Rd. | 100 | 1819 | |
| Cayford, Richard | 1784 | Digby Township | 200 | 1800 | |
| ▲Chadburn, Humphry | 1786 | Halifax-Annapolis Rd. | 200 | 1819 | |
| Chandler, Joshua | 1784 | Digby Township | 300 | 1800 | |
| Chandler, Samuel | 1784 | " " | 100 | 1800 | |
| Chandler, Thomas | 1784 | " " | 100 | 1800 | |
| Chandler, William | 1784 | " " | 100 | 1800 | |
| Chandler, William | 1784 | " " | 200 | 1800 | Captain |
| ▲Charley, George | 1786 | Halifax-Annapolis Rd. | 100 | 1819 | |
| ▲Chesley, Sarah | 1786 | " " | 100 | 1819 | |
| Clarke, James | 1785 | St. Mary's Bay | 1000 | 1796 | |
| ▲Clarke, Scott L. | 1786 | Halifax-Annapolis Rd. | 200 | 1819 | |
| Clawson, Jonathan | 1784 | Digby Township | 350 | 1800 | |
| Clawson, Reuben | 1784 | " " | 250 | 1800 | |
| Clinton, Alexander | 1784 | " " | 300 | 1800 | |
| Cole, William | 1784 | " " | 100 | 1800 | |
| ▲Collins, William | 1786 | Halifax-Annapolis Rd. | 200 | 1819 | |
| Cornwell, Benjamin | 1784 | Digby Township | 250 | 1800 | |
| Cortleyon, Aaron | 1785 | St. Mary's Bay | 1000 | 1796 | |
| □Cosaboom, David | 1784 | Digby Township | 200 | 1800 | |
| □Cosman, John | 1784 | " " | 200 | 1800 | |
| ▲Covert, Elisha | 1786 | Halifax-Annapolis Rd. | 100 | 1819 | |
| □Covert, John | 1784 | Digby Township | 100 | 1800 | |
| □Covert, John, Jr. | 1784 | " " | 100 | 1800 | |
| Covert, Tunis | 1784 | " " | 450 | 1800 | |
| ▲Cox, Esau | 1786 | Halifax-Annapolis Rd. | 200 | 1819 | |
| □Craig, James | 1784 | Digby Township | 300 | 1800 | |
| Crane, Thomas | 1784 | " " | 100 | 1800 | |
| ▲Crasen, William | 1786 | Halifax-Annapolis Rd. | 100 | 1819 | |
| Creighton, James | 1784 | Digby Township | 150 | 1800 | |
| □Cronck, Joseph | 1784 | " " | 400 | 1800 | |
| ▲Cropley, William | 1786 | Halifax-Annapolis Rd. | 100 | 1819 | |
| □Cross, William | 1784 | Digby Township | 300 | 1800 | |
| ▲Crosscupt[Crooscupt]Jona | 1786 | Halifax-Annapolis Rd. | 100 | 1819 | |
| ▲Crosscupt, Ludavick | 1786 | " " " | 100 | 1819 | |
| ▲Crosswell, John | 1786 | " " " | 100 | 1819 | |
| Cudmore, William | 1784 | Digby Township | 100 | 1800 | |
| Cumings, Thomas | 1784 | " " | 300 | 1800 | |
| ▲Cummings, William | 1786 | Halifax-Annapolis Rd. | 100 | 1819 | |
| Cunningham, David | 1784 | Digby Township | 400 | 1800 | |
| ▲Cunninhane, Francis | 1786 | Halifax-Annapolis Rd. | 200 | 1819 | |
| ▲Cureau, Joshua | 1786 | " " " | 200 | 1819 | |
| Davis, Benjamin | 1785 | St Mary's Bay | 1000 | 1796 | |
| ▲Decker, Levi | 1786 | Halifax-Annapolis Rd. | 100 | 1819 | |
| Degan, William | 1784 | Digby Township | 100 | 1800 | |
| ▲Delancy, James | 1791 | Halifax-Annapolis Rd., part possibly in Lunen. Co. | 640 | 1819 | |
| Denton, Stephen | 1784 | Digby Township | 200 | 1800 | |
| ▲De. St. Croix, Joshua Temple | 1791 | Halifax-Annapolis Rd., part possibly in Lunen. Co. | 640 | 1819 | |
| ▲Deveaux, Lewis | 1786 | Halifax-Annapolis Rd. | 200 | 1819 | |
| Dickson, Robert | 1784 | Digby Township | 450 | 1800 | |
| □Dickson, Robert | 1784 | " " | 300 | 1800 | |
| ▲Dimint, Mary | 1786 | Halifax-Annapolis Rd. | 200 | 1819 | |
| Ditmars, Dowe, Jr. | 1784 | Digby Township | 200 | 1800 | |
| Ditmars, Dowie | 1784 | " " | 100 | 1800 | |
| □Ditmars, John | 1784 | " " | 500 | 1800 | |
| ▲Dobbs, John | 1786 | Halifax-Annapolis Rd. | 200 | 1819 | |
| ▲Dobbs, Thomas | 1786 | " " " | 200 | 1819 | |
| Doty, Samuel | 1784 | Digby Township | 100 | 1800 | |
| Doughty, Samuel | 1784 | " " | 100 | 1800 | |

| Name | Date | Situation | Acres | Esch'd | Origin or Rank |
|---|---|---|---|---|---|
| □Dowling, Dennis | 1784 | Digby Township | 100 | 1800 | |
| □Dunbar, Joseph | 1784 | " " | 150 | 1800 | |
| Dunbar, Joseph, Jr. | 1784 | " " | 350 | 1800 | |
| ▲Dunbar, Letitia (Mrs) | 1786 | Halifax-Annapolis Rd. | 200 | 1819 | |
| ▲Dunford, Jonathan | 1786 | " " | 100 | 1819 | |
| □Durling, Daniel | 1784 | Digby Township | 450 | 1800 | |
| Durling, Zebulon | 1784 | " " | 100 | 1800 | |
| Edgar, James | 1784 | " " | 100 | 1800 | |
| Edson, John | 1784 | " " | 500 | 1800 | |
| □Edson, Thomas | 1784 | " " | 300 | 1800 | |
| ▲English, William | 1786 | Halifax-Annapolis Rd. | 100 | 1819 | |
| □Evans, Lemuel | 1784 | Digby Township | 200 | 1800 | |
| Eye, Margaret | 1784 | " " | 150 | 1800 | |
| Fairchild, Eleazer | 1784 | " " | 100 | 1800 | |
| ▲Fanning, Edmund | 1791 | Halifax-Annapolis Rd., part possibly in Lunen. Co. | 640 | 1819 | |
| ▲Fiary, Peter | 1786 | Halifax-Annapolis Rd. | 100 | 1819 | |
| □Fitzgerald, William, Jr. | 1784 | Digby Township | 500 | 1800 | |
| Flavel, Anthony | 1784 | " " | 250 | 1800 | |
| ▲Fleet, William | 1786 | Halifax-Annapolis Rd. | 150 | 1819 | |
| Fountain, Stephen | 1784 | Digby Township | 150 | 1800 | |
| Fowler, Thomas | 1784 | " " | 100 | 1800 | |
| ▲Fraser, James | 1786 | Halifax-Annapolis Rd. | 200 | 1819 | |
| ▲Furgee, Tunesley, Jr. | 1786 | " " " | 100 | 1819 | |
| ▲Furgee, Tunesley, Sr. | 1786 | " " " | 200 | 1819 | |
| ▲Galligher, Andrew | 1786 | " " " | 200 | 1819 | |
| ▲Galligher, Andrew, Jr. | 1786 | " " " | 100 | 1819 | |
| Getchings, Jacob | 1784 | Digby Township | 200 | 1800 | |
| Gevin, John | 1784 | " " | 400 | 1800 | |
| ▲Giggitts, Joseph | 1786 | " " | 100 | 1819 | |
| Gilbert, Samuel | 1784 | Halifax-Annapolis Rd. | 200 | 1800 | |
| □Gilbert, Thomas | 1784 | Digby Township | 200 | 1800 | |
| □Gilbert, Thomas | 1784 | " " | 400 | 1800 | Colonel |
| ▲Gilderslive, Jemime | 1786 | Halifax-Annapolis Rd. | 200 | 1819 | Major |
| Gilliland, William | 1784 | Digby Township | 100 | 1800 | |
| Goldsmith, Stephen | 1784 | " " | 100 | 1800 | |
| Goodman, Isaac | 1784 | " " | 350 | 1800 | |
| Goss, Thomas | 1784 | " " | 100 | 1800 | |
| Gouger, Edward | 1784 | " " | 300 | 1800 | |
| Graham, Alexander | 1784 | " " | 150 | 1800 | |
| Graham, Myers | 1784 | " " | 100 | 1800 | |
| Graham, Patrick | 1784 | " " | 150 | 1800 | |
| ▲Grant, John | 1791 | Halifax-Annapolis Rd., part possibly in Lunen. Co. | 640 | 1819 | |
| □Grant, Sarah (Widow) | 1784 | Digby Township | 500 | 1800 | |
| Grigg, Thomas | 1784 | " " | 300 | 1800 | |
| Grogan, Richard | 1784 | " " | 250 | 1800 | |
| ▲Grove, Michael | 1786 | Halifax-Annapolis Rd. | 100 | 1819 | |
| Hagerman, John | 1784 | Digby Township | 100 | 1800 | |
| Haggarty, Patrick | 1784 | " " | 200 | 1800 | Captain |
| ▲Haines, Mathew | 1786 | Halifax-Annapolis Rd. | 100 | 1819 | |
| ▲Hales, James | 1786 | " " " | 100 | 1819 | |
| ▲Hales, John, Sr. | 1786 | " " " | 50 | 1819 | |
| ▲Hales, John, Sr. | 1786 | " " " | 200 | 1819 | |
| ▲Hales, Jonathan, Jr. | 1786 | " " " | 50 | 1819 | |
| □Hamilton, Archibald | 1784 | Digby Township | 300 | 1800 | |
| ▲Hammel, Isaac | 1786 | Halifax-Annapolis Rd. | 100 | 1819 | |
| ▲Hammill, Abraham | 1786 | " " " | 100 | 1819 | |
| ▲Hammill, Isaac | 1786 | " " " | 100 | 1819 | |
| ▲Hammill, John | 1786 | " " " | 50 | 1819 | |

# LOYALISTS AND LAND SETTLEMENT IN NOVA SCOTIA 33

| Name | Date | Situation | Acres | Esch'd | Origin or Rank |
|---|---|---|---|---|---|
| ▲Hammill, John | 1786 | Halifax-Annapolis Rd. | 200 | 1819 | |
| Handlespike, Conrad | 1784 | Digby Township | 350 | 1800 | |
| ▲Hanning, Thomas | 1786 | Halifax-Annapolis Rd. | 200 | 1819 | |
| ▲Hanson, Christopher | 1786 | " " " | 200 | 1819 | |
| Hardenberg, Derick | 1784 | Digby Township | 100 | 1800 | |
| Hardenbrook, Daniel | 1784 | " " | 100 | 1800 | |
| Harris, Francis | 1784 | " " | 300 | 1800 | |
| Harrison, Christopher | 1784 | " " | 350 | 1800 | |
| Harrison, Thomas, Jr. | 1784 | " " | 100 | 1800 | |
| Hatch, John | 1784 | " " | 150 | 1800 | |
| □Hatfield, Isaac | 1784 | " " | 250 | 1800 | Colonel |
| ▲Haviland, Israel | 1786 | Halifax-Annapolis Rd. | 100 | 1819 | |
| Hawke, Jacob | 1784 | Digby Township | 100 | 1800 | |
| ▲Haynes, Matthew | 1786 | Halifax-Annapolis Rd. | 100 | 1819 | |
| ▲Henderson, Andrew | 1786 | " " " | 160 | 1819 | |
| ▲Hendry, William | 1786 | " " " | 150 | 1819 | |
| ▲Henry, Charles | 1786 | " " " | 100 | 1819 | |
| □Hill, John | 1784 | Digby Township | 250 | 1800 | |
| □Hill, Richard | 1784 | " " | 400 | 1800 | Captain |
| Hill, Zachariah | 1784 | " " | 400 | 1800 | |
| Hilliard, Gershom | 1784 | " " | 250 | 1800 | |
| Hoffman, John | 1784 | " " | 100 | 1800 | |
| Holcomb, Jeconiah | 1784 | " " | 250 | 1800 | |
| □Holdsworth, James H. | 1784 | " " | 100 | 1800 | |
| □Holdsworth, John | 1784 | " " | 100 | 1800 | |
| Holdsworth, Thomas | 1784 | " " | 100 | 1800 | |
| Hollingshead, Anthony | 1784 | " " | 300 | 1800 | |
| Hortwick, Lawrence | 1784 | " " | 200 | 1800 | |
| Houghton, John | 1784 | " " | 200 | 1800 | |
| ▲Houseman, Jonathan | 1786 | Halifax-Annapolis Rd. | 70 | 1819 | |
| ▲Houseman, Jonathan | 1786 | " " " | 150 | 1819 | |
| ▲Houseman, Jonathan | 1786 | " " " | 50 | 1819 | |
| Housman, John | 1784 | Digby Township | 200 | 1800 | |
| □Hoyt, Jesse | 1784 | " " | 500 | 1800 | |
| □Hughston, James | 1784 | " " | 700 | 1800 | |
| Hustead, Jonathan | 1784 | " " | 200 | 1800 | |
| Hutchinson, Isaac | 1784 | " " | 100 | 1800 | |
| □Hutchinson, Thomas | 1784 | " " | 100 | 1800 | |
| Jenkins, (Widow) | 1784 | " " | 300 | 1800 | |
| Jenkins, Griffith | 1784 | " " | 400 | 1800 | |
| ▲Johns, Peters | 1786 | Halifax-Annapolis Rd. | 100 | 1819 | |
| Johnson, (Widow) | 1784 | Digby Township | 200 | 1800 | |
| Johnson, Laurance | 1784 | " " | 350 | 1800 | |
| □Johnson, Martin | 1784 | " " | 400 | 1800 | |
| Johnson, Nicholas | 1784 | " " | 350 | 1800 | |
| Johnston, George | 1784 | " " | 200 | 1800 | |
| □Johnston, William | 1784 | " " | 250 | 1800 | |
| Jones, Edward | 1784 | " " | 350 | 1800 | |
| Jones, Elisha | 1784 | " " | 100 | 1800 | |
| □Jones, Josiah | 1784 | " " | 300 | 1800 | |
| Jones, Mehitable | 1784 | " " | 300 | 1800 | |
| Jones, Nicholas | 1784 | " " | 100 | 1800 | |
| Jones, William | 1784 | " " | 150 | 1800 | |
| Journay, William | 1784 | " " | 100 | 1800 | |
| Kane, John | 1784 | " " | 200 | 1800 | |
| □Kelly, Mathias | 1784 | " " | 150 | 1800 | |
| □Kerr, William | 1784 | " " | 200 | 1800 | |
| Kingsland, William | 1784 | " " | 100 | 1800 | |
| Kipp, Thomas | 1784 | " " | 200 | 1800 | |
| Knox, Thomas | 1785 | St. Mary's Bay | 1000 | 1796 | |
| LaForge, Henry | 1784 | Digby Township | 350 | 1800 | |

## 34  PUBLIC ARCHIVES OF NOVA SCOTIA

| Name | Date | Situation | Acres | Esch'd | Origin or Rank |
|---|---|---|---|---|---|
| ☐Lambertson, John | 1784 | Digby Township | 200 | 1800 | |
| Lambertson, John, Jr. | 1784 | " " | 100 | 1800 | |
| Lambertson, Luke | 1784 | " " | 100 | 1800 | |
| ☐Lambertson, Tunis | 1784 | " " | 100 | 1800 | |
| Langly, Timothy | 1784 | " " | 100 | 1800 | |
| ▲Lawson, David | 1791 | Halifax-Annapolis Rd., part possibly in Lunen. Co. | 640 | 1819 | |
| Leak, John | 1784 | Digby Township | 200 | 1800 | |
| Lebarre [LeBane], Henry | 1784 | " " | 100 | 1800 | |
| ▲Lee, John | 1786 | Halifax-Annapolis Rd. | 200 | 1819 | |
| ▲Lee, Jonathan | 1786 | " " " | 100 | 1819 | |
| Leonard, Robert | 1784 | Digby Township | 100 | 1800 | |
| ☐LeRoy, Francis P. | 1784 | " " | 400 | 1800 | |
| LeSage, Mento | 1784 | " " | 100 | 1800 | |
| ☐Littany, William H. | 1784 | " " | 250 | 1800 | |
| Livesay, William | 1784 | " " | 350 | 1800 | |
| Longshore, Lolly | 1784 | " " | 250 | 1800 | |
| Longworth, Isaac | 1785 | St. Mary's Bay | 1000 | 1796 | |
| ☐Lowe, John | 1784 | Digby Township | 500 | 1800 | |
| ☐Lowe, William | 1784 | " " | 100 | 1800 | |
| Loysadore, Jacob | 1784 | " " | 300 | 1800 | |
| ▲Lumerie, Jonathan | 1786 | Halifax-Annapolis Rd. | 200 | 1819 | |
| ▲Lumerie, Jonathan | 1786 | " " " | 150 | 1819 | |
| ▲Lynes, Ann (Mrs) | 1786 | " " " | 100 | 1819 | |
| ▲Lynes, Ann (Mrs) | 1786 | " " " | 100 | 1819 | |
| ▲McDonald, William | 1786 | " " " | 100 | 1819 | |
| McEwen, James | 1784 | Digby Township | 200 | 1800 | |
| ▲McFarlain, James | 1786 | Halifax-Annapolis Rd. | 100 | 1819 | |
| McGuire, Patrick | 1784 | Digby Township | 200 | 1800 | |
| McKay, John | 1784 | " " | 100 | 1800 | |
| McKinney, William | 1784 | " " | 300 | 1800 | |
| McKown, John | 1784 | " " | 400 | 1800 | |
| ▲McMullen, Neil | 1786 | Halifax-Annapolis Rd. | 200 | 1819 | |
| McMullen, Neil | 1784 | Digby Township | 200 | 1800 | |
| McNeil, Neil | 1784 | " " | 200 | 1800 | |
| ☐Majoribanks, Thomas | 1784 | " " | 400 | 1800 | |
| Mallow, Jeremiah | 1784 | " " | 100 | 1800 | |
| ▲Manavel, Thomas | 1786 | Halifax-Annapolis Rd. | 100 | 1819 | |
| Marple, Richard | 1784 | Digby Township | 100 | 1800 | |
| Meads, Richard | 1784 | " " | 300 | 1800 | |
| ☐Megher, James | 1784 | " " | 300 | 1800 | |
| ▲Miller, George | 1786 | Halifax-Annapolis Rd. | 100 | 1819 | |
| ☐Millidge, Thomas | 1784 | Digby Township | 250 | 1800 | Major |
| Milligan, John | 1784 | " " | 100 | 1800 | |
| ☐Mills, Hope | 1784 | " " | 250 | 1800 | |
| Mills, Hope, Jr. | 1784 | " " | 250 | 1800 | |
| Milner, Jeremiah | 1784 | " " | 100 | 1800 | |
| ▲Moody, James | 1791 | Halifax-Annapolis Rd., part possibly in Lunen. Co. | 640 | 1819 | |
| ☐Moore, Jeremiah | 1784 | Digby Township | 300 | 1800 | |
| Moore, John B. | 1784 | " " | 200 | 1800 | |
| ☐Morehouse, Jonathan | 1784 | " " | 350 | 1800 | |
| Morrison, Malcom | 1784 | " " | 500 | 1800 | |
| Mumford, John | 1784 | " " | 200 | 1800 | |
| Nichols, Henry | 1784 | " " | 250 | 1800 | |
| Nichols, Sarah | 1784 | " " | 250 | 1800 | |
| ☐Northrop, Joshua | 1784 | " " | 200 | 1800 | |
| Nostrandt, Peter | 1784 | " " | 250 | 1800 | |
| ▲Nye, Elizabeth (Mrs) | 1786 | Halifax-Annapolis Rd | 100 | 1819 | |
| O'Reily, Daniel | 1784 | Digby Township | 100 | 1800 | |
| Osborn, Jabez | 1784 | " " | 100 | 1800 | |

# LOYALISTS AND LAND SETTLEMENT IN NOVA SCOTIA 35

| Name | Date | Situation | Acres | Esch'd | Origin or Rank |
|---|---|---|---|---|---|
| Osborn, Thomas | 1784 | Digby Township | 350 | 1800 | |
| Ott, Jacob | 1784 | " " | 350 | 1800 | |
| Outhouse, Nicholas | 1784 | " " | 350 | 1800 | |
| | | | | | |
| Panton, George (Rev.) | 1785 | St. Mary's Bay | 1000 | 1796 | |
| Parker, Simeon | 1784 | Digby Township | 150 | 1800 | |
| Parks, James | 1784 | " " | 250 | 1800 | |
| ▲Parr, William L. | 1791 | Halifax-Annapolis Rd., part possibly in Lunen. Co. | 640 | 1819 | |
| Patchon, Andrew | 1784 | Digby Township | 200 | 1800 | |
| Paterson, Joseph | 1784 | " " | 100 | 1800 | |
| Paul, John | 1784 | " " | 200 | 1800 | |
| ▲Peck, James | 1786 | Halifax-Annapolis Rd. | 200 | 1819 | |
| ▲Perrot, John | 1786 | " " " | 250 | 1819 | Captain |
| ▲Perrott, James | 1786 | " " " | 100 | 1819 | |
| Petite, Benjamin | 1784 | Digby Township | 300 | 1800 | |
| Petite, Isaac | 1784 | " " | 350 | 1800 | |
| Petite, Silas | 1784 | " " | 100 | 1800 | |
| ▲Pheriley, Christopher | 1786 | Halifax-Annapolis Rd. | 100 | 1819 | |
| Philips, Jacob | 1784 | Digby Township | 100 | 1800 | |
| Phillips, Alexander | 1784 | " " | 200 | 1800 | |
| Pilgrim, Alexander | 1784 | " " | 100 | 1800 | |
| Pilgrim, Francis | 1784 | " " | 250 | 1800 | |
| ▲Polhemus, John | 1791 | Halifax-Annapolis Rd., part possibly in Lunen. Co. | 640 | 1819 | |
| Potts, John | 1785 | St. Mary's Bay | 1000 | 1796 | |
| Proctor, Nathaniel | 1784 | Digby Township | 200 | 1800 | |
| Purcell, Pierce | 1784 | " " | 100 | 1800 | |
| Purcell, Simon | 1784 | " " | 100 | 1800 | |
| | | | | | |
| ▲Rattoon, John | 1786 | Halifax-Annapolis Rd. | 200 | 1819 | |
| □Ray, Robert | 1784 | Digby Township | 300 | 1800 | |
| Reading,—(Widow) | 1784 | " " | 300 | 1800 | |
| Reading, Samuel | 1784 | " " | 100 | 1800 | |
| □Reid, [Read], James | 1784 | " " | 200 | 1800 | |
| Remson, Jacob | 1784 | " " | 100 | 1800 | |
| □Remson, Johannes | 1784 | " " | 100 | 1800 | |
| □Remson, Rem | 1784 | " " | 400 | 1800 | |
| Richards, James | 1784 | " " | 200 | 1800 | |
| Ritchie, Andrew | 1784 | " " | 300 | 1800 | |
| □Ritchie, Andrew, Jr. | 1784 | " " | 100 | 1800 | |
| □Ritchie, John | 1784 | " " | 300 | 1800 | |
| □Ritchie, Thomas | 1784 | " " | 100 | 1800 | |
| ▲Robertson [Robinson] Wm. | 1791 | Halifax-Annapolis Rd., part possibly in Lunen. Co. | 640 | 1819 | |
| ▲Robinson, Edward | 1786 | Halifax-Annapolis Rd. | 200 | 1819 | |
| Robinson, Frederick | 1784 | Digby Township | 100 | 1800 | |
| ▲Robinson, John | 1786 | Halifax-Annapolis Rd. | 200 | 1819 | |
| ▲Robinson, Jonathan | 1786 | " " " | 200 | 1819 | |
| ▲Robinson, Jonathan | 1786 | " " " | 100 | 1819 | |
| ▲Robinson, Jonathan | 1786 | " " " | 200 | 1819 | |
| ▲Robinson, William | 1786 | " " " | 200 | 1819 | |
| Roome, John | 1784 | Digby Township | 200 | 1800 | |
| Rowland, David | 1784 | " " | 150 | 1800 | |
| Ruggles, Joseph | 1784 | " " | 100 | 1800 | |
| ▲Ruggles, Timothy | 1791 | Halifax-Annapolis Rd. | 640 | 1819 | Brigadier-general |
| Ryder, John | 1784 | Digby Township | 100 | 1800 | |
| Ryder, Joseph | 1784 | " " | 150 | 1800 | |
| Ryder, Samuel | 1784 | " " | 350 | 1800 | |
| Ryerson, Peter | 1784 | " " | 200 | 1800 | |
| | | | | | |
| ▲Saunders, Pardon | 1791 | Halifax-Annapolis Rd., part possibly in Lunen. Co. | 640 | 1819 | |
| Saunders, William | 1784 | Digby Township | 350 | 1800 | |

36  PUBLIC ARCHIVES OF NOVA SCOTIA

| Name | Date | Situation | Acres | Esch'd | Origin or Rank |
|---|---|---|---|---|---|
| ▭Saxton, John | 1784 | Digby Township | 100 | 1800 | |
| Saxton, Timothy | 1784 | " " | 100 | 1800 | |
| ▲Schutze, Nicholas | 1786 | Halifax-Annapolis Rd. | 50 | 1819 | |
| ▲Seabury, David | 1791 | Halifax-Annapolis Rd., part possibly in Lunen. Co. | 640 | 1819 | |
| Seabury, David | 1785 | St. Mary's Bay | 1000 | 1796 | |
| Seaman, Benjamin | 1785 | " " " | 1000 | 1796 | |
| Seaman, Richard | 1785 | " " " | 1000 | 1796 | |
| Sexton, William | 1784 | Digby Township | 300 | 1800 | |
| Shea, William | 1784 | " " | 250 | 1800 | |
| ▲Sherman, Robert | 1786 | Halifax-Annapolis Rd. | 200 | 1819 | |
| ▭Slocum, John | 1784 | Digby Township | 250 | 1800 | |
| Smith, Alexander | 1784 | " " | 200 | 1800 | |
| Smith, Austen | 1784 | " " | 200 | 1800 | |
| Smith, James | 1784 | " " | 100 | 1800 | |
| Smith, John | 1784 | " " | 100 | 1800 | |
| ▲Sneden, Stephen | 1791 | Halifax-Annapolis Rd., part possibly in Lunen. Co. | 640 | 1819 | |
| ▭Sneeden, Stephen | 1784 | Digby Township | 500 | 1800 | |
| ▲Sniffen, Elizabeth | 1786 | Halifax-Annapolis Rd. | 100 | 1819 | |
| Soales, Daniel | 1784 | Digby Township | 100 | 1800 | |
| Soales, David | 1784 | " " | 100 | 1800 | |
| Stevens, Enos | 1784 | " " | 150 | 1800 | |
| Stevens, Phineas | 1784 | " " | 250 | 1800 | |
| Stewart, Anthony | 1785 | St. Mary's Bay | 1000 | 1796 | |
| ▲Stewart, James | 1791 | Halifax-Annapolis Rd., part possibly in Lunen. Co. | 640 | 1819 | |
| Stewart, Mathew | 1784 | Digby Township | 150 | 1800 | |
| Stilwell, Daniel | 1784 | " " | 100 | 1800 | |
| ▲Strawbridge, George | 1786 | Halifax-Annapolis Rd. | 100 | 1819 | |
| Street, William | 1784 | Digby Township | 100 | 1800 | |
| ▲Sulice, Daniel | 1786 | Halifax-Annapolis Rd. | 200 | 1819 | |
| Sutherland, O'Sullivan | 1784 | Digby Township | 100 | 1800 | |
| ▲Sutherland, O'Sullivan | 1786 | Halifax-Annapolis Rd. | 200 | 1819 | |
| Sye, Roger | 1784 | Digby Township | 200 | 1800 | |
| ▭Syphar, Jacob | 1784 | " " | 250 | 1800 | |
| Talbot, Edward | 1784 | " " | 300 | 1800 | |
| ▲Talbut, Edward | 1786 | Halifax-Annapolis Rd. | 200 | 1819 | |
| Tarrant, Leonard | 1784 | Digby Township | 200 | 1800 | |
| Tate, Thomas | 1784 | " " | 150 | 1800 | |
| ▲Tate, William | 1786 | Halifax-Annapolis Rd. | 100 | 1819 | |
| Taylor, George | 1785 | St. Mary's Bay | 1000 | 1796 | |
| ▭Taylor, John | 1784 | Digby Township | 500 | 1800 | |
| Taylor, William | 1785 | St. Mary's Bay | 1000 | 1796 | |
| ▲Taylor, William | 1791 | Halifax-Annapolis Rd. | 640 | 1819 | |
| Ten Eych, Andrew | 1784 | Digby Township | 100 | 1800 | |
| Ten Eych, Andrew, Jr. | 1784 | " " | 100 | 1800 | |
| Thomas, Ebenezer | 1784 | " " | 200 | 1800 | |
| Thomas, Joseph | 1784 | " " | 200 | 1800 | |
| Thomson, Samuel | 1784 | " " | 200 | 1800 | |
| ▲Todd, Ann | 1786 | Halifax-Annapolis Rd. | 200 | 1819 | |
| ▲Todd, Elizabeth (Miss) | 1786 | " " " | 100 | 1819 | |
| ▲Todd, James | 1786 | " " " | 100 | 1819 | |
| Tongue, Joshua | 1784 | Digby Township | 200 | 1800 | |
| ▲Totten, Gilbert | 1791 | Halifax-Annapolis Rd., part possibly in Lunen. Co. | 640 | 1819 | |
| Totten, Joseph | 1784 | Digby Township | 200 | 1800 | |
| Totten, William | 1784 | " " | 200 | 1800 | Captain |
| Towner, Enoch | 1784 | " " | 150 | 1800 | |
| ▲Townsend, Grigory | 1791 | Halifax-Annapolis Rd., part possibly in Lunen. Co. | 640 | 1819 | |
| ▲Traverne, Caleb | 1786 | Halifax-Annapolis Rd. | 100 | 1819 | |

# LOYALISTS AND LAND SETTLEMENT IN NOVA SCOTIA 37

| Name | Date | Situation | Acres | Esch'd | Origin or Rank |
|---|---|---|---|---|---|
| ▲Tucker, Robert | 1791 | Halifax-Annapolis Rd., part possibly in Lunen. Co. | 640 | 1819 | |
| ▲Tucket, Robert | 1786 | Halifax-Annapolis Rd. | 152 | 1819 | |
| ▲Tyce, Abraham | 1786 | "       "       " | 200 | 1819 | |
| Typenny, Robert | 1784 | Digby Township | 300 | 1800 | Major |
| ▲Valentine, Jacob | 1786 | Halifax-Annapolis Rd. | 100 | 1819 | |
| Valentine, William | 1784 | Digby Township | 100 | 1800 | |
| ▲Van Blaricume, Anthony | 1786 | Halifax-Annapolis Rd | 100 | 1819 | |
| Van Klash, Simeon | 1784 | Digby Township | 300 | 1800 | |
| Van Klech, Livi | 1784 | "       " | 150 | 1800 | |
| Vanloo, Henry | 1784 | "       " | 100 | 1800 | |
| ▲Vanson, Hands | 1786 | Halifax-Annapolis Rd. | 200 | 1819 | |
| Veitch, Andrew | 1784 | Digby Township | 300 | 1800 | |
| Veitch, William | 1784 | "       " | 100 | 1800 | |
| ▢Vroom, John | 1784 | "       " | 400 | 1800 | |
| Wade, Humphrey | 1784 | "       " | 350 | 1800 | |
| Waistcoat, Thomas. | 1784 | "       " | 100 | 1800 | |
| ▢Walker, Adam | 1784 | "       " | 250 | 1800 | |
| Walters, Peter | 1784 | Digby Township | 200 | 1800 | |
| Walters, William | 1784 | "       " | 100 | 1800 | |
| Ward, Ebenezer | 1784 | "       " | 300 | 1800 | |
| ▲Ward, James | 1786 | Halifax-Annapolis Rd. | 200 | 1819 | |
| Ward, Thomas | 1784 | Digby Township | 500 | 1800 | |
| ▲Watts, John | 1786 | Halifax-Annapolis Rd. | 200 | 1819 | Corporal |
| ▲Way, James | 1786 | "       "       " | 100 | 1819 | |
| Wear, Thomas | 1784 | Digby Township | 100 | 1800 | |
| Weeks, Seaman | 1784 | "       " | 350 | 1800 | |
| ▢Welsh, Maurice | 1784 | "       " | 150 | 1800 | |
| Wheeler, Hezekiah | 1784 | "       " | 100 | 1800 | |
| ▲White, Paul | 1786 | Halifax-Annapolis Rd. | 100 | 1819 | |
| ▲White, Paul | 1786 | "       "       " | 200 | 1819 | |
| Whitman, Zebulon | 1784 | Digby Township | 100 | 1800 | |
| Wilkins, Isaac | 1785 | St. Mary's Bay | 1000 | 1796 | |
| Williams, Elijah | 1784 | Digby Township | 200 | 1800 | |
| Wilson, Robert | 1784 | "       " | 100 | 1800 | |
| Wood, George | 1784 | "       " | 100 | 1800 | |
| ▲Wooddrooffe, Jobe | 1786 | Halifax-Annapolis Rd. | 200 | 1819 | |
| Woodruff, Jabez | 1784 | Digby Township | 200 | 1800 | |
| Young, Israel | 1784 | "       " | 300 | 1800 | |
| ▲Young, Martha | 1786 | Halifax-Annapolis Rd. | 100 | 1819 | |

# Cumberland County
## GRANTS

| Name | Date | Situation | Acres | Origin or Rank |
|---|---|---|---|---|
| Ackel, James | 1785 | Cobequid Road | 250 | Westchester, N. Y. |
| Ackerly, Isaac | 1803 | Wentworth Township | 500 | |
| Ackley, David | 1785 | Cobequid Road | 250 | Westchester, N. Y. |
| Ackley, Isaac, Jr. | 1785 | River Remsheg | 200 | " " |
| Ackley, Isaac, Sr. | 1785 | " " | 200 | " " |
| Ackley, Nathaniel | 1785 | Cobequid Road | 500 | " " |
| Ackley, Obadiah | 1785 | River Remsheg | 200 | " " |
| Ackley, Oliver | 1785 | " " | 200 | " " |
| Angevine, John | 1785 | " " | 200 | " " |
| Apps, John | 1784 | Remsheg | 100 | Royal Fencible Am. Reg't |
| Austin, James | 1785 | Cobequid Road | 250 | Westchester, N. Y. |
| Austin, John | 1785 | " " | 250 | " " |
| Baker, John | 1785 | River Remsheg | 200 | " " |
| Baker, Josiah | 1785 | Cobequid Road | 250 | " " |
| Barker, Israel | 1785 | " " | 250 | " " |
| Barrett, Richard | 1784 | Remsheg | 100 | Private R. F. Am. Reg't |
| Baxter, Augustus | 1785 | River Remsheg | 200 | Westchester, N. Y. |
| Baxter, Frederick | 1785 | " " | 200 | " " |
| Baxter, John | 1785 | Cobequid Road | 500 | " " |
| Baxter, Lockwood | 1785 | River Remsheg | 200 | " " |
| Beardsley, Sybal | 1785 | " " | 200 | " " |
| Bebe, Secord | 1803 | Wentworth Township | 500 | |
| Biggin, Thomas | 1784 | Remsheg | 100 | Private R. F. Am. Reg't |
| Bigney, Ann | 1803 | Wentworth Township | 50 | |
| Bigney, Arthur | 1803 | " " | 50 | |
| Bigney, Levi | 1803 | " " | 50 | |
| Bigney, Mark | 1803 | " " | 100 | |
| Bigney, Mary | 1803 | " " | 50 | |
| Bigney, Peter | 1803 | " " | 100 | |
| Bishop, Samuel | 1785 | Cobequid Road | 250 | Westchester, N. Y. |
| Brisband, John | 1785 | " " | 500 | " " |
| Brisbane, James | 1785 | River Remsheg | 200 | " " |
| Brown, Ebenezer | 1785 | " " | 200 | " " |
| Brown, John | 1785 | " " | 200 | " " |
| Brown, Thomas | 1784 | Remsheg | 100 | Private R. F. Am. Reg't |
| Brundidge, Joshua | 1785 | River Remsheg | 200 | Westchester, N. Y. |
| Bryant, John | 1785 | " " | 200 | " " |
| Budd, William | 1785 | " " | 200 | " " |
| Burk, Michael | 1784 | Remsheg | 400 | Corp'l R. F. Am. Reg't |
| Carnell, Thomas | 1785 | River Remsheg | 200 | Westchester, N. Y. |
| Chamberlain, Benjamin | 1785 | Cobequid Road | 500 | " " |
| Chase, James | 1785 | " " | 250 | " " |
| Chase, James | 1785 | River Remsheg | 200 | " " |
| Chatterton, John | 1785 | " " | 200 | " " |
| Chatterton, Samuel | 1803 | Wentworth Township | 500 | |
| Collins, Peter | 1784 | Remsheg | 300 | Corp'l R. F. Am. Reg't |
| Colman, William | 1784 | " | 100 | Private " " " |
| Coon, William | 1785 | Cobequid Road | 500 | Westchester, N. Y. |
| Corbett, John | 1784 | Remsheg | 100 | Private R. F. Am. Reg't |
| Cornell, Samuel | 1785 | River Remsheg | 200 | Westchester, N. Y. |
| Coulbourn, Richard | 1784 | Remsheg | 200 | Private R. F. Am. Reg't |
| Covert, Abraham | 1785 | Cobequid Road | 500 | Lieut. Westchester, N. Y. |
| Cravey, Martin | 1784 | Remsheg | 300 | Serg't R. F. Am. Reg't |

LOYALISTS AND LAND SETTLEMENT IN NOVA SCOTIA 39

| Name | Date | Situation | Acres | Origin or Rank |
|---|---|---|---|---|
| Crawford, John | 1785 | Cobequid Road | 500 | Westchester, N. Y. |
| Creary, Martin | 1785 | " " | 250 | " " |
| | | | | |
| Dallaway, Matthew | 1785 | " " | 250 | " " |
| Derry, James | 1785 | River Remsheg | 200 | " " |
| Derry, John | 1785 | " " | 200 | " " |
| Dickerson, Daniel | 1785 | Cobequid Road | 500 | " " |
| Dotten, James | 1785 | River Remsheg | 200 | " " |
| Dunn, Daniel | 1785 | " " | 200 | " " |
| | | | | |
| Earles, Joseph | 1785 | " " | 200 | " " |
| Edjet, Joel | 1785 | " " | 200 | " " |
| Edjet, John | 1785 | " " | 200 | " " |
| Edmons, John | 1785 | " " | 200 | Westchester, N. Y. |
| Embree, Joseph, Jr. | 1785 | Cobequid Road | 500 | " " |
| Embree, Samuel | 1785 | " " | 500 | Lieut. Westchester, N. Y. |
| | | | | |
| Fanning, Edmund | 1787 | Remsheg River | 800 | Lt.-Col. King's Am. Reg't |
| Fanning, Edmund | 1792 | " " | 1000 | " " " " |
| Ferris, Joshua | 1785 | " " | 200 | Westchester, N. Y. |
| Fillet, James | 1788 | River Macaan, E. | 500 | |
| Forsner, Andrew | 1785 | River Remsheg | 200 | Westchester, N. Y. |
| Foster, William | 1785 | " " | 200 | " " |
| Fountain, Aaron | 1785 | Cobequid Road | 500 | " " |
| Fowler, Amos | 1785 | " " | 250 | " " |
| Fowler, Jonathan | 1785 | River Remsheg | 200 | " " |
| Fowler, Josiah | 1785 | " " | 200 | " " |
| | | | | |
| Ganong, John | 1785 | " " | 200 | " " |
| Gilroy, Barney | 1798 | River Macaan | 500 | 54th. Reg't |
| Gleeson, John | 1785 | Cobequid Road | 500 | Westchester, N. Y. |
| Gooden, Daniel | 1784 | Remsheg | 400 | Serg't R.F. Am. Reg't |
| Gooden, Daniel, Jr. | 1784 | " | 100 | Private " " " |
| Gooden, Enoch | 1784 | " | 200 | Corp'l " " " |
| Gooden, Jonathan | 1784 | " | 200 | Drummer " " " |
| Gooden, Thomas | 1784 | " | 200 | " " " " |
| Goolding, James | 1785 | River Remsheg | 100 | Westchester, N. Y. |
| Goolding, Nathaniel | 1785 | Cobequid Road | 500 | " " |
| Goolding, Zenus | 1785 | River Remsheg | 200 | " " |
| Gordon, John | 1784 | Remsheg | 100 | Private R. F. Am. Reg't |
| Gray, Henry | 1785 | Cobequid Road | 250 | Westchester, N. Y. |
| Griffin, Caleb | 1785 | " " | 500 | " " |
| | | | | |
| Halstead, Samuel | 1785 | River Remsheg | 200 | " " |
| Hammon, George | 1784 | Remsheg | 100 | R. F. Am. Reg't |
| Harper, Thomas | 1784 | " | 100 | " " " |
| Hart, Tucker | 1803 | Wentworth Township | 300 | |
| Hatch, Robert | 1785 | River Remsheg | 200 | Westchester, N. Y. |
| Hatfield, Barnes | 1785 | " " | 200 | Capt. " " |
| Haviland, Gilbert | 1785 | Cobequid Road | 500 | Lieut. " " |
| Haviland, Samuel | 1785 | River Remsheg | 200 | " " |
| Hewson, James | 1785 | " " | 200 | " " |
| Hickey, Laurence | 1784 | Remsheg | 100 | R. F. Am. Reg't |
| Hoag, Nathaniel | 1785 | Cobequid Road | 250 | Westchester, N. Y. |
| Hoeg, Nathaniel | 1785 | River Remsheg | 200 | " " |
| Holiday, Samuel | 1785 | " " | 200 | " " |
| Holmes, Daniel | 1785 | Cobequid Road | 250 | " " |
| Holmes, Samuel | 1785 | River Remsheg | 200 | " " |
| Horton, Joshua | 1785 | Cobequid Road | 250 | " " |
| Horton, Samuel | 1785 | " " | 500 | " " |
| Horton, Samuel | 1785 | River Remsheg | 200 | " " |
| Horton, Solomon | 1785 | " " | 200 | " " |
| Hunt, John | 1785 | " " | 200 | " " |
| Hunter, John | 1785 | Cobequid Road | 500 | " " |
| Husted, Thomas | 1785 | River Remsheg | 200 | " " |

# PUBLIC ARCHIVES OF NOVA SCOTIA

| Name | Date | Situation | Acres | Origin or Rank |
|---|---|---|---|---|
| Jacobs, John | 1785 | River Remsheg | 200 | Westchester, N. Y. |
| Jenkins, Thomas | 1785 | " " | 200 | " " |
| Jennings, Charles | 1785 | Cobequid Road | 250 | " " |
| Jona, John | 1784 | Remsheg | 300 | Corp'l R. F. Am. Reg't |
| Kenady, John | 1784 | " | 100 | " " " |
| Kinshaw, William | 1784 | " | 300 | " " " |
| Kipp, Samuel | 1785 | River Remsheg | 200 | Capt. Westchester, N. Y. |
| Kipp, Samuel | 1787 | " " | 500 | Captain |
| Knapp, Moses | 1785 | " " | 200 | Capt. Westchester, N. Y. |
| Knapp, Moses | 1787 | " " | 500 | Captain |
| Knipp, James | 1785 | " " | 200 | Westchester, N. Y. |
| Larkin, Laurence | 1784 | Remsheg | 250 | Drummer R.F. Am. Reg't |
| Lee, Richard | 1790 | Cumberland Bay | 500 | |
| Lefargee, John | 1785 | River Remsheg | 200 | Westchester, N. Y. |
| Lewes, Shubad | 1785 | Cobequid Road | 500 | " " |
| Lloyd, Michael | 1785 | River Remsheg | 200 | " ". |
| Lloyd, William | 1784 | Remsheg | 100 | Private R. F. Am. Reg't |
| Lofree, William | 1785 | Cobequid Road | 250 | Westchester, N. Y. |
| Lounsbury, James | 1785 | " " | 500 | " " |
| Lovely, Benjamin | 1784 | Remsheg | 300 | R. F. Am. Reg't |
| Low, John | 1785 | River Remsheg | 200 | Westchester, N. Y. |
| Lures, Lank | 1785 | " " | 200 | " " |
| Maby, John | 1785 | Cobequid Road | 500 | " " |
| Maby, Peter | 1785 | " " | 250 | " " |
| McFee, Angus | 1785 | River Remsheg | 200 | " " |
| McNabb, Alexander | 1803 | Wentworth Township | 500 | |
| McNabb, James | 1803 | " " | 500 | |
| McNabb, John | 1803 | " " | 500 | |
| McNabb, Peter | 1803 | " " | 500 | |
| Mead, James | 1785 | Cobequid Road | 250 | Westchester, N. Y. |
| Merrit, James | 1785 | " " | 250 | " " |
| Merrit, Jeremiah | 1785 | River Remsheg | 200 | " " |
| Miller, James | 1785 | Cobequid Road | 250 | " " |
| Mills, Daniel | 1788 | River Macaan, E. | 500 | |
| Mills, David | 1785 | Cobequid Road | 500 | Westchester, N. Y. |
| Mills, Jesse | 1785 | River Remsheg | 200 | " " |
| Mills, Reuben | 1785 | " " | 200 | " " |
| Mills, Samuel | 1785 | " " | 200 | " " |
| Mills, Samuel | 1788 | River Macaan, E. | 500 | |
| Munro, Duncan | 1798 | " " | 500 | 42nd. Reg't |
| Murphy, Patrick | 1803 | Wentworth Township | 48 | |
| Myers, John | 1785 | Cobequid Road | 500 | Westchester, N. Y. |
| Myers, Mincus | 1785 | River Remsheg | 200 | " " |
| Newman, Jeremiah | 1785 | " " | 200 | " " |
| Niles, Nathaniel | 1785 | " " | 200 | " " |
| O'Brien, Luke | 1784 | Remsheg | 100 | R. F. Am. Reg't |
| O'Brien, Miles | 1784 | " | 250 | " " " |
| Ogden, Jesse | 1785 | Cobequid Road | 250 | Westchester, N. Y. |
| Ogden, John | 1785 | " " | 500 | " " |
| Outhouse, Simon | 1785 | " " | 250 | " " |
| Palmer, Gideon | 1785 | " " | 500 | Capt. " " |
| Palmer, Jonathan | 1785 | " " | 500 | " " |
| Parr, John | 1785 | River Remsheg | 200 | " " |
| Philips, Frederick | 1785 | " " | 200 | " " |
| Pierce, Joseph | 1785 | " " | 200 | " " |
| Piers, Alexander | 1785 | " " | 200 | " " |
| Piers, Daniel | 1785 | " " | 100 | " " |
| Piers, Ephraim | 1785 | " " | 200 | " " |

# LOYALISTS AND LAND SETTLEMENT IN NOVA SCOTIA 41

| Name | Date | Situation | Acres | Origin or Rank |
|---|---|---|---|---|
| Piers, Ezekiel | 1785 | River Remsheg | 200 | Westchester, N. Y. |
| Piers, Henry | 1785 | Cobequid Road | 250 | " " |
| Piers, John | 1785 | River Remsheg | 200 | " " |
| Pugsley, Daniel | 1785 | " " | 200 | " " |
| Pugsley, David | 1785 | Cobequid Road | 500 | " " |
| Pugsley, John | 1785 | River Remsheg | 200 | " " |
| Pugsley, John | 1787 | Remsheg River | 1000 | |
| Purdy, Gabriel | 1785 | River Remsheg | 200 | Westchester, N. Y. |
| Purdy, Gabriel | 1785 | " " | 200 | " " |
| Purdy, Henry | 1785 | Cumberland Road | 500 | Capt. " " |
| Purdy, Henry | 1788 | Fort Laurence | 150 | " " " |
| Purdy, Joseph | 1785 | Cobequid Road | 500 | " " |
| Purdy, Nathaniel | 1785 | " " | 250 | " " |
| Purdy, Robert | 1785 | " " | 250 | " " |
| Purdy, Stephen | 1785 | " " | 500 | " " |
| Reynolds, Nathaniel | 1784 | Remsheg | 100 | R. F. Am. Reg't |
| Roblee, John | 1785 | River Remsheg | 200 | Westchester, N. Y. |
| Rundle, Jabez | 1785 | Cobequid Road | 500 | " " |
| Rustin, Jeremiah | 1785 | " " | 500 | " " |
| Rustin, John, Jr. | 1785 | River Remsheg | 200 | " " |
| Rustin, John, Sr. | 1785 | Cobequid Road | 500 | " " |
| Rustin, Peter | 1785 | " " | 500 | " " |
| Ryness, John | 1785 | " " | 250 | |
| Schofield, Jesse | 1785 | River Remsheg | 200 | " " |
| Scofield, Jesse | 1785 | Cobequid Road | 250 | " " |
| Scofield, Paul Carpus | 1785 | River Remsheg | 200 | " " |
| Seaman, Ezekiah | 1785 | Cobequid Road | 250 | " " |
| Seaman, Jacamiah | 1785 | Cobequid Road | 500 | Westchester, N. Y. |
| Seaman, Jacamiah and Seaman, Stephen | 1797 | {Goose River, River Philip | 750, 970 | |
| Seaman, Stephen | 1785 | Cobequid Road | 500 | Westchester, N. Y. |
| Seaman, Stephen, see Seaman, Jacamiah | 1797 | | | |
| Sears, Joseph | 1785 | Cobequid Road | 500 | Westchester, N. Y. |
| Sherwood, John | 1785 | " " | 250 | " " |
| Simmons, Moses | 1785 | " " | 500 | " " |
| Simpson, Obadiah | 1785 | " " | 500 | " " |
| Smith, Absolem | 1785 | River Remsheg | 200 | " " |
| Smith, Elijah | 1785 | Cobequid Road | 500 | |
| Smith, Josiah | 1784 | Remsheg | 500 | Serg't R. F. Am. Reg't |
| Smith, Oliver | 1785 | River Remsheg | 200 | Westchester, N. Y. |
| Snider, Jonathan | 1785 | Cobequid Road | 250 | " " |
| Snider, Zachariah | 1785 | " " | 500 | " " |
| Souls, Thomas | 1803 | Wentworth Township | 500 | |
| Stephens, John | 1785 | River Remsheg | 200 | Westchester, N. Y. |
| Stevens, Andrew | 1803 | Wentworth Township | 50 | |
| Stevens, Ann | 1803 | " " | 50 | |
| Stevens, Aprian | 1803 | " " | 100 | |
| Stevens, Benjamin | 1803 | " " | 100 | |
| Stevens, Lemuel | 1803 | " " | 50 | |
| Stevens, Levi | 1803 | " " | 150 | |
| Stevens, Levi | 1803 | " " | 50 | |
| Stevens, Oliver | 1803 | " " | 100 | |
| Stevens, Ryne Copet | 1803 | " " | 50 | |
| Stults, Henry | 1785 | Cobequid Road | 500 | Westchester, N. Y. |
| Tidd, Daniel | 1785 | River Remsheg | 200 | " " |
| Tidd, David | 1785 | " " | 200 | " " |
| Tidd, Isaac | 1785 | " " | 200 | " " |
| Tidd, James | 1785 | " " | 200 | " " |
| Tidd, John | 1785 | " " | 200 | Ensign. " " |
| Tidd, Moses | 1785 | " " | 200 | |

# PUBLIC ARCHIVES OF NOVA SCOTIA

| Name | Date | Situation | Acres | Origin or Rank |
|---|---|---|---|---|
| Tillit, James | 1785 | River Remsheg | 200 | Westchester, N. Y. |
| Totten, Daniel | 1785 | " " | 200 | " " |
| Totten, Gilbert | 1785 | " " | 200 | Capt. " " |
| Totten, Gilbert | 1787 | " " | 500 | " |
| Totten, James, Jr. | 1785 | " " | 200 | " " |
| Totten, James, Sr. | 1785 | " " | 200 | " " |
| Totten, John | 1785 | " " | 200 | " " |
| Trenchard, Henry | 1785 | Cobequid Road | 500 | " " |
| Trene, Joseph | 1785 | " " | 500 | " " |
| Tuttle, John | 1803 | Wentworth Township | 500 | |
| Tuttle, Peter | 1803 | " " | 500 | |
| Tuttle, Stephen, Jr. | 1803 | " " | 500 | |
| Tuttle, William | 1803 | " " | 500 | |
| Veal, Jacob | 1785 | River Remsheg | 200 | Westchester, N. Y. |
| Vincent, Charles | 1785 | Cobequid Road | 500 | " " |
| Watson, Joseph | 1784 | Remsheg | 100 | R. F. Am. Reg't |
| Weathered, Joshua | 1784 | " | 100 | " " " |
| Webb, Noah | 1785 | River Remsheg | 100 | Westchester, N. Y. |
| Weeks, Wright | 1785 | Cobequid Road | 250 | " " |
| Wheaton, Thomas | 1785 | " " | 500 | " " |
| Wightman, John | 1784 | Remsheg | 100 | R. F. Am. Reg't |
| Williams, Frederick | 1785 | River Remsheg | 200 | Capt. Westchester, N. Y. |
| Williams, John | 1785 | Cobequid Road | 500 | " " |
| Williams, Samuel | 1784 | Remsheg | 150 | R. F. Am. Reg't |
| Williams, Samuel | 1785 | River Remsheg | 200 | Westchester, N. Y. |
| Williams, William | 1785 | " " | 200 | " " |
| Wilson, John | 1785 | Cobequid Road | 250 | " " |
| Winn, Peter | 1785 | River Remsheg | 200 | " " |
| Wood, Samuel | 1785 | Cobequid Road | 250 | " " |
| Worden, Jonathan | 1785 | " " | 250 | " " |
| Wyatt, Nathaniel | 1785 | River Remsheg | 200 | " " |
| Yoxell, Peter | 1784 | Remsheg | 100 | R. F. Am. Reg't |

## Cumberland County
### WARRANTS

| Name | Date | Situation | Acres | Origin or Rank |
|---|---|---|---|---|
| Allen, John | 1787 | Remsheg | 500 | |
| Canfield, Stephen | 1788 | " | 120 | |
| Tuttle, Stephen | 1787 | " | 450 | |

## Halifax County
### GRANTS

| Name | Date | Situation | Acres | Origin or Rank |
|---|---|---|---|---|
| Adams, Philip | 1784 | Preston Township | 200 | |
| Addams, William | 1785 | Merigumish | 100 | Private 82nd. Reg't |
| Alexander, Robert | 1784 | Halifax-Hants Boundary | 500 | |
| Allardice, Archibald | 1784 | Pictou | 500 | Naval Lieutenant |
| Allmon, Wm. James | 1800 | Shubenacadie River | 1000 | |
| Anderson, Andrew | 1785 | Merigumish | 100 | Private 82nd. Reg't |
| Anderson, John | 1784 | Preston Township | 100 | |
| Anderson, Simon | 1785 | Dartmouth | 100 | Soldier |
| Arbuckles, Charles | 1785 | Merigumish | 200 | Corp'l 82nd. Reg't |
| Armstrong, Thomas | 1784 | Windsor Road | 100 | |
| Arthur, James | 1785 | Merigumish | 100 | Private 82nd. Reg't |
| Attwood, Richard | 1784 | Halifax-Hants Boundary | 500 | |
| Atwood, Nathaniel | 1784 | Sheet Harbour | 250 | Royal Garrison Batt. |
| Aylward, James | 1786 | Jedore | 100 | |
| Bacon, Jacob | 1786 | Windsor Road, S. W. | 500 | |
| Bagley, Joseph | 1786 | Preston Township | 200 | |
| Bailie, John | 1785 | Merigumish | 150 | Private 82nd. Reg't |
| Baker, Joseph | 1786 | Jedore | 300 | Blacksmith |
| Bampstead, Jeremiah | 1784 | Preston Township | 200 | |
| Bannaytine, David | 1785 | Merigumish | 200 | Corp'l 82nd. Reg't |
| Barker, John | 1796 | Dartmouth T. & | W.L.'s | |
| Barns, Arthur | 1786 | Jedore | 100 | |
| Bates, Thomas | 1785 | Dartmouth | 100 | Soldier |
| Bean, Enoch | 1785 | S. E. Passage | 400 | |
| Bean, Enoch | 1790 | Cole Harbour, W. | 350 | |
| Beaver, James | 1784 | Ship Harbour, W. | 200 | |
| Bell, James | 1784 | Windsor Road | 200 | |
| Bell, John | 1784 | Preston Township | 200 | |
| Bell, Samuel | 1784 | Windsor Road | 200 | |
| Benham, Thomas | 1784 | Sheet Harbour | 100 | Royal Garrison Batt. |
| Benvie, James | 1785 | Windsor Road, S. W. | 100 | |
| Bermingham, James | 1787 | Preston Township | 100 | |
| Berry, William | 1784 | " " | 200 | (Plym'th,Dep'y Comp |
| Bethell, Rob't | 1799 | Colchester Road | 1250 | { troller, Nav. Offi.Capt |
| | | | | (King'sOrangeRangers |
| Beves, William | 1784 | Preston Township | 200 | |
| Biggny, John | 1784 | Sheet Harbour | 100 | Royal Garrison Batt. |
| Bilboa [Bilboe] Wm. | 1785 | Merigumish | 100 | Drummer 82nd. Reg't |
| Black, John | 1785 | Dartmouth | 50 | Soldier |
| Blakely, Chamber | 1784 | Ship Harbour, W. | 200 | |
| Blowers, Sampson Saltei | 1785 | Halifax | W. L. | |
| Blowers, Sampson Salter | 1786 | Halifax Peninsula | 5 | |
| Blue, Daniel | 1786 | Musquodoboit River | 200 | Quarter Master |
| Blue, Daniel | 1788 | " Harbour | 92 | |
| Boggey, David | 1785 | Merigumish | 100 | Private 82nd. Reg't |
| Bond, George | 1784 | Halifax-Hants Boundary | 500 | Captain E. Florida |
| Bond, John | 1784 | " " " | 1000 | " " " |
| Bond, John | 1784 | " " " | 250 | |
| Bond, John | 1786 | Jedore | 200 | |
| Boothe, John | 1786 | " | 200 | |
| Bowser, John | 1785 | Windsor Road, S. W. | 250 | |
| Boyce, John | 1784 | Preston Township | 150 | |
| Bradaw, John | 1785 | Merigumish | 100 | Private 82nd. Reg't |
| Bradley, John | 1784 | Sheet Harbour | 200 | Royal Garrison Batt. |
| Braeton, Thos. | 1787 | Musquodoboit River, N. | 100 | Soldier |
| Brandon, Samuel | 1787 | Preston Township | 250 | |

## 44   PUBLIC ARCHIVES OF NOVA SCOTIA

| Name | Date | Situation | Acres | Origin or Rank |
|---|---|---|---|---|
| Brannon, Michael | 1785 | Merigumish | 100 | Private 82nd. Reg't |
| Brannon, William | 1785 | " | 100 | "      "      " |
| Brimer, William | 1784 | Preston Township | 100 | |
| Brown, George | 1784 | " " | 500 | |
| Brown, George | 1785 | Merigumish | 200 | Serj't 82nd. Reg't |
| Brown, George | 1785 | " | 100 | Private "      " |
| Brown, Robert | 1784 | Sheet Harbour | 100 | Royal Garrison Batt. |
| Browne, Charles | 1785 | Merigumish | 100 | Private 82nd. Reg't |
| Browne, John | .1785 | Merigumish | 100 | Private 82nd. Reg't. |
| Brownfield, John | 1785 | " | 200 | Corp'l.  "      " |
| Bruce, Moses | 1784 | Halifax-Hants Boundary | 250 | |
| Brumley, Isaac | 1784 | Sheet Harbour | 150 | Royal Garrison Batt. |
| Brutus | 1784 | Preston Township | 50 | |
| Brymer, Alex | 1787 | Bedford | 500 | |
| Brymer, Alexander | 1783 | Halifax | T.L. & W.L | |
| Bryson, John | 1784 | Halifax-Hants Boundary | 250 | |
| Bryson, William | 1784 | "      "      " | 500 | |
| Bryson, William, Jr. | 1784 | "      "      " | 250 | |
| Burchell, James | 1784 | Sheet Harbour | 150 | Royal Garrison Batt. |
| Burns, Berna | 1787 | Musquodoboit River, N. | 100 | Soldier |
| Burns, Edward | 1785 | Windsor Road, S. W. | 100 | |
| Cahill, Mathew | 1787 | Harriet Fields | 200 | |
| Cameron, Alexander | 1785 | E. River—Pictou | 100 | |
| Cameron, Alexander | 1797 | E. River—Pictou | 300 | |
| Cameron, Archibald | 1785 | Merigumish | 150 | Private 82nd. Reg't. |
| Cameron, Archibald | 1785 | " | 100 | "      "      " |
| Cameron, Donald | 1785 | E. River—Pictou | 150 | |
| Cameron, Finlay | 1785 | "      "      " | 400 | |
| Cameron, James | 1797 | "      "      " | 300 | |
| Cameron, John | 1784 | Sheet Harbour | 100 | Royal Garrison Batt. |
| Cameron, Samuel | 1785 | E. River—Pictou | 300 | |
| Cameron, Samuel, Jr. | 1785 | "      "      " | 100 | |
| Campbell, Alexander | 1785 | Merigumish | 100 | Private 82nd. Reg't. |
| Campbell, Alexander | 1786 | Truro.Musquedoboit Rd. | 250 | |
| Campbell, Donald, Jr. | 1785 | Merigumish | 100 | Private 82nd. Reg't. |
| Campbell, Donald, Sr. | 1785 | Merigumish | 100 | Private 82nd. Reg't. |
| Campbell, Edward | 1784 | Sheet Harbour | 150 | Royal Garrison Batt. |
| Campbell, Finlay | 1785 | Merigumish | 100 | Private 82nd. Reg't. |
| Campbell, Matt | 1785 | " | 100 | "      "      " |
| Campin, William | 1785 | " | 100 | "      "      " |
| Carmichael, James | 1785 | " | 200 | Serj't.  "      " |
| Chamberlain, Theophilus | 1784 | Preston Township | 1000 | |
| Chapman, William | 1784 | "      " | 100 | |
| Chisholm, Donald | 1797 | E. River—Pictou | 350 | |
| Chisholm, Donald, Jr. | 1797 | "      "      " | 400 | |
| Chisholm, John | 1797 | "      "      " | 300 | |
| Chisholme, Alexander | 1786 | Dartmouth | 100 | |
| Chisholme, Duncan | 1785 | Merigumish | 100 | Private 82nd. Reg't. |
| Chisholme, John | 1785 | " | 100 | "      "      " |
| Chisholme, John, Jr. | 1785 | E. River—Pictou | 200 | |
| Chisholme, John, Sr. | 1785 | "      "      " | 300 | |
| Clark, Robert | 1785 | "      "      " | 100 | |
| Clark, Robert | 1797 | "      "      " | 150 | |
| Clawson, Robert | 1785 | Merigumish | 100 | Private 82nd. Reg't. |
| Clayton, Henry | 1786 | Jeddore | 100 | |
| Clinton, Patrick | 1785 | Dartmouth | 100 | Soldier |
| Cochrane, Archibald | 1785 | Merigumish | 100 | Private 82nd. Reg't. |
| Cock, Daniel (Rev.) | 1786 | Wilmot River (Stewiacke) | 700 | |
| Coe, John | 1785 | Windsor Road, S. W. | 200 | |
| Coldier, David | 1784 | Preston Township | 100 | |
| Cole, John | 1786 | Truro-Musquedoboit Rd. | 250 | |
| Collins, John | 1784 | Preston Township | 50 | |

# LOYALISTS AND LAND SETTLEMENT IN NOVA SCOTIA 45

| Name | Date | Situation | Acres | Origin or Rank |
|---|---|---|---|---|
| Colly, John | 1785 | Merigumish | 100 | Private 82nd. Reg't. |
| Combs, John | 1784 | Sheet Harbour | 500 | Ensign.RoyalGar.Batt. |
| Connor, Patrick | 1784 | Preston Township | 200 | |
| Conolly, Thomas | 1785 | Merigumish | 100 | Private 82nd. Reg't. |
| Cook, William | 1786 | Truro-Musquedoboit Rd. | 250 | |
| Costley, Robert | 1784 | Halifax-Hants Boundary | 250 | |
| Courtland | 1787 | Preston Township | 50 | Negro |
| Covill, Samuel | 1784 | Halifax-Hants Boundary | 500 | |
| Crawford, Archibald | 1784 | Preston Township | 100 | |
| Crawford, Edward | 1784 | " " | 50 | |
| Crawford, John | 1784 | " " | 200 | |
| Crawford, John | 1784 | " " | 100 | |
| Crawford, Laurence | 1784 | " " | 100 | |
| Creamer, Balthazer | 1784 | " " | 500 | |
| Cresswell, William | 1784 | Windsor Road | 250 | |
| Crispin | 1787 | Preston Township | 50 | Negro |
| Croffs, Thomas | 1784 | " " | 100 | |
| Crum, Nicholas | 1784 | Ship Harbour | 200 | |
| Cullen, Gerrad | 1785 | Merigumish | 200 | Serg't 82nd. Reg't |
| Culton, Robert | 1797 | E. River—Pictou | 100 | |
| Cummings, John | 1785 | Mill River, E. | 250 | |
| Cummins, George | 1785 | Merigumish | 100 | Private 82nd. Reg't |
| Cunard, Abraham | 1786 | Jedore | 150 | |
| Cunard, Abraham | 1792 | Halifax | W. L. | |
| Cunard, Abraham | 1797 | " | W. L. | |
| Cunningham, William | 1784 | Halifax-Hants Boundary | 500 | |
| Currin, John | 1787 | Preston Township | 100 | |
| Currin, Thomas | 1787 | " " | 100 | |
| Curry, Neil | 1784 | Sheet Harbour | 250 | Corp'l Royal Gar. Batt |
| Cusins, John | 1785 | Merigumish | 100 | Private 82nd. Reg't |
| Dansey, James | 1785 | " | 100 | " " " |
| Davis, Isaac | 1785 | Beaver Lake | 200 | |
| De Chazeau, Adam | 1784 | Preston Township | 250 | |
| Denoon, Hugh | 1784 | E. River—Pictou | 500 | New York |
| Denoon, Hugh | 1793 | Pictou | 500 | |
| Denoon, Hugh | 1803 | Cape St. Lewis | 500 | |
| Dewar, Robert | 1785 | Merigumish | 100 | Private 82nd. Reg't |
| Dickson, Alexander | 1785 | " | 100 | " " " |
| Dickson, John | 1785 | " | 100 | " " " |
| Dillman, Christopher | 1790 | Musquodoboit River | 300 | Hessian |
| Dirkham, Dennis | 1785 | Merigumish | 100 | Drummer 82nd. Reg't |
| Disney, William | 1786 | Musquodoboit | 100 | 34th. Reg't |
| Dolphin, Charles | 1784 | Preston Township | 100 | |
| Donaldson, Thomas | 1785 | S. E. Passage | 200 | |
| Donaldson, William | 1784 | Windsor Road | 250 | |
| Donochie, Laurence | 1785 | Merigumish | 100 | Private 82nd. Reg't |
| Drady, John | 1786 | Jedore | 350 | |
| Drumgoold, Robert | 1785 | ShubeneacadieRiver,S.E. | 200 | |
| Drysdale, John | 1787 | Halifax Township | 300 | |
| Dunbar, Alexander | 1797 | East River—Pictou | 200 | |
| Dunbar, Robert | 1797 | " " " | 450 | |
| Dunbar, William | 1797 | " " " | 300 | |
| Dunce, Charles | 1785 | Merigumish | 100 | Private 82nd. Reg't |
| Dunn, Robert | 1785 | " | 200 | Serg't " " |
| Dunnagan, Hugh | 1786 | Jedore, E. | 350 | |
| Dunnagan, Patrick | 1786 | " " | 200 | |
| Dunnagan, Philip | 1786 | " " | 250 | |
| Dunstar, William | 1787 | Preston Township | 100 | |
| Dwyer, Edmund | 1786 | Jedore, E. | 100 | |
| Easler, Peter | 1785 | S. E. Passage | 100 | |
| Edmunson, Christopher | 1787 | Preston Township | 100 | Negro |
| Edward, Thomas | 1784 | Sheet Harbour | 100 | Royal Garrison Batt. |

| Name | Date | Situation | Acres | Origin or Rank |
|---|---|---|---|---|
| Eissan, Michael | 1787 | Jedore, E. | 100 | |
| Ellis, Joseph | 1784 | Halifax-Hants Boundary | 250 | |
| Erlington, William | 1788 | St. Margaret's Bay | 300 | |
| Eves, John | 1785 | Merigumish | 200 | Serg't 82nd. Reg't |
| Fanning, Edmund | 1784 | Halifax Township | 24 | Colonel |
| Fanning, Edmund | 1784 | *Oak I. (Remsheg R.) | 1000 | " |
| Faulkner, John | 1786 | Jedore | 200 | |
| Faulkner, Thomas | 1786 | " | 100 | |
| Fisher, Francis | 1790 | Musquodoboit River | 100 | Hessian |
| Fisher, Maria | 1784 | Preston Township | 100 | |
| Fitzsimons, James | 1784 | Halifax-Hants Boundary | 500 | |
| Flemming [Hemming] Thomas | 1785 | Merigumish | 100 | 82nd. Reg't |
| Flieger, John H. | 1784 | Preston Township | 500 | |
| Foley, Hugh | 1784 | " " | 200 | |
| Foot [Toot] John | 1785 | Merigumish | 200 | |
| Forbes, Alexander | 1784 | Sheet Harbour | 100 | Royal Garrison Batt. |
| Forbes, John | 1797 | East River—Pictou | 400 | |
| Forrest, James | 1784 | Windsor—Halifax Road | 500 | |
| Forsyth, John | 1786 | Dartmouth | 200 | Serg't 42nd. Reg't |
| Foster, Edward | 1797 | Dartmouth | 11 | |
| Fowler, John | 1785 | Merigumish | 200 | Corp'l 82nd. Reg't |
| Fowler, William | 1784 | Windsor Road | 300 | |
| Fraser, James | 1785 | East River—Pictou | 350 | |
| Fraser, James, Jr. | 1785 | " " " | 100 | |
| Fraser, John | 1797 | East River—Pictou | 300 | Lieut. 82nd. Reg't |
| Fraser, Thomas | 1797 | " " " | 200 | 42nd. Reg't |
| Fraser, Thomas | 1797 | " " " | 100 | |
| Fraser, William | 1797 | " " " | 350 | |
| Frazer, Alexander | 1784 | Sheet Harbour | 200 | Royal Garrison Batt. |
| Frazer, John | 1785 | Merigumish | 700 | Lieut. 82nd. Reg't |
| Frazer, John | 1785 | " | 200 | Corp'l  "      " |
| Frederick, John | 1784 | Preston Township | 200 | |
| Frederick, John | 1784 | " " | 100 | |
| Fredson, Charles | 1784 | " " | 50 | |
| Fredson, Cuff | 1784 | " " | 25 | |
| Fredson, William | 1784 | " " | 50 | |
| Freedom, British | 1784 | " " | 50 | |
| Freedome, British | 1785 | Merigumish | 100 | Private 82nd. Reg't |
| Freeman | 1787 | Preston Township | 50 | Negro |
| Freeman, Edward | 1786 | Preston | T. L. | |
| Frelick, Adam | 1784 | Halifax-Hants Boundary | 500 | Captain |
| Fulton, Thomas | 1787 | Preston Township | 200 | |
| Gabriel, Jesse | 1784 | " " | 100 | |
| Gaff, James Lenox | 1784 | Ship Harbour | 200 | |
| Gallagher, John | 1784 | Sheet Harbour | 100 | Royal Garrison Batt. |
| Gallop, Antill | 1784 | Minas Gut | 1000 | |
| Gardiner, Robert | 1785 | Merigumish | 100 | Private 82nd. Reg't |
| Garrett, Joshua | 1786 | Preston Township | 450 | Ensign. |
| †Geddes, Charles | 1788 | Musquodoboit River | 1000 | Watch Maker |
| Gibbs, Zachariah | 1784 | Halifax-Hants Boundary | 1000 | Colonel |
| Gibes, James | 1785 | Merigumish | 100 | Private 82nd. Reg't |
| Giles, Joseph | 1784 | Preston Township | 200 | |
| Gillies, Deffy | 1785 | Merigumish | 200 | Corp'l 82nd. Reg't |
| Gobbiel, Francis | 1785 | " | 100 | Private  "      " |
| Gordon, Alexander | 1785 | " | 100 | "     "    " |
| Gordon, William | 1784 | Preston Township | 200 | |
| Gordon, William | 1785 | Pictou Harbour, E. | 500 | S. Carolina Dragoons |
| Goudge, Thomas | 1786 | Halifax Peninsula | 5 | |
| Gouge, Thomas | 1786 | Jedore | 350 | |
| Gow, Peter | 1785 | Merigumish | 100 | Private 82nd. Reg't |

\* Possibly in Cumberland Co.
† Robert Geddes, also of Musquodoboit River, was a Pre-Loyalist.

# LOYALISTS AND LAND SETTLEMENT IN NOVA SCOTIA 47

| Name | Date | Situation | Acres | Origin or Rank |
|---|---|---|---|---|
| Gowe, William | 1785 | Merigumish | 100 | Private 82nd Reg't |
| Gower, Henry | 1787 | Preston Township | 200 | |
| Grady, Michael | 1785 | Shubenacadie River, S.E. | 100 | King's Rangers |
| Grady, Michael | 1785 | " " " | 100 | " " |
| Graham, James | 1785 | Three Fathom Harbour | 250 | |
| Grant, Daniel | 1787 | Halifax Township | 350 | |
| Grant, John | 1786 | Sheet Harbour | 500 | Ensign. |
| Grant, Peter | 1785 | East River—Pictou | 300 | |
| Grant, William | 1792 | Stewiacke | 450 | |
| Green, Francis | 1796 | Dartmouth T. & | | W.L.'s |
| Green, Henry | 1784 | Halifax-Hants Boundary | 500 | |
| Green, Thomas | 1784 | Ship Harbour, S. W. | 700 | |
| Greenwood, John | 1784 | Preston Township | 55 | |
| Greenwood, Samuel | 1784 | " " | 1000 | |
| Greenwood, Samuel | 1792 | Halifax 2 | | T.L.'s |
| Griffin, Richard | 1785 | Merigumish | 100 | Private 82nd. Reg't |
| Griffith, Joseph | 1784 | Preston Township | 200 | |
| Grimes, Robert | 1784 | " " | 150 | |
| Gschwind, Frederick | 1788 | River Nicumbeau | 400 | Hessian |
| | | | | |
| Hagan, James | 1786 | Jedore | 100 | Seaman |
| Halliburton, John | 1793 | Halifax Peninsula | 10 | |
| Hamilton, James | 1784 | Preston Township | 150 | |
| Handasyde, Elizabeth | 1784 | " " | 250 | |
| Hanson, John | 1784 | Sheet Harbour | 100 | Royal Garrison Batt. |
| Hardin, Ferdinan | 1785 | Merigumish | 100 | Private 82nd. Reg't |
| Hare, Edward | 1786 | Jedore, E. | 500 | |
| Harris [Herris], Henry | 1784 | Windsor Road | 100 | |
| Harrison, Ralph | 1784 | Preston Township | 200 | |
| Hartshorn, Laurence | 1786 | Hammonds Plains | 100 | |
| Hartshorn, Laurence | 1796 | Dartmouth T. & | | W.L.'s |
| Hastings, Joseph Stacey | 1786 | Halifax Peninsula | 5 | |
| Hawkins, Joseph | 1784 | S. E. Passage | 248 | 84th. Reg't |
| Hawkins, Joseph | 1786 | " " | 200 | " " |
| Hayes, John | 1786 | Jedore | 100 | |
| Hayre, Patrick | 1785 | Merigumish | 100 | Private 82nd. Reg't |
| Healy, John | 1786 | Truro.Musquodoboit Rd | 250 | |
| Hemming, see Flemming | 1785 | | | |
| Henderson, Archibald | 1785 | Merigumish | 100 | Private 82nd. Reg't |
| Hennissey, Andrew | 1787 | Windsor Road, S. W. | 500 | |
| Henrachen, Patrick | 1784 | Preston Township | 200 | |
| Hessim, William | 1784 | Windsor Road | 250 | |
| Hickman, Thomas | 1787 | Jedore | 100 | |
| Highlands, Nathaniel | 1784 | Sheet Harbour | 100 | Royal Garrison Batt. |
| Hill, John | 1784 | Preston Township | 200 | |
| Hodger, William | 1785 | Merigumish | 100 | Private 82nd. Reg't |
| Holmes, John | 1785 | " | 100 | " " " |
| Houseal,Bernard M.Rev. | 1786 | Halifax Township | 400 | |
| Hoyt, Benajah | 1784 | Preston " | 350 | |
| Hoyt, Eli | 1784 | Halifax-Hants Boundary | 500 | |
| Hunt, Patrick | 1785 | Merigumish | 100 | Private 82nd. Reg't |
| Hurst, William | 1786 | Preston Township | 100 | N. C. O. |
| Hutchinson, Foster | 1799 | Halifax T. & | | W. L. |
| Hutchinson, Foster | 1800 | Shubenacadie River | 1000 | |
| | | | | |
| Ifes, John | 1785 | Merigumish | 100 | Private 82nd. Reg't |
| Inners, Henry | 1784 | Preston Township | 100 | |
| Ives, John | 1785 | Merigumish | 100 | Drummer 82nd. Reg't |
| | | | | |
| Jack, William | 1785 | " | 100 | Private " " |
| Jackson, John | 1784 | Preston Township | 100 | |
| Jackson, John | 1784 | Sheet Harbour | 100 | Royal Garrison Batt. |
| Jackson, Robert | 1784 | Preston Township | 200 | |
| Jennings, William | 1784 | ". " | 100 | |

PUBLIC ARCHIVES OF NOVA SCOTIA

| Name | Date | Situation | Acres | Origin or Rank |
|---|---|---|---|---|
| Jerret, Robert | 1785 | Merigumish | 100 | Private 82nd. Reg't |
| Johnson, Roger | 1784 | Windsor Road | 1000 | |
| Johnson, Roger | 1785 | " " N. E. | 100 | |
| Johnston, Thomas | 1784 | Preston Township | 200 | |
| Jones, Charles | 1787 | " " | 100 | |
| Jones, James | 1787 | " " | 250 | |
| Jones, Mark | 1784 | " " | 150 | |
| Jones, William | 1784 | Sheet Harbour | 100 | DrummerRoy'lG.Batt. |
| Jordon, William | 1784 | Preston Township | 300 | |
| Kelly, Hugh | 1784 | " " | 500 | |
| Kelly, Hugh | 1786 | Halifax Peninsula | 20 | |
| Kelly, John | 1784 | Preston Township | 350 | |
| Kennedy, Alexander | 1785 | Merigumish | 100 | Private 82nd. Reg't |
| Keys, William | 1786 | Shubenacadie River | 300 | |
| Kidston, Richard | 1785 | Halifax Peninsula | 5 | |
| King, Alexander | 1785 | Merigumish | 100 | Drummer 82nd. Reg't |
| King, Samuel | 1784 | Preston Township | 250 | |
| Kirk, William | 1785 | Merigumish | 100 | Private 82nd. Reg't |
| Knowles, Jeremiah | 1788 | Preston Township | 200 | |
| Lamb, Joseph | 1784 | Ship Harbour, W. | 200 | |
| Lamblash, Peter | 1785 | Merigumish | 100 | Private 82nd. Reg't |
| Landerkin [Landrican] John | 1784 | Halifax-Hants Boundary | 250 | |
| Lang, Archibald | 1784 | Preston Township | 100 | |
| Langley, Joseph | 1786 | Jedore Harbour, N. E. | 350 | 64th. Reg't |
| Law, John | 1784 | Sheet Harbour | 350 | Serg't Royal G. Batt. |
| Leadbetter, Ebenezer | 1784 | Preston Township | 350 | |
| Leader, Ed. | 1786 | Jedore | 100 | |
| Leader, Richard | 1786 | " | 400 | |
| Leckie, Alexander | 1788 | Musquodoboit River | 1000 | |
| Lentler, Andrew | 1786 | Jedore | 200 | |
| Lenzi, Philip | 1786 | Preston Township | 200 | |
| Lenzie, Philip | 1786 | Halifax Peninsula | 10 | |
| Leonard, Michael | 1798 | Halifax | W. L. | |
| Leslie, Alexander | 1786 | Dartmouth | 200 | Corporal |
| Lewis, John | 1784 | Halifax-Hants Boundary | 500 | |
| Lewis, John | 1786 | Jeddore | 100 | (Observer |
| Lexon, Matthew | 1786 | " | 200 | Serg't Marines,H.M.S. |
| Liester | 1787 | Preston Township | 50 | Negro |
| Lindsay, John | 1784 | Windsor Road | 100 | |
| Lively, Reuben | 1784 | Halifax-Hants Boundary | 500 | |
| Lockwood, Thomas | 1785 | Windsor Road, S. W. | 100 | |
| Logan, James | 1784 | Sheet Harbour | 100 | Royal Garrison Batt. |
| Logan, John | 1786 | Wilmot R. (Stewiacke) | 650 | |
| Loggan, Thomas | 1785 | Merigumish | 200 | Corp'l 82nd. Reg't |
| Long, Archibald | 1785 | " | 200 | " " " (N.Y. |
| Loveless, James | 1786 | Preston Township | 500 | Palmer T'n,AlbanyCo. |
| Lunn, John | 1785 | Merigumish | 100 | Private 82nd. Reg't |
| Lynes, Richard | 1784 | Windsor Road | 100 | |
| Lyons, Charles | 1784 | Halifax Harbour, E. | 130 | |
| Lyons, Charles | 1784 | Laurencetown Township | 1870 | |
| McAllister, Samuel | 1784 | Halifax-Hants Boundary | 250 | |
| McAlpine, John | 1796 | Halifax Peninsula | 16½ | |
| McBaw, Samuel | 1785 | Merigumish | 100 | Private 82nd. Reg't |
| McCaddie [McCraddy], John | 1785 | " | 100 | " " " |
| McCallum, Neil | 1785 | " | 100 | " " " |
| McCara, James | 1796 | " | 500 | |
| McCartney, Hugh | 1785 | " | 100 | Private 82nd. Reg't |
| McCasling, Alexander | 1787 | Windsor Road | 200 | |
| MacClellan, John | 1785 | Shubenacadye R., S. E. | 500 | |

LOYALISTS AND LAND SETTLEMENT IN NOVA SCOTIA 49

| Name | Date | Situation | Acres | Origin or Rank |
|---|---|---|---|---|
| McClinchy, Samuel | 1784 | Sheet Harbour | 150 | Royal Garrison Batt. |
| McCrossian, Jeremiah | 1784 | Halifax-Hants Boundary | 250 | |
| McCullum, John | 1784 | " " " | 500 | |
| McCullum, Malcolm | 1784 | Sheet Harbour | 400 | Royal Garrison Batt. |
| McCullum, Malcolm | 1784 | Ship Harbour, W. | 200 | |
| McDermaid, Bryan | 1785 | Merigumish | 100 | Private 82nd. Reg't |
| McDonald, Alexander | 1784 | Sheet Harbour | 100 | Royal Garrison Batt. |
| McDonald, Alexander | 1785 | Merigumish | 500 | Lieut. 82nd. Reg't |
| McDonald, Alexander | 1786 | St. Margaret's Bay | 400 | Sergeant |
| McDonald, Angus | 1784 | Preston Township | 200 | |
| McDonald, Angus | 1785 | Merigumish | 100 | Private 82nd. Reg't |
| McDonald, Angus 2nd. | 1785 | " | 100 | " " " |
| McDonald, Angus 3rd. | 1785 | " | 100 | " " " |
| McDonald, Colin | 1785 | " | 500 | Ensign. " " |
| McDonald, Donald | 1784 | Preston Township | 100 | |
| McDonald, Donald | 1784 | Sheet Harbour | 500 | Ensign. Royal G. Batt. |
| McDonald, Donald, Jr. | 1785 | Merigumish | 100 | Private 82nd. Reg't |
| McDonald, Donald, Sr. | 1785 | " | 100 | " " " |
| McDonald, Duncan | 1784 | Sheet Harbour | 100 | Royal Garrison Batt. |
| McDonald, Duncan | 1785 | East River—Pictou | 100 | |
| McDonald, James | 1785 | " " " | 300 | |
| McDonald, James | 1787 | Halifax Township | 350 | |
| McDonald, John | 1784 | Windsor Road | 250 | |
| McDonald, John | 1785 | East River—Pictou | 250 | |
| McDonald, John | 1785 | Merigumish | 100 | Private 82nd. Reg't |
| McDonald, John | 1786 | Dartmouth Township | 100 | |
| McDonald, John, Jr. | 1785 | East River—Pictou | 250 | |
| McDonald, Hugh | 1784 | Sheet Harbour | 200 | Royal Garrison Batt. |
| McDonald, Hugh | 1785 | East River—Pictou | 100 | |
| McDonald, Hugh | 1786 | St. Margaret's Bay | 400 | Corporal |
| McDonald, Peter | 1785 | Merigumish | 100 | Private 82nd. Reg't |
| McDonald, Roderick | 1785 | " | 100 | " " " |
| McDonald, William | 1784 | Preston Township | 200 | |
| MacDougal, John | 1797 | East River—Pictou | 250 | |
| McDougall, John | 1785 | Merigumish | 100 | Private 82nd. Reg't |
| McEwen, Robert | 1784 | Ship Harbour, W. | 200 | |
| McGahy, James | 1784 | Sheet Harbour | 200 | Royal Garrison Batt. |
| McGavy, Archibald | 1785 | Merigumish | 100 | Private 82nd. Reg't |
| McGeorge, John | 1786 | Truro-Musquodoboit Rd | 250 | |
| McGilvery, Findly | 1784 | Preston Township | 100 | |
| McGilvray, John | 1785 | Merigumish | 100 | Private 82nd. Reg't |
| McGinley, George | 1784 | Windsor Road | 100 | |
| McGuire, Michael | 1785 | Sheet Harbour | 250 | Royal Garrison Batt. |
| McHeffey, Richard | 1785 | Shubenacadie | 700 | |
| McInnis, Miles | 1786 | Musquodoboit River | 200 | |
| MacIntosh, Alexander | 1797 | East River—Pictou | 500 | |
| McKay, Alexander | 1785 | Merigumish | 100 | Private 82nd. Reg't |
| McKay, Archibald | 1784 | Musquodoboit River | 200 | Lt.-Col. Royal Militia |
| McKay, John | 1797 | East River—Pictou | 300 | (Cumb.Co. N.Carolina |
| McKay, Peter | 1784 | Sheet Harbour | 100 | Royal Garrison Batt. |
| McKay, Robert | 1784 | " " | 100 | " " " |
| McKenzie, Alexander | 1785 | Merigumish | 100 | Private 82nd. Reg't |
| McKenzie, Donald | 1784 | Sheet Harbour | 100 | Royal Garrison Batt. |
| McKenzie, Finley | 1786 | Dartmouth Township | 200 | |
| McKenzie, John | 1784 | Sheet Harbour | 100 | Royal Garrison Batt. |
| McKenzie, Robert | 1785 | Merigumish | 100 | Private 82nd. Reg't |
| McKenzie, Thomas | 1797 | East River, Pictou | 100 | |
| Mackey, Thomas | 1784 | Windsor Road | 250 | |
| McKie, Wm. | 1785 | Shubenacadie R., S. E. | 200 | Sergeant |
| McKinnon, Alexander | 1785 | Merigumish | 200 | Corp'l 82nd. Reg't |
| McKinnon, Charles | 1785 | " | 100 | Private " " |
| McKinnon, James | 1787 | Windsor Road | 100 | |
| McLean, Alexander | 1785 | Merigumish | 100 | Private 82nd. Reg't |
| MacLean, Alexander | 1797 | East River—Pictou | 500 | |

# 50 PUBLIC ARCHIVES OF NOVA SCOTIA

| Name | Date | Situation | Acres | Origin or Rank |
|---|---|---|---|---|
| McLean, David | 1797 | East River—Pictou | 500 | |
| McLean, Evan | 1785 | Merigumish | 100 | Private 82nd. Reg't |
| MacLean, Hector | 1797 | East River—Pictou | 400 | |
| McLean, John | 1784 | Sheet Harbour | 100 | Royal Garrison Batt. |
| McLean, John | 1785 | Merigumish | 100 | Drummer 82nd. Reg't |
| McLean, Samuel | 1785 | " | 100 | Private " " |
| MacLellan, James | 1797 | East River—Pictou | 500 | |
| MacLellan, John | 1797 | " " " | 100 | |
| McLeod, Donald | 1784 | Sheet Harbour | 100 | Royal Garrison Batt. |
| McLeod, John | 1784 | " " | 300 | " " " |
| McLeod, Kenneth | 1785 | Merigumish | 100 | Private 82nd. Reg't |
| McLerin, Peter | 1784 | Sheet Harbour | 100 | Royal Garrison Batt. |
| McMinn, Andrew | 1787 | Preston Township | 100 | |
| McMinn, John | 1787 | " " | 100 | |
| McMinn, Thomas | 1787 | " " | 250 | |
| McMullon, Richard | 1784 | Halifax-Hants Boundary | 250 | |
| McNeil, Donald | 1785 | Merigumish | 100 | Private 82nd. Reg't |
| McNeil, John | 1785 | " | 300 | Corp'l " " |
| McNeil, John | 1785 | " | 100 | Private " " |
| McNeil, John, Jr. | 1785 | " | 100 | " " " |
| McNeil, Matt. | 1785 | " | 100 | " " " |
| McNeil, Murd. | 1785 | " | 100 | " " " |
| McNeile, John, Jr. | 1785 | " | 200 | Corp'l " " |
| McPhee, Duncan | 1784 | Sheet Harbour | 200 | Royal Garrison Batt. |
| McPherson, James | 1785 | Merigumish | 100 | Private 82nd. Reg't |
| McPherson, John | 1784 | Sheet Harbour | 100 | Royal Garrison Batt. |
| McPherson, John | 1785 | Merigumish | 100 | Private 82nd. Reg't |
| McQueen, Alexander | 1785 | " | 100 | " " " |
| McVicar, John | 1784 | Ship Harbour, W. | 200 | |
| McVie, William | 1785 | Merigumish | 200 | Corp'l 82nd. Reg't |
| Maguire, John | 1784 | Halifax-Hants Boundary | 500 | |
| Marks, Lawrence | 1784 | Ship Harbour, W. | 200 | |
| Martain, Martain | 1784 | Musquodoboit River | 200 | Cumb. Co. N. Carolina |
| Martain, William | 1784 | " " | 200 | " " " " |
| Martin, Edward | 1784 | Windsor Road | 250 | |
| Martin, Murdock | 1784 | Musquodoboit River | 200 | Cumb. Co. N. Carolina |
| Martin, William | 1784 | Sheet Harbour | 100 | Royal Garrison Batt. |
| Martin, William | 1788 | Preston Township | 100 | |
| Martindale, Henry | 1784 | Halifax-Hants Boundary | 500 | |
| Martindale, Henry, Jr. | 1784 | " " " | 250 | |
| Matheson, Thomas | 1785 | Merigumish | 100 | Private 82nd. Reg't |
| Meek, John | 1784 | Halifax-Hants Boundary | 500 | |
| Meek, Samuel | 1784 | " " " | 500 | |
| Meek, William | 1784 | " " " | 1000 | Captain |
| Merlow, Daniel | 1784 | Bedford Basin | 200 | |
| Miller, Hugh | 1785 | Merigumish | 100 | Private 82nd. Reg't |
| Miller, Robert | 1785 | " | 200 | Corp'l |
| Miller, Tobias | 1784 | Preston Township | 500 | |
| Mills, Robert | 1784 | Sheet Harbour | 200 | Royal Garrison Batt. |
| Molloy, John | 1786 | Halifax | W.L.'s | |
| Moody, John | 1793 | Harriet Fields | 350 | |
| Moody, John | 1793 | " " | 350 | |
| Moore, Peter | 1784 | Sheet Harbour | 100 | Royal Garrison Batt. |
| Morrison, James | 1786 | Jedore | 100 | Blacksmith |
| Morton, John | 1785 | Merigumish | 200 | Corp'l 82nd. Reg't |
| Muir, John | 1785 | " | 100 | Private 82nd. Reg't |
| Muirhead, Andrew | 1785 | " | 100 | " " " |
| Muller, Emanuel | 1784 | Preston Township | 100 | |
| Mullock, Elenor | 1784 | Preston Township | 100 | |
| Mullock, Francis | 1786 | Halifax Peninsula | 10 | |
| Mullock, Francis I. | 1784 | Preston Township | 500 | |
| Mullock, Mary | 1784 | " " | 100 | |
| Munn, James | 1796 | Dartmouth   T. & | W.L.'s | |
| Munro, John | 1785 | Merigumish | 100 | Private 82nd. Reg't |

## LOYALISTS AND LAND SETTLEMENT IN NOVA SCOTIA 51

| Name | Date | Situation | Acres | Origin or Rank |
|---|---|---|---|---|
| Murphy, Andrew | 1786 | Musquodoboit | 100 | Infantry |
| Murphy, John | 1784 | Halifax-Hants Boundary | 500 | |
| Murphy, Philip | 1784 | " " " | 250 | |
| Newgesser, Adam | 1784 | Ship Harbour, W. | 200 | |
| Nicholai, Christopher | 1784 | Windsor Road | 500 | |
| Nichols, James | 1784 | Halifax-Hants Boundary | 500 | Captain |
| Nichols [Nicholl] John | 1787 | Halifax Township | 350 | |
| Nix, John | 1790 | Musquodoboit River | 450 | Hessian |
| Nugent, James | 1784 | Preston Township | 100 | |
| O'Brien, Moses | 1790 | Road to Rawdon | 200 | |
| O'Brien, Robert | 1784 | Preston Township | 500 | |
| Olding, Nicholas Perdue | 1784 | Sheet Harbour | 650 | Lieut. Royal G. Batt. |
| Oswald, George | 1785 | Merigumish | 200 | Corp'l 82nd. Reg't |
| Paine, Michael | 1788 | Preston Township | 200 | |
| Parker, George | 1787 | Halifax | 150 | |
| Patterson, Daniel | 1786 | St. Margaret's Bay | 150 | |
| Patterson, John | 1785 | Merigumish | 100 | Private 82nd. Reg't |
| Paxton, Joseph | 1786 | Jedore | 100 | |
| Peacock, James | 1785 | Merigumish | 200 | Sergeant 82nd. Reg't |
| Pearson, Thomas | 1784 | Halifax-Hants Boundary | 500 | Colonel |
| Peebles, John | 1787 | Halifax Wharf Lot | | |
| Pegg, George | 1787 | Preston Township | 100 | |
| Pence, Conrad | 1785 | Windsor Road, S. W. | 500 | |
| Porter, William | 1785 | Dartmouth | 1000 | Deputy Commissary |
| Potts, Thomas | 1786 | Jeddore | 150 | (General |
| Prince, John | 1784 | Dartmouth Township | 170 | |
| Prince, John | 1785 | Halifax Peninsula | 20 | |
| Prior, Edward | 1786 | Jeddore | 500 | |
| Prior, Edward, Jr. | 1786 | " | 100 | |
| Proctor, Samuel | 1784 | Halifax-Hants Boundary | 250 | |
| Putman, James | 1795 | {East River—Pictou | {700 | |
| | | {Preston Township | {300 | |
| Putman, James | 1797 | Halifax | T. L. | |
| Readman, John | 1787 | Preston Township | 100 | |
| Reeves, John | 1796 | Dartmouth T. & | W.L.'s | |
| Reid, Robert | 1785 | Merigumish | 100 | Private 82nd. Reg't |
| Reily, Cornelius | 1784 | Windsor Road | 250 | |
| Reynard, Ann (Mrs.) | 1788 | Between Bear and Port- | | |
| | | agee Coves | 100 | |
| Richard, I. | 1784 | Preston Township | 50 | |
| Riddle, William | 1785 | Merigumish | 100 | Private 82nd. Reg't |
| Ring, Joseph | 1785 | Jeddore | 100 | |
| Ritten, Houre William | 1784 | Ship Harbour | 200 | Royal Garrison Batt. |
| Robertson, Alexander | 1785 | Merigumish | 1500 | Lt.-Col. 82nd. Reg't |
| Robertson, George | 1785 | " | 100 | Private " " |
| Robertson, James | 1785 | " | 200 | Corp'l " " |
| Robertson, James | 1797 | East River—Pictou | 350 | |
| Robertson, John | 1797 | " " " | 450 | |
| Robertson, William | 1797 | " " " | 200 | |
| Robinson, Benjamin | 1796 | Dartmouth T. & | W.L.'s | |
| Robinson, Charles | 1785 | Merigumish | 200 | Serg't 82nd. Reg't |
| Robinson, James | 1785 | Windsor Road, S. W. | 200 | |
| Robinson, William | 1785 | Merigumish | 100 | Drummer 82nd. Reg't |
| Robson, John | 1785 | " | 200 | Corp'l " " |
| Robson, Mary | 1792 | Halifax | W. L. | |
| Rogers, Andrew | 1787 | Preston Township | 100 | |
| Rogers, Jasper | 1787 | " " | 250 | |
| Rogers, William | 1784 | " " | 200 | |
| Rottenken, Frederick | 1784 | " " | 200 | |
| Rull, Benj. | 1786 | Jeddore | 200 | |

## PUBLIC ARCHIVES OF NOVA SCOTIA

| Name | Date | Situation | Acres | Origin or Rank |
|---|---|---|---|---|
| Russell, Joseph | 1784 | Preston Township | 500 | |
| Rust, Nathaniel | 1786 | " " | 250 | |
| Ruth, Mark | 1784 | Sheet Harbour | 400 | Serg't Royal G. Batt. |
| Rutledge, Simon | 1784 | Sheet Harbour | 350 | Royal Garrison Batt. |
| Ryan, Thomas | 1785 | Merigumish | 100 | Private 82nd. Reg't |
| Ryland, Peter | 1784 | Halifax-Hants Boundary | 250 | |
| Sadler, John | 1790 | Rawdon Road | 100 | |
| Sadler, John | 1790 | Rawdon, S. E. | 100 | |
| Sam | 1787 | Preston Township | 50 | Negro |
| Sange, Christian | 1784 | Ship Harbour | 200 | |
| Saunderson, John | 1784 | Halifax-Hants Boundary | 500 | Captain |
| Savage, Dominah | 1787 | Preston Township | 100 | |
| Scantlon, John | 1786 | Jeddore | 100 | |
| Schenk, Henry | 1790 | Musquodoboit River | 250 | Hessian |
| Scofeld, Zebulon | 1784 | Preston Township | 150 | |
| Scott | 1787 | " " | 50 | Negro |
| Scott, John | 1785 | Merigumish | 200 | Corp'l 82nd. Reg't |
| Scott, Robert | 1784 | Halifax-Hants Boundary | 250 | |
| Shady, Conrad | 1784 | Ship Harbour | 200 | |
| Sharp, William | 1785 | Merigumish | 100 | Private 82nd. Reg't |
| Sharpless, John | 1784 | Sheet Harbour | 100 | Royal Garrison Batt. |
| Shaw, Alexander | 1785 | Merigumish | 100 | Private 82nd. Reg't |
| Shaw, Donald | 1797 | East River—Pictou | 300 | |
| Shaw, Ralph | 1784 | Windsor Road | 200 | |
| Sheehee, John | 1792 | Harriet Fields | 100 | |
| Shelton, Ebenezer | 1784 | Preston Township | 200 | |
| Shepherd, John | 1784 | Sheet Harbour | 100 | Royal Garrison Batt. |
| Shields, John | 1786 | Windsor Road, N. E. | 200 | Corporal |
| Shrive, Thomas | 1784 | Minas Gut | 500 | Lt. Prince of Wales |
| Shrum, John | 1784 | Preston Township | 200 | (Reg't |
| Shults, George | 1784 | " " | 200 | |
| Shuthers, James | 1785 | Merigumish | 200 | Serg't 82nd. Reg't |
| Sideman, Henry | 1786 | Jeddore | 100 | |
| Simmons, Jonathan | 1784 | Sheet Harbour | 100 | Royal Garr'son Batt. |
| Simpson, David | 1785 | Merigumish | 200 | Serg't 82nd. Reg't |
| Simpson, Joseph | 1784 | Halifax-Hants Boundary | 250 | |
| Skey, Patrick | 1785 | Merigumish | 100 | Private 82nd. Reg't |
| Skirvine, David | 1785 | " | 100 | " " " |
| Small, John | 1785 | " | 100 | " " " |
| Smith, Benjamin | 1787 | Preston Township | 200 | |
| Smith, George | 1784 | " " | 250 | |
| Smith, John | 1784 | " " | 50 | |
| Smith, Robert | 1785 | Merigumish | 200 | Serg't 82nd. Reg't |
| Smith, Titus | 1784 | Preston Township | 500 | |
| Snell, Daniel | 1784 | Halifax-Hants Boundary | 250 | |
| Snell, David | 1784 | " " " | 250 | |
| Snell, George | 1784 | " " " | 500 | |
| Sniden, George | 1784 | Preston Township | 100 | |
| Solomon, John | 1784 | Windsor Road, N. E. | 500 | |
| Sovereign, John | 1785 | Merigumish | 100 | Private 82nd. Reg't |
| Spainler, Sebastion | 1787 | Preston Township | 200 | |
| Stafford, David | 1784 | " " | 50 | |
| Stangell, George | 1790 | Musquodoboit River | 250 | Hessian |
| Steel, Richard | 1788 | Sandwich Point | 100 | |
| Stephenson— | 1786 | Jeddore | 200 | Serjeant |
| Stevens, Francis | 1786 | Halifax Peninsula | 5 | |
| Stevens, Thomas | 1786 | " " | 5 | |
| Stevenson, John | 1785 | Merigumish | 100 | Private 82nd. Reg't |
| Stewart, Alexander | 1785 | " | 200 | Corp'l " " |
| Stewart, Anthony | 1784 | Halifax Peninsula | 5 | |
| Stewart, Charles | 1784 | Sheet Harbour | 100 | Royal Garrison Batt. |
| Stewart, Charles | 1785 | Merigumish | 100 | Private 82nd. Reg't |
| Stewart, John | 1784 | Sheet Harbour | 100 | Royal Garrison Batt. |

# LOYALISTS AND LAND SETTLEMENT IN NOVA SCOTIA 53

| Name | Date | Situation | Acres | Origin or Rank |
|---|---|---|---|---|
| Stewart, Kenneth | 1784 | Musquodoboit River | 200 | Cumb. Co. N. Carolina |
| Stewart, Robert | 1785 | Merigumish | 200 | Serg't 82nd. Reg't |
| Stewart, Robert | 1786 | Jeddore Harbour | 300 | 64th. Reg't |
| Stewart, William | 1784 | Preston Township | 100 | |
| Stone, Thomas | *1785 | Windsor Road, S. W. | 300 | |
| Storey, Joseph | 1784 | Sheet Harbour | 100 | Royal Garrison Batt. |
| Stormy, Frederick | 1785 | Jeddore | 100 | |
| Story, John | 1793 | Musquodoboit | 700 | |
| Strong | 1787 | Preston Township | 50 | Negro |
| Stuart, James | 1786 | Dartmouth | 100 | |
| Summerset | 1787 | Preston Township | 50 | Negro |
| Sumner, John | 1786 | Jeddore | 100 | 70th. Reg't of Foot |
| Sutherland, Alexander | 1784 | Sheet Harbour | 800 | Lieut. Royal G. Batt. |
| Sutherland, David | 1784 | " " | 100 | Royal Garrison Batt. |
| Sutherland, Erick | 1784 | " " | 200 | " " " |
| Sutherland, James | 1784 | " " | 750 | Lieut. Royal G. Batt. |
| Sutherland, John | 1784 | " " | 100 | Royal Garrison Batt. |
| Sutherland, William | 1784 | " " | 750 | Lieut. Royal G. Batt. |
| Sutherland, William | 1784 | " " | 100 | Royal Garrison Batt. |
| Sutle, Thomas | 1787 | Preston Township | 300 | |
| Swift, Ed. | 1786 | Jeddore | 100 | |
| Swilling, John | 1786 | " | 100 | |
| Symtor, William | 1785 | Merigumish | 100 | Private 82nd. Reg't |
| | | | | |
| Taylor, Alexander | 1784 | Preston Township | 100 | |
| Thompson, John | 1784 | " " | 200 | |
| Thomson, Andrew | 1784 | Windsor Road | 1000 | |
| Thornton, Abraham | 1784 | Halifax-Hants Boundary | 250 | |
| Thornton, Eli | 1784 | " " " | 250 | |
| Thornton, Thomas | 1784 | " " " | 250 | |
| Thyne, Robert | 1785 | Merigumish | 100 | Private 82nd. Reg't |
| Todd, John | 1784 | Preston Township | 150 | |
| Tolbet, Matthew | 1785 | Merigumish | 100 | Private 82nd. Reg't |
| Toney | 1787 | Preston Township | 50 | Negro |
| Townsend, Thomas | 1785 | Merigumish | 100 | Private 82nd. Reg't |
| †Townsend, William | 1784 | Preston Township | 50 | |
| Tremain, Jonathan | 1796 | Dartmouth | T. & W.L.'s | |
| Tremain, Jonathan | 1799 | " | 2¾ | |
| Tremaine, Jonathan | 1786 | Hammond Plains | 200 | |
| Trustate, James | 1785 | Merigumish | 100 | Private 82nd. Reg't |
| Tybe, Joseph | 1787 | Preston Township | 100 | |
| Tybon, Nicholas | 1784 | " " | 150 | |
| Tybon, William | 1784 | " " | 100 | |
| | | | | |
| Underwood, Benjamin | 1786 | Harriet Fields | 200 | |
| | | | | |
| Wallace, Michael | 1795 | Halifax | T.L.'s | |
| Wallace, Michael | 1796 | Dartmouth | W. L. | |
| Wallace, William | 1784 | Halifax-Hants Boundary | 500 | |
| Walter, Richard | 1784 | Sheet Harbour | 100 | Royal Garrison Batt. |
| Ward, Patrick | 1784 | Windsor Road | 250 | |
| Watson, Joshua | 1785 | Dartmouth | 200 | Soldier |
| Watson, Joshua, Jr. | 1785 | " | 100 | " |
| Weaver, George | 1784 | Ship Harbour | 200 | |
| Weirgan, Patrick | 1788 | Preston Township | 200 | |
| Wells, Benjamin | 1784 | " " | 200 | |
| Wells, Thomas | 1785 | Shubenaccadie R., S. E. | 200 | Sergeant |
| Wentworth, Benning | 1798 | Halifax | T. L. | |
| West, William | 1785 | Merigumish | 200 | Private 82nd. Reg't |
| Westphall, George | 1784 | Preston Township | 500 | |
| White, Joseph | 1787 | " " | 200 | |
| White, William | 1784 | Sheet Harbour | 150 | Royal Garrison Batt. |

\* Draft Grant in Public Archives is dated 1784.
† Possibly escheated in 1815. See error in escheat No. 149.

| Name | Date | Situation | Acres | Origin or Rank |
|---|---|---|---|---|
| Whitear, Benjamin | 1786 | S. E. Passage | 500 | |
| Wier, Benjamin | 1784 | Halifax-Hants Boundary | 500 | |
| Wier, William | 1784 | " " " | 500 | |
| Williams | 1787 | Preston Township | 50 | Negro |
| Williams, Edward | 1787 | " " | 300 | |
| Williams, John | 1788 | Musquodoboit Harbour | 400 | |
| Williams, Thomas | 1784 | Halifax-Hants Boundary | 250 | |
| Wilson, Archibald | 1785 | Merigumish | 200 | Corp'l 82nd. Reg't |
| Wilson, Robert | 1785 | " | 100 | Private " " |
| Wilson, Roger | 1784 | Halifax-Hants Boundary | 250 | |
| Wisker, John | 1784 | Sheet Harbour | 200 | Royal Garrison Batt. |
| Witecar [Whitaker] Thos. | 1786 | Jeddore Harbour, N. E. | 300 | 64th. Reg't |
| Withrow, David | 1784 | Halifax-Hants Boundary | 250 | |
| Withrow, Jacob | 1784 | " " " | 250 | |
| Withrow, John | 1784 | " " " | 500 | |
| Wood, Thomas | 1785 | Merigumish | 100 | Private 82nd. Reg't |
| Wood, William | 1785 | " | 100 | Drummer " " |
| Worrell, Margaret | 1785 | Shubenaccadie River | 300 | |
| Wright, John | 1785 | Merigumish | 100 | Private 82nd. Reg't |
| Wright, Thomas | 1794 | Petpeswick | 300 | |
| | | | | |
| Young, Nathan | 1786 | Dartmouth | 150 | |
| Young, Reuben | 1784 | Ship Harbour | 200 | |
| Young, Thomas | 1787 | Preston Township | 300 | |

## Halifax County
### WARRANTS

| Name | Date | Situation | Acres | Origin or Rank |
|---|---|---|---|---|
| Bollard, John | 1786 | Jedore | 100 | |
| Brenton, James | 1785 | Halifax | W. L. | |
| Breton, John | 1785 | Dartmouth | 100 | |
| Burns, John | 1785 | " | 200 | |
| Cameron, Archibald | 1785 | " | 200 | |
| Flecter [Fletcher], Thos. | 1786 | Gay's River | 500 | |
| Hettle, Thomas | 1785 | Dartmouth | 200 | |
| McLean, Donald | 1787 | Pictou Harbour | 500 | Dr. |
| Maffat, William | 1785 | Dartmouth | 400 | |
| Martin, William | 1784 | Gay's River | 500 | |
| Philip [Phillips] William | 1786 & 1788 | Halifax Co. | 100 | Royal Reg't of Artill'y |
| Ramminton, Eliz. (Mrs.) | 1786 | Lake Egmont (?) | 300 | |
| Rowland, Roger | 1786 | Jedore | 100 | |
| Scoles, William | 1788 | Sandwich Point | 50 | 33rd. Reg't of Foot |
| Weirgan, Patrick | 1786 | Pope's Head Har. | 250 | |
| Weizer, Frederick | 1786 | Jeddore | 100 | |

LOYALISTS AND LAND SETTLEMENT IN NOVA SCOTIA 55

## Halifax County
### ESCHEATS

Column for "Amount escheated" is filled in only when this amount differs from the amount of the grant.

| Name | Date | Situation | Acres | Esch'd | Amt. of Esch't | Origin or Rank |
|---|---|---|---|---|---|---|
| Abraham | 1786 | Shubenacadie River | 50 | 1810 | | |
| Adam | 1786 | " " | 50 | 1810 | | |
| Adams, John | 1784 | Preston Township | 200 | 1815 | | |
| Allan, Ebebezer | 1784 | " " | 350 | 1820 | | |
| Allan, Silas | 1784 | " " | 400 | 1815 | 200 | |
| Anderson, Andrew | 1786 | Shubenacadie River | 100 | 1810 | | |
| Anderson, James | 1786 | " " | 100 | 1810 | | |
| Andrew | 1786 | " " | 50 | 1810 | | |
| Annand, Jennet | 1786 | " " | 100 | 1810 | | |
| Annand, William | 1786 | " " | 100 | 1810 | | |
| Anster, Nathaniel | 1786 | " " | 100 | 1810 | | |
| | | | | | | |
| Batz, Nicholas | 1784 | Harriet Fields | 100 | 1820 | | |
| Becker, George | 1784 | " " | 100 | 1820 | | |
| Beech, Peter | 1784 | Preston Township | 100 | 1815 | | |
| Begg, Andrew | 1786 | Shubenacadie River | 200 | 1810 | | |
| Begg, Thomas | 1786 | " " | 100 | 1810 | | |
| Belding, Stephen | 1784 | Preston Township | 200 | 1815 | | |
| Bell, Magdalena | 1785 | Harriet Fields | 60 | 1817 | | Widow |
| Bellfountain, John | 1784 | Preston Township | 200 | 1815 | | |
| Bishop, William | 1784 | Halifax-Lunenburg Rd. | 100 | 1812 | | Hessian |
| Bissett, George | 1784 | Preston Township | 200 | 1815 | | (Corps |
| Bob | 1786 | Shubenacadie River | 50 | 1810 | | |
| Bower, Jobe | 1784 | Preston Township | 200 | 1815 | | |
| Bowman, William | 1784 | Halifax-Hants Boundary | 500 | 1810 | | |
| Brempton, Charles | 1784 | Preston Township | 100 | 1815 | | |
| Bristoe | 1784 | " " | 50 | 1815 | | Negro |
| Brun, Andrew | 1785 | Harriet Fields | 210 | 1817 | | |
| Brun, Jacob | 1785 | " " | 100 | 1817 | | |
| Brust, John | 1786 | Shubenacadie River | 100 | 1810 | | |
| Byrns, Patrick | 1786 | | 200 | 1810 | | |
| | | | | | | |
| Calehar, Sarah | 1786 | " " | 200 | 1810 | | |
| Cammerdinger, Louis | 1785 | Harriet Fields | 210 | 1817 | | |
| Carter, Christian | 1784 | Preston Township | 500 | 1815 | | |
| Cawfield, Daniel | 1786 | Truro Road | 450 | 1814 | | |
| Cawfield, Daniel | 1786 | Truro-Musquodoboit Rd. | 450 | 1814 | | |
| *Cawfield, John | 1787 | " " | 250 | 1815 | | |
| Cezar | 1786 | Shubenacadie River | 50 | 1810 | | |
| Ciely, Hannah | 1786 | Shubenacadie River | 200 | 1810 | | |
| Cohen, Jacob | 1786 | " " | 250 | 1810 | | |
| Coldier, Walter | 1784 | Preston Township | 100 | 1815 | | |
| Collins, Charles | 1784 | " " | 100 | 1815 | | |
| Cook, John | 1786 | Shubenacadie River | 100 | 1810 | | |
| Cox, Samuel | 1784 | Preston Township | 200 | 1815 | | |
| Crawford, Daniel | 1784 | " " | 150 | 1815 | 173† | |
| Crawford, Edward | 1784 | " " | 350 | 1815 | 300 | |
| Creed, Matthew | 1784 | " " | 100 | 1815 | | |
| Croffs, Thomas | 1784 | " " | 300 | 1815 | 200 | |
| Crittingdone, Eben. | 1784 | " " | 200 | 1815 | | |

* This is part of a grant to Barnard Thompson and others, 1350 acres, 1787. It is recorded in the escheat as 1785.
† Error in escheat No. 207.

56  PUBLIC ARCHIVES OF NOVA SCOTIA

| Name | Date | Situation | Acres | Esch'd | Amt. of Esch't | Origin or Rank |
|---|---|---|---|---|---|---|
| Davis, Peter | 1784 | Preston Township | 400 | 1815 | | |
| DeBold, Christopher | 1784 | Halifax-Lunenburg Rd. | 100 | 1812 | | Hessian |
| Deddy | 1786 | Shubenacadie River | 50 | 1810 | | (Corps |
| Dell, Thomas | 1784 | Preston Township | 200 | 1820 | | |
| Derwin, Daniel | 1784 | " " | 100 | 1815 | | |
| Deys, John | 1784 | Harriet Fields | 100 | 1820 | | |
| Dick | 1786 | Shubenacadie River | 50 | 1810 | | |
| Dignall, Michael | 1786 | " " | 200 | 1810 | | |
| Dixon, Alexander | 1786 | " " | 150 | 1810 | | |
| Dixon, John | 1784 | Preston Township | 200 | 1815 | | |
| Dolbear, William | 1785 | Harriet Fields | 240 | 1817 | | |
| Donnelly, Leckie | 1785 | Shubenacadie River | 200 | 1811 | | 70thRegt |
| Dunbar, Alexander | 1784 | Preston Township | 200 | 1815 | | (of Foot |
| Dunn, James | 1786 | Shubenacadie River | 150 | 1810 | | |
| Dunn, John | 1786 | " " | 100 | 1810 | | |
| Eliza | 1786 | " " | 50 | 1810 | | |
| Ey, George | 1784 | Harriet Fields | 100 | 1820 | | |
| Fausel, John | 1784 | Halifax-Lunenburg Road | 200 | 1812 | | Hessian |
| Ferser, John | 1784 | Preston Township | 100 | 1815 | | (Corps |
| Findly, Francis | 1784 | " " | 100 | 1815 | | |
| Finucane, Donnatt | 1785 | Merigumish | 500 | 1810 | | 82d Regt |
| Fisher, John | 1784 | Harriet Fields | 100 | 1820 | | |
| Flach, John | 1784 | " " | 100 | 1820 | | |
| Fletcher, John | 1786 | Shubenacadie River | 100 | 1810 | | |
| Frank | 1786 | " " | 50 | 1810 | | |
| Fredson, Charles | 1784 | Preston Township | 100 | 1815 | 50 | |
| Fredson, Peter | 1784 | " " | 150 | 1815 | | |
| Fredson, William | 1784 | " " | 100 | 1815 | 50 | |
| Freston, Cuff | 1784 | " " | 50 | 1815 | 25 | |
| Friswell, Richard | 1786 | Shubenacadie River | 100 | 1810 | | |
| Galaper, Andrew | 1785 | Harriet Fields | 220 | 1817 | | |
| Gass, John | 1784 | Preston Township | 100 | 1815 | | |
| George | 1786 | Shubenacadie River | 50 | 1810 | | |
| German, Louis | 1784 | Harriet Fields | 100 | 1820 | | |
| Gilbert, James | 1786 | Shubenacadie River | 100 | 1810 | | |
| Gilfellen, Robert | 1784 | Preston Township | 100 | 1815 | | |
| Gilling, William | 1786 | Shubenacadie River | 200 | 1810 | | |
| Gottlieb, George | 1784 | Harriet Fields | 100 | 1820 | | |
| Greenhill, William | 1784 | Preston Township | 200 | 1815 | | |
| Greenwood, John | 1784 | " " | 250 | 1815 | 145 | |
| Gschwind, Frederick | 1784 | Harriet Fields | 500 | 1820 | | |
| Hall, James | 1786 | Shubenacadie River | 200 | 1810 | | |
| Hamilton, Samuel | 1786 | " " | 200 | 1810 | | |
| Handasyde, Charles | 1784 | Preston Township | 200 | 1815 | 100 | |
| Harvey, Edward | 1784 | " " | 100 | 1815 | | |
| Hays, Mary | 1785 | Harriet Fields | 70 | 1817 | | |
| Head, John | 1786 | Hammonds Plains | 200 | 1812 | | Soldier |
| Heffner, John | 1784 | Harriet Fields | 100 | 1820 | | |
| Henkelman, I. Henry | 1784 | " " | 1000 | 1820 | | Lieut. |
| Henry, James | 1784 | Preston Township | 100 | 1815 | | |
| Herbig, Michael | 1784 | Harriet Fields | 100 | 1820 | | |
| Hettler, Christopher | 1784 | Halifax-Lunenburg Road | 100 | 1812 | | Hessian |
| Hettler, Christopher | 1784 | Harriet Fields | 100 | 1820 | | (Corps |
| Heywood, William | 1786 | Shubenacadie River | 100 | 1810 | | |
| Hicks, William | 1784 | Preston Township | 50 | 1815 | | |
| Hilly, William | 1784 | " " | 100 | 1815 | | |
| Hind, John | 1784 | Halifax-Lunenburg Road | 150 | 1812 | | Hessian |
| Hinds, Henry | 1786 | Hammonds Plains | 100 | 1814 | | (Corps |
| Hirchfield, Frederick | 1786 | Shubenacadie River | 200 | 1810 | | (Corp. |
| Hoffman, John | 1784 | Halifax-Lunenburg Road | 300 | 1812 | | Hessian |

## LOYALISTS AND LAND SETTLEMENT IN NOVA SCOTIA 57

| Name | Date | Situation | Acres | Esch'd | Amt. of Esch't | Origin or Rank |
|---|---|---|---|---|---|---|
| Hollis, Thomas | 1785 | Harriet Fields | 270 | 1817 | | Corp. |
| Houzeal, Michael | 1784 | Preston Township | 700 | 1815 | | |
| Howell, Matthew | 1784 | " " | 200 | 1815 | | |
| Hoyt, Isaac | 1784 | " " | 350 | 1815 | 195 | |
| Hufman, Anthony | 1784 | " " | 200 | 1815 | | |
| Hunt, Thomas | 1784 | " " | 150 | 1815 | | |
| | | | | | | |
| Igler, Michael | 1784 | " " | 100 | 1815 | | |
| | | | | | | |
| James | 1786 | Shubenacadie River | 50 | 1810 | | |
| John | 1786 | " " | 50 | 1810 | | |
| John, Jr. | 1786 | " " | 50 | 1810 | | |
| Jordon, William | 1784 | Preston Township | 500 | 1815 | 200 | |
| Joseph see Thomas Joseph | 1786 | | | | | |
| Kauffman, Christopher | 1784 | Harriet Fields | 200 | 1820 | | |
| Kerr, Elizabeth | 1786 | Shubenacadie River | 200 | 1810 | | |
| Kettle, Isaac | 1784 | Preston Township | 200 | 1815 | | |
| King, William | 1786 | Shubenacadie River | 200 | 1810 | | |
| Klein, John | 1784 | Harriet Fields | 100 | 1820 | | |
| Klein, William | 1784 | " " | 100 | 1820 | | |
| Knafft, Jacob | 1784 | " " | 100 | 1820 | | |
| Knight, John | 1784 | Preston Township | 100 | 1815 | | |
| Knorr, John | 1785 | Harriet Fields | 100 | 1817 | | |
| Koch, William | 1784 | " " | 100 | 1820 | | |
| Kohler, Christopher | 1784 | " " | 100 | 1820 | | (Corps |
| Kuhlman, John | 1784 | Halifax-Lunenburg Road | 100 | 1812 | | Hessian |
| | | | | | | |
| Langley, Jacob | 1784 | Preston Township | 200 | 1815 | | |
| Larnard, Jesse | 1784 | " " | 200 | 1820 | | |
| Laudner, John | 1784 | Harriet Fields | 100 | 1820 | | |
| Laycock, John | 1786 | Shubenacadie River | 200 | 1810 | | |
| Ledder, Edmund | 1786 | " " | 100 | 1810 | | |
| Leithauser, M. | 1784 | Harriet Fields | 100 | 1820 | | |
| Leonard, Richard Reed | 1786 | Shubenacadie River | 200 | 1810 | | |
| Leopold, Christopher | 1784 | Harrietfields | 100 | 1820 | | |
| Lesh, John | 1784 | " | 100 | 1820 | | |
| Leslie, Robert | 1784 | Preston Township | 200 | 1815 | | |
| Lewis, John | 1786 | Shubenacadie River | 100 | 1810 | | |
| Lewis, Paul | 1784 | Preston Township | 200 | 1815 | | |
| Lindlow, Jacob | 1784 | Harrietfields | 100 | 1820 | | |
| Lindsey, John | 1784 | Preston Township | 300 | 1815 | | |
| Lishlar, G. | 1784 | Harrietfields | 100 | 1820 | | |
| Lishler, George | 1784 | Halifax-Lunenburg Road | 100 | 1812 | | Hessian |
| Lounds, James | 1785 | Harrietfields | 160 | 1817 | | (Corps |
| Lounds, Matthew | 1785 | " | 100 | 1817 | | |
| Lounds, Thomas | 1785 | " | 100 | 1811 | | |
| Lucas, Benjamin | 1784 | Preston Township | 100 | 1815 | | |
| | | | | | | |
| McFall, John | 1784 | " " | 100 | 1815 | | |
| McGraw, Duncan | 1784 | Halifax-Lunenburg Road | 100 | 1812 | | Hessian |
| McGreedy, John | 1786 | Shubenacadie River | 200 | 1810 | | (Corps |
| McPherson, John | 1786 | Shubenacadie | 100 | 1810 | | |
| May, John | 1784 | Harrietfields | 100 | 1820 | | |
| Melone, John | 1784 | Preston Township | 100 | 1815 | | |
| Meloney, John | 1784 | " " | 200 | 1815 | | |
| Milford, Deborah | 1786 | Shubenacadie River | 200 | 1810 | | |
| Milford, Mary | 1786 | " " | 200 | 1810 | | |
| Millar, Jacob | 1785 | Harrietfields | 180 | 1817 | | |
| Miller, David | 1784 | Preston Township | 100 | 1812 | 50 | |
| Miller, John | 1784 | " " | 100 | 1815 | | |
| Miller, Robert | 1786 | Shubenacadie | 100 | 1810 | | |
| Milton [Melton] Wm. | 1784 | Ship Harbour, W. | 200 | 1810 | | |

| Name | Date | Situation | Acres | Esch'd | Amt. of Esch't | Origin or Rank |
|---|---|---|---|---|---|---|
| Mitchall, John | 1786 | Shubenacadie | 100 | 1810 | | |
| Morris, Kenney [Henry] | 1784 | Preston Township | 100 | 1815 | | |
| Morrison, George | 1784 | " " | 150 | 1815 | | |
| Muller, Henry | 1784 | Harrietfields | 100 | 1820 | | |
| Mullock, Joshua R. | 1786 | Shubenacadie | 100 | 1810 | | |
| Munro, James | 1786 | " | 100 | 1810 | | |
| Munro, John | 1786 | " | 100 | 1810 | | |
| Murphy, Daniel | 1784 | Preston Township | 200 | 1820 | | |
| Murray, Mary | 1786 | Shubenacadie River | 200 | 1810 | | |
| *Negro, James | 1784 | Preston Township | 100 | 1815 | | |
| Nero | 1786 | Shubenacadie River | 50 | 1810 | | |
| Nolte, George | 1784 | Harrietfields | 100 | 1820 | | |
| O'Brien, Edward B. | 1786 | Shubenacadie River | 100 | 1810 | | |
| Oldendorf, Charles | 1784 | Halifax-Lunenburg Road | 150 | 1812 | | Hessian |
| Oldendorf, Charles | 1784 | Harrietfields | 100 | 1820 | | (Corps |
| Parker, Zachary | 1784 | Preston Township | 200 | 1815 | | |
| Penhorn, John | 1786 | Shubenacadie River | 200 | 1810 | | |
| Peter | 1786 | " " | 50 | 1810 | | |
| Peter | 1786 | " " | 50 | 1810 | | |
| Prince | 1786 | " " | 50 | 1810 | | |
| Purcell, Robert | 1786 | " " | 200 | 1810 | | |
| Quimmer, Philip | 1785 | Harrietfields | 200 | 1817 | | Serjeant |
| Reading, Michael | 1786 | Shubenacadie River | 100 | 1810 | | |
| Reed, Richard, see Leonard, Rich'd Reed | 1786 | | | | | |
| Rench, John | 1786 | Shubenacadie River | 150 | 1810 | | |
| Robinson, George | 1784 | Preston Township | 100 | 1815 | | |
| Robson, George | 1784 | Harrietfields | 190 | 1817 | | |
| Rohring, George | 1784 | " | 100 | 1820 | | |
| Ross, Thomas | 1784 | Preston Township | 200 | 1815 | | |
| Russell, Martin | 1786 | Shubenacadie River | 200 | 1810 | | |
| Ryan, Thomas | 1786 | " " | 200 | 1810 | | |
| Saby | 1786 | " " | 50 | 1810 | | |
| Sam | 1786 | " " | 50 | 1810 | | |
| Samuel | 1786 | " " | 50 | 1810 | | |
| Schaffer, John | 1784 | Harrietfields | 100 | 1820 | | |
| Scott | 1786 | Shubenacadie River | 50 | 1810 | | |
| Seales, Michael | 1784 | Preston Township | 200 | 1815 | 100 | |
| Shelly | 1786 | Shubenacadie River | 50 | 1810 | | |
| Shier, Henry | 1785 | Harrietfields | 190 | 1817 | | |
| Shier, James | 1785 | " | 100 | 1817 | | |
| Shreiber, Andrew | 1784 | Halifax-Lunenburg Road | 100 | 1812 | | Hessian |
| Simpson, George | 1786 | Shubenacadie River | 200 | 1810 | | (Corps |
| Smart | 1786 | " " | 50 | 1810 | | |
| Smith, Charles | 1785 | Harrietfields | 100 | 1817 | | |
| Smith, David | 1784 | " | 100 | 1820 | | |
| Smith, Henry | 1784 | " | 100 | 1820 | | |
| Smith, John | 1784 | Preston Township | 100 | 1815 | | |
| Smith, Titus | 1786 | Shubenacadie River | 100 | 1810 | | |
| Sneider, John | 1784 | Harrietfields | 100 | 1820 | | |
| Spoeder, John | 1784 | Halifax-Lunenburg Road | 100 | 1812 | | Hessian |
| Squire | 1786 | Shubenacadie River | 50 | 1810 | | (Corps |
| Steeving, John | 1785 | Harrietfields | 100 | 1817 | | |
| Stevenson, John | 1785 | " | 100 | 1817 | | |
| Stewart, Charles | 1784 | Preston Township | 100 | 1815 | | |
| Stewart, William | 1784 | " " | 200 | 1815 | 100 | |

* Possibly "James, a negro", but negroes seldom received this quantity of land.

## LOYALISTS AND LAND SETTLEMENT IN NOVA SCOTIA 59

| Name | Date | Situation | Acres | Esch'd | Amt. of Esch't | Origin or Rank |
|---|---|---|---|---|---|---|
| Stimmos, John | 1786 | Shubenacadie River | 200 | 1810 | | |
| Stobo, John | 1786 | " " | 50 | 1810 | | |
| Stobo, Robert | 1786 | " " | 200 | 1810 | | |
| Stove, Francis | 1786 | " " | 100 | 1810 | | |
| Strafsman, Henry | 1784 | Halifax-Lunenburg Road | 100 | 1812 | | Hessian |
| Street, John | 1786 | Shubenacadie River | 200 | 1810 | | (Corps |
| | | | | | | |
| Terry | 1786 | " " | 50 | 1810 | | |
| Thomas, Joseph | 1786 | " " | 50 | 1810* | | |
| Thompson, Richard | 1786 | " " | 200 | 1810 | | |
| Thompson, William | 1787 | Halifax-Truro Road | 200 | 1817 | | |
| Thrope, Thomas | 1784 | Preston Township | 100 | 1815 | | |
| Toby | 1786 | Shubenacadie River | 50 | 1810 | | |
| Todwin, Abraham | 1784 | Preston Township | 100 | 1815 | 200† | |
| Townsend, William | 1784 | " " | 100 | 1802 | 50‡ | |
| Tweed, Leonard | 1786 | Shubenacadie River | 200 | 1810 | | |
| | | | | | | |
| Uhmann, Peter | 1784 | Harrietfields | 100 | 1820 | | |
| | | | | | | |
| Vaughn, Samuel | 1784 | Preston Township | 100 | 1815 | | (Lieut. |
| Vieth, Adolphus | 1784 | Halifax-Lunenburg Road | 600 | 1812 | | Hessian (Corps |
| Wakenfield, John | 1784 | Preston Township | 200 | 1815 | | |
| Webster, Thomas | 1784 | " " | 100 | 1815 | | |
| Welsh, John | 1784 | " " | 100 | 1815 | | |
| Westin, John | 1784 | Harrietfields | 100 | 1820 | | |
| White, William | 1784 | Preston Township | 100 | 1815 | | |
| Wideman, John | 1784 | Halifax-Lunenburg Road | 100 | 1812 | | Hessian (Corps |
| Wieshuhn [Wisholm], Henry | 1784 | Preston Township | 200 | 1815 | | |
| Wood, Abner | 1784 | " " | 100 | 1815 | | |
| Woolett, Anthony | 1784 | " " | 50 | 1802 | 100x | |

\* Possibly Thomas and Joseph.
† Error in Escheat Number 207.
‡ Possible error in escheat Number 149. See Anthony Woolett.
x Possible error in escheat 149. See, Townsend, William.

## Hants County
### GRANTS

| Name | Date | Situation | Acres | Origin or Rank |
|---|---|---|---|---|
| Almond, John | 1785 | Rawdon Township | 250 | |
| Bane, John | 1787 | Rawdon, E. | 250 | St. Augustine |
| Barron, Alexander | 1786 | Rawdon Township, E. | 250 | |
| Berwick, John | 1787 | Rawdon, E. | 100 | St. Augustine |
| Blair, Andrew | 1798 | Rawdon | 500 | |
| Bond, George | 1798 | " | 300 | |
| Bond, John | 1798 | " | 300 | |
| Brown, John | 1786 | Rawdon Township, E. | 250 | |
| Carter, James (John) | 1786 | "    "    " | 250 | |
| Clarke, John | 1786 | Windsor Township | 500 | |
| Conner, James | 1785 | Windsor Road, N. E. | 250 | |
| *Cotnam, Deborah, Widow | 1785 | Minas Basin | 1000 | Salem |
| †Dalrymple, James | 1816 | Douglas Township | 500 | 84th. Reg't |
| †Ettinger, Lewis | 1816 | "    " | 500 | "    " |
| Evans, Margaret | 1787 | Rawdon, E. | 300 | St. Augustine |
| Evans, Samuel | 1787 | "    " | 100 | "    " |
| Fenton, Richard | 1787 | "    " | 400 | S. Carolina Soldier |
| †Ferguson, Alexander | 1816 | Douglas Township | 500 | 84th. Reg't |
| †Ferguson, Alexander | 1816 | "    " | 333½ | "    " |
| Ferguson, James | 1785 | Rawdon Township | 250 | |
| †Ferguson, John | 1816 | Douglas Township | 400 | 84th. Reg't |
| †Fraser,—(Widow) and Fraser, Donald | 1816 | "    " | 250 | "    " |
| †Gill, William | 1816 | "    " | 200 | "    " |
| Gilmore, George (Rev.) | 1786 | Windsor Road, S. W. | 500 | |
| †Grant, Donald | 1816 | Douglas Township | 500 | 84th. Reg't |
| Grant, John | 1783 | River Piziquid | 3000 | Reduced Captain |
| †Grant, John | 1816 | Douglas Township | 250 | 84th. Reg't |
| †Grant, Peter | 1816 | "    " | 500 | "    " |
| Hammell, Daniel | 1785 | Minas Basin, S. | 1000 | |
| Hayward, Henry | 1785 | Windsor Road | 500 | |
| Heafler [Heflar] John | 1798 | Rawdon | 400 | |
| Heafler [Heflar] Philip | 1798 | " | 400 | |
| †Hennegar, Christian | 1816 | Douglas Township | 500 | 84th. Reg't |
| Hockenhull, John | 1798 | Rawdon Road | 750 | |
| Horn, Simeon | 1787 | Rawdon, E. | 100 | |
| Ingram, William | 1787 | "    " | 300 | |
| Johnson, Roger | 1784 | Chevery | 1000 | |
| Jones, James (Rev.) | 1786 | Windsor Road, S. | 500 | |
| Kidston, Richard, Jr. | 1797 | Shubenaccadie | 1000 | |
| Kidston, Richard, Sr. | 1797 | " | 1000 | |
| King, Henry | 1798 | Rawdon | 400 | |

\* Her husband (d. 1780) had served 35 years in the 40th. Reg't, "Chiefly in this province", being latterly a Captain. When he became infirm he sold his commission and settled in Salem, New England, from which place he was driven to Nova Scotia during the Revolution. P. A. N. S., *Land papers, Memorial.*

† These grantees had been entitled to lands in the grant to Col. John Small in trust for the 2nd. battalion of the 84th. Regiment. This was escheated in 1798, and the grant to James Dalrymple and 34 others, 1816, reestablished titles to land of some of the remaining members of the regiment or the widows.

LOYALISTS AND LAND SETTLEMENT IN NOVA SCOTIA 61

| Name | Date | Situation | Acres | Origin or Rank |
|---|---|---|---|---|
| †Laffin, Thomas | 1816 | Douglas Township | 500 | 84th. Reg't |
| Lane, Henry | 1785 | Petit R., Minas Basin | 500 | Ensign. |
| Laws, John | 1787 | Rawdon, E. | 200 | St. Augustine |
| Lemand, James | 1786 | Rawdon Township, E. | 250 | |
| Lemand, John | 1786 | " " " | 250 | |
| Lemmon, James | 1798 | Rawdon | 250 | |
| †McDonald, Alexander | 1816 | Douglas Township | 300 | 84th. Reg't |
| †McDonald, Donald | 1816 | " " | 300 | " " |
| †McDonald, Donald | 1816 | " " | 240 | ' " |
| †McDonald, John, Jr. | 1816 | " " | 150 | " " |
| †McDonald, John, Sr. | 1816 | " " | 500 | " " |
| McDonald, Randle | 1787 | Rawdon, E. | 500 | St. Augustine |
| †McDougal[d],[Anne] (Widow) | 1816 | Douglas Township | 500 | 84th. Reg't |
| †McDougal[d], Donald | 1816 | " " | 350 | " " . |
| †McDougal, Donald | 1816 | " " | 250 | " " |
| †McKenzie, Donald | 1816 | " " | 300 | " " |
| †McKenzie, Duncan | 1816 | " " | 300 | " " |
| †McKenzie, Malcolm | 1816 | " " | 300 | " " |
| McKisah [McKizick], Daniel | 1787 | Rawdon, E. | 200 | St. Augustine |
| †McNeil, John | 1816 | Douglas Township | 500 | 84th. Reg't |
| †McPhee, Alexander | 1816 | " " | 500 | " " |
| †McPhee, Donald | 1816 | " " | 500 | " " |
| †McPhee, Evan | 1816 | " " | 500 | " " |
| †McPhee, James | 1816 | " " | 350 | " " |
| Marshall, John | 1787 | Rawdon, E. | 150 | |
| Marsham, Jeremiah | 1786 | Windsor Road, S. W. | 500 | |
| Monohan, Michael | 1785 | " " , N. E. | 500 | |
| Mott, James | 1787 | Rawdon, E. | 100 | St. Augustine |
| †Murdock, Findley | 1816 | Douglas Township | 500 | 84th. Reg't |
| Pace,—(Widow) | 1787 | Rawdon, E. | 200 | St. Augustine |
| Pace, Derias | 1787 | " " | 300 | " " |
| Parker, Thomas | 1787 | " " | 100 | " " (Georgia. |
| Philips, Daniel | 1787 | " " | 400 | Capt. Royal Militia, |
| †Rafter, John | 1816 | Douglas Township | 250 | 84th. Reg't |
| Ross, David | 1781 | Newport Township | 1000 | Rhode Island |
| Steward, Gilbert | 1781 | " " | 1000 | " " |
| Stewart, Anthony | 1784 | Windsor Road, S. W. | 1000 | |
| Sterling, John | 1787 | Rawdon, E. | 100 | |
| †Taggart, Stephen | 1816 | Douglas Township | 500 | 84th. Reg't |
| †Thompson, Alexander | 1816 | " " | 411 | " " |
| †Thompson, Donald | 1816 | " " | 150 | " " |
| †Thompson, James | 1816 | " " | 150 | " " |
| †Welsh, Thomas | 1816 | " " | 368 | " " |
| Wheelwright, Joseph | 1785 | Minas Basin (Man of War's Land) | 700 | |
| Wilkins, Isaac | 1791 | Hfx-Windsor Rd., N. E. | 1500 | New York |
| Wilkins, Isaac | 1793 | Windsor Road | 40 | |
| Wilkins, Martin | 1791 | Hfx-Windsor Rd., N. E. | 500 | |

† These grantees had been entitled to lands in the grant to Col. John Small in trust for the 2nd battalion of the 84th Regiment. This was escheated in 1798, and the grant to James Dalrymple and 34 others, 1816, reestablished titles to land of some of the remaining members of the regiment or their widows

## Hants County
### WARRANTS

| Name | Date | Situation | Acres | Origin or Rank |
|---|---|---|---|---|
| Campbell, Colin | 1791 | Hants County | 500 | Lieut. 74th. Reg't |
| Fisher, Philip | 1786 | Nine Mile River | 100 | Hessian |
| Gammerdinger, Ludovick | 1786 | " " " | 100 | " |
| Hengel, George | 1786 | " " " | 100 | " |
| *McNeil, Daniel | 1797 | Minas Basin | 1000 | Captain |
| Moore, Joseph | 1791 | Shubenaccadie R., N. W. | 200 | |
| Shenk, Henry | 1786 | Nine Mile River | 100 | Hessian |

\* To replace barren land at Country Harbour.

## Hants County
### ESCHEATS

| Name | Date | Situation | Acres | Esch'd | Origin or Rank |
|---|---|---|---|---|---|
| Amiel, Robert | 1785 | Minas Basin | 500 | 1810 | Lieut. |
| 84th. Reg't 2d. Batt., see Small, John (Capt.) | 1784 | | | | |
| McCree, George | 1784 | Windsor Road, S. W. | 1000 | 1814 | |
| Small, John* (In trust for 2d. Batt., 84th. Reg't) | 1784 | Douglass | 105,000 | 1798 | (2nd. Batt. Col. 84th Regt |
| Steel, John | 1785 | Minas Basin | 500 | 1810 | Capt. R. N. |
| Wanton, William | 1785 | " " | 1000 | 1810 | |

\* Escheat No. 135 missing from records of Court of Escheats.

# King's County
## GRANTS

| Name | Date | Situation | Acres | Origin or Rank |
|---|---|---|---|---|
| *Anderson, Thom·s | 1787 | Parrsborough Township | 300 | |
| Arnold, John | 1784 | Advocate Harbour | 1000 | |
| *Ascough, Richard | 1787 | Parrsborough Township | 700 | Lieutenant |
| Babbett, John see LeVong, Peter | 1787 | | | |
| Barclay, Beverly Rob'n | 1797 | Aylesford | 1000 | |
| Barclay, Delancy | 1797 | " | 1000 | |
| Barclay, Henry | 1797 | " | 1000 | |
| Barclay, Thomas | 1797 | " | 1000 | |
| Barclay, Thomas, Jr. | 1797 | " | 1000 | |
| Benedict, Jabez | 1786 | Wilmot Township | 200 | |
| Bower, Daniel | 1784 | Parrsborough | 700 | Captain |
| Boyd, Francis | 1783 | Point Concmie | 500 | |
| Braley, John see Lamb, Isaac | 1787 | | | |
| Brenton, William | 1786 | Upper Wilmot | 500 | Newport, R. I. |
| Brown, Daniel Isaac | 1784 | Parrsborough | 1000 | Major |
| Buchannon, John | 1784 | Swan Creek | 700 | Lieut. Royal Navy |
| Bullen, Nathaniel | 1784 | Parrsborough | 500 | Doctor |
| Burn, Finley | 1785 | Parrsborough Township | 700 | Captain |
| Butler, Edmund | 1785 | " " | 700 | |
| Clark, Alexander | 1784 | " " | 500 | Adjutant |
| Cloud, Rebecca | 1785 | " " | 500 | |
| Cole, Edward | 1785 | " " | 1000 | Colonel |
| Connolly, John | 1785 | " " | 1000 | Lieut.-Colonel |
| *Crowe, Robert Richard | 1787 | " " | 700 | Captain |
| De Meyern,— | 1787 | " " | 700 | Capt. King's Orange |
| Dumain, William | 1785 | " " | 200 | (Rangers |
| Dunkham, Asher | 1785 | " " | 500 | Lieutenant |
| Finney, Francis | 1784 | " " | 500 | Ensign |
| Fordice, John | 1784 | Chignecto River | 500 | Refugee |
| Fowler, Elijah | 1785 | Parrsborough Township | 500 | Lieutenant |
| Fowler, John | 1786 | Wilmot " | 300 | |
| Fraser, Francis | 1784 | Swan Creek | 700 | Captain Pioneers |
| Frasier, John | 1784 | " " | 500 | Surg. Orange Rangers |
| Frasier, William | 1784 | " " | 500 | Lieut. 42nd. Reg't |
| Frazer, Francis | 1784 | Parrsborough Township | 500 | Lieutenant |
| Halliburton, John, Jr. | 1786 | Upper Wilmot | 500 | |
| Harriott, Thomas | 1785 | Parrsborough Township | 200 | |
| *Hartshorne, Laurance | 1787 | " " | 700 | |
| Hathaway, Luther | 1785 | " " | 500 | Lieutenant |
| Head, Michael | 1787 | " " | 1000 | |
| Hemmington, John | 1787 | Parrsboro Parish | 400 | |
| Henry, Patrick | 1785 | Parrsborough Township | 500 | Lieutenant |
| Henry, William | 1788 | " " | 250 | |
| Hetfield, John | 1784 | " " | 700 | Captain |
| Inglis, Charles | 1790 | Aylesford | 967 | Bishop of N. S. |
| Inglis, John | 1795 | " | 200 | |

* Grants could not be found in the Department of Lands and Forests; but maps and escheats show they were granted.

# PUBLIC ARCHIVES OF NOVA SCOTIA

| Name | Date | Situation | Acres | Origin or Rank |
|---|---|---|---|---|
| Kerr, James | 1784 | Parrsboro | 700 | Captain |
| Kipp, Isaac | 1785 | Parrsborough Township | 1000 | Major |
| *Kitchum, Jedediah and Smith, Petitiah | 1787 | " " | 500 | |
| *Lamb, Isaac and Braley, John | 1787 | " " | 500 | |
| Lawrence, Elisha | 1785 | " " | 2000 | Lieut.-Colonel |
| Leonard, Samuel | 1784 | " " | 700 | Captain |
| Leonard, Thomas | 1784 | River Chignecto | 1000 | Major |
| *Le Vong, Peter and Babbett, John | 1787 | Parrsborough Township | 500 | |
| Lewis, Caleb | 1784 | Chignecto River | 500 | Refugee |
| Lindsay, Samuel | 1784 | Parrsborough Township | 700 | Captain |
| Longstreet, John | 1786 | Parrsborough | 231 | |
| Longstreet, John | 1787 | Cumberland Road | 250 | |
| McDonald, Alexander | 1784 | Parrsborough Township | 700 | Captain |
| McGill, John | 1784 | " " | 700 | |
| McKochran, Archibald | 1784 | Swan Creek | 500 | Lt. N. Carolina Vol's |
| Magee, Henry | 1786 | Wilmot Township | 500 | |
| Mitchel, James | 1785 | Parrsborough Township | 280 | |
| Moore, Thomas | 1785 | " " | 400 | |
| *Moore, Thomas Wm. | 1787 | " " | 1000 | Captain |
| *Morris, Luther | 1787 | " " | 500 | |
| Morrison, George and Morrison, Hugh | 1787 | Aylesford Township | 1000 | |
| *Mumford, Joseph | 1787 | Parrsborough Township | 500 | |
| Munro, John | 1785 | " " | 500 | Lieutenant |
| *Murray,— | 1787 | " " | 1000 | Captain |
| Nowlan, John | 1785 | " " | 500 | Quarter Master |
| Nutting, John | 1783 | Minas Basin | 2000 | |
| Ormsby, Mathew | 1786 | Wilmot Township | 300 | |
| Pattinson, Thomas | 1784 | Parrsborough Township | 1000 | Lieut.-Colonel |
| Pearce, Henry | 1786 | Wilmot Township | 100 | |
| Pearce, William | 1786 | " " | 100 | |
| Potts, Edward | 1788 | Parrsborough Township | 560 | Captain |
| *Potts, Thomas | 1787 | " " | 400 | |
| *Pritchard Francis Toml'n | 1787 | " " | 500 | |
| Pritchard, Thomas I. | 1784 | " " | 500 | Lieutenant |
| Ratchford, James | 1785 | " " | 200 | |
| Raymond, James | 1784 | " " | 700 | Captain |
| Reid, John | 1785 | " " | 500 | Lieutenant |
| Reid, William | 1785 | " " | 500 | " |
| Shreeve, Thomas | 1790 | Cumberland Road, E Side (not reg'd) | 587 | First Minister, Parrsborough Parish |
| Smith, John | 1785 | Parrsborough Township | 700 | |
| Smith, Petitiah see Kitchum, Jedidiah | 1787 | | | |
| Spicer, Robert | 1785 | " " | 500 | Lieutenant |
| Stewart, James | 1785 | " " | 700 | Captain |
| *Sutherland, Adam | 1787 | " " | 500 | |
| Taylor, Eliazer | 1784 | " " | 500 | Lieutenant |
| *Taylor, John Parr | 1787 | " " | 500 | |
| Thompson, William | 1785 | " " | 500 | |
| VanCortland Jacob Ogden | 1790 | Aylesford | 500 | Ensign |
| VanCortland, Philip | 1790 | " | 1600 | Maj.3d. Batt.N.J.Vol's |

* Grants not in the Department of Lands and Forests; but map s and escheats show they were granted

LOYALISTS AND LAND SETTLEMENT IN NOVA SCOTIA 65

| Name | Date | Situation | Acres | Origin or Rank |
|---|---|---|---|---|
| VanCortland, Philip, Jr. | 1790 | Aylesford | 500 | Ensign |
| Vandyke, John | 1785 | Parrsborough Township | 1000 | Major |
| *Van Dyke, John, Jr. see Van Dyke, Ralph | 1787 | | | |
| *Van Dyke, Ralph & Van Dyke, John, Jr. | 1787 | "          " | 700 | |
| Vought, John | 1784 | "          " | 700 | Captain |
| Vought, John | 1786 | "          " | 180 | " |
| Ward, Edmund | 1785 | "          " | 700 | " |
| †West, John | 1784 | Wilmot Township | 500 | |
| West, John | 1786 | "          " (Partly in Annapolis County) | 250 | |
| Wightman, John | 1784 | Parrsborough Township | 500 | Lieutenant |
| Wilkins, James | 1784 | Annapolis Road | 500 | |
| Wilkins, James | 1784 | "          " S. | 500 | |
| Wilson, Samuel | 1785 | Parrsborough Township | 700 | Captain |
| Woodcock, Joseph | 1788 | "          " | 560 | |
| *Yelverton, Thomas | 1784 | Parrsborough | 700 | Captain |

\* Grants not in the Department of Lands and Forests; but maps and escheats show they were granted
† Registered, 1785.

# King's County
## WARRANTS

| Name | Date | Situation | Acres |
|---|---|---|---|
| Shreeve, Thomas (Rev.) | 1788 | Cumberland Road | 550 |

# King's County
## ESCHEATS

| Name | Date | Situation | Acres | Esch'd | Origin or Rank |
|---|---|---|---|---|---|
| Barnston, Letitia | 1785 | Parrsborough Township | 500 | 1814 | |
| Bissionett, Sarah | 1785 | "          " | 700 | 1814 | |
| Bowlsby, Charles | 1785 | "          " | 250 | 1814 | |
| Bowlsby, John | 1785 | "          " | 250 | 1814 | |
| Cameron, Daniel | 1784 | Swan Creek | 500 | 1796 | Lt. DeLancey's 1st Batt. |
| Campbell, Alexander | 1784 | Mill River | 600 | 1796 | Lieut. |
| Campbell, Donald | 1784 | "          " | 600 | 1796 | Ensign |
| Currie, Neill | 1784 | "          " | 600 | 1796 | Quarter Master |
| Fletcher, Duncan | 1784 | Swan Creek | 700 | 1796 | Capt. R. Am. |
| French, Adolphus | 1785 | Parrsborough Township | 500 | 1814 | (Reg't. |

| Name | Date | Situation | Acres | Esch'd | Origin or Rank |
|---|---|---|---|---|---|
| Hollenbury,— | 1784 | Mill River | 600 | 1796 | Lt H.M.Navy |
| Longstreet, John | 1785 | Parrsborough Township | 700 | 1814 | Captain |
| †Lowden [Loudon] John | 1785 | " " | 500 | 1814 | Lieut. |
| McArthur, Neil | 1784 | Swan Creek | 700 | 1796 | Capt. N. C. |
| McDonald, John | 1784 | Mill River | 600 | 1796 | Lt.   (Vol's |
| McDonald, John | 1786 | Parrsborough Township | 500 | 1814 | " |
| McDougald, Archibald | 1784 | Mill River | 600 | 1796 | Ensign |
| McKethin, Dougald | 1784 | " " | 600 | 1796 | Lieut. |
| McLean, Donald | 1784 | Minas B. (NearSwanCreek) | 700 | 1796 | (ey's 1st Batt. |
| McMullan, Alexander | 1784 | Swan Creek | 500 | 1796 | Lt. DeLanc- |
| McPherson, Charles | 1784 | " " | 700 | 1796 | Capt. " |
| *Raymond, William | 1787 | Parrsborough Township | 700 | 1814 | |
| *Shreve, Catherine | 1787 | " " | 500 | 1814 | |
| Stevens, Thomas | 1784 | Advocate Harbour | 500 | 1814 | |
| Taylor, William | 1785 | Parrsborough Township | 500 | 1814 | |
| ‡Vought, Christopher | 1784 | " " | 700 | 1814 | Captain |
| Walker, Richard | 1785 | " " | 1000 | 1814 | |
| Ward, Moses | 1785 | " " | 500 | 1814 | |
| Wemyss, Peter | 1785 | Minas B. (NearSwanCreek) | 700 | 1796 | |

* Grants could not be found in the Department of Lands and Forests. Escheat No. 201 shows it was granted.
† In grant called "Thomas", in escheat, "John".
‡ In grant called "Christopher", in escheat, "Charles".

LOYALISTS AND LAND SETTLEMENT IN NOVA SCOTIA 67

## Lunenburg County
### GRANTS

| Name | Date | Situation | Acres | Origin or Rank |
|---|---|---|---|---|
| Allen, John | 1788 | Chester | T. L. | |
| Anderson, James | 1785 | Chester Township | 150 | |
| Anderson, James | 1788 | Chester | T. L. | |
| Anderson, James | 1788 | " | T. L. | |
| Apthorpe, James | 1785 | Chester Township | 500 | |
| Armiger, Moses | 1785 | " " | 100 | |
| Bangs, Seth | 1788 | Chester | T. L. | |
| Bangs, Seth, Jr. | 1788 | " | T. L. | |
| Bedisson, Robert | 1788 | " | T. L. | |
| Behem, John | 1785 | Chester Township | 100 | |
| Bell, William | 1788 | Chester | T. L. | |
| Bradley, James | 1785 | Chester Township | 100 | |
| Bremner, John | 1785 | " " | 200 | |
| Brown, John | 1788 | Chester | T. L. | |
| Brunn, Jacob | 1788 | " | T. L. | |
| Burton, William | 1785 | Chester Township | 200 | New York |
| Campbell, John | 1785 | " " | 100 | |
| Campbell, William | 1785 | " " | 200 | |
| Cole, John | 1785 | " " | 100 | |
| Cook, Josiah | .1785 | " " | 100 | Gunner Royal Reg't of (Artillery |
| Cooper, Elias | 1788 | Chester | T. L. | |
| Cooper, Sarah | 1788 | " | T. L. | |
| Cummings, Patrick | 1785 | Chester Township | 200 | |
| Cummings, Patrick | 1788 | Chester | T. L. | |
| Daniel, Feuler | 1785 | Chester Township | 300 | |
| DeBeust, Philip | 1785 | " " | 500 | |
| DeBlois, George | 1787 | Lunenburg | T. L. | |
| Denny, Michael | 1785 | Chester Township | 100 | |
| Downes, Dier | 1788 | Chester | T. L. | |
| Downes, Mary | 1788 | " | T. L. | |
| Dunn, James | 1785 | Chester Township | 100 | |
| Edwards, Amelia. | 1785 | " " | 100 | |
| Elliot, Thomas | 1785 | " " | 200 | |
| English, Roger | 1788 | Chester | T. L. | |
| Ferguie, Andrew | 1788 | " | T. L. | |
| Fleiger, John Henry | 1792 | Mahone Bay—Islands | 330 | |
| Fraiser, John | 1785 | Chester Township | 100 | |
| Fraser, Robert | 1785 | " " | 100 | |
| Fraser, Robert | 1785 | " " | 100 | |
| Giles, William | 1785 | " " | 100 | |
| Grant, George | 1792 | Mahone Bay—Islands | 330 | |
| Gray, Andrew | 1788 | Chester | T. L. | |
| Green, James | 1788 | " | T. L. | |
| Green, James | 1788 | " | T. L. | |
| Grigg, William | 1788 | " | T. L. | |
| Hall, Andrew | 1785 | Chester Township | 100 | |
| Hardacker, James | 1785 | " " | 100 | |
| Hartman, Jacob | 1785 | New Dublin Township | 150 | |
| Hay, Sarah | 1788 | Chester | T. L. | |

# 68  PUBLIC ARCHIVES OF NOVA SCOTIA

| Name | Date | Situation | Acres | Origin or Rank |
|---|---|---|---|---|
| Haywood, Benjamin | 1788 | Chester | | T. L. |
| Hill, James | 1785 | Chester Township | 500 | |
| Johnson, Obadiah | 1788 | Chester | | T. L. |
| Keith, Hellen | 1788 | " | | T. L. |
| Kennedy, Thomas | 1785 | Chester Township | 100 | |
| Kennedy, William | 1784 | Chester | | T.L. & Wharf L. |
| Kensleagh, Frederick | 1788 | Chester Township | 100 | |
| Kingshorne, John | 1785 | Chester | | W. L. & Wharf L. |
| Knowles, Robert | 1785 | Chester Township | 100 | |
| Letson, John | 1788 | Chester | | T. L. |
| Letson, Robert | 1788 | Chester | | T. L. |
| Letson, Susannah | 1788 | " | | T. L. |
| Lishman, Edward | 1785 | Chester Township | 200 | Gunner H. M. Royal |
| Lishman, Edward | 1785 | " " | 100 | (Reg't of Artillery |
| McHerman, Daniel | 1785 | " " | 200 | |
| Macleod, James | 1785 | " " | 500 | |
| Mahaney, James | 1785 | " " | 250 | |
| Marshall, John | 1785 | " " | 200 | |
| Martin, John | 1785 | " " | 200 | |
| Mead, Richard | 1788 | Chester | | T. L. |
| Mead, Robert | 1788 | " | | T. L. (Artillery |
| Melvin, James | 1785 | Chester Township | 100 | Gunner Royal Reg't of |
| Mitchell, Alexander | 1785 | " " | 100 | " " " " |
| Molloy, John | 1785 | " " | 200 | |
| Moorhead, Samuel | 1785 | " " | 100 | Gunner R. Reg't |
| Morris, William | 1784 | Mahone Bay | 700 | (Artillery |
| Morris, William | 1788 | Chester | | T. L. |
| Morton, Joseph | 1785 | Chester Township | 200 | |
| Murphy, Michael | 1788 | Chester | | T. L. |
| Murphy, Timothy | 1788 | " | | T. L. |
| Murray, James | 1788 | " | | T. L. |
| Norris, John | 1785 | Chester Township | 100 | Royal Reg't of Artillery |
| O'Brien, Lewis | 1788 | Chester | | T. L. |
| Parker, George | 1785 | Chester Township | 150 | |
| Pattelo, Alexander | 1785 | " " | 150 | |
| Patten, Elizabeth | 1785 | " " | 100 | |
| Portous, John | 1785 | " " | 100 | |
| Ramsey, Joseph | 1788 | Chester | | T. L. |
| Redman, Joel | 1785 | Chester Township | 200 | |
| Richardson, John | 1785 | " " | 400 | |
| Richardson, Thomas | 1785 | " " | 100 | |
| Robertson, James | 1785 | " " | 100 | |
| Ruff, Arthur | 1785 | " " | 100 | |
| Ruff, Arthur | 1785 | " " | 200 | |
| Russell, Joseph | 1785 | " " | 500 | |
| Russell, William | 1785 | " " | 500 | |
| Sanderson, John | 1785 | " " | 100 | |
| Sharpe, James | 1785 | " " | 150 | |
| Shoals, John | 1786 | Lunenburg  T. L.'s & | W. L. | Captain |
| Smith, Daniel | 1785 | Chester Township | 250 | |
| Smith, David | 1788 | Chester | | T. L. |
| Smith, Walter | 1785 | Chester Township | 100 | |
| Spears, Robert | 1785 | Chester—Windsor Road | 500 | Quarter Master R. F. |
| Sterling, Frederick | 1785 | Chester Township | 500 | (Am. Reg't. |
| Storey, James | 1785 | " " | 200 | |
| Swanscombe, Richard | 1785 | " " | 100 | |

LOYALISTS AND LAND SETTLEMENT IN NOVA SCOTIA 69

| Name | Date | Situation | Acres | Origin or Rank |
|---|---|---|---|---|
| Thompson, Alexander | 1788 | Chester | T. L. | |
| Thompson, James | 1785 | Chester Township | 100 | |
| Thompson, Thomas | 1788 | Chester | T. L. | |
| Townsend, John | 1785 | Chester Township | 100 | (Artillery |
| Turner, Francis | 1785 | " " | 100 | Gunner R. Reg't of |
| Walker, F. | 1788 | Chester | T L. | |
| Walker, John | 1785 | Chester Township | 100 | |
| Walker, Justice | 1785 | Lunenburg | 200 | |
| Wallace, Alexander | 1785 | Chester Township | 100 | |
| Weidle, George | 1785 | Lunenburg | 200 | |
| Wentworth, Benning | 1796 | " | 543 | New Hampshire |
| Wilkey, Morris | 1785 | Chester Township | 100 | |
| Willis, David | 1785 | " " | 100 | |
| Wilson, Thomas | 1785 | " " | 100 | |
| Woodruff, Smith | 1788 | Chester | T. L. | |

## Lunenburg County
### WARRANTS

| Name | Date | Situation | Acres | Origin or Rank |
|---|---|---|---|---|
| Bell, John | 1787 | New Dublin Township | 300 | |
| Collins, John | 1787 | " " " | 200 | |
| Stemple, John Hendrick | 1787 | " " " | 100 | |
| Stephenson, Alexander | 1787 | " " " | 200 | |
| Stewart, John | 1787 | " " " | 200 | |
| Traynor, Maurice | 1787 | " " " | 200 | |

## Lunenburg County
### ESCHEATS

| Name | Date | Situation | Acres | Esch'd | Origin or Rank |
|---|---|---|---|---|---|
| Allan, John | 1784 | Chester Township | 250 | 1813 | |
| Allan, John | 1784 | " " | 200 | 1813 | |
| Amory, John | 1784 | " " | 300 | 1813 | |
| Anderson, James | 1784 | " " | 300 | 1813 | |
| Anderson, William | 1784 | " " | 100 | 1813 | |
| Bangs, Seth | 1784 | " " | 300 | 1813 | |
| Barnett, Joseph | 1784 | " " | 250 | 1813 | |
| Bayan, James | 1784 | " " | 100 | 1813 | |
| Bell, William | 1784 | " " | 500 | 1813 | |
| Bethel [Robert] | 1784 | " " | 700 | 1813 | Captain |
| Bosworth, Thomas | 1784 | " " | 250 | 1813 | |
| Bowie, William | 1784 | " " | 150 | 1813 | |

| Name | Date | Situation | Acres | Esch'd | Origin or Rank |
|---|---|---|---|---|---|
| Brinley, William | 1791 | Halifax-Annapolis Road* | | 1819 | |
| Brown, Duncan | 1784 | Chester Township | 100 | 1813 | |
| Brown, John | 1784 | " " | 700 | 1813 | |
| Burton, Peter | 1784 | " " | 500 | 1813 | |
| Calder, David | 1784 | " " | 200 | 1813 | |
| Cochran, John | 1784 | " " | 300 | 1813 | |
| Cody, Richard | 1784 | " " | 300 | 1813 | |
| Cole, William | 1784 | " " | 100 | 1813 | |
| Collins, William | 1784 | " " | 400 | 1813 | |
| Conkey, Israel | 1784 | " " | 300 | 1813 | |
| Cook, Joseph | 1784 | " " | 100 | 1813 | |
| Cooper, Elias | 1784 | " " | 700 | 1813 | |
| Curens, John | 1784 | " " | 300 | 1813 | |
| Cushing, James | 1784 | " " | 200 | 1813 | |
| Delaney, Robert | 1784 | " " | 100 | 1813 | |
| Downs, Dier | 1784 | " " | 200 | 1813 | |
| Dykman, James | 1784 | " " | 250 | 1813 | |
| Earle, John | 1784 | " " | 400 | 1813 | |
| English, Robert | 1784 | " " | 500 | 1813 | |
| Erwin, John | 1784 | " " | 350 | 1813 | |
| Etter, Benjamin | 1784 | " " | 100 | 1813 | |
| Etter, Francklin | 1784 | " " | 800 | 1813 | |
| Fargie, Andrew | 1784 | " " | 500 | 1813 | |
| Fife, Adam | 1784 | " " | 700 | 1813 | |
| Ford, Littleton | 1784 | " " | 100 | 1813 | |
| Garland, James | 1784 | " " | 100 | 1813 | |
| Gibson, William | 1784 | " " | 150 | 1813 | |
| Gordon, William | 1784 | " " | 500 | 1813 | |
| Graham, John | 1784 | " " | 100 | 1813 | |
| Grant, Daniel | 1784 | " " | 100 | 1813 | |
| Gray, Andrew | 1784 | " " | 400 | 1813 | |
| Green, James | 1784 | " " | 1000 | 1813 | |
| Grumble, George | 1784 | " " | 200 | 1813 | |
| Hall, William | 1784 | " " | 600 | 1813 | |
| Hay, Sarah | 1784 | " " | 500 | 1813 | |
| Hill, George | 1784 | " " | 100 | 1813 | |
| Hopkins, William | 1784 | " " | 100 | 1813 | |
| Hume, William | 1784 | " " | 200 | 1813 | |
| Hutt, Jacob | 1784 | " " | 100 | 1813 | |
| Johnston, Obadiah | 1784 | " " | 750 | 1813 | |
| Johnston, Thomas | 1784 | " " | 500 | 1813 | |
| Keith, Mary Helen | 1784 | " " | 500 | 1813 | |
| Kennedy, Dennis | 1784 | " " | 400 | 1813 | |
| Kennedy, William | 1784 | " " | 250 | 1813 | |
| Kinghorne, John | 1784 | " " | 500 | 1813 | |
| Leonard, Timothy | 1784 | " " | 250 | 1813 | |
| Letson, Robert | 1784 | " " | 400 | 1813 | |
| McCoy, Roderick | 1784 | " " | 100 | 1813 | |
| McCree, Hugh | 1784 | " " | 100 | 1813 | |
| McDonald, James | 1784 | " " | 100 | 1813 | |

* Those escheats in Annapolis County marked "Part possibly in Lunenburg County", were lands granted to William Brinley and others. Neither the draft grant nor the maps show which of the grantees received their lands in Annapolis County, and which in Lunenburg County, so all are listed under "Escheats, Annapolis Co."

LOYALISTS AND LAND SETTLEMENT IN NOVA SCOTIA 71

| Name | Date | Situation | Acres | Esch'd | Origin or Rank |
|---|---|---|---|---|---|
| McEnnis, Denagh | 1784 | Chester Township | 100 | 1813 | |
| McEven, John | 1784 | " " | 300 | 1813 | |
| McLean, Hector | 1784 | " " | 100 | 1813 | |
| McNeal, Alexander | 1784 | " " | 300 | 1813 | |
| Matthews, William | 1784 | " " | 200 | 1813 | |
| Mead, Richard | 1784 | " " | 100 | 1813 | |
| Mead, Robert | 1784 | " " | 1000 | 1813 | |
| Miller, William | 1784 | " " | 500 | 1813 | Captain |
| Mullock, Elenor | 1784 | " " | 100 | 1813 | |
| Mullock, Francis | 1784 | " " | 600 | 1813 | |
| Mullock, Mary | 1784 | " " | 100 | 1813 | |
| Nelson, William | 1784 | " " | 200 | 1813 | |
| Nevin, John | 1784 | " " | 200 | 1813 | |
| Norris, Francis | 1784 | " " | 400 | 1813 | |
| O'Bryan, Lewis | 1784 | " " | 450 | 1813 | |
| Ormsby, John | 1784 | " " | 100 | 1813 | |
| Powdill, Richard | 1784 | " " | 200 | 1813 | |
| Ramsay, James | 1784 | " " | 100 | 1813 | |
| Ramsay, Joseph | 1784 | " " | 500 | 1813 | |
| Ranson, Thomas | 1784 | " " | 200 | 1813 | |
| Shaw, Thomas | 1784 | " " | 700 | 1813 | |
| Stewart, Alexander | 1784 | " " | 250 | 1813 | |
| Smith, David | 1784 | " " | 250 | 1813 | |
| Smith, Duncan | 1784 | " " | 250 | 1813 | |
| Stell, Richard | 1784 | " " | 200 | 1813 | |
| Stout, John B. | 1784 | " " | 300 | 1813 | |
| Swift, John | 1784 | " " | 250 | 1813 | Virginia |
| Symonds, James | 1784 | " " | 100 | 1813 | |
| Thickpenny, Anthony | 1784 | " " | 300 | 1813 | |
| Thompson, James | 1784 | " " | 250 | 1813 | |
| Thomson, Alexander | 1784 | " " | 400 | 1813 | |
| Thomson, Thomas | 1784 | " " | 400 | 1813 | |
| Utholf, Henry | 1784 | " " | 600 | 1813 | |
| Williams, George | 1784 | " " | 100 | 1813 | |
| Winterton, William | 1784 | " " | 650 | 1813 | |
| Woodruff, Smith | 1784 | " " | 300 | 1813 | |

## Queen's County
### GRANTS

| Name | Date | Situation | Acres | Origin or Rank |
|---|---|---|---|---|
| Allikson, Charles | 1784 | Port Mouton | 150 | British Legion |
| Anderson, John | 1784 | " " | 200 | " " |
| Beaily, Seth | 1784 | " " | 200 | " " |
| Benham, William | 1784 | " " | 200 | " " |
| Blair, Waid | 1784 | " " | 100 | " " |
| Blowers, S. S. | 1784 | Great Port Joli | 1000 | |
| Bolds, John | 1784 | Port Mouton | 250 | British Legion |
| Bowers, Joseph | 1784 | " " | 200 | " " |
| Branton, John | 1784 | " " | 100 | " " |
| Brown, Thomas | 1784 | " " | 150 | " " |
| Buchanan, William | 1785 | " " | 600 | |
| Buchanna, David | 1784 | " " | 200 | British Legion |
| Buchannan, William | 1784 | " " | 100 | " " |
| Burrows, Benjamin | 1784 | " " | 150 | " " |
| Caivling, George | 1784 | " " | 100 | " " |
| Cameron, Allan | 1785 | Port Hebert, E. | 100 | |
| Cameron, Daniel | 1785 | " " " | 200 | |
| Campbell, John | 1784 | Port Mouton | 100 | British Legion |
| Campbell, Niel | 1784 | " " | 200 | " " |
| Campbell, William | 1784 | " " | 500 | " " |
| Cartor, John | 1784 | " " | 200 | " " |
| Christy, Angus | 1784 | " " | 250 | " " |
| Christy, John | 1784 | " " | 100 | " " |
| Clark, Andrew | 1784 | " " | 100 | " " |
| Clark, James | 1785 | " " | 100 | |
| Conley, John | 1784 | " " | 100 | British Legion |
| Conley, Patt | 1784 | " " | 100 | " " |
| Conley, Thomas | 1784 | " " | 300 | " " |
| Coop, John | 1784 | " " | 200 | " " |
| Crage, John | 1784 | " " | 200 | " " |
| Curling, John | 1784 | " " | 100 | " " |
| Curtin, John | 1784 | " " | 100 | " " |
| Cutt, Donald | 1785 | Port Hebert, E. | 100 | |
| Cutt, John | 1785 | " " " | 100 | |
| Davis, Thomas | 1784 | Port Mouton | 150 | British Legion |
| Duncan, John | 1784 | " " | 100 | " " |
| Ealey, Joseph | 1784 | " " | 100 | " " |
| Figg, John | 1785 | " " | 100 | |
| Fox, Thomas | 1784 | " " | 100 | British Legion |
| Fraser, John | 1785 | " " | 300 | |
| Ganong [Genong], Marques | 1784 | " " | 250 | British Legion |
| Gibbins, John | 1784 | " " | 100 | " " |
| Gibbons, George | 1784 | " " | 100 | " " |
| Gill, Joseph | 1784 | " " | 100 | " " |
| Glass, James | 1784 | " " | 200 | " " |
| Grant, Margaret | 1784 | " " | 150 | " " |
| Green, Francis | 1792 | Catherine River | 427 | Boston |
| Griffith, William | 1784 | Port Mouton | 100 | British Legion |
| Griffon, James | 1784 | " " | 100 | " " |

LOYALISTS AND LAND SETTLEMENT IN NOVA SCOTIA 73

| Name | Date | Situation | Acres | Origin or Rank |
|---|---|---|---|---|
| Hackett, Alexander | 1784 | Port Mouton | 100 | British Legion |
| Haggon, Andrew | 1784 | " " | 100 | " " |
| Hall, Thomas | 1784 | " " | 100 | " " |
| Hamett, George | 1784 | " " | 200 | " " |
| Handfand, Philip | 1784 | " " | 100 | " " |
| Harris, Robert | 1784 | " " | 100 | " " |
| Hays, Mickle | 1784 | " " | 250 | " " |
| Hays, William | 1784 | " " | 250 | " " |
| Henderson, John | 1785 | Port Hebert, E. | 200 | |
| Hovenden, John | 1784 | Port Mouton | 600 | British Legion |
| Hunter, George | 1785 | Port Hebert, E. | 200 | |
| Hutchins, Joseiah | 1784 | Port Mouton | 100 | British Legion |
| James, Thomas | 1784 | Port Mouton | 200 | British Legion |
| Jarett, James | 1784 | " " | 100 | " " |
| Jenkins, George | 1784 | " " | 600 | " " |
| Keatton, Redmon | 1784 | " " | 100 | " " |
| Kenney, Frederick | 1784 | " " | 200 | " " |
| Kitichison, William | 1784 | " " | 200 | " " |
| Lauzier, Ebrum | 1784 | " " | 200 | " " |
| Liggatt, William | 1784 | " " | 100 | " " |
| Lisley, Jasper | 1784 | " " | 100 | " " |
| McAlpine, John | 1785 | Great Port Jolly | 500 | |
| McCalep, Patrick | 1784 | Port Mouton | 100 | British Legion |
| McDonald, Christina | 1785 | Port Hebert, E. | 100 | |
| McDonald, Donald | 1785 | " " " | 200 | |
| McDonald, John | 1784 | Port Mouton | 100 | British Legion |
| McDonald, John | 1785 | Port Hebert, E. | 200 | |
| McGinnis, Donald | 1785 | " " " | 200 | |
| McGonegall, John | 1785 | " " " | 100 | |
| McKay, Gilbert | 1785 | " " " | 200 | |
| McKay, John | 1785 | " " " | 200 | |
| McKay, Neil | 1785 | " " " | 200 | |
| MacKay, Richard | 1784 | Port Mouton | 100 | British Legion |
| McKenzey [McKenzie], John | 1784 | " " | 100 | " " |
| McLachlan, Alexander | 1785 | Port Hebert, E. | 100 | |
| McLean, Duncan | 1785 | " " " | 200 | |
| McLean, John | 1785 | " " " | 100 | |
| McLeod, John and Stuart, McNeil | 1785 | " " " | 200 | |
| McMullon, Neil | 1784 | Port Mouton | 100 | British Legion |
| McPherson, Allan | 1785 | " " | 650 | " " |
| McPherson, Donald | 1784 | " " | 1050 | " " |
| Millar, William | 1784 | " " | 200 | " " |
| Millaker, John | 1784 | " " | 100 | " " |
| Mimme, John | 1784 | " " | 100 | " " |
| Mitchell, Alexander | 1785 | Port Hebert, E. | 200 | |
| Mitchell, Colin | 1785 | Port Hebert | 200 | |
| Moore, Paul | 1785 | Port Mouton | 150 | |
| Mulloy, Charles | 1784 | " " | 150 | British Legion |
| Mungand, Peter | 1784 | " " | 150 | " " |
| Neason, Jacob | 1784 | " " | 200 | " " |
| Parker, William | 1785 | " " | 150 | |
| Pars, Zephyneah | 1784 | " " | 100 | British Legion |
| Pool, Thomas | 1784 | " " | 600 | " " |
| Powers, Henry | 1784 | " " | 100 | " " |
| Rabbins, William | 1784 | " " | 550 | " " |
| Reid, William | 1784 | " " | 100 | " " |

## PUBLIC ARCHIVES OF NOVA SCOTIA

| Name | Date | Situation | Acres | Origin or Rank |
|---|---|---|---|---|
| Rogers, John | 1784 | Port Mouton | 100 | British Legion |
| Rubendick, John | 1784 | " " | 100 | " " |
| Rudley, Drew | 1784 | " " | 100 | " " |
| Ryon, John | 1784 | " " | 100 | " " |
| Scott, Thomas | 1784 | " " | 350 | " " |
| Seymison, Edward | 1785 | " " | 100 | |
| Shion, Daniel | 1784 | " " | 100 | British Legion |
| Sinklair[Sinclair] Kathrin | 1784 | " " | 200 | "        " Grant |
| Smith, Daniel | 1784 | " " | 300 | " " |
| Smith, Edward | 1784 | " " | 550 | " " |
| Sommers, Edward | 1785 | " " | 100 | |
| Stanley, Thomas | 1784 | " " | 650 | British Legion |
| Stare, John | 1784 | " " | 200 | " " |
| Sterns, Jonathan | 1784 | Great Port Joli | 1000 | |
| Stewart, Charles | 1784 | Port Mouton | 300 | British Legion |
| Stewart, James | 1784 | " " | 500 | " " |
| Stroud, Andrew | 1784 | " " | 100 | " " |
| Stuart, Neil see McLeod, John | 1785 | | | |
| Styne, Henry | 1784 | " " | 100 | " " |
| Thomas, John | 1784 | Little Port Joli | 500 | Plymouth, Mass. |
| Thompson, Nathaniel | 1784 | Port Mouton | 100 | British Legion |
| Tochar, John | 1785 | Port Hebert, E. | 200 | |
| Trager, Jacob | 1784 | Port Mouton | 150 | British Legion |
| Travis, Nathaniel | 1784 | " " | 100 | " " |
| Trigg, John | 1784 | " " | 150 | " " |
| Vernan[Vernon]Christian | 1784 | " " | 200 | " " |
| Vernun[Vernon] Nathan'l | 1784 | " " | 750 | " " |
| Walker, John | 1784 | " " | 100 | " " |
| Wallace, Heigh | 1784 | " " | 100 | " " |
| Warten, Israel | 1784 | " " | 200 | " " |
| Welsh [Weilsh] Andrew | 1784 | " " | 100 | " " |
| Wilson, John | 1784 | " " | 100 | " " |

## Queen's County

### WARRANTS

| Name | Date | Situation | Acres | Origin or Rank |
|---|---|---|---|---|
| Alder, James | 1786 | Great Port Jolly | 100 | |
| Boyd, James | 1786 | " " " | 200 | |
| Cameron, Murdock | 1786 | " " " | 200 | |
| Denham, Thomas | 1786 | " " " | 200 | |
| Duffee, William | 1786 | " " " | 200 | |
| Ferguson, John | 1786 | " " " | 200 | |
| Fraser, James | 1786 | " " " | 200 | |
| French, James | 1786 | " " " | 100 | |
| Gordon, Alexander | 1786 | " " " | 200 | |

LOYALISTS AND LAND SETTLEMENT IN NOVA SCOTIA 75

| Name | Date | Situation | Acres | Origin or Rank |
|---|---|---|---|---|
| McCarly, Timothy | 1786 | Great Port Jolly | 100 | |
| McDonald, Alexander | 1786 | " " " | 100 | |
| McFarlane, Peter | 1786 | " " " | 200 | |
| McKenzie, John, Jr. | 1786 | " " " | 200 | |
| McKenzie, John, Sr. | 1786 | " " " | 200 | |
| McLean, Donald | 1786 | " " " | 200 | |
| McLean, James | 1786 | " " " | 200 | |
| McLeod, Barbara | 1786 | " " " | 180 | |
| Maxwell, David | 1786 | " " " | 250 | |
| Orr,—(Widow) | 1786 | " " " | 200 | |
| Robertson, John | 1786 | " " " | 200 | |
| Robertson, Neil | 1786 | " " " | 200 | |
| Scott, George | 1786 | " " " | 250 | |
| Thomas, John | 1786 | Little Port Joli | 500 | |

# Shelburne County
## GRANTS

| Name | Date | Situation | Acres | Origin or Rank |
|---|---|---|---|---|
| Abbot, Benjamin | 1785 | Argyle Township | 100 | |
| Abbot, Benjamin, Jr. | 1785 | " " | 150 | |
| Abbot, Moses | 1785 | " " | 100 | |
| Ackerman, Gilbert | 1788 | Tusket River | 300 | |
| Ackerman, John | 1786 | Shel. Anna. Road | 200 | |
| Ackerman, John | 1786 | " " " | 200 | |
| Ackerson, Abraham | 1786 | " " " | 200 | |
| Ackerson[Akerson] Jacob | 1788 | Tusket River | 300 | |
| Ackerson, John | 1785 | Shel Meadow S.ofKingSt | 5 | |
| Ackerson[Akerson]Rich'd | 1788 | Tusket River | 300 | |
| Ackland, Philip | 1784 | Shelburne | W. H. L. | |
| Ackland, Philip | 1784 | " | T. L. | |
| Ackland, Philip | 1785 | Port Hebert Har. | 200 | |
| Acres, Thomas | 1785 | Lake Rodney, S. | 100 | |
| Adams, Thomas | 1786 | Shel. Anna. Rd. | 200 | |
| Adams, William | 1784 | Shelburne | W. L. | |
| Adams, William | 1784 | | W. L. | |
| Aiken, Andrew | 1784 | " | W. H. L. | |
| Aiken, Justice | 1784 | " | T. L. | |
| Aiken, Justice | 1785 | McNutt's Island | 50 | |
| Aikman, John | 1790 | Sable R. (Not reg'd) | 100 | |
| Akerson, Jacob see Ackerson, Jacob | 1788 | | | |
| Akerson, Richard see Ackerson, Richard | 1788 | | | |
| Allen, James | 1784 | Shelburne | 50 | |
| Allen, James | 1784 | " | T. L. | |
| Allen, James | 1784 | " | W. H. L | |
| Allen, James | 1785 | Argyle Township | 150 | |
| Allen, Thomas | 1784 | Shelburne | T. L. | |
| Allsworth, Samuel | 1784 | " | W. H. L. | |
| Alstine, Joseph | 1784 | " | T. L | |
| Anant, [Arrant] Stephen | 1784 | " | 50 | |
| Andrews, John | 1784 | " | T. L. | |
| Andrews, John | 1784 | Port Roseway River, E. | 50 | |
| Anderson, Andrew | 1785 | Jordan River, E. | 100 | |
| Anderson, Archibald | 1786 | Cape Negro River | 100 | |
| Anderson, John | 1784 | Shelburne | 50 | |
| Anderson, John | 1784 | " | T. L. | |
| Anderson, John | 1784 | " | T. L. | |
| Anderson, John | 1787 | Birch Town | 50 | |
| Anderson, John | 1790 | Sable R. (Not reg'd) | 200 | |
| Anderson, Walter | 1785 | Jordan River, E. | 200 | |
| Andrews, Robert | 1786 | Shel. Anna. Rd. | 200 | |
| Andrews, Samuel | 1788 | Tusket River | 250 | |
| Andrews, William | 1796 | Cocquiwit Harbour | 215 | |
| Appleby, Robert | 1785 | Port Roseway, E. | 20 | |
| Archibald, Edward | 1784 | Shelburne | T. L. | |
| Archibald, Edward | 1784 | " | 50 | |
| Arrant, Stephen see also Anant, Stephen | 1784 | " | W. H. L. | |
| Ashby, Joseph | 1785 | Port Hebert Harbour | 200 | |
| Aston, John | 1786 | Shel. Anna. Road | 200 | |
| Atkins,— | 1784 | Shelburne | T. L. | 17th. Dragoons |
| Auld, William | 1785 | Jordan River, E. | 100 | |

LOYALISTS AND LAND SETTLEMENT IN NOVA SCOTIA 77

| Name | Date | Situation | Acres | Origin or Rank |
|---|---|---|---|---|
| Babcock, David | 1788 | Tusket River | 300 | |
| Bagnall, Samuel | 1786 | Cape Negro River | 200 | |
| Bailey, John | 1784 | Shelburne | T. L. | |
| Bailey, John | 1787 | Herring Falls | 50 | |
| Bain, David | 1787 | Birch Town | 50 | |
| Baine, David | 1785 | Lake Rodney, S. | 100 | |
| Banta, Simon | 1788 | Tusket River | 300 | |
| Banta, Weart | 1785 | McNutt's Island | 50 | |
| Barclay, Andrew | 1784 | Shelburne | T. L. | |
| Barclay, Andrew | 1785 | McNutt's Island | 50 | |
| Barley, Andrew | 1784 | Shelburne | W. H. L. | |
| Barnes [Barns] John | 1786 | Shel. Anna. Road | 200 | |
| Barnett, James | 1784 | Shelburne | 50 | |
| Barnett, William | 1784 | " | T. L. | |
| Baron, James | 1784 | " | T. L. | |
| Barr, John | 1784 | " | 50 | |
| Barren, James | 1784 | " | 50 | |
| Barringate, Daniel | 1786 | Shel. Anna. Road | 200 | |
| Barrow, Thomas | 1787 | Birch Town | 100 | |
| Barry, Robert | 1784 | Shelburne | 50 | |
| Barry, Robert | 1784 | " | T. L. | |
| Bartlett, Edward and Wood, R. A. | 1790 | Sable River (Not Reg'd) | 100 | |
| Batt, Thomas | 1784 | Shelburne | 50 | |
| Batt, Thomas | 1784 | " | W. H. L. | |
| Batt, Thomas | 1784 | " | T. L. | |
| Baxter, John | 1784 | " | T. L. | |
| Baxter, Samuel | 1784 | " | T. L. | |
| Bazil, Richard | 1787 | Birch Town | 10 | |
| Bealie, George | 1784 | Shelburne | 50 | |
| Beamorld, John | 1787 | Birch Town | 100 | |
| Bean, John | 1785 | Cape Negro River | 100 | |
| Beasley, William | 1785 | Jordan River, E. | 100 | |
| Beatie, George | 1784 | Shelburne | T. L. | |
| Beatie, George 2nd. | 1784 | " | T. L. | |
| Bedford, John | 1784 | " | 50 | |
| Bentley, Felix | 1784 | " | T. L. | |
| Bergh, Adam | 1784 | " | T. L. | |
| Bermingham, Richard | 1784 | " | W. H. L | |
| Berry, Daniel | 1784 | " | W. H. L | |
| Berry, Robert | 1784 | " | W. H. L | |
| Bertram, Alexander | 1787 | Port Roseway Har., W. | 200 | |
| Bingay, Thomas | 1790 | Sable River (Not reg'd) | 200 | |
| Binny, James | 1786 | Cape Negro River | 100 | |
| Birge, Joseph | 1784 | Shelburne | W. H. L | |
| Birge, Joseph | 1785 | McNutt's Island | 50 | |
| Birmingham, Richard | 1784 | Shelburne | 50 | |
| Birmingham, Richard | 1786 | Shel. Anna. Road | 200 | |
| Black, Joseph | 1785 | McNutt's Island | 50 | |
| Black, William | 1784 | Shelburne | 50 | |
| Black, William | 1784 | " | T. L. | |
| Black, William | 1785 | McNutt's Island | 50 | |
| Blackbourn, Hugh | 1786 | Shel. Anna. Road | 200 | |
| Blackwell, John | 1784 | Shelburne | W. H. L. | |
| Blades, Henry | 1787 | Birch Town | 100 | |
| Blair, John | 1784 | Shelburne | T. L. | |
| Blair, John | 1786 | Shel. Anna. Road | 200 | |
| Blaricam [Van Blarcom] Ryah V. | 1784 | Shelburne | T. L. | |
| Blauvelt, Theunis | 1788 | Tusket River | 300 | |
| Blucke, Stephen | 1787 | Port Roseway Har., W. | 200 | |
| Boice, Gideon | 1787 | " " " " | 100 | |
| Boltby [Boultby] Edward | 1784 | Shelburne | W. L. | |
| Bolten, Henry | 1784 | " | 50 | |
| Bolton, Henry | 1784 | Port Roseway Har., W. | 50 | Albany, N. Y. |

# 78 PUBLIC ARCHIVES OF NOVA SCOTIA

| Name | Date | Situation | Acres | Origin or Rank |
|---|---|---|---|---|
| Bolton, Henry | 1784 | Shelburne | | W. L. |
| Bolton, Henry | 1784 | " | | Wharf L. |
| Bond, Joseph | 1786 | " | | W. L. |
| Bonsfield, Michael | 1786 | Cape Negro River | 200 | |
| Bonta, Weart | 1786 | " " " | 200 | |
| Boole, Francis | 1790 | Sable River (Not reg'd) | 200 | |
| Bougart, John | 1784 | Shelburne | | T. L. |
| Bough, James | 1787 | Birch Town | 200 | |
| Bouldby, Edward | 1784 | Shelburne | 50 | |
| Boultby, Edward see Boltby, Edward | 1784 | | | |
| Bousfield, Michael | 1787 | Shelburne | | T. L. & W. L. |
| Bower, Bartholomew | 1784 | " | | W. L. |
| Bower, Bartholomew | 1784 | " | | Wharf L. |
| Bowett, Thomas | 1785 | Shelburne E. Meadows | 5 | |
| Bowman, George | 1784 | Port Roseway Har., E. | 50 | |
| Bowman, George | 1784 | Shelburne | | W. H. L |
| Boyd, John | 1790 | Sable River (Not reg'd) | 500 | Dr. |
| Boyd, William Robert | 1784 | Shelburne | | W. H. L. |
| Bradburne, Alexander | 1784 | " | | W. H. L. |
| Bradburne, Alexander | 1784 | " | 50 | |
| Bradley, Alexander | 1784 | " | | T. L. |
| Brady, Joseph | 1784 | " | | T. L. |
| Brady, Mary | 1787 | Port Roseway Har., W. | 200 | |
| Braine, Samuel | 1787 | " " " " | 200 | |
| Braine, Thomas | 1787 | " " " " | 200 | |
| Brainthwaite, William | 1787 | " " " " | 200 | |
| Branding, Charles | 1786 | Cape Negro River | 200 | |
| Branthwaite, William | 1786 | Shelburne | | W. L. |
| Brayne, Thomas | 1784 | " | | T. L. |
| Brazil, Richard | 1784 | " | | T. L. |
| Breen, Hugh | 1786 | " | | W. L. |
| Breen, Hugh & Co. | 1784 | " | | T. L. |
| Brewer, Joseph | 1784 | " | | T. L. |
| Brewer, Ross | 1784 | Port Roseway River, E. | 50 | |
| Brewer, Ross | 1784 | Shelburne | | W. H. L |
| Brewer, Ross | 1784 | " | | T. L. |
| Briges, Joseph | 1785 | Lake Rodney, S. | 100 | |
| Briggs, William | 1784 | Shelburne | | W. H. L |
| Briggs, William | 1786 | Shel. Anna. Road | 200 | |
| Bright, Moses | 1787 | Birch Town | 200 | |
| Brindley, Edward | 1785 | Port Roseway, E. | 20 | |
| Brindley, Edward | 1788 | Tusket River | 300 | |
| Brindly, Edward | 1784 | Shelburne | | T. L. |
| Brinley, Edward | 1784 | " | | W. H. L |
| Brinley, Edward | 1786 | Shel. Anna. Rd. | 200 | |
| Brockelsby, William | 1787 | Birch Town | 100 | |
| Brocks, Daniel James | 1786 | Shel. Anna. Road | 200 | |
| Brook, Francis | 1784 | Shelburne Harbour, E. | 100 | |
| Broom, John | 1784 | Shelburne | 50 | |
| Broom, John | 1784 | " | | T. L. |
| Brown, Andrew | 1785 | Jordan River, E. | 100 | |
| Brown, Andrew | 1786 | Shel. Anna. Road | 200 | |
| Brown, Charles | 1784 | Shelburne | 50 | |
| Brown, Charles, Sr. | 1784 | " | | W. H. L |
| Brown, David | 1784 | " | | T. L. |
| Brown, John | 1784 | " | | T. L. |
| Brown, John | 1784 | " | | W. H. L |
| Brown, John | 1786 | Shel. Anna. Road | 200 | |
| Brown, John | 1787 | Herring Falls | 50 | |
| Brown, Michael | 1786 | Shel. Anna. Road | 200 | |
| Brown, Nicholas | 1784 | Shelburne | | T. L. |
| Brown, Nicholas | 1784 | " | | W. H. L |
| Brown, Nicholas | 1785 | Port Roseway, E. | 20 | |

## LOYALISTS AND LAND SETTLEMENT IN NOVA SCOTIA 79

| Name | Date | Situation | Acres | Origin or Rank |
|---|---|---|---|---|
| Brown, Nicholas | 1787 | Birch Town | 50 | |
| Brown, Richard | 1784 | Shelburne | T. L. | |
| Brown, William | 1784 | " | T. L. | |
| Brown, William | 1784 | " | T. L. | |
| Brown, William | 1787 | (Pt. Hebert R. (not reg'd) | 200 | |
| | | Jordan R. E. (not reg'd | 500 | |
| Browne, Richard | 1786 | Cape Negro River | 200 | |
| Bruce, Andrew | 1786 | Shelburne | W. L. | |
| Bruff, Charles Oliver | 1784 | " | 50 | |
| Bruff, Charles Oliver | 1784 | " | T. L. | |
| Bruff, Charles Oliver | 1784 | " | W. H. L | |
| Buchan, Robert | 1785 | Jordan River, E. | 100 | |
| Buchan, Robert | 1786 | Shel. Anna. Road | 200 | |
| Buchanan, David | 1786 | " " | 200 | |
| Buchanan, Donald | 1785 | Jordan River, E. | 100 | |
| Burk, William | 1784 | Shelburne | 50 | |
| Burk, William | 1784 | " | T. L. | |
| Burling, Samuel | 1785 | Port Roseway Har., W. | 350 | |
| Burn, Benedict see Byrn, Benedict | 1784 | | | |
| Burn, Matthew | 1786 | Cape Negro River | 200 | |
| Burn, William | 1787 | Shel. Liverpool Road | 500 | Doctor |
| Burne, Matthew | 1784 | Shelburne | 50 | |
| Burnside, Thomas | 1786 | Shel. Anna. Road | 200 | |
| Burton, Joe Hugh | 1784 | Shelburne | W. H. L. | |
| Burton, Joseph Hughes | 1784 | " | T. L. | |
| Burton, Peter | 1784 | " | T. L. | |
| Burton, Peter | 1784 | " | W. H. L | |
| Burton, Robert | 1786 | Shel. Anna. Road | 200 | |
| Burton, William | 1784 | Shelburne | W. H. L | |
| Bushton, William | 1784 | " | 50 | |
| Butler, John | 1784 | " | 50 | |
| Butler, John | 1784 | " | T L. | |
| Butler, Samuel | 1784 | " | T. L. | |
| Butler, Samuel | 1784 | " | W. H. L | |
| Bydell, Joseph | 1785 | Jordan River, E. | 100 | |
| Byrn [Burn] Benedict | 1784 | Shelburne | T. L. | |
| Byrne, Christopher | 1790 | Sable River (Not reg'd) | 100 | |
| Byrne, Matthew | 1784 | Shelburne | T. L. | |
| Calder, Andrew | 1784 | Shelburne | 50 | |
| Calder, Andrew | 1784 | " | W. H. L | |
| Caldwell, William | 1784 | " | W. H. L. | |
| Caldwell, William | 1785 | Port Hebert Harbour | 100 | |
| Caldwell, William | 1786 | Shelburne Harbour, E. | 50 | |
| Callow, Thomas | 1787 | Birch Town | 200 | |
| Cameron, Alexander | 1784 | Shelburne | 50 | |
| Cameron, Alexander | 1784 | " | T. L. | |
| Cameron, Donal | 1784 | " | T. L. | Sergeant |
| Cameron, Donald | 1785 | Jordan River, E. | 100 | |
| Cameron, Evan | 1784 | Shelburne | T. L. | |
| Cameron, Ewen | 1784 | " | 50 | |
| Cames, John | 1784 | Port Roseway Har., E. | 50 | |
| Campbell, Alexander | 1784 | Shelburne | 50 | |
| Campbell, Alexander | 1784 | " | W. H. L | |
| Campbell, Archibald | 1784 | " | 50 | |
| Campbell, Archibald | 1784 | " | T. L. | |
| Campbell, Archibald | 1785 | Jordan River, E. | 100 | |
| Campbell, Colin | 1785 | Port Roseway | 250 | |
| Campbell, Colin | 1786 | Shelburne | W. L. | |
| Campbell, Daniel | 1785 | Jordan River, E. | 100 | |
| Campbell, Dugal | 1784 | Shelburne | W. H. L | |
| Campbell, Dugald | 1784 | " | 50 | |
| Campbell, Farquhar | 1785 | Cape Negro River | 100 | |

80    PUBLIC ARCHIVES OF NOVA SCOTIA

| Name | Date | Situation | Acres | Origin or Rank |
|---|---|---|---|---|
| Campbell, George | 1784 | Shelburne | | T. L. |
| Campbell, George | 1784 | " | | W. H. L. |
| Campbell, George | 1787 | Birch Town | 50 | |
| Campbell, John | 1785 | Jordan River, E. | 100 | |
| Campbell, John | 1785 | " " " | 100 | |
| Campbell, Lean | 1785 | " " " | 200 | |
| Campbell, Robert | 1784 | Port Roseway River, E. | 50 | |
| Campbell, Robert | 1784 | Shelburne | | W. H. L. |
| Campbell, Samuel | 1784 | " | 50 | |
| Campbell, Samuel | 1784 | " | | W. H. L |
| Campbell, Samuel | 1784 | " | | Wharf L. |
| Campbell, William | 1785 | Jordan River, E. | 100 | |
| Cannall, John | 1786 | Shel. Anna. Road | 200 | |
| Cannell, Robert | 1786 | " " " | 200 | |
| Carberry, William | 1786 | Cape Negro River | 200 | |
| Carland, Patrick | 1785 | Port Hebert Harbour | 225 | |
| Carleton, Christopher | 1790 | Sable River (Not reg'd) | 100 | |
| Carleton, Thomas | 1786 | Shel. Anna. Road | 200 | |
| Carman, Jonathan | 1785 | Jordan River, E. | 100 | |
| Carpenter, John | 1784 | Shelburne | 50 | |
| Carson, William | 1784 | " | | W. H. L |
| Carson, William | 1785 | McNutt's Island | 50 | |
| Castle, William | 1784 | Shelburne | 50 | |
| Castle, William | 1784 | " | | W. H. L. |
| Catherwood, David | 1784 | Jordan River, E. | 250 | |
| Catherwood, David | 1784 | Shelburne | | T. L. |
| Catherwood, David | 1784 | " | | W. H. L. |
| Catherwood, David | 1787 | Shel. Liverpool Road | 500 | |
| Chambers, John | 1786 | Shel. Anna. Road | 200 | |
| Chetwynd, Thomas | 1784 | Shelburne | | T. L. |
| Chisholm, George | 1784 | Port Roseway River, E. | 50 | |
| Chisholm, George | 1784 | Shelburne | | T. L. |
| Chisholm, George | 1784 | " | | W. H. L. |
| Christian, Arrach | 1785 | Cape Negro River | 100 | |
| Christie, John | 1785 | Port Roseway, E. | 20 | |
| Christy, Charles | 1786 | Shel. Anna. Road | 200 | |
| Christy, Matthew | 1786 | " " " | 200 | |
| Church, Charles | 1784 | Shelburne | | T L. |
| Church, Charles | 1784 | " | | W. H. L. |
| Clapp, Margaret | 1790 | Sable River (Not reg'd) | 200 | |
| Clark, Archibald | 1784 | Shelburne | 50 | |
| Clark, Robert A. | 1790 | Sable River (Not reg'd) | 200 | |
| Clark, William | 1784 | Shelburne | | T. L. |
| Clark, William | 1784 | " | | W. H. L. |
| Clarke, Robert | 1785 | Jordan River, E. | 200 | Lieut. |
| Clarke, William | 1785 | McNutt's Island | 50 | |
| Clarke, William | 1790 | Sable River (Not reg'd) | 100 | |
| Claudon, John George | 1784 | Shelburne | | T. L. |
| Cleghorne, Robert A. | 1790 | Sable River (Not reg'd) | 200 | |
| Clerk, James | 1784 | Shelburne | | T. L. |
| Clibbing, James | 1784 | " | | T. L. |
| Clipping, James | 1784 | " | 50 | |
| Clisby, John | 1784 | " | 50 | |
| Clisby, John | 1784 | " | | T. L. |
| Clowden, John George | 1784 | " | 50 | |
| Clowden, John George | 1784 | " | | W. H. L. |
| Cochran, Michael | 1787 | Birch Town | 100 | |
| Cock, James | 1784 | Shelburne | 50 | |
| Cock, James | 1784 | " | | W. H. L. |
| Cockain, Alexander | 1784 | " | 250 | |
| Cockane, Alexander | 1784 | " | | T. L. |
| Cockane, Alexander | 1784 | " | | W. L. |
| Cockran, Alexander | 1784 | " | | Wharf L. |
| Cockray, John | 1790 | Sable River (Not reg'd) | 200 | |

# LOYALISTS AND LAND SETTLEMENT IN NOVA SCOTIA 81

| Name | Date | Situation | Acres | Origin or Rank |
|---|---|---|---|---|
| Collins, Thomas | 1785 | Jordan River, E. | 100 | |
| Combauld, Richard | 1788 | Tusket River | 300 | |
| Commins, James | 1784 | Shelburne | T. L. | |
| Conley, James | 1785 | Cape Negro River | 200 | |
| Connoll, James | 1784 | Shelburne | W. L. | |
| Cook, George | 1786 | Shel. Anna. Road | 200 | |
| Cook, Michael | 1784 | Shelburne | T. L. | |
| Cook, William | 1784 | " | 50 | |
| Cook, William | 1784 | " | T. L. | |
| Cook, William | 1784 | " | W. H. L. | |
| Cooper, James | 1786 | Shel. Anna. Road | 200 | |
| Cooper, John | 1784 | Shelburne | W. H. L. | |
| Cooper, John | 1787 | Birch Town | 50 | |
| Copeland, William | 1790 | Sable River (Not reg'd) | 100 | |
| Corbett, William | 1786 | Shel. Anna. Road | 200 | |
| Cormick, James | 1785 | Jordan River, E. | 200 | |
| Cornwall, Melancthon | 1784 | Shelburne | T. L. | |
| Coulby, John | 1790 | Sable River (Not reg'd) | 420 | |
| Courtney, James | 1784 | Port Roseway River, W. | 500 | |
| Courtney, James | 1784 | Shelburne | W. L. | |
| Courtney, James | 1784 | " | Wharf L. | |
| Courtney, James | 1787 | Herring Falls | 50 | |
| Courtney, Richard | 1784 | Port Roseway River, E. | 50 | |
| Courtney, Richard | 1784 | Port Roseway River, W. | 500 | |
| Courtney, Richard | 1784 | Shelburne | W. L. | |
| Courtney, Richard | 1784 | " | T. L. | |
| Courtney, Richard | 1784 | " | Wharf L. | |
| Courtney, Thomas | 1784 | Port Roseway River, W. | 500 | |
| Courtney, Thomas | 1784 | Shelburne | W. L | |
| Courtney, Thomas | 1784 | " | W. L. | |
| Courtney, Thomas | 1784 | " | Wharf L. | |
| Covell, Robert | 1786 | Cape Negro River | 100 | |
| Cowan, George | 1786 | " " " | 200 | |
| Cowdrey, Joseph | 1785 | Jordan River, E. | 100 | |
| Cowling, John | 1784 | Shelburne | W. H. L. | |
| Cox, James | 1784 | " | T. L. & | W. L. |
| Cox, James | 1786 | Cape Negro River | 200 | |
| Craig, John | 1784 | Shelburne | W. H. L. | |
| Craig, John | 1786 | Cape Negro River | 200 | |
| Crain, Timothy | 1784 | Shelburne | W. H. L. | |
| Crawford, James | 1784 | " | 50 | |
| Crawford, Margaret | 1784 | " | 50 | |
| Crawford, Margaret | 1784 | " | W. L. | |
| Crawford, Margaret | 1785 | Port Hebert Harbour | 200 | |
| Crawford, Peter | 1784 | Shelburne | T. L. | |
| Crawford, Robert | 1786 | Shel. Anna. Road | 200 | |
| Creutt, Joseph | 1784 | Shelburne | W. H. L. | |
| Crocker, Mary | 1790 | Sable River (Not reg'd) | 250 | |
| Cromwall, Melancton | 1784 | Shelburne | 50 | |
| Crow, Joshua | 1790 | Sable River (Not reg'd) | 250 | |
| Crow, Peter | 1785 | Jordan River, E. | 100 | |
| Crowe, Jonathan | 1785 | " " " | 100 | |
| Cumming, William | 1785 | " " " | 100 | |
| Cummings, William | 1785 | " " " | 100 | |
| Cunningham, Cornelius | 1786 | Shel. Anna. Road | 200 | |
| Cunningham, John | 1785 | Jordan River, E. | 200 | Lieut. |
| Cunningham, John | 1785 | " " " | 100 | |
| Cunningham, John | 1786 | Shel. Anna. Road | 200 | |
| Cunningham, Paul | 1786 | Cape Negro River | 200 | |
| Cunningham, Paul | 1787 | Birch Town | 50 | |
| Currie, Alexander | 1785 | Jordan River, E. | 200 | |
| Curry, Alexander | 1784 | Shelburne | 50 | |
| Curry, Alexander | 1784 | " | T. L. | |
| Curry, Alexander | 1784 | " | W. H. L. | |

82  PUBLIC ARCHIVES OF NOVA SCOTIA

| Name | Date | Situation | Acres | Origin or Rank |
|---|---|---|---|---|
| Curry, John | 1785 | Jordan River, E. | 100 | |
| Cuzzens, John | 1786 | Shel. Anna. Road | 200 | |
| Daily, James | 1784 | Shelburne | | T. L. |
| Daley, Dennis | 1786 | Shelburne Anna. Road | 200 | |
| Daley, James | 1784 | Shelburne | 50 | |
| Daley, James | 1786 | Cape Negro River | 100 | |
| Dalton, Thomas | 1784 | Shelburne | | T. L. |
| Dampsey, Roger | 1786 | Cape Negro River | 100 | |
| Davenport, Isaac | 1786 | Shel. Anna. Road | 200 | |
| Davenport, Samuel | 1784 | Shelburne | | Wharf L |
| Davenport, Samuel | 1785 | Port Roseway, E. | 20 | |
| Davenport, Samuel | 1786 | Shel. Anna. Road | 200 | |
| Davidson, John | 1787 | Birch Town | 50 | |
| Davidson, Robert | 1784 | Shelburne | | W. H. L. |
| Davidson, Robert | 1784 | " | | W. L. |
| Davidson, Robert | 1787 | Herring Falls | 50 | |
| Davis, Benjamin | 1784 | Shelburne | | Wharf L. |
| Davis, Benjamin, Jr. | 1784 | " | | W. H. L |
| Davis, Benjamin, Sr. | 1784 | " | | W. H. L. |
| Davis, George | 1786 | Cape Negro River | 100 | |
| Davis, John | 1784 | Shelburne | | W. H. L. |
| Davis, John | 1784 | " | | W. L. |
| Davis, John | 1785 | Port Hebert Harbour | 200 | |
| Davis, John | 1787 | Herring Falls | 50 | |
| Davis, Thomas | 1787 | Birch Town | 100 | |
| Davison, John | 1784 | Shelburne | | W. H. L |
| Dean, John | 1784 | " | 50 | |
| Dean, William | 1784 | " | | T. L. |
| Decker, Benjamin | 1784 | " | | W. L. |
| Decker, Isaac | 1788 | Tusket River | 300 | |
| Decker, Isaac and Smith, Job | 1788 | " " | 300 | |
| Deffandorf, George | 1790 | Sable River (Not reg'd) | 200 | |
| Deffandorf, Jacob | 1790 | " " " " | 100 | |
| Deffendrass, John | 1784 | Shelburne | | T. L. |
| Defendress, George | 1784 | " | | T. L. |
| Deker, Isaac | 1784 | " | | T. L. |
| Demelt, Isaac | 1784 | " | | W. H. L. |
| Demill, Isaac | 1786 | Cape Negro River | 200 | |
| Demilt, Isaac | 1787 | Birch Town | 50 | |
| Demsey, Roger | 1784 | Shelburne | | W. H. L. |
| Denham, Thomas | 1784 | " | 50 | |
| Dennin, John | 1787 | Birch Town | 50 | |
| Denny, Charles | 1784 | Shelburne | | W. L. |
| Derevier, John | 1784 | " | 50 | |
| De. Revier, John | 1784 | " | | W. H. L. |
| De Revier, John | 1784 | " | | T. L. |
| Devereaux, William | 1785 | McNutt's Island | 50 | |
| Devereux, William | 1784 | Shelburne | | W. H. L. |
| Dick, James | 1785 | Jordan River, E. | 200 | |
| Dickie, James | 1784 | Shelburne | | W. H. L. |
| Dickie, Walter | 1784 | " | | T. L. |
| Dickie, William | 1784 | " | 50 | |
| Dickinson, John | 1786 | Cape Negro River | 200 | |
| Dickinson, Roger | 1784 | Shelburne | | W. H. L. |
| Dickinson, Roger | 1785 | McNutt's Island | 50 | |
| Dickinson, Roger and Lindsay, M. | 1790 | Sable River (Not reg'd) | 100 | |
| Dingley, Thomas | 1787 | Birch Town | 100 | |
| Doale, Francis | 1787 | Herring Falls | 50 | |
| Dogherty, Hugh | 1784 | Shelburne | | T. L. |
| Dogherty, Hugh | 1784 | " | | W. H. L. |
| Dogherty, Hugh | 1785 | Port Hebert Harbour | 200 | |

## LOYALISTS AND LAND SETTLEMENT IN NOVA SCOTIA    83

| Name | Date | Situation | Acres | Origin or Rank |
|---|---|---|---|---|
| Dole, James | 1784 | Shelburne | | T. L. |
| Donaldson, James | 1784 | " | | W. L. |
| Donaldson, Samuel | 1786 | " | | W. L. |
| Dorney, L. & Jappie, P. | 1787 | Birch Town | 550 | |
| Dorney, Luke | 1787 | " " | 50 | |
| Doughty, Timothy | 1784 | Shelburne | | W. H. L. |
| Douglas, George | 1786 | Cape Negro River | 200 | |
| Douglas, William | 1785 | Port Roseway | 350 | |
| Douglass, James | 1785 | Jordan River, E. | 200 | |
| Dove, Alexander | 1787 | Birch Town | 50 | |
| Dower, Alexander | 1784 | Shelburne | | T. L. |
| Dowey, George | 1785 | Cape Negro River | 200 | |
| Downey, Luke | 1784 | Shelburne | | T. L. |
| Downy, Henry | 1784 | " | | W. H. L. |
| Doyle, Francis | 1786 | Cape Negro River | 200 | |
| Drescoll, James | 1784 | Shelburne | | T. L. |
| Drogartie, Anthony | 1785 | Cape Negro River | 200 | |
| Duddy, John | 1784 | Shelburne | | T. L. |
| Dunbar, Robert | 1784 | | | T. L. |
| Duncan, James | 1784 | " | | T. L. |
| Duncan, James | 1784 | " | | T. L. |
| Dundas, George | 1784 | " | | T. L. |
| Dundass, George | 1784 | " | 50 | |
| Dundass, George | 1785 | Jordan River, E. | 200 | |
| Dunlap, Alexander | 1784 | Shelburne | 50 | |
| Dunlap, Alexander | 1784 | " | | W. H. L. |
| Dunlap, Alexander | 1786 | Cape Negro River | 200 | |
| Dunn, James | 1786 | Argyle Township | 250 | |
| Dunn, Walter | 1784 | Shelburne Harbour, E. | 100 | |
| Durant, Christopher | 1784 | Shelburne | | W. H. L. |
| Durant, Christopher | 1786 | Cape Negro River | 200 | |
| Durfee, Joseph | 1784 | Shelburne | | W. H. L. |
| Durfey, Joseph | 1784 | Port Roseway Har., W. | 550 | |
| Durfey, Robert | 1784 | Shelburne | | T. L. |
| Eagle, Hugh | 1784 | " | 50 | |
| Eagle, Hugh | 1784 | " | | T. L. |
| Eagleson, Charles | 1784 | " | | W. L. |
| Eaking, George | 1786 | Shel. Anna. Road | 200 | |
| Earle, Peter | 1788 | Tusket River | 300 | |
| Early, John | 1786 | Shel. Anna. Road | 200 | |
| Eary, William | 1784 | Shelburne | | W. H. L. |
| Eckland, Henry | 1786 | Shel. Anna. Road | 200 | |
| Edmonds, John | 1784 | Shelburne | | W. H. L. |
| Edmonds, John | 1785 | McNutt's Island | 50 | |
| Edmunds, John | 1786 | Cape Negro River | 100 | |
| Edwards, John | 1785 | " " " | 100 | |
| Edwards, John | 1786 | " " " | 200 | |
| Edwards, Joseph | 1787 | Birch Town | 200 | |
| Edwards, Samuel | 1787 | Port Roseway Har., W. | 50 | |
| Edwards, William | 1786 | Shel. Anna. Road | 200 | |
| Egan, Thomas | 1790 | Sable River (Not reg'd) | 100 | |
| Ellis, James | 1784 | Shelburne | | W. H. L. |
| Ellis, Thomas and Nelson, W. | 1790 | Sable River (Not reg'd) | 100 | |
| Ellison,—(Mrs.) | 1784 | Shelburne | | T. L. |
| Ellison, Abraham | 1784 | " | 50 | |
| Ellison, Eliakim | 1785 | Port Roseway, E. | 20 | |
| Ellison, Jane | 1787 | Port Roseway Har., W. | 200 | |
| Ellison, Mary | 1787 | " " " " | 75 | |
| Ellison, Sarah | 1787 | " " " " | 75 | |
| Elvens, Henry | 1784 | Shelburne | | T. L. |
| English, Joseph | 1784 | " | | T. L. |
| English, Joseph | 1787 | Herring Falls | 50 | |

| Name | Date | Situation | Acres | Origin or Rank |
|---|---|---|---|---|
| Enslow, Isaac | 1784 | Shelburne | 50 | |
| Enslow, Isaac | 1784 | " | | T. L. |
| Etherington, John | 1785 | McNutt's Island | 50 | |
| Evan, Margaret | 1784 | Shelburne | | T. L. |
| Evans, James | 1786 | Shel. Anna. Road | 200 | |
| Evat, John | 1784 | Shelburne | | T. L. |
| Every, Richard | 1784 | Shelburne Harbour, E. | 100 | |
| Fairclon, George | 1786 | Shel. Anna. Road | 200 | |
| Fairley, Alexander | 1784 | Shelburne | | T. L. |
| Fairly, Alexander | 1784 | " | | W. H. L. |
| Fanning, Edward | 1784 | " | 50 | |
| Fanning, Edward | 1784 | " | | T. L. |
| Farish, George | 1787 | Port Roseway Har., W. | 200 | |
| Farish, Greggs | 1787 | "      "      "      " | 200 | |
| Farren, James | 1784 | Shelburne | 50 | |
| Farrens, John | 1784 | " | 50 | |
| Farrer, Lancelot | 1787 | Port Roseway Har., W. | 200 | |
| Farrer, Thomas | 1787 | "      "      "      " | 200 | |
| Ferguson, James | 1784 | "      "      "   E. | 50 | |
| Ferguson, [Furgeson] Jas. | 1785 | Lake Rodney, S. | 100 | |
| Ferguson, John | 1784 | Shelburne | 50 | |
| Ferguson, John | 1784 | " | | T. L. |
| Fernandes, Mary | 1787 | Port Roseway Har., W. | 200 | |
| Ferrar, Thomas | 1784 | Shelburne | | Wharf L. |
| Finley, Jonathan | 1784 | " | | W. H. L. |
| Fisher, Peter | 1785 | Jordan River, E. | 200 | |
| Fisher, Peter | 1788 | Tusket River | 300 | |
| Fitzgerald, Thomas | 1784 | Shelburne | | T. L. |
| Fitzpatrick, John | 1790 | Sable River (Not reg'd) | 200 | |
| Fitzroy, Michael | 1784 | Shelburne | 50 | |
| Flinn, Osborne | 1785 | Jordan River, E. | 100 | |
| Flood, John | 1785 | Cape Negro River | 100 | |
| Fogarthy, John | 1784 | Shelburne | | T. L. |
| Fogarty, John | 1784 | Port Roseway Har., E. | 50 | |
| Fogarty, John | 1784 | Shelburne | | W. H. L. |
| Foles, Younger | 1785 | Jordan River, E. | 100 | |
| Forbes, William | 1785 | "      "      " | 100 | |
| Ford, John | 1786 | Shel. Anna. Road | 200 | |
| Foreman, William P. | 1784 | Shelburne | | T. L. |
| Forgay, James | 1785 | Shelburne E. Meadows | 5 | |
| Forsyth, Thomas | 1785 | Jordan River, E. | 100 | |
| Fosset, William | 1790 | Sable River (Not reg'd) | 100 | |
| Foster, William | 1790 | "      "      "      " | 100 | |
| Fox, Robert | 1785 | McNutt's Island | 50 | |
| Foy, Sarah Ann | 1784 | Shelburne | | T. L. |
| Fraser, Alexander | 1784 | Port Roseway River, E. | 50 | |
| Fraser, Alexander | 1784 | "      "      "      " | 50 | |
| Fraser, Alexander | 1785 | Lake Rodney, S. | 100 | |
| Fraser, Alexander | 1787 | Birch Town | 50 | |
| Fraser, Daniel | 1785 | Port Hebert Harbour | 200 | |
| Fraser, Hugh | 1785 | "      "      " | 200 | |
| Fraser, John | 1785 | Cape Negro River | 200 | |
| Fraser, Simon | 1787 | Birch Town | 50 | |
| Frasier, James | 1784 | Shelburne | | W. H. L. |
| Frazier, Alexander | 1784 | " | | T. L. | Captain |
| Frazier, Daniel | 1784 | " | 50 | |
| Frazier, Daniel | 1784 | " | | T. L. |
| Frazier, Hugh | 1784 | " | 50 | |
| Frazier, Hugh | 1784 | " | | T. L. |
| Frazier, James | 1784 | " | 50 | |
| Frazier, James | 1784 | " | | T. L. |
| Frazier, James | 1784 | " | | T. L. |
| Frazier, Simon | 1784 | " | | T. L. |

| Name | Date | Situation | Acres | Origin or Rank |
|---|---|---|---|---|
| French, George | 1786 | Shel. Anna. Road | 200 | |
| French, Robert | 1784 | Port Roseway River, E. | 50 | |
| French, Robert | 1784 | Shelburne | | T. L. |
| French, Robert | 1784 | " | | W. H. L. |
| French, Robert | 1786 | Cape Negro River | 100 | |
| Frietz, Abraham | 1784 | Shelburne | | W. H. L. |
| Frost, Andrew | 1785 | Argyle Township | 100 | |
| Frost, Daniel | 1785 | " " | 113 | |
| Frost, James | 1785 | " " | 150 | |
| Frost, Jeremiah | 1785 | " " | 100 | |
| Frost, Joshua | 1785 | " " | 350 | |
| Frost, Stephen | 1785 | Argyle Township | 100 | |
| Frude, Peter | 1790 | Sable River (Not reg'd) | 200 | |
| Full, Thomas | 1785 | Port Hebert Harbour | 200 | |
| Furguson, James see Ferguson, James | 1785 | | | |
| Galbreath, Joseph | 1786 | Cape Negro River | 100 | |
| Gamage, James | 1784 | Shelburne | 50 | |
| Gamage, James | 1784 | " | | W. H. L. & T. L. |
| Gammage, James | 1785 | Port Hebert Harbour | 200 | |
| Gammill, Matthew | 1784 | Shelburne | 50 | |
| Garder, John | 1784 | " | | W. H. L. |
| Gardiner, John | 1784 | " | | T. L. |
| Gardner, John | 1784 | " | 50 | |
| Gardner, John | 1785 | Port Hebert Harbour | 200 | |
| Garland, Alexander | 1784 | Shelburne | 50 | |
| Garland, Alexander | 1786 | Cape Negro River | 100 | |
| Garnett, John | 1784 | Shelburne | | T. L. |
| Gates, James | 1787 | Birch Town | 50 | |
| Gautier, James | 1784 | Shelburne | | W. L. & T. L. |
| Gay, Alexander | 1786 | " | | W. L. |
| Gearing, Patrick | 1786 | Shel. Anna. Road | 200 | |
| Geary, Robert A. | 1790 | Sable River (Not reg'd) | 100 | |
| Gibson, Andrew | 1784 | Shelburne | | T. L. |
| Gibson, Andrew | 1786 | Cape Negro River | 100 | |
| Gilbert, Francis | 1784 | Shelburne | | T. L. |
| Gilbert, Sarah | 1790 | Sable River (Not reg'd) | 200 | |
| Gilchrist, William | 1790 | " " " " | 100 | |
| Gildert, Mary | 1786 | Shel. Anna. Road | 200 | |
| Goddard, Daniel | 1784 | Shelburne | 50 | |
| Goddard, Daniel | 1784 | " | | W. L. |
| Goddard, Henry | 1785 | Port Hebert Harbour | 100 | |
| Goddard, Job | 1784 | Shelburne | 50 | |
| Goddard, Job | 1784 | " | | W. H. L. |
| Goddard, Job | 1785 | Port Hebert Harbour | 200 | |
| Goddard, John | 1784 | Shelburne | 50 | |
| Goddard, John | 1784 | " | | T. L. |
| Goddard, Lemuel | 1784 | " | | T. L. |
| Goddard, Lemuel, Jr. | 1785 | McNutt's Island | 50 | |
| Goddard, Lemuel, Sr. | 1785 | " " | 50 | |
| Goff, John | 1784 | Shelburne | | T. L. |
| Goodin, Henry | 1785 | Argyle Township | 150 | |
| Goodin, Jedidiah | 1785 | " " | 349 | |
| Gordon, Michael | 1784 | Shelburne | | T. L. |
| Gordon, Michael | 1786 | Shel. Anna. Road | 200 | |
| Goswell, George | 1784 | Shelburne | | T. L. |
| Govan, John | 1790 | Sable River (Not reg'd) | 100 | |
| Gow, Robert | 1784 | Shelburne | | W. H. L. |
| Gow, Robert | 1788 | Shelburne Harbour, W. | 50 | |
| Graham, James | 1784 | " " | | T. L. |
| Graham, John | 1784 | " " | | W. L. |
| Graham, John | 1784 | " " | | Wharf L. |
| Graham, William | 1784 | " " | 50 | |

## PUBLIC ARCHIVES OF NOVA SCOTIA

| Name | Date | Situation | Acres | Origin or Rank |
|---|---|---|---|---|
| Graham, William | 1784 | Shelburne | T. L. | |
| Grandine, Daniel | 1784 | " | 50 | |
| Grandine, Daniel | 1784 | " | T. L. | |
| Grandine, Daniel | 1784 | " | W. H. L. | |
| Grandine, Samuel | 1784 | " | 50 | |
| Grandine, Samuel | 1784 | " | W. H. L. | |
| Grant, Alexander | 1784 | " | W. H. L. | |
| Grant, James | 1784 | " | T. L. | |
| Grant, James | 1784 | " | W. H. L. | |
| Grant, James | 1785 | McNutt's Island | 50 | |
| Grant, Lewis | 1784 | Shelburne | T. L. | |
| Grant, Peter | 1784 | " | T. L. | |
| Grant, Peter | 1784 | " | T. L. | |
| Grant, Peter | 1784 | " | W. H. L. | |
| Grant, Peter, Jr. | 1784 | " | 50 | |
| Grant, Peter, Sr. | 1784 | " | 50 | |
| Grassman, Casper | 1784 | " | 50 | |
| Grassman, Caspar | 1784 | " | T. L. | |
| Grassman, Caspar | 1784 | " | W. H. L. | |
| Graves, John | 1784 | Shelburne | W. H. L. | |
| Graves, Thomas | 1784 | Port Roseway Har., E. | 50 | |
| Graves, Thomas | 1784 | Shelburne | T. L. | |
| Gray, George | 1790 | Sable River (Not reg'd) | 200 | |
| Gray, Isaac | 1784 | Shelburne | T. L. | |
| Gray, Isaac | 1787 | Birch Town | 50 | |
| Gray, James | 1787 | " " | 200 | |
| Gray, Peter | 1784 | Shelburne | 50 | |
| Gray, Peter | 1784 | " | W. H. L. | |
| Gray, Reuben | 1784 | " | W. L. | |
| Gray, Robert | 1784 | " T. L. & | Wharf L. | Captain |
| Gray, Robert | 1785 | Jordan River, E. | 200 | Captain |
| Gray, Robert | 1787 | Sable River, E. | 500 | |
| Gray, Robert | 1788 | Shelburne (12 miles out) | 400 | |
| Gray, Robert | 1788 | Tusket River | 700 | Captain |
| Green, Edward | 1790 | Sable River (Not reg'd) | 200 | |
| Greest, Henry | 1787 | Port Roseway Har., W. | 200 | |
| Gregory, George | 1784 | Shelburne | 50 | |
| Gregory, George | 1784 | " | W. H. L. | |
| Grosvenor, Benjamin | 1784 | " | 50 | |
| Grosvenor, Benjamin | 1784 | " | T. L. | |
| Guest, Henry | 1784 | " | W. H. L. | |
| Halburt, Titus | 1786 | Cape Negro River | 200 | |
| Hale & Low | 1784 | Shelburne | T. L. | |
| Hale, William | 1784 | " | T. L. | |
| Hale, William | 1784 | " | T. L. & | Wharf L. |
| Hale, William | 1785 | McNutt's Island | 50 | |
| Hale, William | 1787 | Blue Island | 65 | |
| Hall, Richard | 1784 | Shelburne | W. H. L. | |
| Hall, Richard | 1786 | Shel. Anna. Road | 200 | |
| Hall, Richard | 1786 | " " " | 200 | |
| Hall, Richard | 1786 | " " " | 200 | |
| Hall, Richard | 1786 | " " " | 200 | |
| Hall, Richard | 1786 | " " " | 200 | |
| Hamilton, Charles | 1784 | Shelburne Harbour, E. | 100 | |
| Hamilton, James | 1786 | Cape Negro River | 400 | |
| Hamilton, John | 1786 | " " " | 200 | |
| Hamilton, John, Jr. | 1786 | " " " | 100 | |
| Hammond, Timothy | 1785 | Jordan River, E. | 100 | |
| Handley, Patrick | 1786 | Shel. Anna. Road | 200 | |
| Hannah, Edward | 1784 | Shelburne | 50 | |
| Hannah, Jean | 1790 | Sable River (Not reg'd) | 200 | |
| Hannah, Nathaniel | 1784 | Shelburne | 50 | |

## LOYALISTS AND LAND SETTLEMENT IN NOVA SCOTIA 87

| Name | Date | Situation | Acres | Origin or Rank |
|---|---|---|---|---|
| Hanny, Nathaniel | 1784 | Shelburne | T. L. | |
| Hanny, Nathaniel | 1784 | " | W. H. L. | |
| Hard, David | 1784 | " | 50 | |
| Harding, Elizabeth | 1787 | Birch Town | 50 | |
| Harding, George | 1784 | Shelburne | 50 | |
| Harding, George | 1784 | " | T. L. | |
| Harding, George | 1784 | Sable River (Not reg'd) | 100 | |
| Harding, Jasper | 1784 | Shelburne | 50 | |
| Harding, Jasper | 1790 | Sable River (Not reg'd) | 100 | |
| Harding, Joseph | 1784 | Shelburne | T. L. | |
| Harding, Richard | 1784 | " | T. L. | |
| Harding, Richard | 1790 | Sable River (Not reg'd) | 100 | |
| Harding, Robert | 1784 | Shelburne | W. H. L. | |
| Harding, Robert A. | 1790 | Sable River (Not reg'd) | 100 | |
| Hardy, George | 1787 | Birch Town | 100 | |
| Hardy, William | 1790 | Sable River (Not reg'd) | 100 | |
| Hare, Thomas | 1786 | Shelburne | T. L. | Captain |
| Hargill, William | 1787 | Port Roseway Har., W. | 50 | |
| Hargin, Samuel | 1790 | Sable River (Not reg'd) | 100 | |
| Hargrave, William | 1784 | Shelburne | Wharf L. | |
| Hargraves, George | 1787 | Birch Town | 100 | |
| Hargraves, William | 1784 | Jordan River | 50 | |
| Hargraves, William | 1784 | "   " E. | 250 | |
| Hargraves, William | 1784 | Shelburne {W. L. | Wharf L. & T. L.} | Captain |
| Hargraves, William | 1784 | Shelburne | Wharf L. | |
| Hargraves, William | 1784 | " | T. L. | |
| Hargraves, William | 1787 | Port Roseway Har., W. | 100 | |
| Hargraves, William | 1787 | Shel. Liverpool Road | 500 | |
| Harris, Sarah | 1786 | Shel. Anna. Road | 200 | |
| Hart, Charles | 1784 | Port Roseway Har., E. | 50 | |
| Hart, Charles | 1790 | Sable River (Not reg'd) | 100 | |
| Harter, John | 1784 | Port Roseway Har., E. | 50 | |
| Harter, John | 1784 | Shelburne | T. L. | |
| Harter, John | 1786 | Cape Negro River | 200 | |
| Hartley, Thomas | 1784 | Shelburne | 50 | |
| Hartley, Thomas | 1786 | Shel. Anna. Road | 200 | |
| Hartly, Thomas | 1784 | Shelburne | W. L. | |
| Hartshorne, Laurence | 1784 | " | W. L. | |
| Hartshorne, Lawrence | 1784 | " | T. L. | |
| Hartzaugh, George | 1786 | Shel. Anna. Road | 200 | |
| Harvey, William | 1784 | Shelburne | W. L. | |
| Harvey, William, Jr. | 1784 | " | W. L. | |
| Hatten. Robert | 1784 | " | W. H. L. | |
| Haverson, John | 1785 | Jordan River, E. | 100 | |
| Havila,—(Widow) | 1784 | Shelburne | T. L. | |
| Hay, Hugh | 1784 | " | T. L. | |
| Hay, Hugh | 1784 | " | W. H. L. | |
| Hay, Hugh | 1786 | Cape Negro River | 200 | |
| Hayden, Joseph | 1784 | Shelburne | W. L. | |
| Hayes, James | 1784 | " | T. L. | |
| Hayman, Adam | 1786 | Shel. Anna. Road | 200 | |
| Haynes, Mary | 1787 | Port Roseway Har., W. | 200 | |
| Haynes, Robert | 1785 | Jordan River, E. | 100 | |
| Hazzard, Stephen | 1784 | Shelburne | 50 | |
| Hazzard, Stephen | 1784 | " | T. L. | |
| Hazzard. Stephen | 1784 | " | W. H. L. | |
| Heath, Joseph | 1784 | " | T. L. | |
| Hely, Timothy | 1790 | Sable River (Not reg'd) | 200 | |
| Helyear, Samuel | 1787 | Birch Town | 100 | |
| Hemion, Henry | 1786 | Shel. Anna. Road | 200 | |
| Henrigan, John | 1790 | Sable River (Not reg'd) | 100 | |
| Henston, James | 1790 | "   "   "   " | 100 | |
| Herbert, Samuel | 1787 | Birch Town | 50 | |

# PUBLIC ARCHIVES OF NOVA SCOTIA

| Name | Date | Situation | Acres | Origin or Rank |
|---|---|---|---|---|
| Herring, Abraham | 1785 | Shelburne, E. Meadows | 5 | |
| Hervey, William | 1784 | Port Roseway Har., E. | 50 | |
| Hetfield, James | 1788 | Tusket River | 250 | |
| Hewat, Andrew | 1785 | Jordan River, E. | 200 | Captain |
| Hewett, Andrew | 1788 | Shelburne (12 miles out) | 600 | |
| Hewitt, Andrew | 1784 | " | T. L. | |
| Higgins, John | 1786 | Shel. Anna. Road | 200 | |
| Higgins, William | 1785 | Jordan River, E. | 200 | |
| Hill, Joshua | 1784 | Shelburne | T. L. | |
| Hill, Joshua | 1787 | Birch Town | 50 | |
| Hill, William | 1784 | Shelburne | T. L. | |
| Hillard, Christopher | 1785 | Jordan River, E. | 100 | |
| Hind, David | 1784 | Shelburne | T. L. | |
| Hipson, Francis | 1785 | Argyle Township | 150 | |
| Hoaron, Hugh | 1786 | Shel. Anna. Road | 200 | |
| Hobbs, Ebenezer | 1785 | Argyle Township | 100 | |
| Hobbs, Lemuel | 1785 | " " | 100 | |
| Hobbs, Maurice | 1785 | " " | 100 | |
| Hodgins, William | 1787 | Birch Town | 100 | |
| Hodgkinson, Henry | 1784 | Shelburne | W. H. L. | |
| Hodgsings, Robert | 1784 | " | W. H. L. | |
| Hodgson, Thomas | 1784 | " | W. H. L. | |
| Hodson, Thomas | 1784 | " | T. L. | |
| Hodson, Thomas | 1787 | Birch Town | 50 | |
| Hogarth, Andrew | 1784 | Shelburne | 50 | |
| Hogarth, Andrew | 1784 | " | T. L. | |
| Hogarth, Andrew | 1784 | " | W. H. L. | |
| Hokes, John | 1784 | Port Roseway Har., E. | 50 | |
| Holden, William | 1787 | Birch Town | 100 | |
| Holderness, William | 1784 | Shel. Har.-N. W. Branch | 50 | |
| Holderness, William | 1784 | Shelburne | T. L. | |
| Holdstead, John | 1785 | Shelburne, E. Meadows | 5 | |
| Holdstead, William | 1785 | " " " | 5 | |
| Holland, James | 1785 | Jordan River, E. | 100 | |
| Hollingsly, Richard | 1784 | Shelburne | 50 | |
| Holmes, Joseph | 1784 | " | 50 | |
| Holmes, Joseph | 1784 | " | W. L. | |
| Horton, Jonathan | 1788 | Tusket River | 175 | |
| Horton, Richard | 1786 | Cape Negro River | 100 | |
| Hose [Howe], Joseph | 1784 | Shelburne | T. L. | |
| Hossiter, Herman | 1784 | " | T. L. | |
| Houston, Robert | 1784 | " | T. L. | |
| Howlings, Thomas | 1784 | " | W. L. | |
| Hoyster, Herman | 1784 | " | W. H. L. | |
| Hubbs, Zephiniah | 1784 | " | T. L. | |
| Hudson, Thomas | 1785 | Lake Rodney, S. | 100 | |
| Hueston, Alexander | 1784 | Shelburne | 50 | |
| Hueston, Robert | 1784 | " | 50 | |
| Huggeford, John | 1785 | Port Roseway, E. | 20 | |
| Huggerford, John | 1784 | Shelburne | T. L. | |
| Hughes, Charles | 1787 | Birch Town | 100 | |
| Hughes, James | 1784 | Shelburne | 50 | |
| Hughes, John | 1786 | Shel. Anna. Road | 200 | |
| Hughes, Robert | 1784 | Shelburne | 50 | |
| Hughes, Robert | 1784 | " | T. L. | |
| Hughes, Robert | 1784 | " | W. H. L. | |
| Hughes, William | 1784 | " | W. H. L. | |
| Hughes, William | 1785 | McNutt's Island | 50 | |
| Hughes, William | 1790 | Sable River (Not reg'd) | 100 | |
| Hughs, John | 1784 | Shelburne | W. H. L. | |
| Hull, William | 1784 | " | W. H. L. | |
| Huns, Enoch | 1784 | " | 50 | |
| Hunt, Enoc | 1784 | " | T. L. | |
| Hunt, Enoch | 1784 | " | W. H. L. | |

# LOYALISTS AND LAND SETTLEMENT IN NOVA SCOTIA 89

| Name | Date | Situation | Acres | Origin or Rank |
|---|---|---|---|---|
| Hunt, Enoch | 1786 | Shel. Anna. Road | 200 | |
| Hunt, Gilbert | 1787 | Port Roseway Har., W. | 100 | |
| Hunt, Thomas | 1784 | Shelburne | W. H. L. | |
| Hunter, Francis | 1784 | " | 50 | |
| Hunter, Francis | 1784 | " | T. L. | |
| Hurd, David | 1784 | " | W. H. L. | |
| Hurry, Mary | 1784 | " | T. L. | |
| Ingham, Elizabeth | 1786 | Cape Negro River | 200 | |
| Ingleson, Charles | 1784 | Shelburne | W. H. L. | |
| Inglis, William | 1785 | Jordan River, E. | 200 | |
| Innes, Robert | 1785 | " " " | 100 | |
| Innes, Stephen | 1784 | Shelburne | T. L. | |
| Irvine, Daniel | 1790 | Sable River (Not reg'd) | 100 | |
| Irwin, James | 1784 | Shelburne Harbour, E. | 100 | |
| Irwin, James | 1786 | Shel. Anna. Road | 200 | |
| Irwin, John | 1785 | Jordan River, E. | 100 | |
| Jackson, Basil | 1785 | " " " | 100 | |
| Jackson, Jas. (& 3 others) | 1785 | McNutt's Island | 50 | Negro Pilot |
| Jackson, London (" " ) | 1785 | " " | 50 | " " |
| Jackson, Samuel | 1784 | Shelburne | 50 | |
| Jackson, William | 1784 | " | 50 | |
| Jackson, William | 1784 | " | W. H. L. | |
| Jackway, John | 1784 | " | W. H. L. | |
| Jackways, John | 1785 | Port Hebert Harbour | 200 | |
| Jappie, P. see Dorney, Luke | 1787 | | | |
| Jaram, Francis | 1790 | Sable River (Not reg'd) | 100 | |
| Jardine, John | 1785 | Jordan River, E. | 100 | |
| Jeans, Daniel | 1784 | Shelburne | W. H. L. | |
| Jeans, Jenkinson | 1784 | " | 50 | |
| Jeans, Jenkinson | 1784 | " | T. L. | |
| Jefferson, Joseph | 1786 | Cape Negro River | 100 | |
| Jeffries, David | 1786 | " " " | 100 | |
| Jenkins, Peter | 1790 | Sable River (Not reg'd) | 100 | |
| Jessup, Jeremiah | 1786 | Shel. Anna. Road | 200 | |
| Johnson, George | 1784 | Shelburne | T. L. | |
| Johnson, Herman | 1784 | " | T. L. | |
| Johnson, John | 1784 | " | T. L. | |
| Johnson, William | 1784 | " | T. L. | |
| Johnston, George | 1784 | " | 50 | |
| Johnston, George | 1784 | " | W. H. L. | |
| Johnston, Harmon | 1784 | " | W. H. L | |
| Johnston, Joseph | 1786 | Shel. Anna. Road | 200 | |
| Johnston, Patience | 1786 | " " " | 200 | |
| Johnston, William | 1784 | Shelburne | 50 | |
| Johnston, William | 1784 | " | W. H. L. | |
| Johnstone, John | 1784 | " | W. L. | |
| Jolliff, Richard | 1784 | " | 50 | |
| Jolliffe, Richard | 1784 | " | T. L. | |
| Jones, Abraham | 1784 | " | 180 | |
| Jones, Abraham | 1784 | " | W. L. | |
| Jones, James | 1784 | " | T. L. | |
| Jones, John | 1784 | Port Roseway River, E. | 50 | |
| Jones, John | 1784 | Shelburne | T. L. | |
| Jones, John | 1784 | " | T. L.. | |
| Jones, John | 1784 | " | T. L. | |
| Jones, John | 1787 | Herring Falls | 50 | |
| Jones, John | 1790 | Sable River (Not reg'd) | 100 | |
| Jones, Robert | 1785 | Jordan River, E. | 100 | |
| Jones, Thomas | 1784 | Shelburne | W. H. L. | |
| Jones, Thomas | 1784 | " | W. H. L. | |

## PUBLIC ARCHIVES OF NOVA SCOTIA

| Name | Date | Situation | Acres | Origin or Rank |
|---|---|---|---|---|
| Keans, John | 1784 | Shelburne | 50 | |
| Kearny, Patrick | 1790 | Sable River (Not reg'd) | 100 | |
| Keely, John | 1784 | Shelburne | W. H. L. | |
| Keenon, James | 1785 | Jordan River, E. | 100 | |
| Kelley—see O'Kelley | | | | |
| Kelley, Michael | 1786 | Shel. Anna. Road | 200 | |
| Kelley, William | 1785 | Jordan River, E. | 100 | |
| Kelly, Hugh | 1790 | Sable River (Not reg'd) | 100 | |
| Kelly, James | 1784 | Shelburne Harbour, E. | 100 | |
| Kendrick, Daniel | 1784 | Shelburne | 50 | |
| Keneda [Kennedy] John | 1790 | Sable River (Not reg'd) | 100 | |
| Kennedy, John | 1784 | Port Roseway River, E. | 50 | |
| Kennedy, John | 1784 | Shelburne | 50 | |
| Kennedy, John | 1784 | " | W. H. L | |
| Kennedy, Hugh | 1784 | " | 50 | |
| Kepling, Kellin | 1784 | " | W. H. L. | |
| Kidder, William | 1790 | Sable River (Not reg'd) | 200 | |
| Killigrove, Henry | 1787 | Port Roseway Har., W. | 50 | |
| King, Eleanor | 1786 | Cape Negro River | 200 | |
| King, Eleanor | 1787 | Birch Town | 50 | |
| King, Henry | 1784 | Shelburne | T. L. | |
| King, Henry | 1786 | Shel. Anna. Road | 200 | |
| King, John | 1784 | Shelburne | 50 | |
| King, John | 1784 | " | T. L. | |
| King, John | 1784 | " | T. L. | |
| King, John | 1784 | " | T. L. & | W. H. L. |
| King, Patrick | 1784 | " | W. H. L. | |
| King, Robert | 1784 | Shelburne Harbour, E. | 100 | |
| Kingston, John | 1784 | Shelburne | 50 | |
| Kingston, John | 1784 | " | T. L. | |
| Kirk, Samuel | 1785 | Port Roseway, E. | 20 | |
| Knapp, David | 1784 | Shelburne | 50 | |
| Knapp, David | 1784 | " | W. H. L | |
| Knight, Samuel | 1790 | Sable River (Not reg'd) | 100 | |
| Knox, Henry Edward | 1784 | Shelburne | T. L. | |
| Knox, Henry Edward | 1784 | " | 50 | |
| | | | | |
| Lacey, Richard | 1784 | " | 50 | |
| Lacey, Richard | 1784 | " | T. L. | |
| Lackey, [Lakey] John | 1784 | " | T. L. | |
| Lafferty, Daniel | 1784 | " | 50 | |
| Lamb, Richard | 1786 | Cape Negro | 100 | |
| Lamey, Michael | 1784 | Shelburne | T. L. | |
| Lander, Mary | 1786 | Cape Negro | 100 | |
| Lang, James | 1784 | Shelburne | 50 | |
| Leonex, Peter | 1784 | " | W. H. L | |
| Largin, Michael | 1785 | Jordan River, E. | 200 | Lieut. |
| Largin, Michael | 1786 | Shelburne | W. L. | |
| Laurens, Peter | 1784 | " | T. L. | |
| Lavender, William | 1787 | Birch Town | 100 | |
| Lawrence, Thomas | 1787 | Port Roseway Har., W. | 200 | |
| Lawson, Douglas | 1784 | Shelburne | T. L. | |
| Lawson, Dougles | 1784 | Shelburne District | 100 | |
| Layton, John | 1784 | Shelburne | W. H. L | |
| Leach, Rich'd & 3 others | 1785 | McNutt's Island | 50 | Negro Pilot |
| Lear, Christopher | 1785 | " " | 50 | |
| Lear, Christopher | 1786 | Cape Negro | 200 | |
| Lear, Jesse | 1784 | Shelburne | 50 | |
| Leary, Michael | 1784 | " | W. H. L. | |
| Leckie, Alexander | 1784 | " | W. L. | |
| Leckie, James | 1784 | " | 50 | |
| Lederew, Margaret | 1784 | " | W. H. L | & T. L. |
| Leighton, John | 1784 | " | T. L. | |
| Leighton, John | 1790 | Sable River (Not reg'd) | 100 | |

# LOYALISTS AND LAND SETTLEMENT IN NOVA SCOTIA 91

| Name | Date | Situation | Acres | Origin or Rank |
|---|---|---|---|---|
| Leister, James | 1784 | Shelburne | Wharf L. | |
| Lennen, Andrew | 1784 | " | 50 | |
| Lenox, David | 1785 | Shelburne, E. Meadows | 5 | |
| Lenox, Peter | 1784 | Shelburne | 50 | |
| Lent, Abraham | 1784 | " | 50 | |
| Lent, Abraham | 1784 | " | W. H. L | |
| Lent, Abraham | 1784 | " | T. L. | |
| Lent, Abraham | 1788 | Tusket River | 230 | |
| Lent, James | 1788 | " " | 175 | |
| Lenzi, James | 1785 | Jordan River, E. | 100 | |
| Leonard, Jeremiah | 1786 | Cape Negro | 100 | |
| Leonard, Thomas | 1784 | Shelburne | T. L. | |
| Leonard, Thomas | 1784 | " | W. L. | |
| Leonard, Thomas, Jr. | 1784 | " | W. L. | |
| Leslie, James | 1784 | " | W. H. L. | |
| Lewis, Erasmus | 1790 | Sable River (Not reg'd) | 100 | |
| Lewis, John | 1786 | Shel. Anna. Road | 200 | |
| Lighton, John | 1784 | Shelburne | 50 | |
| Lindsay, M. see Dickinson, Roger | 1790 | | | |
| Linen, Andrew | 1784 | " | W. H. L. | |
| Lippincut, James | 1784 | " | W. L. | |
| Little, James | 1784 | " | W. H. L. | |
| Little, Peabodie | 1785 | Port Hebert Harbour | 100 | |
| Long, James | 1784 | Shelburne | W. H. L. | |
| Lord, Stephen | 1785 | Cape Negro River | 100 | |
| Loring, Benjamin | 1784 | Shelburne | 50 | Surgeon to H. M. |
| Loring, Benjamin | 1784 | " T. L. | & W. L. | (General Hospital |
| Lorton, Lewis | 1785 | Shelburne, E. Meadows | 5 | |
| Lotham, John | 1790 | Sable River (Not reg'd) | 500 | |
| Lounds, John | 1784 | Shelburne | Wharf L. | |
| Lourie, Robert | 1784 | Shelburne Harbour, E. | 100 | |
| Low,—see Hale & Low | 1784 | | | |
| Lowe, Charles | 1784 | Shelburne | W. H. L. | |
| Lowe, Charles | 1785 | McNutt's Island | 50 | |
| Lowe, George | 1784 | Shelburne | T. L. | |
| Lowndes, John | 1784 | " | W. L. | |
| Lownds, John | 1784 | " | 50 | |
| Lownds, John | 1784 | " | T. L. | |
| Lowney, John | 1786 | Cape Negro | 200 | |
| Lowrie, Mary | 1785 | Jordan River, E. | 300 | |
| Lowtharp, Isaac | 1784 | Shelburne | 50 | |
| Luke, George | 1784 | " | 50 | |
| Luke, George | 1784 | " | W. H. L. | |
| Lumley, Thomas | 1786 | Shel. Anna. Road | 200 | |
| Luther, Henry | 1784 | Shelburne | T. L. | |
| Luther, Henry | 1784 | " | T. L. | |
| Lyle, Gavin | 1785 | Cape Negro River | 200 | |
| Lyman, Oliver | 1784 | Shelburne | T. L. | |
| Lynch, Peter | 1784 | " | T. L. | |
| Lynch, Peter | 1784 | " | T. L. | |
| Lynch, Peter | 1784 | " | W. L. | |
| Lynch, Peter | 1784 | " | Wharf L. | |
| Lynch, Peter | 1785 | McNutt's Island | 50 | |
| Lyndsay, Michael | 1784 | Shelburne | T. L. | |
| Lyon, Charles | 1784 | " | 50 | |
| Lyon, Charles | 1784 | " | W. H. L. | |
| McAfee, John | 1784 | Shelburne | T. L. | |
| Macafee, John | 1784 | " | T. L. | |
| McAlpin, Donald | 1784 | Port Roseway Har., E. | 50 | |
| McAlpine, Donald | 1784 | Shelburne | W. H. L. | |
| McAlpine, Dugald | 1785 | Jordan River, E. | 100 | |
| McAlpine, John | 1784 | Shelburne | 50 | |

## PUBLIC ARCHIVES OF NOVA SCOTIA

| Name | Date | Situation | Acres | Origin or Rank |
|---|---|---|---|---|
| McAlpine, John | 1784 | Shelburne | 50 | |
| McAlpine, John | 1784 | " | T. L. | |
| McAlpine, John, 1st. | 1784 | " | W. H. L. | |
| McBride, Thomas | 1784 | " | W. L. | |
| McCarty, James | 1785 | Jordan River, E. | 100 | |
| McCarty, Timothy | 1784 | Shelburne | 50 | |
| McCarty, William | 1784 | " | W. H. L. | |
| McCollock, Robert | 1784 | " | T. L. | |
| McCormeck, Nathaniel | 1785 | Jordan River, E. | 100 | |
| McCracking, John | 1784 | Shelburne | W. H. L | |
| McCrea, William | 1784 | " | 50 | |
| McCrea, William | 1784 | " | T. L. | |
| MacCremmen, Donald | 1785 | Jordan River, E. | 200 | Lieut. |
| McCrummin, Daniel | 1784 | Port Roseway River, E. | 50 | |
| McCrunmine, Donald | 1784 | Shelburne | W. H. L. | |
| McCullom, John | 1784 | " | W. H. L. | |
| McCullough, Robert | 1784 | Port Roseway Har., E. | 50 | |
| McDonald, Alexander | 1785 | Jordan River, E. | 200 | |
| McDonald, Alexander | 1785 | " " " | 100 | |
| McDonald, Angus | 1785 | " " " | 100 | |
| McDonald, Angus | 1785 | " " " | 100 | |
| McDonald, Archibald | 1785 | " " " | 100 | |
| McDonald, Archibald | 1785 | " " " | 100 | |
| McDonald, James | 1785 | " " " | 100 | |
| McDonald, John | 1784 | Shelburne | 50 | |
| McDonald, John | 1785 | Jordan River, E. | 100 | |
| McDonald, John | 1785 | " " " | 100 | |
| McDonald, John, 4th. | 1785 | " " " | 100 | |
| McDonald, Neal | 1784 | Shelburne | T. L. | |
| McDonald, Neal | 1784 | " | W. H. L. | |
| McDonald, Neil | 1787 | Birch Town | 50 | |
| McDonald, Norman | 1785 | Jordan River, E. | 100 | |
| McDonald, Roderick | 1785 | " " " | 100 | |
| McDonald, Ronald | 1784 | Shelburne | 50 | |
| McDonald, Soyle | 1784 | " | W. H. L. | |
| McDonnaugh, Patrick | 1784 | " | T. L. | |
| McDonnell, Michael | 1786 | Shel. Anna. Road | 200 | |
| McDougal, Alexander | 1784 | Shelburne | T. L. | |
| McDougal, Roderick | 1785 | Jordan River, E. | 100 | |
| McDougall, Archibald | 1785 | " " " | 100 | |
| McEwen, James | 1784 | Shelburne | T. L. | |
| McEwen, John | 1784 | " | W. H. L. | |
| McEwen, William | 1784 | " | T. L. | |
| McEwen, William | 1785 | Port Hebert Harbour | 100 | |
| McFarlane, Arch'd | 1787 | Port Roseway Har., W. | 200 | |
| McGaughey, Robert | 1784 | Shelburne Harbour, E. | 100 | |
| McGilveray, John | 1785 | Jordan River, E. | 100 | |
| McGowan, John | 1790 | Sable River (Not reg'd) | 200 | |
| McGrath, James | 1784 | Shelburne | 50 | |
| McGrath, James | 1784 | " | W. H. L. | |
| McGray, John | 1786 | Great Tusket Island | 500 | |
| McIntire, Donald | 1785 | Cape Negro River | 200 | |
| McIntosh, Finley | 1785 | Jordan River, E. | 100 | |
| McIntyre, Angus | 1785 | " " " | 100 | |
| McIntyre, John | 1785 | " " " | 100 | |
| McIntyre, Ronald | 1790 | Sable River (Not reg'd) | 100 | |
| McInulty, Jenkin | 1786 | Shel. Anna. Road | 200 | |
| McIver, Donald | 1785 | Jordan River, E. | 100 | |
| McKay, John | 1784 | Shelburne | W. H. L. | |
| MacKay, Donald | 1785 | Jordan River, E. | 200 | |
| McKay, John | 1785 | Shelburne Township | 230 | |
| McKegan, William | 1785 | Jordan River, E. | 100 | |
| McKenney, John | 1786 | Yarmouth Township | 666 | Navy Pilot |
| McKenney, Murdock | 1784 | Shelburne | T. L. | |

## LOYALISTS AND LAND SETTLEMENT IN NOVA SCOTIA 93

| Name | Date | Situation | Acres | Origin or Ran |
|---|---|---|---|---|
| McKensey, Keneth | 1784 | Shelburne | W. H. L. | |
| McKenzie, Alexander | 1784 | " | T. L. | |
| McKenzie, Alexander | 1785 | Shelburne Township | 230 | |
| McKenzie, David | 1785 | " " | 230 | |
| McKenzie, John | 1784 | Shelburne | 50 | |
| MacKenzie, John | 1785 | Jordan River, E. | 100 | |
| McKenzie, Kenneth | 1784 | Shelburne | 50 | |
| McKenzie, Murdock | 1784 | " | 50 | |
| McKenzie, Norman | 1785 | Jordan River, E. | 100 | |
| McKenzie, Roderick | 1784 | Shelburne | 50 | |
| McKenzie, Roderick | 1784 | " | T. L. | |
| McKenzie, Roderick | 1784 | " | W. H. L. | |
| McKenzie, Valentine | 1786 | Cape Negro River | 200 | |
| Mackey, Alexander | 1787 | Birch Town | 50 | |
| McKie, James | 1790 | Sable River (Not reg'd) | 100 | |
| Mackie, John | 1786 | Shel. Anna. Road | 200 | |
| Mackie [Mackay] Robert | 1786 | " " " | 200 | |
| McKinlay, John | 1785 | McNutt's Island | 50 | |
| McKinlay, John | 1786 | Shel. Anna. Road | 200 | |
| McKinley, Colin | 1784 | Shelburne | 50 | |
| McKinley, Colin | 1784 | " | T. L. | |
| McKinley, Collin | 1784 | " | W. H. L. | |
| McKinley, John | 1784 | " | W. H. L. | |
| McKinney, Gilbert | 1784 | " | 50 | |
| McKinney, Gilbert | 1784 | " | T. L. | |
| McKinney, James | 1784 | " | 50 | |
| McKinney, John | 1784 | " | W. H. L. | |
| McKinney, Joshua | 1784 | " | T. L. | |
| McKinnon, Charles | 1785 | Jordan River, E. | 100 | |
| McKinnon, John | 1785 | Argyle Township | 100 | |
| McKinnon, Ronald | 1785 | " " | 100 | |
| McKinnon, William | 1785 | " " | 100 | |
| McKinzie, William | 1784 | Shelburne | T. L. | |
| McLachlan, William | 1786 | Shel. Anna. Road | 200 | |
| McLauchlin, Charles | 1785 | Jordan River, E. | 200 | |
| McLaw, Charles | 1784 | Shelburne | 50 | |
| McLay, John | 1785 | Cape Negro River | 200 | |
| McLean,— | 1784 | Shelburne | T. L. | Captain |
| McLean, Alexander | 1785 | Jordan River, E. | 100 | |
| McLean, Alexander, 2nd. | 1785 | " " " | 100 | |
| McLean, Alexander, 3rd. | 1785 | " " " | 100 | |
| McLean, Duncan | 1785 | " " " | 100 | |
| McLean, Lodowick | 1785 | " " " | 100 | |
| McLean, Neil | 1785 | " " " | 200 | |
| McLean, Neil | 1785 | " " " | 200 | |
| McLean, Timothy | 1785 | Shelburne Township | 400 | |
| McLeod, Angus | 1784 | Shelburne | 50 | |
| McLeod, Angus | 1784 | " | W. L. | |
| McLeod, Angus | 1784 | " | W. L. | |
| McLeod, Angus | 1785 | Jordan River, E. | 100 | |
| McLeod, Donald | 1784 | Shelburne | 50 | |
| McLeod, John | 1784 | " | 50 | |
| McLeod, John | 1785 | Jordan River, E. | 100 | |
| McLeod, John | 1785 | " " " | 100 | |
| McLeod, William | 1784 | Shelburne | 50 | |
| McMaster, Daniel | 1786 | Shel. Anna. Road | 200 | |
| McMasters, James | 1784 | Shelburne | W. L. | |
| McMasters, James | 1786 | Shel. Anna. Road | 200 | |
| McMillan, Duncan | 1790 | Sable River (Not reg'd) | 500 | |
| McMillan, Hugh | 1790 | " " " " | 100 | |
| McMillan, John | 1785 | Jordan River, E. | 100 | |
| McMurray, John | 1790 | Sable River (Not reg'd) | 100 | |
| McNabb, William | 1784 | Shelburne | T. L. | |

## PUBLIC ARCHIVES OF NOVA SCOTIA

| Name | Date | Situation | Acres | Origin or Rank |
|---|---|---|---|---|
| McNeal, John | 1784 | Shelburne | | T. L. |
| McNeil, Charles | 1784 | " | | W. L. |
| McNeil, Charles | 1787 | Sable River | 1000 | Major |
| McNeil, John | 1787 | Birch Town | 50 | Joiner |
| McNeil, John | 1787 | " " | 50 | |
| McNeil, Charles | 1786 | Shel. Anna. Road | 200 | |
| McNichol, John | 1786 | Cape Negro River | 100 | |
| McNichole, John | 1784 | Shelburne | | W. H. L. |
| McNiel, Daniel | 1784 | " | | T. L. |
| McNiel, John | 1784 | " | | W. H. L. |
| McNutt, Benjamin | 1785 | McNutt's Island | 250 | |
| McNutt, Francis | 1784 | Shelburne | | T. L. |
| McNutt, John | 1784 | " | | T. L. |
| McNutt, Joseph | 1784 | " | | T. L. |
| McNutt, Martin | 1785 | Shelburne Township | 400 | |
| McPherson, John | 1785 | Jordan River, E. | 200 | |
| McQuaid, John | 1784 | Shelburne Harbour, E. | 100 | |
| MacQuhae, Robert | 1785 | Port Roseway, E. | 20 | |
| McQuhae, Robert | 1786 | Shel. Anna. Road | 200 | |
| McRoberts, James | 1784 | Shelburne | | T. L. |
| McSparling, Isaac | 1784 | " | 50 | |
| McSparling, Isaac | 1784 | " | | W. H. L. |
| MacVicker, John | 1785 | Jordan River, E. | 200 | |
| McVillan, Eleanor | 1785 | " " " | 200 | |
| McWater, John | 1784 | Shelburne | | T. L. |
| McWater, Thomas | 1786 | Shel. Anna. Road | 200 | |
| McWilliam, Archibald | 1784 | Shelburne | | T. L. |
| Maffat, James | 1784 | " | | T. L. |
| Mahan, Timothy | 1787 | Birch Town | 50 | |
| Mahany, John | 1784 | Shelburne | | W. H. L. |
| Mahony, John | 1784 | " | | T. L. |
| Mangham, Joseph | 1784 | Shelburne Harbour, E. | 100 | |
| Mann, Samuel | 1784 | Shelburne | | T. L. |
| Mann, Samuel | 1785 | McNutt's Island | 50 | |
| Marchea, William | 1784 | Shelburne | | W. H. L. |
| Marshall, Samuel | 1784 | " | | W. H. L. |
| Marshall, Samuel | 1787 | Blue Island | 65 | |
| Martin, John | 1785 | Jordan River, E. | 100 | |
| Martin, Robert | 1784 | Shelburne | 50 | |
| Martin, Robert | 1784 | " | | T. L. |
| Martin, Robert | 1784 | " | | T. L. |
| Martin, Robert | 1784 | " | | W. H. L. |
| Martin, Thomas | 1785 | Jordan River, E. | 200 | |
| Mason, Charles | 1784 | Shelburne | | W. H. L. |
| Mason, Charles | 1784 | Cape Negro RiverFalls | 227 | |
| Mason, Charles | 1786 | Shelburne District | 250 | |
| Mason, John | 1784 | Shelburne | | T. L.'s |
| Mason, John | 1784 | " | | W. H. L. |
| Mater, Valentine | 1784 | " | | W. L. |
| Mathieson, John | 1785 | Jordan River, E. | 200 | |
| Maybee, Isaac | 1788 | Tusket River | 200 | |
| Mellows, David Henry | 1784 | Shelburne | | T. L. |
| Menzie, Alexander | 1784 | " | | W. H. L. |
| Menzie, John | 1785 | McNutt's Island | 50 | |
| Menzies, John | 1784 | Shelburne | | T. L. |
| Menzies, John | 1784 | " | | W. H. L. |
| Merrit, Robert | 1784 | Shelburne | | W. H. L. |
| Merrit, Robert | 1785 | McNutt's Island | 50 | |
| Milby, William | 1784 | Shelburne | | T. L. |
| Milby, William | 1784 | " | | W. H. L. |
| Milby, William | 1786 | Shel. Anna. Road | 200 | |
| Milby, William and Milby, Zadock | 1784 | Shelburne | | Wharf L. |
| Milby, Zadock, see Milby, Wm. | 1784 | | | |

LOYALISTS AND LAND SETTLEMENT IN NOVA SCOTIA 95

| Name | Date | Situation | Acres | Origin or Rank |
|---|---|---|---|---|
| Milby, Zadock | 1786 | Shel. Anna. Road | 200 | |
| Miles, Thomas | 1787 | Birch Town | 100 | |
| Millar, Charles | 1784 | Shelburne | | T. L. |
| Miller, Ann | 1786 | Shel. Anna. Road | 200 | |
| Miller, Charles | 1784 | Shelburne | 50 | |
| Miller, Charles | 1784 | " | | W. H. L. |
| Miller, Hugh | 1784 | " | | W. L. |
| Miller, Isaac | 1784 | " | | T. L. |
| Miller, John | 1784 | " | 50 | |
| Miller, John | 1784 | " | | T. L. |
| Miller, John | 1784 | " | | T. L. |
| Miller, John | 1784 | Shelburne | | T. L. |
| Miller, John | 1785 | Port Hebert Harbour | 200 | |
| Miller, John | 1787 | Birch Town | 50 | |
| Miller, Matthew | 1786 | Shel. Anna. Road | 200 | |
| Miller, Thomas | 1784 | Shelburne | | T. L. |
| Miller, William | 1786 | Cape Negro River | 200 | |
| Mills, Francis | 1786 | Shel. Anna. Road | 200 | |
| Mills, Nathaniel | 1784 | Shelburne | 50 | |
| Mills, Nathaniel | 1784 | " | | T. L. |
| Mills, Nathaniel | 1784 | " | | W. H. L. |
| Milson, Edward | 1790 | Sable River (Not reg'd) | 100 | |
| Milworth [Midworth] Bromley | 1786 | Shel. Anna. Road | 200 | |
| Minns, William | 1784 | Shelburne | | W. H. L. |
| Minshull, John | 1786 | " | | W. L. |
| Moffat, James | 1784 | " | 50 | |
| Moffat, James | 1784 | " | | W. H. L. |
| Moffatt, James | 1785 | Port Hebert Harbour | 200 | |
| Moffatt, Robert | 1785 | " " " | 100 | |
| Molloy, Thomas | 1786 | Shel. Anna. Road | 200 | |
| Monroe, William | 1784 | Shelburne | | W. H. L |
| Moody, William | 1790 | Sable River (Not reg'd) | 100 | |
| Mooney, William | 1784 | Port Roseway Har., E. | 50 | |
| Moony, Patrick | 1784 | Shelburne | | W. H. L. |
| Moore, Jasper | 1786 | Shel. Anna. Road | 200 | |
| Moore, John | 1784 | Shelburne | 50 | |
| Moore, John | 1784 | " | | T. L. |
| Moran, Thomas | 1790 | Sable River (Not reg'd) | 100 | |
| Morewise, John | 1784 | Shelburne | | T. L. |
| Morgan,— | 1784 | " | | T. L. | 17th. Dragoons. |
| Morgan, Caleb | 1787 | Port Roseway Har., W. | 200 | |
| Morgan, Willoby | 1784 | Shelburne | | W. H. L. |
| Morgan, Willoughby | 1784 | Shelburne Harbour, W. | 100 | |
| Morgan, Willoughby | 1784 | Shelburne | | T. L. |
| Morris, Noah | 1784 | " | | T. L. |
| Morris, Robert | 1784 | " | | T. L. |
| Morris, Robert | 1784 | " | | W. L. |
| Morris, Robert | 1784 | " | | W. L. |
| Morris, Robert | 1787 | Port Roseway Har., W. | 200 | |
| Morris, Robert | 1788 | Tusket River | 220 | |
| Morrison, Charles | 1785 | Cape Negro River | 200 | |
| Morrison, Edward | 1784 | Shelburne | 50 | |
| Morrison, Edward | 1786 | Cape Negro River | 100 | |
| Morrison, Peter | 1785 | Jordan River, E. | 100 | |
| Morrison, Samuel | 1790 | Sable River (Not reg'd) | 100 | |
| Morse, Ebenezer | 1784 | Shelburne | 50 | |
| Morse, Ebenezer | 1786 | Cape Negro River | 200 | |
| Moseley, Benjamin | 1786 | " " " | 100 | |
| Moseley, George | 1784 | Port Roseway River, E. | 50 | |
| Mosely, George | 1784 | Shelburne | | T. L. |
| Mosher, Elijah | 1785 | Jordan River, E. | 100 | |
| Mountain, Richard | 1785 | " " " | 200 | |

## PUBLIC ARCHIVES OF NOVA SCOTIA

| Name | Date | Situation | Acres | Origin or Rank |
|---|---|---|---|---|
| Muir, James | 1784 | Shelburne | 50 | |
| Muir, William | 1786 | Cape Negro River | 100 | |
| Mulhall, Richard | 1784 | Shelburne | | T. L. |
| Mullock, William | 1788 | Tusket River | 175 | |
| Munns, Alexander | 1784 | Shelburne | | T. L. |
| Munns, James | 1784 | " | 50 | |
| Munns, James | 1784 | Shelburne | | T. L. |
| Munro, Burnett | 1785 | Lake Rodney, S. | 100 | |
| Munro, Daniel | 1784 | Shelburne | 50 | |
| Munro, Daniel | 1784 | " | | T. L. |
| Munro, Nathaniel | 1785 | Lake Rodney, S. | 100 | |
| Munro, Nathaniel | 1787 | Birch Town | 50 | |
| Munro, William | 1785 | Lake Rodney, S. | 100 | |
| Munroe, Nathaniel | 1784 | Shelburne | | W. H. L. |
| Munroe, William | 1784 | " | 50 | |
| Murchy, William | 1787 | Herring Falls | 50 | |
| Murfey, James | 1784 | Shelburne | | T. L. |
| Murphy, Francis | 1786 | Cape Negro River | 100 | |
| Murphy, James | 1784 | Shelburne | | W. H. L. |
| Murphy, John | 1786 | Shel. Anna. Road | 200 | |
| Murphy, Patrick | 1784 | Shelburne | | W. H. L. |
| Murphy, Patrick | 1785 | Jordan River, E. | 100 | |
| Murray, Alexander | 1784 | Shelburne | | W. H. L. |
| Murray, Alexander | 1786 | Shelburne Harbour, E. | 50 | |
| Murray, Alexander | 1790 | Sable River (Not reg'd) | 100 | |
| Murray, Archibald | 1790 | "    "    "    " | 100 | |
| Murray, John | 1790 | "    "    "    " | 100 | |
| Murray, William | 1790 | "    "    "    " | 200 | |
| Murrow, John | 1787 | Port Roseway Har., W. | 200 | |
| Musgrave, Bartholomew | 1784 | Shelburne | | T. L. |
| Musgrave, Bartholomew | 1784 | " | | W. H. L. |
| Musgrave, Bartholomew | 1785 | McNutt's Island | 50 | |
| Musgrave, Bartholomew | 1790 | Sable River (Not reg'd) | 100 | |
| Myer, Frederick | 1784 | Shelburne | 50 | |
| Myer, Frederick | 1787 | Port Roseway Har., W. | 200 | |
| Myer, Jeremiah | 1784 | Shelburne | 50 | |
| Myers, Fredrick | 1784 | " | | T. L. |
| Myers, Thomas | 1786 | Shel. Anna. Road | 200 | |
| Nairn, David | 1784 | Shelburne | | W. H. L. |
| Nairns, David | 1784 | " | 50 | |
| Neale, James | 1787 | Port Roseway Har., W. | 50 | |
| Needham, Sebastian | 1784 | Shelburne | | T. L. |
| Needham, Sebastine | 1784 | " | | W. H. L. |
| Neilson, Robert | 1784 | " | | T. L. |
| Nelson, Robert | 1784 | " | | W. H. L. |
| Nelson, Robert | 1786 | Cape Negro River | 100 | |
| Nelson, Robert | 1787 | Herring Falls | 50 | |
| Nelson, W. see Ellis, Thomas | 1790 | | | |
| Nesbitt, Archibald | 1784 | Shelburne | | T. L. |
| Nesbitt, Archibald | 1785 | Lake Rodney, S. | 100 | |
| Nesbitt, Archibald | 1787 | Birch Town | 50 | |
| Newport, Sampson | 1786 | Cape Negro River | 100 | |
| Nichilson, Neal | 1784 | Port Roseway Har., E. | 50 | |
| Nichol, Duncan | 1785 | Jordan River, E. | 200 | |
| Nicholl, Edward | 1784 | Shelburne | | T. L. |
| Nicholls, John | 1784 | " | | T. L. |
| Nichols, John | 1784 | " | | W. H. L. |
| Nichols, John | 1785 | Port Hebert Harbour | 100 | |
| Nichols, John | 1785 | "    "    " | 100 | |
| Nicholson, Donald | 1784 | Shelburne | | T. L. |
| Nicholson, Peter | 1784 | " | 50 | |
| Nicholson, Peter | 1785 | Jordan River, E. | 100 | |

# LOYALISTS AND LAND SETTLEMENT IN NOVA SCOTIA 97

| Name | Date | Situation | Acres | Origin or Rank |
|---|---|---|---|---|
| Nostrum, John | 1784 | Shelburne | W. H. L. | |
| Nowland, Richard | 1785 | Port Hebert Harbour | 100 | |
| Nugent, Arthur B. | 1788 | Tusket River | 300 | |
| Nunn, Samuel | 1784 | Shelburne | 50 | |
| Nunn, Samuel | 1784 | " | T. L. | |
| Nunn, Samuel | 1784 | " | W. H. L. | |
| Nutter, Valentine | 1784 | " | T. L. | |
| Nutter, Valentine | 1784 | " | T. L. | |
| | | | | |
| Oakes, William | 1786 | Cape Negro River | 100 | |
| O'Brian, Thomas | 1787 | Birch Town | 50 | |
| O'Brien, Thomas | 1784 | Shelburne | T. L. | |
| O'Brien, Thomas | 1786 | Shel. Anna. Road | 200 | |
| Odell, John | 1787 | Birch Town | 100 | |
| Ogden, David | 1788 | Tusket River | 500 | |
| Ogden, Isaac | 1784 | Shelburne | T. L. | |
| Ogden, John | 1786 | Shel. Anna. Road | 200 | |
| Ogden, Nicholas | 1784 | Jordan Bay, E. | 200 | |
| Ogden, Nicholas | 1784 | Jordan River, E. | 200 | |
| Ogden, Nicholas | 1784 | Shelburne | Wharf L. | |
| Ogden, Nicholas | 1784 | " | W. H. L. | |
| Ogden, Nicholas | 1788 | Tusket River | 575 | |
| O'Kelley, Michael | 1786 | Cape Negro River | 200 | |
| Oliver, Charles | 1784 | Shelburne | W. H. L. | |
| Oliver, Joseph | 1784 | Shelburne | 50 | |
| Oliver, Joseph | 1784 | " | T. L. | |
| O'Neal, Barnaby | 1787 | Birch Town | 100 | |
| O'Neal, John | 1784 | Shelburne | 50 | |
| Orcut, Joseph | 1784 | " | T. L. | |
| Orr, John | 1785 | McNutt's Island | 50 | |
| Owens, William | 1786 | Shel. Anna. Road | 200 | |
| | | | | |
| Pagan, William | 1784 | Shelburne | W. L. | |
| Palmer, Alpheus | 1785 | McNutt's Island | 50 | |
| Palmer, Alpheus | 1785 | Port Roseway, E. | 20 | |
| Palmer, Alphius | 1784 | Shelburne | W. H. L. | |
| Palmer, Benjamin | 1784 | " | 50 | |
| Palmer, Benjamin | 1786 | Shel. Anna. Road | 200 | |
| Palmer, Lewis | 1784 | Shelburne | W. H. L. | |
| Palmer, Lewis | 1785 | Port Roseway, E. | 20 | |
| Panton, George (Rev.) | 1788 | Tusket River | 500 | |
| Parbert, George | 1784 | Shelburne | T. L. | |
| Parker, Joshua | 1784 | " | 50 | |
| Parker, Joshua | 1784 | " | T. L. | |
| Parker, Joshua | 1784 | " | W. H. L. | |
| Parker, Peter | 1784 | " | 50 | |
| Parker, Peter | 1784 | " | T. L. | |
| Parker, Peter | 1785 | Port Hebert Harbour | 200 | |
| Parkerhide, William | 1784 | Shelburne | W. H. L. | |
| Parkley, William | 1786 | Cape Negro River | 200 | |
| Parney, Thomas | 1784 | Shelburne | T. L. | |
| Parsons, William | 1786 | Shel. Anna. Road | 200 | |
| Pashley, George | 1784 | Shelburne | 50 | |
| Pashley, George | 1784 | " | T. L. | |
| Pashley, George | 1784 | " | W. H. L. | |
| Pashley, George | 1787 | Birch Town | 350 | |
| Passhley, George | 1785 | Birch Town Creek, E. | 300 | Captain |
| Patient, John | 1784 | Shelburne | 50 | |
| Patten, George | 1784 | " | 50 | |
| Patten, George | 1784 | " | W. H. L. | |
| Patten, John | 1786 | " | W. L. | |
| Patterson, Robert | 1784 | " | T. L. | |
| Patterson, Robert | 1784 | " | W. L. | |
| Patton, George | 1784 | " | Wharf L. | |

| Name | Date | Situation | Acres | Origin or Rank |
|---|---|---|---|---|
| Peck, William | 1785 | Port Hebert Harbour | 100 | |
| Pecker, Jeremiah | 1784 | Shelburne | | T. L. |
| Pecker, Jeremiah | 1784 | " | | W. H. L. |
| Pecker, Jeremiah | 1786 | Shel. Anna. Road | 200 | |
| Pecker, Jeremiah | 1787 | Herring Falls | 50 | |
| Peel, George | 1790 | Sable River (Not reg'd) | 200 | |
| Peffendorf—, see Deffendorf | | | | |
| Pell, Jonathan | 1785 | Shel. Anna. Road | 250 | |
| Pell, Joseph | 1785 | " " " | 100 | |
| Pell, Joshua | 1785 | " " " | 500 | |
| Pell, Joshua, Jr. | 1785 | " " " | 200 | |
| Pell, Samuel | 1784 | Shelburne | | W. H. L. |
| Pendergrass, Matthew | 1784 | " | 50 | |
| Pendergrass, Matthew | 1784 | " | | T. L. |
| Pendergrass, Matthew | 1784 | " | | W. H. L. |
| Pendergrass, Thomas | 1784 | " | 50 | |
| Pendergrass, Thomas | 1784 | " | | T. L. |
| Penny, Richard | 1786 | Cape Negro River | 250 | |
| Penny, Richard | 1787 | Birch Town | 50 | |
| Penny, Samuel | 1784 | Shelburne | | T. L. |
| Perry, Jacob | 1785 | Shelburne—E. Meadows | 5 | |
| Perry, Jacob | 1788 | Tusket River | 300 | |
| Perry, Samuel | 1784 | Shelburne | | W. H. L. |
| Perry, Silas | 1784 | " | 50 | |
| Perry, Sturges | 1784 | " | | W. H. L. |
| Perry, Sturgus | 1784 | " | 50 | |
| Perry, Sturgus | 1784 | " | 50 | |
| Petit, John Samuel | 1790 | Sable River (Not reg'd) | 100 | |
| Petrie, Ninian | 1784 | Shelburne | | T. L. |
| Pettit, John | 1784 | " | | W. H. L. |
| Pettit, John Samuel | 1784 | " | | W. H. L. |
| Pettit, Mary | 1787 | Port Roseway Har., W. | 200 | |
| Philips, Patrick | 1790 | Sable River (Not reg'd) | 200 | |
| Phillips, David | 1784 | Shelburne | 50 | |
| Phillips, David | 1784 | " | | W. H. L. |
| Phillips, John | 1786 | Cape Negro River | 200 | |
| Phillips, Martha | 1784 | Shelburne | | W. H. L. |
| Phillips, Mary | 1786 | Cape Negro River | 100 | |
| Pitcher, Moses | 1785 | McNutt's Island | 50 | |
| Pitcher, Moses | 1785 | Port Roseway, E. | 20 | |
| Porter, Andrew | 1784 | Shelburne | | T. L. |
| Porterfield, William | 1790 | Sable River (Not reg'd) | 500 | |
| Potter, James | 1784 | Shelburne | 50 | |
| Potter, James | 1784 | " | | W. H. L. |
| Potter, James | 1784 | " | | Wharf L. |
| Potter, John | 1784 | " | | W. H. L. |
| Potter, Thomas | 1786 | Cape Negro River | 200 | |
| Powell, Henry | 1784 | Shelburne | 50 | |
| Powell, Henry | 1784 | " | 50 | |
| Powell, Nathaniel | 1784 | " | | T. L. |
| Powell, William | 1784 | Shelburne Harbour, E. | 100 | |
| Powell, William | 1787 | Birch Town | 100 | |
| Power, Thomas | 1784 | Shelburne | 50 | |
| Power, Thomas | 1784 | " | | W. L. |
| Pride, Ira | 1790 | Sable River (Not reg'd) | 450 | |
| Prim, John | 1784 | Shelburne | 50 | |
| Prim, John | 1784 | " | | W. H. L. |
| Prior, James | 1784 | " | | W. H. L. |
| Prior, James | 1785 | McNutt's Island | 50 | |
| Procter, Isaac | 1785 | Jordan River, E. | 100 | |
| Prout, Timothy | 1784 | Shelburne | 50 | |
| Prout, Timothy | 1784 | " | | T. L. |
| Prynn, John | 1784 | " | | T. L. |

# LOYALISTS AND LAND SETTLEMENT IN NOVA SCOTIA 99

| Name | Date | Situation | Acres | Origin or Rank |
|---|---|---|---|---|
| Purdy, John | 1790 | Sable River (Not reg'd) | 100 | |
| Purney, Thomas | 1784 | Shelburne | 50 | |
| Purney, Thomas | 1784 | " | W. H. L. | |
| Pyncheon, Joseph | 1784 | " | 50 | |
| Pynchon, Joseph | 1784 | " | T. I. | |
| Pynchon, Joseph | 1784 | " | T. L.'s & | W. H. L. |
| Quinn, Hugh | 1785 | Cape Negro River | 200 | |
| Ramsay, James | 1786 | Shel. Anna. Road | 200 | |
| Rand, Nathaniel | 1784 | Shelburne | T. L. | |
| Rand, Nathaniel | 1785 | McNutt's Island | 50 | |
| Randall, Amos | 1786 | Cape Negro River | 100 | |
| Randall, William | 1784 | Shelburne | T. L. | |
| Randall, William | 1784 | " | W. H. L. | |
| Randolph, Sarah | 1784 | " | T. L. | |
| Rankey, Frederick | 1790 | Sable River (Not reg'd) | 100 | |
| Rapalie, George | 1784 | Shelburne | W. H. L. | |
| Rayne, James | 1784 | " | T. L. | |
| Read, William | 1785 | Jordan River, E. | 200 | |
| Reath, James | 1784 | Shelburne | 50 | |
| Reath, Kenneth | 1784 | " | 50 | |
| Reder [Rider] John | 1790 | Sable River (Not reg'd) | 230 | |
| Redhead, William | 1786 | Shel. Anna. Road | 200 | |
| Redman, Michael | 1788 | Tusket River | 175 | |
| Reed, Alexander | 1784 | Shelburne | 50 | |
| Reed, Alexander | 1784 | " | W. H. L. | |
| Rees, Thomas | 1790 | Sable River (Not reg'd) | 100 | |
| Reeth, Archibald | 1790 | " " " " | 100 | |
| Reid, Alexander | 1784 | Shelburne | T. L. | |
| Reid, Collin | 1784 | " | 50 | |
| Reid, Hugh | 1790 | Sable River (Not reg'd) | 100 | |
| Reider, Michael | 1786 | Shel. Anna. Road | 200 | |
| Reilly, Terence | 1787 | Port Roseway Har., W. | 200 | |
| Reith, James | 1784 | Shelburne | T. L. | |
| Ressler, Frederick | 1786 | Shel. Anna. Road | 200 | |
| Restine, Joseph | 1785 | McNutt's Island | 50 | Pilot, Negro |
| Revell, Richard | 1784 | Shelburne | 50 | |
| Revell, Richard | 1784 | " | T. L. | |
| Reville, Richard | 1784 | " | W. H. L. | |
| Reyne, James | 1784 | Shelburne | W. H. L. | |
| Rice, Joseph | 1784 | " | W. H. L. | |
| Rich,—(Widow) | 1790 | Sable River (Not reg'd) | 100 | |
| Rich, James | 1784 | Shelburne | T. L. | |
| Rich, James | 1787 | Port Roseway Har., W. | 200 | |
| Richards, Edward | 1790 | Sable River (Not reg'd) | 200 | |
| Richards, Nathaniel | 1784 | Shelburne | W. L. | |
| Richards, Nicholas | 1788 | Tusket River | 200 | |
| Richardson, John | 1785 | Cape Negro River | 100 | |
| Richardson, Thomas | 1784 | Shelburne | 50 | |
| Richmond, William | 1784 | " | W. H. L. | |
| Richmond, William | 1785 | Port Roseway, E. | 20 | |
| Rick, Joseph | 1787 | Birch Town | 50 | |
| Ricker, Nathaniel | 1785 | Argyle Township | 150 | |
| Ricker, Paul | 1785 | " " | 150 | |
| Rickets, Josiah | 1787 | Birch Town | 100 | |
| Riely, Patrick | 1784 | Shelburne | W. H. L. | |
| Rigby, William | 1784 | " | T. L. | |
| Robb, John | 1790 | Sable River (Not reg'd) | 200 | |
| Roberts, Benjamin | 1785 | Argyle Township | 250 | |
| Roberts, James | 1786 | Yarmouth Township | 666 | Navy Pilot |
| Roberts, John | 1786 | Cape Negro River | 250 | |
| Robertson, Alexander | 1784 | Shelburne | T. L. | Captain |
| Robertson, Anthony | 1785 | Port Hebert Harbour | 100 | |

# 100  PUBLIC ARCHIVES OF NOVA SCOTIA

| Name | Date | Situation | Acres | Origin or Rank |
|---|---|---|---|---|
| Robertson, James | 1784 | Shelburne | 50 | |
| Robertson, James | 1785 | Jordan River, E. | 200 | |
| Robertson, John | 1786 | Cape Negro River | 200 | |
| Robertson, Peter | 1784 | Shelburne | | W. H. L. |
| Robertson, Peter | 1785 | Port Hebert Harbour | 100 | |
| Robertson, Peter | 1785 | " " " | 100 | |
| Robertson, William | 1784 | Shelburne | 50 | |
| Robertson, William | 1785 | Port Hebert Harbour | 200 | |
| Robins, William | 1785 | Jordan River, E. | 200 | Lieut. |
| Robinson, Alexander see Robinson, James | 1784 | | | |
| Robinson, James | 1784 | Shelburne | | T. L. |
| Robinson, James and Robinson, Alexander | 1784 | Herring Falls | 920 | |
| Robinson, James and 3 others | 1785 | McNutt's Island | 50 | Pilot Negro |
| Robinson, William | 1784 | Shelburne | 50 | |
| Robinson, William | 1784 | " | | T. L. |
| Robinson, William | 1784 | " | | W. H. L. |
| Robinson, William | 1784 | " | | W. H. L. |
| Robison, Robert | 1786 | Shel. Anna. Road | 200 | |
| Rogers, Barney | 1785 | Jordan River, E. | 100 | |
| Rogers, Peter | 1785 | " " " | 100 | |
| Rohl, Andrew | 1784 | Shelburne | | T. L. |
| Roll, Andrew | 1784 | " | | W. H. L. |
| Rose, Alexander | 1784 | " | | T. L. |
| Rose, Alexander | 1787 | Birch Town | 50 | |
| Rose, James | 1784 | Port Roseway Har., E. | 50 | |
| Rose, James | 1784 | Shelburne | | T. L. |
| Rose, Jonathan | 1784 | " | | T. L. |
| Rose, William | 1784 | " | 50 | |
| Rose, William | 1784 | " | | W. L. |
| Rose, William | 1784 | " | | W. H. L. |
| Ross, Alexander | 1784 | " | 50 | |
| Ross, Alexander | 1784 | " | | W. H. L. |
| Ross, Alexander | 1790 | Sable River (Not reg'd) | 100 | |
| Ross, Andrew | 1784 | Shelburne | 50 | |
| Ross, Andrew | 1784 | " | | T. L. |
| Ross, Andrew | 1784 | " | | W. H. L. |
| Ross, Andrew | 1785 | Port Hebert Harbour | 100 | |
| Ross, Donald | 1784 | Shelburne | | W. L. |
| Ross, James | 1785 | Jordan River, E. | 100 | |
| Ross, William | 1790 | Sable River (Not reg'd) | 100 | |
| Rowe, Peter | 1785 | Jordan River, E. | 100 | |
| Rowland, William | 1787 | Port Roseway Harbour, | W. 50 | |
| Rowlands, Thomas | 1785 | Port Hebert Harbour | 200 | |
| Rowlet, John | 1786 | Shelburne | | W. L. |
| Rowlett, John | 1787 | Port Roseway Har., W. | 200 | |
| Rude, Jacob | 1790 | Sable River (Not reg'd) | 200 | |
| Russel, James | 1787 | Birch Town | 50 | |
| Russell, James | 1786 | Cape Negro River | 100 | |
| Ruton, David | 1788 | Tusket River | 300 | |
| Ryan, Cornelius | 1786 | Shel. Anna. Road | 200 | |
| Ryan, James | 1784 | Port Roseway Har., E. | 50 | |
| Ryan, James | 1784 | Shelburne | 50 | |
| Ryan, Peter | 1784 | " | | T. L. |
| St. Clair, John | 1784 | " | 50 | |
| St. Clair, Henry | 1785 | Jordan River, E. | 200 | |
| Sargent, John | 1784 | Shelburne | | T. L. & W. L. |
| Sarvånt, Abraham | 1788 | Tusket River | 300 | |
| Saunders, Samuel | 1786 | Yarmouth Township | 666 | Navy Pilot |
| Saville, John | 1784 | Shelburne | | W. L. |
| Sayer, Samuel | 1786 | Cape Negro River | 200 | |

## LOYALISTS AND LAND SETTLEMENT IN NOVA SCOTIA

| Name | Date | Situation | Acres | Origin or Rank |
|---|---|---|---|---|
| Schneider, William, Jr. | 1784 | Shelburne | T. L. | |
| Schooly, Robert | 1786 | Cape Negro River | 200 | |
| Sciely, Thomas | 1785 | Argyle Township | 200 | |
| Scott, George | 1784 | Shelburne | 50 | |
| Scott, George | 1784 | " | W. H. L. | |
| Scott, George | 1785 | Port Hebert Harbour | 200 | |
| Scott, George | 1786 | Shel. Anna. Road | 200 | |
| Seaman, John | 1784 | Shelburne | W. L. | |
| Seaman, Henry | 1784 | " | W. L. | |
| Seers, Jonathan | 1788 | Tusket River | 500 | |
| Seers, Samuel | 1784 | Shelburne | T. L. | |
| Sellers, Archibald | 1784 | " | T. L. | |
| Sentner, Philip | 1784 | " | W. H. L. | |
| Serjeant, John | 1785 | Port Roseway, E. | 20 | Lieut. |
| Shakespear, Stephen | 1784 | Port Roseway River, W. | 501 | |
| Shakespear, Stephen | 1784 | Shelburne | 50 | |
| Shakespear, Stephen | 1784 | " | T.L.'s, & Wharf | W. L.'s L. |
| Shaw, John | 1785 | Cape Negro River | 100 | |
| Shaw, Thomas | 1784 | Shelburne | 50 | |
| Shaw, Thomas | 1784 | " | T. L. | |
| Shaw, Thomas | 1784 | " | W. H. L. | |
| Shaw, Thomas | 1786 | Cape Negro | 200 | |
| Shipman, William | 1785 | Jordan River, E. | 200 | Ensign |
| Shorto, Samuel | 1787 | Birch Town | 100 | |
| Silbey, John | 1784 | Shelburne | T. L. | |
| Silbey, John | 1784 | " | T. L. | |
| Silby, John | 1784 | " | W. H. L. | |
| Simpson, James | 1784 | Port Roseway Har., E. | 50 | |
| Sinclair, John | 1784 | Shelburne | W. H L. | |
| Siveally, John | 1786 | Cape Negro River | 200 | |
| Slater, James | 1787 | Birch Town | 100 | |
| Sloane, James | 1788 | Tusket River | 200 | |
| Smart, John | 1784 | Shelburne | 50 | |
| Smart, John | 1784 | " | W. H. L. | |
| Smith, Benjamin | 1784 | " | 50 | |
| Smith, Benjamin | 1784 | " | W. H. L. | |
| Smith, Daniel | 1787 | Birch Town | 200 | |
| Smith, David | 1785 | Jordan River, E. | 100 | |
| Smith, Ephraim | 1786 | Shel. Anna. Road | 200 | |
| Smith, Erich | 1786 | Cape Negro River | 100 | |
| Smith, Jacob | 1790 | Sable River (Not reg'd) | 100 | |
| Smith, James | 1785 | Jordan River, E. | 100 | |
| Smith, Job see Decker, Isaac | 1788 | | | |
| Smith, John | 1784 | Shelburne | T. L. | |
| Smith, John | 1787 | Birch Town | 100 | |
| Smith, Thomas | 1785 | Jordan River, E. | 100 | |
| Smith, William | 1787 | Birch Town | 100 | |
| Smith, Whitford | 1784 | Shelburne | 50 | |
| Smith, Whitford | 1784 | " | T. L. | |
| Smith, Whitford | 1784 | " | W. H. L. | |
| Smithers, James | 1787 | Birch Town | 50 | |
| Saville, John | 1784 | Shelburne | 50 | |
| Somerville, Robert | 1786 | " | W. L. | |
| Sommers, William | 1784 | " | T. L. | |
| Southerland, William | 1784 | Shelburne | T. L. | |
| Southerland, William | 1784 | " | W. H. L. | |
| Sparling, Peter | 1784 | " | 50 | |
| Sparling, Peter | 1784 | " | T. L. | |
| Sparling, Peter, Jr. | 1784 | " | T. L. | |
| Speakman, John | 1785 | Jordan River, E. | 100 | |
| Spearings, Henry | 1784 | Shelburne | 50 | |
| Spears, Robert | 1785 | Jordan River, E. | 100 | |

102   PUBLIC ARCHIVES OF NOVA SCOTIA

| Name | Date | Situation | Acres | Origin or Rank |
|---|---|---|---|---|
| Speed, Paul | 1784 | Shelburne | 50 | |
| Speed, Paul | 1784 | " | W. H. L. | |
| Spencer, John | 1784 | " | 50 | |
| Spencer, John | 1784 | " | T. L. | |
| Spencer, John | 1784 | " | W. H. L. | |
| Spencer, John | 1787 | Port Roseway Har., W. | 200 | |
| Spicer, Francis | 1787 | Birch Town | 100 | |
| Spier, Agnes | 1790 | Sable River (Not reg'd) | 200 | |
| Spier, Hugh | 1790 | "    "    "    " | 100 | |
| Spier, John | 1790 | "    "    "    " | 100 | |
| Spike, John | 1790 | "    "    "    " | 100 | |
| Springall, Gregory | 1786 | Shelburne | W. L. | |
| Springall, Gregory | 1786 | Shel. Anna. Road | 200 | |
| Sproul, Andrew | 1784 | Shelburne | T. L. | |
| Sproull, Andrew | 1786 | Shel. Anna. Road | 200 | |
| Squires, William | 1787 | Birch Town | 100 | |
| Stacey, Matthew | 1784 | Shelburne | W. H. L. | |
| Stacey, Matthew | 1786 | Cape Negro River | 200 | |
| Stalker, John | 1785 | "    "    " | 200 | |
| Stanhope, Henry Edwin | 1784 | Shelburne | T. L. | Captain |
| Stanton, John | 1785 | Port Hebert Harbour | 100 | |
| Stanton, Lathan | 1785 | "    "    " | 100 | |
| Stayner, Daniel | 1784 | Shelburne | W. H. L. | |
| Steel, Andrew | 1790 | Sable River (Not reg'd) | 100 | |
| Stephens, Alexander | 1787 | Birch Town | 100 | |
| Stephens, John | 1790 | Sable River (Not reg'd) | 100 | |
| Stephens, William | 1785 | Argyle Township | 200 | |
| Stephenson, John | 1784 | Shelburne | T. L. | |
| Stephenson, John | 1786 | Shel. Anna. Road | 200 | |
| Stevenson, John | 1784 | Shelburne | T. L. | |
| Steward (Stewart) John | 1784 | " | W. H. L. | |
| Stewart, Abraham | 1785 | Shelburne, E. Meadows | 5 | |
| Stewart, Alexander | 1787 | Birch Town | 200 | |
| Stewart, John | 1784 | Shelburne | 50 | |
| Stewart, John | 1784 | " | T. L. | |
| Stiles, William | 1787 | Port Roseway Har., W. | 200 | |
| Stokes, James | 1784 | Shelburne | T. L. | |
| Stokes, John | 1784 | " | W. H. L. | |
| Storey, John | 1785 | Cape Negro River | 100 | |
| Stout, Delina | 1785 | Port Hebert Harbour | 100 | |
| Stranger, Daniel | 1790 | Sable River (Not reg'd) | 100 | |
| Street, Patrick | 1786 | Shelburne | W. H. L. | |
| Stuart, John | 1784 | " | T. L. | |
| Stuart, John | 1786 | Cape Negro River | 200 | |
| Stuart, [Stewart] John | 1786 | Shel. Anna. Road | 200 | |
| Sullivan, Bartholemew | 1784 | Jordan River, E. | 200 | |
| Sullivan, Florence | 1784 | Shelburne | W. L. | |
| Sullivan, Florence | 1784 | Shelburne Township | 50 | |
| Sutcliffe, William | 1790 | Sable River (Not reg'd) | 100 | |
| Sutherland, Adam | 1786 | Shel. Anna. Road | 200 | |
| Sutherland, John | 1787 | Birch Town | 200 | |
| Swazey, John | 1785 | Jordan River, E. | 100 | |
| Swinburgh, Christian | 1786 | Shel. Anna. Road | 200 | |
| Swords, James | 1784 | Shelburne | T. L. | |
| Swords, Thomas | 1784 | " | T. L. | |
| Tail, John | 1787 | Birch Town | 200 | |
| Talbut, John | 1784 | Shelburne | W. H. L. | |
| Tankard, Matthew | 1784 | " | 50 | |
| Tankard, Matthew | 1784 | " | T. L. | |
| Tankard, Matthew | 1784 | " | W. H. L. | |
| Tankard, Matthew | 1786 | Cape Negro River | 200 | |
| Tanley, Thomas | 1786 | Shel. Anna. Road | 200 | |
| Taylor, Ann | 1785 | Port Hebert Harbour | 100 | |

## LOYALISTS AND LAND SETTLEMENT IN NOVA SCOTIA 103

| Name | Date | Situation | Acres | Origin or Rank |
|---|---|---|---|---|
| Taylor, Charles | 1784 | Shelburne | T. L. & | W. L. |
| Taylor, Charles | 1788 | Tusket River | 300 | |
| Taylor, David | 1790 | Sable River (Not reg'd) | 100 | |
| Taylor, James | 1784 | Shelburne Harbour, E. | 100 | |
| Tellfair, Charles | 1784 | Shelburne | T. L. | |
| Tench, John | 1784 | Port Roseway River, E. | 50 | |
| Tench, John | 1784 | Shelburne | T. L. & | W. L. |
| Tenner, Thomas | 1784 | " | W. H. L. | |
| Tennor, Thomas | 1784 | " | 50 | |
| Terrill, John | 1784 | " | W. L. | |
| Thomas, Edmond | 1787 | Birch Town | 200 | |
| Thomas, Edward | 1786 | Shel. Anna. Road | 200 | |
| Thomas, George | 1784 | Port Roseway River, E. | 50 | |
| Thomas, George | 1784 | Shelburne | W. L. | |
| Thomas, George | 1785 | Port Roseway, E. | 20 | |
| Thomas, Jonathan | 1784 | Shelburne | 50 | |
| Thomas, Jonathan | 1786 | Cape Negro River | 200 | |
| Thomas, Nathaniel Ray | 1784 | Shelburne | T. L. | |
| Thomas, Nathaniel Ray | 1784 | " | W. H. L. | |
| Thomas, Richard | 1785 | Port Hebert Harbour | 200 | |
| Thomas, Richard | 1787 | Herring Falls | 50 | |
| Thomas, William | 1784 | Shelburne | 50 | |
| Thomas, William | 1784 | " | T. L. | |
| Thompson, Archibald | 1785 | Shelburne, E. Meadows | 5 | |
| Thompson, David | 1784 | Port Roseway Har., E. | 100 | |
| Thompson, David | 1784 | Shelburne | Wharf L. | |
| Thompson, David | 1784 | " | W. H. L. | |
| Thompson, James | 1784 | " | T. L. | |
| Thompson, James | 1784 | " | W. H. L. | |
| Thompson, John | 1790 | Sable River (Not reg'd) | 100 | |
| Thompson, Robert | 1786 | Shel. Anna. Road | 200 | |
| Thompson, William | 1790 | Sable River (Not reg'd) | 200 | |
| Thornhill, Poler | 1787 | Birch Town | 100 | |
| Tolbot, John | 1784 | Shelburne | T. L. | |
| Tolbut, John | 1784 | " | 50 | |
| Tolly, Joseph | 1784 | " | T. L. | |
| Tompkins, Abraham | 1787 | Port Roseway Har., W. | 200 | |
| Townsend, John | 1790 | Sable River (Not reg'd) | 200 | |
| Townsend, Richard | 1784 | Shelburne | Wharf L. | |
| Townsend, Timothy | 1790 | Sable River (Not reg'd) | 200 | |
| Trighlith, Edward | 1784 | Shelburne | 50 | |
| Tribe, William | 1784 | " | 50 | |
| Tulley, Thomas | 1784 | " | W. H. L. | |
| Tullock, Peter | 1784 | " | T. L. | |
| Tullough, Peter | 1784 | " | W. H. L. | |
| Turnbull, Robert | 1784 | " | T. L. | |
| Turnbull, Robert | 1786 | Cape Negro River | 100 | |
| Turnbull, Robert, Sr. | 1786 | " " " | 200 | |
| Turnbull, Thomas | 1784 | Shelburne | T. L. | |
| Turnbull, Thomas | 1786 | Cape Negro River | 200 | |
| Turnbull, Walter | 1786 | " " " | 100 | |
| Tuttick, Peter | 1790 | Sable River (Not reg'd) | 200 | |
| Tyson, Cornelius | 1784 | Shelburne | T. L. | |
| Van Blarcom, Ryah see Blaricam, Ryah V. | 1784 | | | |
| Van Buskirk, Abraham | 1784 | Port Roseway Har., W. | 500 | |
| Van Buskirk, Abraham | 1784 | Shelburne | Wharf L. | & W. L. |
| Van Buskirk, Andrew | 1788 | Tusket River | 300 | |
| Van Buskirk, Jacob | 1787 | Port Roseway Har., W. | 200 | Captain |
| Van Buskirk, Jacob | 1788 | Tusket River | 300 | |
| Van Buskirk, John | 1788 | " " | 300 | |
| Van Buskirk, William | 1788 | " " | 250 | |
| Van Blarckom, Peter | 1785 | Shelburne, E. Meadows | 5 | |

## 104   PUBLIC ARCHIVES OF NOVA SCOTIA

| Name | Date | Situation | Acres | Origin or Rank |
|---|---|---|---|---|
| Van Blarckom, Peter | 1788 | Tusket River | 300 | |
| Van Cortland, Philip | 1788 | " " | 300 | Major N. J. Vol's |
| Van Cortland, Philip | 1788 | Shelburne (12 miles out) | 200 | Major |
| Van Emburgh, Adonijah | 1788 | Tusket River | 300 | |
| Van Emburgh, Gilbert | 1788 | " " | 300 | |
| Van Emburgh, James | 1785 | Shelburne, E. Meadows | 5 | |
| Van Emburgh, James | 1788 | Tusket River | 300 | |
| Van Emburgh, John | 1788 | " " | 200 | |
| Van Morden [Norden] Stephen | 1785 | Shelburne, E. Meadows | 5 | |
| Van Norden, Cornelius | 1788 | Tusket River | 275 | |
| Van Norden, Gabriel | 1788 | " " | 300 | |
| Van Norden, John | 1788 | " " | 190 | |
| Van Norden [Morden] John | 1790 | Sable River (Not reg'd) | 250 | |
| Van Norden, Stephen, see Van Morden, Stephen | 1785 | | | |
| Van Norden, Stephen | 1788 | Tusket River | 300 | |
| Vanright, John | 1784 | Shelburne | 50 | |
| Van Ripen, Cornelius | 1785 | Shelburne, E. Meadows | 5 | |
| Van Vaert, John | 1785 | " " | 5 | |
| Van Vousin, David | 1786 | Shel. Anna. Road | 200 | |
| Vassey, Joseph | 1784 | Shelburne | T. L. | |
| Veitch, Gavin | 1785 | Jordan River, E. | 200 | |
| Vent, Joshua | 1784 | Shelburne | T. L. | |
| Vinckler, Joseph | 1785 | Jordan River, E. | 100 | |
| Wainwright, John | 1784 | Shelburne | T. L. | |
| Wainwright, John | 1785 | Lake Rodney, S. | 100 | |
| Walker, John | 1784 | Shelburne | 50 | |
| Walker, John | 1785 | Cape Negro River | 100 | |
| Walker, Richard | 1785 | Port Hebert Harbour | 200 | |
| Wall, Patrick | 1784 | Shelburne | 50 | |
| Wall, Patrick | 1785 | Wright's Road | 13 | Captain |
| Walsh, Joseph | 1784 | Shelburne | W. H. L. | |
| Walter, William | 1786 | Shel. Anna. Road | 200 | |
| Walter, William (Rev.) | 1784 | Shelburne | W. H. L. | |
| Ward, Eyre | 1784 | " | W. H. L. | |
| Ward, Ira | 1784 | " | 50 | |
| Ward, Ira | 1784 | " | T. L. | |
| Ward, William | 1784 | " | W. L. | |
| Wardell, Ann | 1787 | Birch Town | 50 | |
| Wardell, John | 1784 | Shelburne | T. L. | |
| Warden, William | 1784 | " | T. L. | |
| Warden, William | 1784 | " | W. H. L. | |
| Warden, William | 1787 | Herring Falls | 50 | |
| Waters, John | 1786 | Cape Negro River | 200 | |
| Watson, Catherine | 1787 | Port Roseway, W. | 200 | |
| Watson, Daniel | 1786 | Cape Negro River | 100 | |
| Watson, George | 1784 | Shelburne | 50 | |
| Watson, George | 1784 | " | T. L. | |
| Watson, John | 1784 | " | 50 | |
| Watson, John | 1784 | " | T. L. | |
| Watson, John | 1784 | " | T. L. | |
| Watson, John | 1784 | " | W. H. L. | |
| Watson, John, Jr. | 1790 | Sable River (Not reg'd) | 100 | |
| Watson, John, Sr. | 1790 | " " " " | 100 | |
| Watson, Joshua | 1784 | Jordan River, E. | 200 | |
| Watson, Joshua | 1784 | Port Roseway Har., E. | 50 | |
| Watson, Joshua | 1784 | Shelburne | T. L. | |
| Watson, Joshua | 1784 | " | T. L., W. L., & | Wharf. L. |
| Watson, Joshua | 1784 | " | Wharf L. | |
| Watt, William | 1785 | Cape Negro River | 100 | |
| Webber, Oliver | 1786 | " " " | 100 | |

# LOYALISTS AND LAND SETTLEMENT IN NOVA SCOTIA 105

| Name | Date | Situation | Acres | Origin or Rank |
|---|---|---|---|---|
| Weir, Archibald | 1790 | Sable River (Not reg'd) | 100 | |
| Weir, William | 1786 | Shelburne | | W. L. |
| Weiser, Frederick | 1785 | Lake Rodney, S. | 100 | |
| Weisner, Leonard | 1784 | Shelburne | 50 | |
| Weisner, Leonard | 1784 | " | | T. L. |
| Welch, John | 1790 | Sable River | 100 | |
| Wells, Benjamin | 1784 | Shelburne | 50 | |
| Wells, Benjamin | 1786 | Cape Negro River | 200 | |
| Wells [Wills] Dudley | 1786 | Shel. Anna. Road | 200 | |
| Welsh, Joseph | 1784 | Shelburne | | T. L. |
| Welsh, Joseph | 1785 | Port Hebert Harbour | 200 | |
| Welsh, Joseph | 1787 | Birch Town | 50 | |
| Welton, Richard | 1784 | Shelburne | | T. L. |
| Westland, Thomas | 1784 | " | 50 | |
| Westland, Thomas | 1784 | " | | T. L. |
| White, Amos | 1784 | Shelburne | | T. L. |
| White, Amos | 1784 | " | | W. H. L. |
| White, Briton, Sr. | 1784 | " | | T. L. |
| White, Caleb | 1784 | " | | W. L. |
| White, Charles | 1785 | Port Hebert Harbour | 200 | |
| White, Charles | 1790 | Sable River (Not reg'd) | 100 | |
| White, Duncan | 1784 | Shelburne | 50 | |
| White, Duncan | 1784 | " | | T. L. |
| White, Duncan | 1784 | " | | W. H. L. |
| White, Duncan | 1787 | Birch Town | 50 | |
| White, Duncan | 1790 | Sable River (Not reg'd) | 100 | |
| White, Gideon | 1784 | Port Roseway River, E. | 50 | |
| White, Gideon | 1784 | Shelburne | | T. L. |
| White, James | 1784 | " | | T. L. |
| White, James | 1784 | " | | W. L. |
| White, James | 1786 | Cape Negro River | 200 | |
| White, Richard | 1784 | Port Roseway Harbour | 50 | |
| White, Richard | 1784 | Shelburne | | W. H. L. |
| White, Richard | 1785 | Jordan River, E. | 200 | |
| Whithall, David | 1785 | Cape Negro River | 100 | |
| Whiting, Thomas | 1784 | Shelburne | 50 | |
| Whiting, Thomas | 1786 | Cape Negro River | 250 | |
| Whitman, John | 1786 | Shel. Anna. Road | 200 | |
| Whitmore, Rachael | 1784 | Shelburne | | T. L. |
| Whitten, Richard | 1784 | " | 50 | |
| Whitton, Richard | 1784 | " | | W. H. L. |
| Whitton, Richard | 1786 | Shel. Anna. Road | 200 | |
| Whitworth, Charles | 1786 | Shelburne | | W. L. |
| Wier, Archibald | 1784 | " | | T. L. |
| Wier, Archibald | 1784 | " | 50 | |
| Wier, Thomas | 1785 | Port Hebert Harbour | 100 | |
| Wilkins, Isaac | 1784 | Jordan River, E. | 5000 | |
| Wilkins, Isaac | 1784 | Port Roseway Har., E. | 500 | N. Y. |
| Wilkins, Isaac | 1785 | Gunning Cove | 72 | |
| Wilkins, Isaac | 1787 | Shel. Liverpool Road | 200 | |
| Wilkins, Martin S. | 1787 | Shel. Liverpool Road | 500 | |
| Wilkins, Robert | 1784 | Shelburne | | T. L. & W. L. |
| Wilkins, Robert | 1786 | Cape Negro River | 200 | |
| Williams, Daniel | 1784 | Shelburne | 50 | |
| Williams, Daniel | 1784 | " | | T. L. |
| Williams, John | 1784 | " | 50 | |
| Williams, John | 1784 | " | | W. H. L. |
| Williams, John | 1785 | Lake Rodney, S. | 100 | |
| Williams, John | 1786 | Shel. Anna. Road | 200 | |
| Williams, John | 1787 | Birch Town | 50 | |
| Williams, Richard | 1784 | Shelburne | | T. L. |
| Williams, Richard | 1784 | " | 50 | |
| Williams, Richard | 1785 | Port Hebert Harbour | 100 | |
| Williams, Samuel | 1787 | Birch Town | 50 | |

| Name | Date | Situation | Acres | Origin or Rank |
|---|---|---|---|---|
| Williams, Samuel | 1784 | Shelburne | | T. L. |
| Williamson, Richard | 1785 | Port Hebert Harbour | 100 | |
| Williamson, Tunis | 1784 | Shelburne | | W. L. |
| Williamson, William | 1784 | " | | W. L. |
| Wilson, Andrew | 1786 | Shel. Anna. Road | 200 | |
| Wilson, James | 1784 | Shelburne | 50 | |
| Wilson, James | 1784 | " | 50 | |
| Wilson, James | 1784 | " | | T. L. |
| Wilson, James | 1784 | " | | W. H. L. |
| Wilson, John | 1784 | " | 50 | |
| Wilson, John | 1784 | " | | T. L. |
| Wilson, John | 1786 | Cape Negro Harbour | 200 | |
| Wilson, Michael | 1785 | Jordan River, E. | 100 | |
| Wilson, William | 1784 | Shelburne | 50 | |
| Wilson, William | 1784 | " | | T. L. |
| Winn, Francis | 1786 | Shel. Anna. Road | 200 | |
| Witherspoon, William | 1784 | Shelburne | | W. L. |
| Wood, Benjamin | 1784 | " | | T. L. |
| Wood, Benjamin | 1784 | " | | W. H. L. |
| Wood, R. A. see Bartlett, Edward | 1790 | | | |
| Wood, Robert | 1784 | " | | T. L. |
| Wood, Robert and Bartlett, Edward | 1790 | Sable River (Not reg'd) | 100 | |
| Wood, Thomas | 1790 | " " " " | 200 | |
| Wright, James | 1784 | Shelburne | | W. H. L. |
| Wright, Thomas | 1790 | Sable River (Not reg'd) | 200 | |
| Yates, James | 1787 | Birch Cove | 50 | |
| Yelvin, Henry | 1784 | Shelburne | 50 | |
| Yelvin, Henry | 1784 | " | | W. H. L. |
| Yonks, Cune | 1784 | " | | W. L. |
| Young, David | 1785 | Jordan River, E. | 200 | |
| Young, Edward | 1784 | Shelburne | | T. L. & W. H. L. |
| Young, Henry | 1785 | Argyle Township | 100 | |
| Young, Robert | 1784 | Shelburne | 50 | |
| Young, Robert | 1784 | " | | T. L. |
| Young, William | 1784 | " | 50 | |
| Young, William | 1784 | " | | T. L. |
| Yule, Peter | 1786 | Shel. Anna. Road | 200 | |

## Shelburne County
### WARRANTS

| Name | Date | Situation | Acres | Origin or Rank |
|---|---|---|---|---|
| Aarons, Jacob | 1787 | Shelburne Township | 20 | Negro |
| Ackerson, Edward | 1786 | Port Roseway River, W. | 200 | |
| Ackerson, John | 1786 | " " " " | 200 | |
| Adams, William | 1785 | Shelburne, near Common | 95 | |
| Addington, Andrew | 1786 | Birch Town Creek | 100 | |
| Aitkins, Andrew | 1787 | Shelburne Township | 40 | Negro |
| Alexander, Thomas | 1786 | Birch Town Creek | 100 | |
| Anderson, Archibald | 1786 | Port Roseway River, W. | 200 | |
| Anderson, Isaac | 1787 | Shelburne Township | 40 | Negro |
| Anderson, Peter | 1785 | Cape Negro Harbour, E. | 38 | |

## LOYALISTS AND LAND SETTLEMENT IN NOVA SCOTIA 107

| Name | Date | Situation | Acres | Origin or Rank |
|---|---|---|---|---|
| Asbey, James | 1787 | Argyle Township | 180 | |
| Aysh, William | 1787 | Shelburne Township | 40 | Negro |
| Backus, Thomas | 1787 | " " | 40 | Negro |
| Baley, Charles and Morant, John | 1787 | " " | 38 | Negro |
| Baley, George and Ramsey, Elenor | 1787 | " " | 28 | Negro |
| Bell, Joseph | 1785 | " " | 10 | |
| Bell, Joseph | 1786 | Birch Town Creek | 200 | |
| Bell, Robert | 1788 | Green Harbour | 140 | |
| Bennet, Joseph | 1787 | Shelburne Township | 40 | Negro |
| Bennet, William | 1786 | Tusket River, S. | 200 | |
| Bennet, William | 1787 | Argyle Township | 200 | |
| Berges, Jefry | 1787 | Shelburne Township | 26 | Negro |
| Blackwell, John | 1785 | Cape Negro Har., W. | 305 | |
| Blanchard, Lewis | 1786 | Tusket River, S. | 200 | |
| Blewer, Jacob | 1786 | Pell's Road | 197 | |
| Blewer, John | 1786 | " " | 196 | |
| Blewer, Peter | 1786 | " " | 200 | |
| Bloy, London | 1787 | Shelburne Township | 40 | Negro |
| Bogart, Abraham | 1786 | Tusket River, S. | 200 | |
| Bolton, Samuel | 1787 | Shelburne Township | 40 | Negro |
| Bouflerie, Jacob | 1785 | Cape Negro Harbour, E. | 160 | |
| Bower, Bartholomew | 1786 | Port Roseway River, W. | 200 | |
| Bowers, Adam | 1786 | Pell's Road | 200 | |
| Bowers, Charles | 1786 | " " | 200 | |
| Bowlby, Edward | 1786 | " " | 140 | |
| Bowler, Arthur | 1787 | Shelburne Township | 32 | Negro |
| Bowman, Robert | 1786 | Birch Town Creek | 100 | |
| Bracey, Jonas | 1787 | Shelburne Township | 20 | Negro |
| Brannon, Daniel | 1786 | Pell's Road | 178 | |
| Brinley, Thomas | 1786 | Port Roseway River, W. | 200 | |
| Broughton, Benjamin | 1787 | Shelburne Township | 40 | Negro |
| Brown, David | 1786 | Port Roseway River, W. | 200 | |
| Brown, John | 1787 | Shelburne Township | 40 | Negro |
| Brown, Doct. (?) John | 1787 | " " | 40 | Negro |
| Brown, John | 1788 | Green Harbour | 200 | |
| Brown, Patty | 1787 | Shelburne Township | 40 | Negro |
| Brown, Simon | 1787 | " " | 20 | " |
| Brown, William | 1788 | Green Harbour | 50 | |
| Bruce, Andrew | 1786 | Tusket River, S. | 200 | |
| Bullock, Robert | 1786 | Pell's Road | 200 | |
| Burnham, John | 1788 | Green's Harbour | 150 | |
| Bush, Isaac | 1787 | Shelburne Township | 40 | Negro |
| Bush, Richard | 1787 | " " | 40 | " |
| Byrne, Benedit | 1785 | Cape Negro Harbour, E. | 400 | |
| Cameron, Alexander, Sr. | 1786 | Port Roseway River, W. | 200 | |
| Cameron, Alexander | 1786 | " " " " | 200 | |
| Cameron, Daniel | 1785 | Cape Negro Harbour, E. | 37 | |
| Cameron, Duncan | 1786 | Port Roseway River, W. | 200 | |
| Cameron, Evan | 1785 | Cape Negro Harbour, E. | 114 | |
| Cameron, John | 1786 | Port Roseway River, W. | 200 | |
| Campbell, Ezekiel | 1787 | Shelburne Township | 40 | Negro |
| Campbell, Oliver | 1785 | " " | ½&12rds. | |
| Campbell, Samuel | 1785 | " " | 25 | |
| Campbell, Samuel | 1788 | Cape Negro River | 1000 | |
| Carpenter, John | 1786 | Tusket River, S. | 200 | |
| Carr, John | 1788 | Green Harbour | 70 | |
| Carrol, Daniel | 1785 | Shelburne Township | 1 | |
| Channell, Scipio | 1787 | " " | 40 | Negro |
| Cheese, William | 1787 | " " | 40 | " |
| Christian, Sally | 1787 | " " | 20 | " |

108  PUBLIC ARCHIVES OF NOVA SCOTIA

| Name | Date | Situation | Acres | Origin or Rank |
|---|---|---|---|---|
| Church, Limuch | 1787 | Shelburne Township | 40 | Negro |
| Colethurst, Rachel | 1787 | " " | 40 | " |
| Connor, Philis | 1787 | " " | 40 | " |
| Cook, Henry | 1787 | " " | 40 | " |
| Cooling, Michael | 1788 | Green Harbour | 70 | |
| Cooper, John | 1787 | Shelburne Township | 40 | Negro |
| Corcorn, Matthew | 1788 | Green Harbour | 100 | |
| Cornbauld, Richard | 1786 | Tusket River, S. | 200 | |
| Couch, Henry | 1786 | Birch Town Creek | 100 | |
| Coughtery, Richard | 1786 | Port Roseway River, W. | 200 | |
| Cox, Edward | 1787 | Shelburne Township | 40 | Negro |
| Cox, Ned | 1787 | " " | 40 | " |
| Coyle, Patrick | 1788 | Green Harbour | 100 | |
| Craig, John | 1786 | Shelburne Township | 50 | |
| Creig, John | 1786 | Tusket River, S. | 200 | |
| Crocheron, Jane | 1786 | " " " | 200 | |
| Cromwell, Peggy | 1787 | Shelburne Township | 20 | Negro |
| Cunningham, Charles | 1786 | Tusket River, S. | 200 | |
| Cunningham, William | 1785 | Shelburne, near Common | 275 | |
| Dailey, John | 1786 | Shelburne Township | 200 | |
| Davis, Thomas | 1787 | " " | 40 | Negro |
| Davis, William | 1787 | " " | 40 | " |
| Day, Joseph | 1786 | Port Roseway River, W. | 200 | |
| Dean, Nicholas | 1788 | Green Harbour | 50 | |
| Dean, William | 1788 | " " | 50 | |
| Derkenderen, James | 1786 | Pell's Road | 200 | |
| Dickson, Absolum | 1787 | Shelburne Township | 40 | Negro |
| Dickson, Samuel | 1787 | " " | 40 | " |
| Dixon, Charles | 1787 | " " | 40 | " |
| Dole, James | 1786 | Tusket River South | 200 | |
| Dorris, John | 1786 | Pell's Road | 197 | |
| Driscoll, James | 1786 | Birch Town Creek | 100 | |
| Dunbar, George | 1786 | Port Roseway River, W. | 200 | |
| Duncan, James | 1786 | " " " " | 200 | |
| Dunfire, David | 1786 | Birch Town Creek | 100 | |
| Dunlop, Francis | 1788 | Green Harbour | 70 | |
| Dunscomb, Daniel | 1787 | Barrington Township | 750 | |
| Earl, Hanah | 1787 | Shelburne Township | 20 | Negro |
| Elliot, Edward | 1787 | " " | 40 | " |
| Elvin, Henry | 1786 | Birch Town Creek | 200 | |
| Evans, Thomas | 1787 | Shelburne Township | 40 | Negro |
| Farmer, Jupiter | 1787 | " " | 40 | " |
| Farrar, Benjamin | 1786 | Birch Town Creek | 180 | |
| Ferguson, John | 1785 | Cape Negro Harbour, E. | 150 | |
| Finlay, Jonathan | 1785 | " " " | 25 | |
| Fisher, George | 1786 | Shelburne Township | 200 | |
| Ford, Charles | 1787 | " " | 40 | Negro |
| Ford, Demps | 1787 | " " | 40 | " |
| Fox, Robert | 1786 | Pell's Road | 200 | |
| Francis, Peter see Robinson, Neil | 1787 | | | |
| Freeman, Thomas | 1787 | Shelburne Township | 39 | Negro |
| Freitz, Catherine | 1786 | Pell's Road | 160 | |
| Freitz, Peter | 1786 | " " | 200 | |
| French, Adolphus | 1786 | Tusket River, S. | 200 | |
| French, Adolphus | 1787 | Argyle Township | 200 | |
| French, John | 1787 | " " | 200 | |
| Frost, Benjamin | 1787 | Shelburne Township | 20 | Negro |
| Fullerton, Alexander | 1786 | Pell's Road | 178 | |
| Garnett, Bristol | 1787 | Shelburne Township | 40 | Negro |

## LOYALISTS AND LAND SETTLEMENT IN NOVA SCOTIA 109

| Name | Date | Situation | Acres | Origin or Rank |
|---|---|---|---|---|
| Gavel, John | 1786 | Tusket River, S. | 200 | |
| Gay, Alexander | 1786 | " " " | 200 | |
| George, Elizabeth | 1787 | Shelburne Township | 20 | Negro |
| Gernon, James | 1786 | Tusket River, S. | 200 | |
| Gibbons, John | 1787 | Shelburne Township | 40 | Negro |
| Givin, Harry | 1787 | " " | 20 | " |
| Glasgow, Jonathan | 1787 | " " | 40 | " |
| Goddard, Elias Kingston | 1786 | Port Roseway River | 200 | |
| Goddard, Lemuel, Sr. | 1786 | " " " | 400 | |
| Goddard, Lemuel, Jr. | 1786 | " " " | 200 | |
| Godfrey, Ely | 1787 | Shelburne Township | 40 | Negro |
| Godfrey, Jeffry | 1787 | " " | 13 | " |
| Gow, Robert | 1785 | Cape Negro Harbour, E. | 200 | |
| Grant, Alexander | 1786 | Port Roseway River, W. | 200 | |
| Grant, Alexander | 1788 | Green Harbour | 70 | |
| Grant, Peter | 1786 | Birch Town Creek | 200 | |
| Grath, James | 1788 | Green Harbour | 200 | |
| Gray, Harry | 1787 | Shelburne Township | 39 | Negro |
| Gray, Isaac | 1786 | Birch Town Creek | 200 | |
| Gray, Robert | 1786 | Port Roseway River, W. | 200 | |
| Gray, Robert | 1788 | Green Harbour | 220 | |
| Greenwood, William | 1785 | Cape Negro Harbour, E. | 235 | |
| Grosvenor, Benjamin | 1786 | Pell's Road | 193 | |
| Groves, John | 1788 | Green Harbour | 70 | |
| Hale, William | 1785 | Cape Negro Harbour, E. | 2 | |
| Hall, Richard | 1786 | Tusket River, S. | 200 | |
| Halstead, William | 1786 | " " " | 200 | |
| Hamilton, James | 1788 | Green Harbour | 50 | |
| Harden, Peter | 1787 | Shelburne Township | 40 | Negro |
| Harper, William | 1786 | Birch Town Creek | 200 | |
| Harris, Betsy see Rivers, Rachael | 1787 | | | |
| Harrison, Francis | 1787 | Shelburne Township | 40 | Negro |
| Harrison, Samuel | 1788 | Green Harbour | 500 | |
| Harvey, John | 1786 | Birch Town Creek | 200 | |
| Hatfield, James | 1787 | Argyle Township | 200 | |
| Hays, William | 1788 | Green Harbour | 50 | |
| Hazel, Abraham | 1787 | Shelburne Township | 40 | Negro |
| Hesieter, Herman | 1786 | Birch Town Creek | 250 | |
| Hector, James | 1787 | Shelburne Township | 40 | Negro |
| Henderson, John | 1785 | Cape Negro Harbour, E. | 28 | |
| Henderson, John | 1788 | Cape Negro River | 500 | |
| Henry, Elizabeth | 1787 | Shelburne Township | 36 | Negro |
| Henry, John | 1788 | Green Harbour | 70 | |
| Herbert, Willis | 1787 | Shelburne Township | 40 | Negro |
| Hervey, William | 1786 | Tusket River, S. | 200 | |
| Hetfield, Jacob | 1786 | " " " | 200 | |
| Hetfield, James | 1786 | " " " | 200 | |
| Hetfield, Job | 1786 | " " " | 200 | |
| Hewit, John | 1788 | Green Harbour | 500 | |
| Hickman, David | 1788 | " " | 70 | |
| Hildrith, Isaac | 1785 | Shelburne, near Common | 360 | |
| Hill, Joshua | 1786 | Pell's Road | 150 | |
| Hoalstead, Moses | 1787 | Shelburne Township | 40 | Negro |
| Holderness, William | 1788 | Green Harbour | 160 | |
| Holmes, Joseph | 1786 | Shelburne Township | 200 | |
| Holstead, James | 1787 | " " | 20 | Negro |
| Holstead, William | 1787 | Argyle Township | 200 | |
| Horton, Jonathan | 1786 | Tusket River, S. | 200 | |
| Howard, Ansel | 1787 | Shelburne Township | 40 | Negro |
| Humphreys, James | 1786 | Tusket River, S. | 200 | |
| Huskins, Job | 1788 | Green Harbour | 140 | |

## 110  PUBLIC ARCHIVES OF NOVA SCOTIA

| Name | Date | Situation | Acres | Origin or Rank |
|---|---|---|---|---|
| Huskins, John | 1788 | Green Harbour | 250 | |
| Hutchins, Mathew | 1787 | Argyle Township | 200 | |
| Innis, Stephen | 1786 | Pell's Road | 200 | |
| Jackson, John | 1787 | Shelburne Township | 40 | Negro |
| Jackson, Judeth | 1787 | " " | 20 | " |
| Jappie, Paul | 1785 | Cape Negro Harbour, E. | 5 | |
| Jenkins, Richard | 1788 | Green Harbour | 180 | |
| Jenner, Thomas | 1785 | Cape Negro Harbour, E. | 15 | |
| Johnson, Diana | 1787 | Shelburne Township | 20 | Negro |
| Johnson, George | 1787 | " " | 20 | " |
| Johnson, James | 1787 | " " | 40 | " |
| Johnson, John | 1786 | Pell's Road | 197 | |
| Johnson, Levin | 1787 | Shelburne Township | 40 | Negro |
| Johnson, Lucas | 1785 | Cape Negro Harbour, E. | 45 | |
| Johnson, Peter | 1787 | Shelburne Township | 35 | Negro |
| Johnson, Prince | 1787 | " " | 40 | " |
| Johnson, Tobias | 1787 | " " | 40 | " |
| Johnson, Tobias | 1787 | " " | 40 | " |
| Johnson, Thomas | 1787 | " " | 40 | " |
| Johnston, George | 1786 | Pell's Road | 245 | |
| Johnston, Patience | 1786 | " " | 200 | |
| Jones, Abraham, Jr. | 1786 | Tusket River, S. | 200 | |
| Jones, Abraham, Sr. | 1786 | " " " | 200 | |
| Jones, Francis | 1787 | Shelburne Township | 40 | Negro |
| Jones, John | 1787 | " " | 40 | " |
| Jones, Shadrick | 1787 | " " | 40 | " |
| Jones, William | 1786 | Birch Town Creek | 100 | |
| Jorden, Luke | 1787 | Shelburne Township | 40 | Negro |
| Joy, John | 1787 | " " | 40 | " |
| Keeley, John | 1786 | Birch Town Creek | 200 | |
| Kelly, Barnard | 1788 | Green Harbour | 50 | |
| Kelly, John | 1788 | " " | 50 | |
| Kelly, Moses | 1787 | Shelburne Township | 40 | Negro |
| Kelly, Thomas | 1786 | Birch Town Creek | 200 | |
| Ketfield, Nathaniel | 1786 | " " " | 100 | |
| King, Isaac | 1785 | Cape Negro Harbour, E. | 150 | |
| King, John | 1786 | Tusket River, S. | 200 | |
| Kirk, Samuel | 1784 | Shelburne District | 200 | |
| Kirk, Samuel | 1787 | Argyle Township | 200 | |
| Knowland, Christopher | 1788 | Green Harbour | 70 | |
| Lacey, James | 1786 | Tusket River, S. | 200 | |
| Lamb, William | 1788 | Green Harbour | 140 | |
| Lamey, Michael | 1785 | Cape Negro Harbour, E. | 60 | |
| Langley, Jane | 1787 | Shelburne Township | 30 | Negro |
| Lansfield, Attained Anthony | 1788 | Green Harbour | 180 | |
| Laroza, William | 1786 | Tusket River, S. | 200 | |
| Laurance, Richard | 1787 | Shelburne Township | 20 | Negro |
| Lawrence, Nicholas | 1786 | Tusket River, S. | 200 | |
| Lawrence, Philip | 1787 | Shelburne Township | 10 | Negro |
| Lawson, Edward | 1787 | " " | 20 | " |
| Lawson, Jacob | 1787 | " " | 20 | ' |
| Lawson, Joseph | 1787 | " " | 20 | " |
| Lawson, Solomon | 1787 | " " | 40 | " |
| Lawton, Richard | 1787 | " " | 40 | " |
| Laveander, Robert | 1786 | Port Roseway River, W. | 200 | |
| Leckie, Alexander, Jr. | 1786 | Tusket River, S. | 200 | |
| LeDrew, Margaret | 1786 | Pell's Road | 130 | |
| Lent, Abraham | 1786 | Tusket River, S. | 200 | |
| Lent, James | 1786 | " " " | 200 | |

LOYALISTS AND LAND SETTLEMENT IN NOVA SCOTIA 111

| Name | Date | Situation | Acres | Origin or Rank |
|---|---|---|---|---|
| Leonard, James | 1787 | Argyle Township | 150 | |
| Leonard, John | 1786 | Tusket River South | 200 | |
| Leonard, Thomas | 1786 | " " " | 200 | |
| Leonard, William | 1786 | " " " | 200 | |
| Lewis, David | 1786 | " " " | 200 | |
| Lippincott, Jacob | 1786 | " " " | 200 | |
| Lippincott, James | 1786 | " " " | 200 | |
| Low, Ceser | 1787 | Shelburne Township | 40 | Negro |
| Lowe, Charles | 1786 | Tusket River, S. | 200 | |
| Lowe, John | 1788 | Green Harbour | 50 | |
| Lyman, Oliver | 1786 | Pell's Road | 200 | |
| Mabey, Isaac | 1786 | Tusket River, S. | 200 | |
| McAlpine, John | 1788 | Green Harbour | 100 | |
| McAuslen, Alexander | 1786 | Tusket River, S. | 200 | |
| McCarty, John | 1786 | " " " | 200 | |
| McDonald, John | 1788 | Green Harbour | 70 | |
| McDonald, Soirl | 1785 | Cape Negro Harbour, E. | 35 | |
| McEwan, John | 1788 | Green Harbour | 200 | |
| McGregor, Donald | 1788 | " " | 100 | |
| McIlroy, Hugh | 1786 | Birch Town Creek | 100 | |
| McKay, John | 1787 | Shelburne Township | 40 | Negro |
| McKenzie, John | 1786 | Pell's Road | 187 | |
| McKerlie, John see McPhail, John | 1789 | | | |
| McKinney, John & Sons | 1785 | Cape Negro Harbour, E. | 500 | |
| McLeod, Daniel | 1788 | Green Harbour | 140 | |
| McLeod, Donald | 1786 | Tusket River, S. | 200 | |
| McLeod, John | 1786 | " " " | 200 | |
| McNeill, James | 1786 | Birch Town Creek | 200 | |
| McNeill, John | 1786 | " " " | 100 | |
| McPhail, John and McKerlie, John | 1789 | Sable River, N. E. | 500 | |
| McPhie, John | 1786 | Port Roseway River, W. | 200 | |
| McSparrow, Isaac | 1786 | Birch Town Creek | 200 | |
| Mahan, John | 1788 | Green Harbour | 50 | |
| Mahan, Henry | 1786 | Tusket River, S. | 200 | |
| Mahan, Timothy | 1786 | Pell's Road | 202 | |
| Mahan, Timothy | 1786 | " " | 224 | |
| Mahon, Thomas | 1788 | Green Harbour | 250 | |
| Marks, Conrad | 1786 | Pell's Road | 88 | |
| Marsh, Joseph | 1786 | Tusket River, South | 200 | |
| Marsh, Thomas | 1786 | " " " | 200 | |
| Marston, Benjamin | 1785 | Shelburne Township | 1 & 20 | rds. |
| Mann, Samuel | 1786 | Tusket River, S. | 200 | |
| Mason, Samuel | 1786 | Birch Town Creek | 200 | |
| Mather, Andrew | 1786 | Port Roseway River, W. | 200 | |
| Michler, Daniel | 1786 | Pell's Road | 226 | |
| Middleton, Thomas | 1786 | Tusket River, S. | 200 | |
| Miller, Doublin | 1787 | Shelburne Township | 20 | Negro |
| Miller, James | 1785 | Shelburne near Common | 210 | |
| Miller, Richard | 1787 | Shelburne Township | 40 | Negro |
| Miller, William | 1788 | Green Harbour | 50 | |
| Mills, Ranty | 1787 | Shelburne Township | 40 | Negro |
| Mills, Thomas | 1787 | " " | 40 | " |
| Mitchell, Thomas | 1788 | Green Harbour | 140 | |
| Moesley, George | 1786 | Birch Town Creek | 200 | |
| Molineux, William | 1785 | Cape Negro Harbour, E. | 210 | |
| Moluck, William | 1786 | Tusket River, S. | 200 | |
| Monnon, Edward | 1788 | Green Harbour | 50 | |
| Moore, Lewis | 1787 | Shelburne Township | 20 | Negro |
| Moore, Samuel | 1787 | " " | 40 | Negro |

## 112 PUBLIC ARCHIVES OF NOVA SCOTIA

| Name | Date | Situation | Acres | Origin or Rank |
|---|---|---|---|---|
| Morant, John | | | | |
| see Baley, Charles | 1787 | | | |
| Morris, Nathaniel | 1786 | Port Roseway River, W. | 200 | |
| Morris, Noah | 1786 | Shelburne Township | 200 | |
| Morris, Robert | 1786 | Tusket River, S. | 200 | |
| Morris, Robert | 1787 | Shelburne Township | 40 | Negro |
| Morris, William | 1786 | Port Roseway River, W. | 200 | |
| Mossman, Susannah | 1787 | Shelburne Township | 20 | Negro |
| Munn, Alexander | 1786 | Port Roseway River, W. | 200 | |
| Munn, Samuel | 1786 | Pell's Road | 193 | |
| Murray, Moses | 1787 | Shelburne Township | 20 | Negro |
| Musgrave, William and Sparling, Peter | 1785 | Cape Negro Harbour, E. | 97 | |
| Newcomb, James | 1787 | Shelburne Township | 40 | Negro |
| Nicholson, Caleb | 1785 | Cape Negro Harbour, E. | 250 | |
| Norman, Joseph | 1786 | Pell's Road | 210 | |
| Nutter, Valentine | 1786 | Tusket River, S. | 200 | |
| O'Neal, William | 1787 | Shelburne Township | 27 | Negro |
| Omand, John | 1785 | Cape Negro Harbour, E. | 37 | |
| Palmer, Lewis | 1786 | Pell's Road | 200 | |
| Pandarvis, Lewis | 1787 | Shelburne Township | 40 | Negro |
| Parclay, Daniel | 1787 | " " | 40 | " |
| Patrick, Thomas | 1787 | " " | 40 | " |
| Patterson, Robert | 1786 | Tusket River, S. | 200 | |
| Paul, John | 1787 | Shelburne Township | 40 | Negro |
| Peck, John | 1785 | Cape Negro Harbour, E. | 28 | |
| Pell, Joshua | 1785 | Shelburne Township | 5½ | |
| Perkins, Cato | 1787 | " " | 40 | Negro |
| Perry, Prince | 1787 | " " | 40 | " |
| Perry, Samuel | 1785 | Cape Negro Harbour, E. | 375 | |
| Perry, Samuel, Jr. | 1785 | " " " " | 65 | |
| Perry, Silas | 1785 | " " " " | 55 | |
| Perry, Stephen | 1785 | " " " " | 55 | |
| Perry, Thomas | 1785 | " " " " | 305 | |
| Peters, Stephen | 1787 | Shelburne Township | 20 | Negro |
| Pharo, Peter | 1787 | " " | 40 | " |
| Phripp, Daniel | 1787 | " " | 40 | " |
| Pool, Benjamin | 1787 | " " | 29 | " |
| Post, Isaac | 1786 | Port Roseway River, W. | 200 | |
| Potts, John | 1786 | Shelburne Township | 300 | |
| Prentice, Peter | 1787 | " " | 20 | Negro |
| Price, Joseph | 1786 | Tusket River, S. | 200 | |
| Price, Joseph | 1787 | Argyle Township | 200 | |
| Prior, John | 1787 | Shelburne Township | 40 | Negro |
| Propyt, Richard | 1787 | " " | 40 | " |
| Raimant, Dover | 1787 | " " | 20 | " |
| Rain, James | 1786 | " " | 200 | |
| Ramsey, Elenor see Baley, George | 1787 | | | |
| Raven, Joseph | 1787 | " " | 40 | Negro |
| Ray, James | 1787 | " " | 40 | " |
| Reach, Kenneth | 1786 | Tusket River, S. | 200 | |
| Read, Moses | 1786 | " " " | 200 | |
| Redman, Michael | 1786 | " " " | 200 | |
| Reid, James | 1787 | Shelburne Township | 40 | Negro |
| Reilly, Paul | 1785 | Cape Negro Harbour, E. | 25 | |
| Reilly, Terrance | 1786 | Tusket River, S. | 200 | |
| Richards, Nathaniel | 1786 | " " " | 200 | |
| Rick, Christopher | 1787 | Shelburne Township | 40 | Negro |
| Right, Caithness | 1787 | " " | 20 | " |
| Rippon, Austin | 1787 | " " | 20 | " |

LOYALISTS AND LAND SETTLEMENT IN NOVA SCOTIA 113

| Name | Date | Situation | Acres | Origin or Rank |
|---|---|---|---|---|
| Rivers, Rachael and Harris, Betsy | 1787 | Shelburne Township | 40 | Negro |
| Roach, Richard | 1787 | " " | 40 | " |
| Robinson, Neil and Francis, Peter | 1787 | " " | 40 | " |
| Robinson, Prince | 1787 | " " | 40 | " |
| Robinson, William | 1787 | " " | 40 | " |
| Rose, John | 1786 | Pell's Road | 220 | |
| Ross, Friend | 1785 | Cape Negro Harbour, E. | 53 | |
| Ross, Friend | 1786 | Port Roseway River, W. | 200 | |
| Russell, Hannah | 1787 | Shelburne Township | 40 | Negro |
| St. Jago, John | 1787 | " " | 40 | " |
| Salsberry, John | 1787 | " " | 40 | " |
| Salsberry, Peter | 1787 | " " | 40 | " |
| Sanders, David | 1787 | " ". | 40 | " |
| Sanders, Thomas | 1787 | " " | 40 | " |
| Savage, Abraham | 1786 | Pell's Road | 200 | |
| Sawyer, Berry | 1787 | Shelburne Township | 40 | Negro |
| Schneider, George Philip | 1786 | Pell's Road | 226 | |
| Seaburne, John | 1787 | Shelburne Township | 40 | Negro |
| Seaman, John | 1786 | Tusket River, S. | 200 | |
| Sellers, Archibald | 1786 | Port Roseway River, W. | 200 | |
| Shalter, Isaac | 1787 | Shelburne Township | 40 | Negro |
| Sharp, John | 1786 | Port Roseway River, W. | 200 | |
| Shelleman, John | 1786 | Birch Town Creek | 100 | |
| Shephard, Thomas | 1787 | Shelburne Township | 40 | Negro |
| Sheppard, Benjamin | 1787 | " " | 40 | " |
| Shields, Thomas | 1787 | " " | 40 | " |
| Sloan, Richard | 1787 | " " | 40 | " |
| Smith, Elisha and Smith, Theodore | 1785 | Cape Negro Harbour, E. | 505 | |
| Smith, Job | 1786 | Tusket River, S. | 200 | |
| Smith, Joseph | 1785 | Cape Negro Harbour, E. | 250 | |
| Smith, Luke | 1787 | Shelburne Township | 27 | Negro |
| Smith, Peter J. | 1786 | Pell's Road | 200 | |
| Smith, Sandy | 1787 | Shelburne Township | 20 | Negro |
| Smith, Theodore see Smith, Elisha | 1785 | | | |
| Smith, William | 1787 | " " | 40 | " |
| Snowball, Nathaniel, Sr. | 1787 | " " | 40 | " |
| Sorrell, William | 1786 | Tusket River, S. | 200 | |
| Sorrels, Henry | 1786 | " " " | 200 | |
| Sparling, Peter see Musgrave. William | 1785 | | | |
| Spurr, Cyres | 1787 | Shelburne Township | 40 | Negro |
| Steel, Patrick | 1786 | Birch Town Creek | 200 | |
| Stephanis, Gothelf | 1788 | Green Harbour | 50 | |
| Stevens, Abraham | 1785 | Shelburne Township | ⅛ and 12 rds | |
| Steward, James | 1787 | " " | 40 | Negro |
| Stoakes, James | 1786 | Birch Town Creek | 200 | |
| Stokes, James | 1786 | Pell's Road | 200 | |
| Stout, David | 1785 | Cape Negro Har., E. | 250 | |
| Strahan, James | 1786 | Birch Town Creek | 100 | |
| Strumm, Jacob | 1786 | Pell's Road | 197 | |
| Stubbords, Matthew | 1788 | Green Harbour | 70 | |
| Sullivan, Bartholomew | 1785 | Shelburne Township | ½ and 16 rds | |
| Sutherland, Daniel | 1785 | Cape Negro Harbour, E. | 150 | |
| Sullivan, Demps | 1787 | Shelburne Township | 40 | Negro |
| Swaine, Ephraim | 1785 | Cape Negro Harbour, E. | 155 | |
| Swain, John | 1785 | " " " | 159 | |
| Taskew, Nathan | 1787 | Shelburne Township | 40 | Negro |
| Taylor, John | 1787 | " " | 40 | " |

# 114 PUBLIC ARCHIVES OF NOVA SCOTIA

| Name | Date | Situation | Acres | Origin or Rank |
|---|---|---|---|---|
| Temple, John | 1786 | Tusket River South | 200 | |
| Tench, John | 1786 | " " " | 200 | |
| Thomas, Amos | 1787 | Shelburne Township | 40 | Negro |
| Thomas, John | 1787 | " " | 30 | " |
| Thompson, Charles | 1787 | " " | 40 | " |
| Thompson, James | 1787 | " " | 40 | " |
| Thompson, Jane | 1787 | " " | 40 | " |
| Thomson, John | 1785 | Shelburne near Common | 100 | |
| Timpson, Benjamin | 1788 | Green Harbour | 50 | |
| Tocker, Jacob | 1786 | Tusket River, S. | 200 | |
| Toney, Jane | 1787 | Shelburne Township | 20 | Negro |
| Tooker, Jacob | 1787 | Argyle Township | 150 | |
| Townsend, Benjamin | 1786 | Tusket River, S. | 200 | |
| Townsend, Jacob | 1786 | " " " | 200 | |
| Townsend, Richard, Jr. | 1786 | " " " | 200 | |
| Townsend, Richard, Sr. | 1786 | " " " | 200 | |
| Townsend, Thomas | 1786 | " " " | 200 | |
| Townsend, Timothy | 1786 | | 200 | |
| Trowel, Joseph | 1787 | Shelburne Township | 40 | Negro |
| Truet, Anthony | 1787 | " " | 40 | " |
| Truin, Henry | 1787 | " " | 40 | " |
| Tulloch, Robert | 1786 | Birch Town Creek | 200 | |
| Tully, Christopher | 1786 | Port Roseway River, W. | 200 | |
| Tunnercliffe, Joseph | 1786 | Pell's Road | 175 | |
| Turnbull, Robert | 1785 | Cape Negro Harbour, E. | 40 | |
| Turnbull, Walter | 1785 | " " " " | 33 | |
| Turner, Nathaniel | 1787 | Shelburne Township | 40 | Negro |
| Turner, Robert | 1787 | " " | 40 | " |
| | | | | |
| Upham, John | 1787 | " " | 33 | " |
| | | | | |
| Van Buskirk, Abraham | 1786 | Tusket River, South | 200 | Lt. Col. |
| Van Tuyle, Dennis | 1787 | Argyle Township | 200 | |
| Van Tuyle, Dennis | 1786 | Tusket River, S. | 200 | |
| Venters, London | 1787 | Shelburne Township | 40 | Negro |
| Vernon, Nathaniel | 1786 | Pell's Road | 200 | |
| | | | | |
| Waistcoat, Joseph | 1787 | Shelburne Township | 40 | Negro |
| Warden, George | 1786 | Port Roseway River, W. | 200 | |
| Waring, John | 1787 | Shelburne Township | 40 | Negro |
| Washington, Harry | 1787 | " " | 40 | " |
| Watson, John | 1788 | Green Harbour | 50 | |
| Wells, William | 1787 | Shelburne Township | 40 | Negro |
| Welsh, James | 1786 | Port Roseway River, W. | 200 | |
| Welsh, Thomas | 1788 | Green Harbour | 156 | |
| White, Aaron | 1786 | Tusket River, S. | 200 | |
| White, Elizabeth | 1787 | Shelburne Township | 20 | Negro |
| White, Samuel | 1787 | " " | 40 | " |
| Whitten, Samuel | 1787 | " " | 40 | " |
| Wicks, Peter | 1787 | " " | 40 | " |
| Wilkie, John | 1786 | Port Roseway River, W. | 200 | |
| Wilkins, Toney | 1787 | Shelburne Township | 40 | Negro |
| Wilkinson, Charles | 1787 | " " | 40 | " |
| Wilkinson, Moses | 1787 | " " | 40 | " |
| Williams, Arthur | 1786 | Tusket River, S. | 200 | |
| Williams, Billy | 1787 | Shelburne Township | 40 | Negro |
| Williams, Cesar | 1787 | " " | 34 | " |
| Williams, Jacob | 1786 | Tusket River, S. | 200 | |
| Williams, John | 1786 | " " " | 200 | |
| Williams, John | 1787 | Argyle Township | 200 | |
| Williameon, William | 1786 | Tusket River, S. | 200 | |
| Willoughby, Edward | 1787 | Shelburne Township | 40 | Negro |
| Willson, Luke | 1787 | " " | 40 | " |
| Wilson, Andrew | 1786 | Tusket River, S. | 200 | |

LOYALISTS AND LAND SETTLEMENT IN NOVA SCOTIA 115

| Name | Date | Situation | Acres | Origin or Rank |
|---|---|---|---|---|
| Winants, John | 1786 | Tusket River, S. | 200 | |
| Wise, George | 1787 | Shelburne Township | 40 | Negro |
| Withers, Michael | 1788 | Green Harbour | 50 | |
| Wood, Francis | 1786 | Tusket River, S. | 200 | |
| Woods, Richard | 1788 | Green Harbour | 100 | |
| Worth, Benjamin | 1788 | " " | 200 | |
| Worthley, John | 1786 | Tusket River, S. | 200 | |
| Worthley, John | 1787 | Argyle Township | 200 | |
| Wright, James Nichols | 1786 | Pell's Road | 219 | |
| York, Charlotte | 1787 | Shelburne Township | 40 | Negro |
| York, Ishmeal | 1787 | " " | 40 | " |
| Young, Edward | 1786 | " " | 200 | |
| Young, James | 1787 | " " | 40 | " |
| Young, William | 1788 | Green Harbour | 50 | |

## Shelburne County
### ESCHEATS

| Name | Date | Situation | Acres | Esch'd | Origin or Rank |
|---|---|---|---|---|---|
| Alexander, Thomas | 1785 | Port Roseway, W. | 250 | 1819 | |
| Alstine, Joseph | 1785 | " " " | 250 | 1819 | |
| Anderson, John | 1785 | Cape Negro River | 300 | 1819 | |
| Antonio, John | 1785 | Shelburne Township | 200 | 1819 | |
| Apple, Christopher | 1785 | " " | 100 | 1819 | |
| Armour, William | 1785 | Cape Negro River | 200 | 1819 | |
| Ayton, George | 1784 | Seal Island | 1000 | 1821 | |
| Barclay, Andrew | 1785 | Port Roseway, W. | 500 | 1819 | Captain |
| Bean, John | 1785 | Cape Negro River | 200 (100 esch'd) | 1819 | |
| Beattie, George | 1785 | Port Roseway, W. | 500 | 1819 | |
| Black, William | 1785 | " " " | 250 | 1819 | |
| Blight, Richard | 1785 | Shelburne Township | 100 | 1819 | |
| Bode, Charles | 1785 | " " | 200 | 1819 | |
| Boyd, James | 1785 | " " | 100 | 1819 | |
| Boye, Nicholas | 1785 | " " | 200 | 1819 | |
| Brigford, Robert | 1785 | Cape Negro River | 200 | 1819 | |
| Brissley, Thomas | 1785 | " " " | 100 | 1819 | |
| Brown, John | 1785 | Shelburne Township | 100 | 1819 | |
| Brown, Samuel | 1785 | " " | 100 | 1819 | |
| Brown, William | 1785 | Cape Negro River | 200 | 1819 | |
| Burke, Thomas | 1785 | Shelburne Township | 100 | 1819 | |
| Campbell, Archibald | 1785 | " " | 100 | 1819 | |
| Carley, Thomas | 1785 | " " | 100 | 1819 | |
| Carnes, George | 1785 | " " | 100 | 1819 | |
| Carton, Daniel | 1785 | " " | 100 | 1819 | |
| Castle, William | 1784 | Port Roseway River | 501 | 1819 | |
| Chisholm, Andrew | 1785 | Cape Negro River | 200 | 1819 | |
| Christie, Alexander | 1785 | " " " | 100 | 1819 | |
| Clarke, Hugh, Jr. | 1785 | " " " | 100 | 1819 | |
| Clarke, Hugh, Sr. | 1785 | " " " | 100 | 1819 | |
| Climpson, William | 1785 | " " " | 100 | 1819 | |

116   PUBLIC ARCHIVES OF NOVA SCOTIA

| Name | Date | Situation | Acres | Esch'd | Origin or Rank |
|---|---|---|---|---|---|
| Colquhoun, Peter | 1785 | Shelburne Township | 200 | 1819 | |
| Conlin, Henry | 1785 | " " | 100 | 1819 | |
| Connoly, James | 1785 | " " | 100 | 1819 | |
| Connor, Hugh | 1785 | Cape Negro River | 100 | 1819 | |
| Connor, Mary | 1785 | Shelburne Township | 200 | 1819 | |
| Cook, Alexander | 1785 | " " | 200 | 1819 | |
| Cooper, William | 1785 | Port Roseway, W. | 300 | 1819 | |
| Crow, William | 1785 | Cape Negro River | 200 | 1819 | |
| Cummins, James | 1785 | " " " | 200 | 1819 | |
| Dale, Robert | 1785 | Shelburne Township | 200 | 1819 | |
| Dole, James | 1784 | Port Roseway River | 501 | 1819 | |
| Donaldson, James | 1785 | " " W. | 350 | 1819 | |
| Dove, Alexander | 1785 | " " " | 250 | 1819 | |
| Dowde, Charles | 1785 | Shelburne Township | 100 | 1819 | |
| Drum, Philip | 1785 | " " | 100 | 1819 | |
| Dryer, John | 1785 | " " | 200 | 1819 | |
| Dunahow, Gilbert | 1785 | Cape Negro River | 100 | 1819 | |
| Dunshee, John | 1785 | Port Roseway, W. | 250 | 1819 | |
| Early, Thomas | 1785 | Shelburne Township | 100 | 1819 | |
| Ellis, James | 1785 | Port Roseway, W. | 250 | 1819 | |
| Enslow, Isaac | 1785 | Shelburne Township | 200 | 1819 | |
| Ettrer, John Christopher | 1785 | Cape Negro River | 100 | 1819 | |
| Fegan, William | 1785 | Shelburne Township | 100 | 1819 | |
| Fitzimons, Henry | 1785 | Cape Negro River | 100 | 1819 | |
| Forbes, Alexander | 1785 | " " " | 100 | 1819 | |
| Fraser, Elizabeth | 1785 | " " " | 100 | 1819 | |
| Fraser, Francis Lovatt | 1785 | " " ' | 100 | 1819 | |
| Fraser, John | 1785 | " " " | 100 | 1819 | |
| Fraser, Thomas | 1785 | " " " | 100 | 1819 | |
| Gardonier, Jacob | 1785 | Port Roseway, W. | 350 | 1819 | |
| Gibson, Thomas | 1785 | Shelburne Township | 100 | 1819 | |
| Glass, John | 1785 | Cape Negro River | 100 | 1819 | |
| Goodick, Alexander | 1785 | Shelburne Township | 200 | 1819 | |
| Gordon, John | 1785 | Port Roseway, W. | 200 | 1819 | |
| Gorman, Edmund | 1785 | " " " | 350 | 1819 | |
| Grier, Charles | 1785 | Shelburne Township | 200 | 1819 | |
| Guyon, Peter | 1785 | " " | 200 | 1819 | |
| Hall, Henry | 1785 | " " | 100 | 1819 | |
| Hall, James | 1785 | " " | 100 | 1819 | |
| Hay, John | 1785 | " " | 100 | 1819 | |
| Henley, Thomas | 1785 | " " | 100 | 1819 | |
| Hill, Robert | 1785 | " " | 100 | 1819 | |
| Hogg, Alexander | 1785 | " " | 200 | 1819 | |
| Hoose, John | 1785 | " " | 200 | 1819 | |
| Huston, Robert | 1785 | Cape Negro River | 100 | 1819 | |
| Irwin, John | 1785 | Shelburne Township | 200 | 1819 | |
| Jackson, John | 1785 | Cape Negro River | 100 | 1819 | |
| Jefferson, John | 1785 | Shelburne Township | 200 | 1819 | |
| Johnson, Robert | 1785 | " " | 100 | 1819 | |
| Jones, John | 1785 | Cape Negro River | 200 | 1819 | |
| Jordan, Jeremiah | 1785 | " " " | 100 | 1819 | |
| Kearny, Mary | 1785 | Shelburne Township | 100 | 1819 | |
| Keisling, George | 1785 | " " | 200 | 1819 | |
| Kennedy, Hugh | 1785 | " " | 100 | 1819 | |
| Kennedy, John | 1785 | " " | 100 | 1819 | |

# LOYALISTS AND LAND SETTLEMENT IN NOVA SCOTIA 117

| Name | Date | Situation | Acres | Esch'd | Origin or Rank |
|---|---|---|---|---|---|
| Kinley, Thomas | 1785 | Cape Negro River | 100 | 1819 | |
| Kirt, [Kirk] John | 1785 | Shelburne Township | 100 | 1819 | |
| | | | | | |
| Langdon, John | 1785 | " " | 100 | 1819 | |
| Langton, James | 1785 | " " | 100 | 1819 | |
| Leybourn, Robert | 1785 | " " | 100 | 1819 | |
| Loughran, Hugh | 1785 | " " | 200 | 1819 | |
| Louthan, James | 1785 | " " " | 100 | 1819 | |
| Lownds, John | 1784 | Port Roseway River | 501 | 1819 | |
| Lyle, John | 1785 | Cape Negro River | 200 | 1819 | |
| Lynch, Peter | 1784 | Port Roseway River | 501 | 1819 | |
| | | | | | |
| McCandry, Alexander | 1785 | Shelburne Township | 100 | 1819 | |
| McCoy, Angus | 1785 | Cape Negro River | 200 | 1819 | |
| McDonald, Alexander | 1785 | " " " | 100 | 1819 | |
| McDonald, Alexander | 1785 | Port Roseway, W. | 450 | 1819 | |
| McDonald, Neil | 1785 | " " " | 250 | 1819 | |
| MacKay, Thomas | 1785 | Cape Negro River | 200 | 1819 | |
| McLachlan [McLaughlin] Fardy | 1785 | Shelburne Township | 100 | 1819 | |
| McLean, James | 1785 | Port Roseway, W. | 250 | 1819 | |
| McLean, John | 1785 | Cape Negro River | 100 | 1819 | |
| McMisker, Neil | 1785 | " " " | 100 | 1819 | |
| McNab, Alexander | 1785 | Shelburne Township | 200 | 1819 | |
| McNab, Donald | 1785 | Cape Negro River | 100 | 1819 | |
| Maden, Michael | 1785 | " " " | 100 | 1819 | |
| Mahannah, Jeremiah | 1785 | " " " | 100 | 1819 | |
| Marshall, Robert | 1785 | Shelburne Township | 100 | 1819 | |
| Martin, John | 1785 | " " | 100 | 1819 | |
| Martin, William | 1785 | Cape Negro River | 100 | 1819 | |
| Mazie, Thomas | 1785 | " " " | 200 | 1819 | |
| Miller, Frederick | 1785 | Shelburne Township | 100 | 1819 | |
| Miller, James | 1785 | Cape Negro River | 200 | 1819 | |
| Miller, John | 1784 | Port Roseway River | 501 | 1819 | |
| Miller, Robert | 1785 | Cape Negro River | 100 | 1819 | |
| Mills, Nathaniel | 1785 | Port Roseway, W. | 500 | 1819 | |
| Monro, John | 1785 | Cape Negro River | 200 | 1819 | |
| Morrison, George | 1785 | Port Roseway, W. | 250 | 1819 | |
| *Mullen, John | 1785 | Shelburne Township | 100 | 1819 | |
| Mulligan, Peter | 1785 | Shelburne Township | 100 | 1819 | |
| Murphy, Arthur | 1785 | " " | 200 | 1819 | |
| Murphy, Michael | 1785 | Cape Negro River | 100 | 1819 | |
| Murray, Daniel | 1785 | Shelburne Township | 200 | 1819 | |
| | | | | | |
| Neil, Sebastian | 1785 | " " | 200 | 1819 | |
| Nelson, James | 1785 | Cape Negro River | 100 | 1819 | |
| Nutter, Valentine | 1784 | Port Roseway River | 501 | 1819 | |
| | | | | | |
| Olenberg, Philip | 1785 | Shelburne Township | 200 | 1819 | |
| O'Neal, John, Jr. | 1785 | Port Roseway, W. | 250 | 1819 | |
| O'Neal, John, Sr. | 1785 | " " " | 350 | 1819 | |
| Orr, John | 1785 | Cape Negro River | 100 | 1819 | |
| Oxford, Peter | 1785 | Shelburne Township | 100 | 1819 | |
| | | | | | |
| Parish, William | 1785 | Cape Negro River | 100 | 1819 | |
| Patton, John | 1785 | Port Roseway, W. | 500 | 1819 | |
| Peachey, Richard | 1785 | Cape Negro River | 100 | 1819 | |
| Pegan, William | 1785 | Shelburne Township | 100 | 1819 | |
| Pendergrass, Mathew | 1784 | Port Roseway River | 501 | 1819 | |
| Pendergrass, Thomas | 1784 | " " " | 501 | 1819 | |

\* Of the grant to John Mullen and others, (10,900 acres, Shelburne Township), all land was escheated except that held by Donald and Hugh McKay. They were not original grantees, and it is not known from whom they secured their lands. So all the grantees are listed in the escheats. In making a list of the total number of escheats, therefore, two must be subtracted.

| Name | Date | Situation | Acres | Esch'd | Origin or Rank |
|---|---|---|---|---|---|
| Perry, John | 1785 | Port Roseway River | 500 | 1819 | |
| Phillips, John | 1785 | Cape Negro River | 100 | 1819 | |
| Phillips, Matthew | 1785 | Shelburne Township | 100 | 1819 | |
| Pike, Benjamin | 1785 | Cape Negro River | 100 | 1819 | |
| Prentice, Archibald | 1785 | " " " | 100 | 1819 | |
| Punnel, Charles | 1785 | " " " | 100 | 1819 | |
| Rapp, John | 1785 | Shelburne Township | 200 | 1819 | |
| Rene, John | 1785 | " " | 200 | 1819 | |
| Rex, George | 1785 | Cape Negro River | 200 | 1819 | |
| Richie [Ritchie] John | 1785 | " " " | 200 | 1819 | |
| Robertson, John | 1785 | Shelburne Township | 200 | 1819 | |
| Robinson, William | 1785 | Port Roseway, W. | 200 | 1819 | |
| Ross, Malcolm | 1785 | Cape Negro River | 200 | 1819 | |
| Selkrig, Alexander | 1785 | Port Roseway, W. | 300 | 1819 | |
| Shackleton, Mark | 1785 | Shelburne Township | 100 | 1819 | |
| Shakespear, David | 1784 | Port Roseway, W. | 501 | 1819 | |
| Shanley, William | 1785 | Cape Negro River | 100 | 1819 | |
| Shedden, John | 1785 | " " " | 200 | 1819 | |
| Shene, Donald | 1785 | " ' " | 100 | 1819 | |
| Sherry, Francis | 1785 | Shelburne Township | 100 | 1819 | |
| Smithers, James | 1785 | Port Roseway, W. | 500 | 1819 | |
| Standford, Richard | 1785 | Shelburne Township | 100 | 1819 | |
| Sullivan, Patrick | 1785 | " " | 200 | 1819 | |
| Swords, James | 1785 | Port Roseway, W. | 250 | 1819 | |
| Swords, Thomas | 1785 | " " " | 250 | 1819 | |
| Taylor, Margaret | 1785 | Shelburne Township | 100 | 1819 | |
| Taylor, Peter | 1785 | Cape Negro River | 200 | 1819 | |
| Thompson, Ezekiel | 1785 | " " " | 100 | 1819 | |
| Thompson, William | 1785 | " " ' | 200 | 1819 | |
| Thurston, Robert | 1785 | " " " | 100 | 1819 | |
| Torrance[Forrance]Hugh | 1785 | Shelburne Township | 200 | 1819 | |
| Turner, Joseph | 1785 | " " | 200 | 1819 | |
| Wall, Patrick | 1785 | Port Roseway, W. | 500 | 1819 | Captain |
| Walsh [Welch] James | 1785 | " " " | 250 | 1819 | |
| Ward, Patrick | 1785 | Shelburne Township | 100 | 1819 | |
| Watson, David | 1785 | " " | 200 | 1819 | |
| Webster, Thomas | 1785 | Cape Negro River | 100 | 1819 | |
| Westwood, Samuel | 1785 | " " " | 100 | 1819 | |
| Wier, William | 1785 | Port Roseway, W. | 250 | 1819 | |
| Williamson, George | 1785 | Shelburne Township | 100 | 1819 | |
| Wise, Joshua | 1785 | Port Roseway, W. | 500 | 1819 | |
| Wood, Benjamin | 1785 | " " " | 500 | 1819 | |

LOYALISTS AND LAND SETTLEMENT IN NOVA SCOTIA 119

## Sydney County
### GRANTS

| Name | Date | Situation | Acres | Origin or Rank |
|---|---|---|---|---|
| Adams, James | 1785 | Guysborough Township | 100 | |
| Adams, James | 1790 | Guysborough | T. L. | |
| Adams, John | 1784 | *Bay of St. Lewis | 200 | |
| Addison, Thomas | 1785 | Guysborough Township | 100 | |
| Addison, Thomas | 1790 | Guysborough | T. L. | |
| Agnew, Eliz. (Widow) | 1785 | Manchester Township | 100 | St. Augustine |
| Aickins, Samuel | 1785 | Guysborough " | 350 | |
| Aikin, Samuel | 1790 | Guysborough | T. L. | |
| Aikin, Samuel | 1790 | " (Not reg'd) | 5 | |
| Aikins, Samuel | 1790 | " " " | W. L. | |
| Allan, John | 1784 | Country Harbour, E. | 100 | King's Carolina |
| Allern, William | 1784 | Bay of St. Lewis | 100 | (Rangers |
| Allis, John | 1790 | Guysborough (Not reg'd) | T. L. | (Regiment |
| Ambrose, John | 1785 | Manchester Township | 200 | Duke of Cumberland's |
| Anderson, Matthew | 1784 | Country Harbour, E. | 200 | Corporal Royal North |
| Anderson, Robert | 1785 | Guysborough Township | 150 | (Carolina Regiment |
| Anderson, Robert | 1790 | Guysborough (Not reg'd) | T. L. | |
| Anderson, Thomas | 1785 | Guysborough Township | 200 | |
| Anderson, Thomas | 1790 | Guysborough | T. L. | |
| Armstrong, David | 1790 | Guysborough (Not reg'd) | T. L. | |
| Armstrong, David A. | 1790 | " " " | 5 | |
| Armstrong, Henry | 1790 | " " " | 5 | |
| Armstrong, Henry | 1790 | " " " | T. L. | |
| Armstrong, Robert | 1785 | Manchester Township | 100 | Duke Cumb.'s Reg't |
| Armstrong, Robert | 1790 | Guysborough | T. L. | |
| Armstrong, W. | 1790 | " (Not reg'd)) | 5 | |
| Armstrong, William | 1790 | " " " | T. L. | |
| Armsworthy, Baptist | 1785 | Manchester Township | 100 | Duke Cumb.'s Reg't |
| Armsworthy, Baptist | 1790 | Guysborough | T. L. | |
| Ash, Charles | 1787 | Tracadie | 40 | Negro |
| Auddy, John | 1784 | Country Harbour, E. | 100 | R.N.C. Reg't |
| | | | | |
| Bachus, Robert | 1787 | Tracadie | 40 | Negro |
| Backer, John | 1784 | Country Harbour, E. | 300 | Sergeant K.C. Rangers |
| Bailey, Thomas | 1787 | Tracadie | 40 | Negro |
| Baker, Adam | 1785 | Guysborough Township | 150 | |
| Baker, Adam | 1790 | Guysborough | T. L. | |
| Baker, George | 1787 | Tracadie | 40 | Negro |
| Baldwin, Richard | 1784 | Bay of St. Lewis | 100 | |
| Ball, Peter | 1790 | Guysborough (Not reg'd) | 5 | |
| Ballentine, James | 1790 | " " " | 5 | |
| Pallingtine, James | 1784 | Country Harbour, E. | 100 | K.C. Rangers |
| Balmor, James | 1785 | Manchester Township | 1000 | Major |
| Bange, Joseph | 1785 | Guysborough " | 100 | |
| Barker, John I. | 1784 | Country Harbour, F. | 100 | R.N.C. Reg't |
| Barnel, William | 1785 | Manchester Township | 100 | St. Augustine |
| Baronhawk, John | 1784 | Bay of St. Lewis | 200 | Lieut. |
| Barret, Thomas | 1785 | Manchester | 500 | |
| Barrett, Robert | 1790 | Guysborough | T. L. | |
| Barthy, Archibald | 1784 | Country Harbour, E. | 100 | South Carolina Reg't |
| Barton, Anthony | 1787 | Tracadie | 40 | Negro |
| Bassett, James | 1784 | Country Harbour, E. | 100 | S. C. Reg't |
| Bates, Ezekiel | 1784 | " " " | 100 | K.C. Rangers |
| Bathoon, Daniel | 1784 | " " " | 100 | R.N.C. Reg't |

*Near the River Antigonish.

| Name | Date | Situation | Acres | Origin or Rank |
|---|---|---|---|---|
| Batley, Philip | 1787 | Tracadie | 40 | Negro |
| Bayard, Abraham | 1787 | " | 40 | " |
| Bayn, Alexander | 1785 | Guysborough Township | 250 | |
| Bayne, Alexander | 1790 | Guysborough | T. L. | |
| Baxter, Thomas | 1790 | " (Not reg'd) | 5 | |
| Baxter, Thomas | 1790 | " " " | T. L. | |
| Beasley, Jacob | 1790 | Manchester Township | 100 | St. Augustine |
| Bedford, Levan | 1785 | Guysborough " | 250 | |
| Beetman, William | 1785 | " . " | 100 | |
| Beetman, William | 1790 | Guysborough (Not reg'd) | T. L. | |
| Belcher, William | 1785 | Guysborough Township | 100 | |
| Belcher, William | 1790 | Guysborough (Not reg'd) | 5 | |
| Belchley, William | 1790 | " | T. L. | |
| Berden, York | 1787 | Tracadie | 40 | Negro |
| Berry, John | 1784 | Country Harbour, E. | 100 | K.C. Rangers |
| Bevin, John | 1784 | " " " | 150 | Drummer R. N. C. |
| Bevins, John | 1784 | Bay of St. Lewis | 100 | (Reg't |
| Black, Malcolm | 1784 | Country Harbour E. | 200 | Serg't R.N.C. Reg't |
| Black, Peter | 1784 | " " " | 100 | K.C. Rangers |
| Black, Quaco | 1784 | " " " . | 100 | R.N.C. Reg't |
| Black, Ralph | 1785 | Guysborough Township | 100 | |
| Black, Ralph | 1790 | Guysborough | T. L. | |
| Bleven, John | 1784 | Country Harbour, E. | 200 | Serg't R.N.C. Reg't |
| Boggs, James | 1785 | Guysborough Township | 900 | |
| Boggs, James | 1790 | Guysborough (Not reg'd) | T. L. | |
| Boggs, Samuel | 1790 | " | 5 | |
| Bollen, James | 1790 | " " " | T. L. | |
| Bolten, William | 1784 | Country Harbour, E. | 100 | K.C. Rangers |
| Bolton, Isaac | 1787 | Tracadie | 40 | Negro |
| Boss, (Ross?) Jacob | 1784 | Country Harbour, E. | 100 | K.C. Rangers |
| Bossaw, James A. | 1784 | " " " | 800 | Lieut. S.C. Reg't |
| Boswell, William | 1785 | Manchester Township | 100 | Duke Cumb.'s Reg't |
| Boswell, William | 1790 | Guysborough (Not reg'd) | T. L. | |
| Bowers, Joseph | 1787 | Tracadie | 40 | Negro |
| Bowers, Martin | 1785 | Guysborough Township | 100 | |
| Bowers, Martin | 1790 | Guysborough (Not reg'd) | T. L. | |
| Bowey, James | 1790 | " " " | T. L. | |
| Bowie, James | 1785 | Guysborough Township | 100 | |
| Bowie, James | 1790 | Guysborough (Not reg'd) | 5 | |
| Bowlin, John | 1784 | Country Harbour, E. | 200 | Serg't S.C. Reg't |
| Bowling, James | 1785 | Guysborough Township | 100 | |
| Boyd, George Frederick | 1784 | Milford Haven | 700 | Dr. 84th. Reg't |
| Boyd, Henry | 1784 | Country Harbour, E. | 100 | K.C. Rangers |
| Boyd, John | 1784 | " " " | 100 | S.C. Reg't |
| Boyle, Roger | 1784 | " " " | 100 | K.C. Rangers |
| Boylen, Patrick | 1784 | Bay of St. Lewis | 100 | |
| Bradey, Jacob | 1787 | Tracadie | 40 | Negro |
| Bradford, Richard | 1784 | Country Harbour, E. | 200 | Corp'l, R.N.C. Reg't |
| Bradley, David | 1785 | Manchester Township | 100 | Duke Cumb.'s Reg't |
| Bradley, David | 1790 | Guysborough | T. L. | |
| Bradley, John | 1784 | Country Harbour, E. | 100 | R.N.C. Reg't |
| Bradshaw, John | 1784 | " " " | 100 | S.C. Reg't |
| Bratton, John | 1787 | Tracadie | 40 | Negro |
| Brearley, John | 1784 | Bay of St. Lewis | 650 | |
| Brewen, Rachael | 1787 | Tracadie | 40 | Negro |
| Brickstock, Roger | 1785 | Manchester Township | 100 | Duke Cumb.'s Reg't |
| Bristol, Edward | 1785 | Guysborough " | 150 | |
| Bristol, Edward | 1790 | Guysborough (Not reg'd) | T. L. | |
| Britt, John | 1784 | Country Harbour, E. | 100 | S.C. Reg't |
| Brittain, Joseph | 1784 | " " " | 200 | Corp'l S.C. Reg't |
| Brogan, Solomon | 1785 | Guysborough Township | 100 | |
| Brogan, Solomon | 1790 | Guysborough | T. L. | |
| Brogan, Solomon | 1790 | " (Not reg'd) | W. L. | |
| Brooks, Tim | 1790 | " " " | 5 | |

LOYALISTS AND LAND SETTLEMENT IN NOVA SCOTIA 121

| Name | Date | Situation | Acres | Origin or Rank |
|---|---|---|---|---|
| Brooks, Timothy | 1785 | Manchester Township | 100 | Duke Cumb.'s Reg't |
| Brooks, Timothy | 1790 | Guysborough (Not reg'd) | T. L. | |
| Brooks, Timothy | 1790 | " | T. L. | |
| Brown, Aaron | 1785 | Guysborough Township | 150 | |
| Brown, Aaron | 1790 | Guysborough (Not reg'd) | T. L. | |
| Brown, Alexander | 1790 | " " " | 5 | |
| Brown, Daniel | 1787 | Tracadie | 40 | Negro |
| Brown, George | 1785 | Manchester Township | 100 | Duke Cumb.'s Reg't |
| Brown, George | 1790 | Guysborough | T. L. | |
| Brown, George | 1790 | " | T. L. | |
| Brown, John | 1784 | Country Harbour, E. | 100 | K.C. Rangers |
| Brown, John | 1785 | Guysborough Township | 100 | |
| Brown, William | 1785 | " " | 200 | |
| Brown, William | 1785 | Manchester " | 100 | Duke Cumb.'s Reg't |
| Brown, William | 1790 | Guysborough | T. L. | |
| Brown, William | 1790 | " (Not reg'd) | T. L. | |
| Brown, William | 1790 | " " " | W. L. | |
| Browne, John | 1790 | " | T. L. | |
| Brownley, Robert | 1790 | " | T. L. | |
| Brownlie, Robert | 1785 | Manchester Township | 100 | Duke Cumb.'s Reg't |
| Brownrigg, Richard F. | 1790 | Guysborough (Not reg'd) | T. L. | |
| Brownspriggs, Thomas | 1787 | Tracadie | 40 | Negro |
| Bruce, George | 1785 | Manchester Township | 100 | Duke Cumb.'s Reg't |
| Bruce, George | 1790 | Guysborough | T. L. | |
| Bruce, George | 1790 | " | T. L. | |
| Bruce, Robert | 1790 | " (Not reg'd) | 5 | Major |
| Brush, Ludovic Jacob | 1785 | Guysborough Township | 250 | |
| Bryan, Thomas | 1785 | Manchester " | 100 | Duke Cumb.'s Reg't |
| Bryen, Timothy | 1784 | Country Harbour, E. | 100 | Dr. R.N.C. Reg't |
| Bumgardner, John | 1790 | Guysborough | T. L. | |
| Bumgardner, John | 1790 | " | T. L. | |
| Bumgarner, John | 1785 | Manchester Township | 100 | Duke Cumb.'s Reg't |
| Bundey, James | 1785 | " " | 100 | " " " |
| Bundy, James | 1790 | Guysborough (Not reg'd) | 5 | |
| Bundy, James | 1790 | " " " | T. L. | |
| Bundy, James | 1790 | " | T. L. | |
| Burk, Richard | 1785 | Guysborough Township | 100 | |
| Bush, Jacob | 1790 | Guysborough | T. L. | |
| Bush, John | 1785 | Guysborough Township | 300 | |
| Bush, John Godfrey | 1790 | Guysborough | T. L. | |
| Butler, Jonathan | 1784 | Country Harbour, E. | 150 | R.N.C. Reg't |
| Butt, John | 1790 | Guysborough | 5 | |
| Byrd, Robert | 1785 | Manchester Township | 100 | St. Augustine |
| Byron, Thomas | 1790 | Guysborough | T. L. | |
| Cachell, John | 1784 | Country Harbour, E. | 200 | Corp'l R.N.C. Reg't |
| Cahel, Thomas | 1784 | Bay of St. Lewis | 100 | |
| Calder, David | 1785 | Guysborough Township | 100 | |
| Caldhan, William | 1790 | Guysborough (Not reg'd) | T. L. | |
| Cameron, Archibald | 1784 | Country Harbour, E. | 650 | Lieut. K.C. Rangers |
| Campbell, Alexander | 1784 | " " " | 750 | " R.N.C. Reg't |
| Campbell, Colin | 1788 | Guysborough Township | 1000 | Major |
| Campbell, Colin | 1790 | Guysborough | T. L. | " |
| Campbell, Donald | 1784 | Country Harbour, E. | 550 | Ensign. R.N.C. Reg't |
| Campbell, George | 1785 | Manchester Township | 100 | St. Augustine |
| Campbell, John | 1784 | Country Harbour, E. | 300 | Serg't. K.C. Rangers |
| Campbell, John | 1785 | Guysborough Township | 100 | |
| Campbell, John | 1790 | Guysborough (Not reg'd) | 5 | |
| Campbell, John | 1790 | " | T. L. | |
| Campbell, Mur. | 1790 | " (Not reg'd) | 5 | |
| Campbell, Murdock | 1785 | Guysborough Township | 200 | |
| Campbell, Murdock | 1790 | Guysborough | T. L. | |
| Campbell, W. | 1790 | " (Not reg'd) | 5 | |
| Campbell, Walter | 1784 | Country Harbour, E. | 100 | R.N.C. Reg't |

## PUBLIC ARCHIVES OF NOVA SCOTIA

| Name | Date | Situation | Acres | Origin or Rank |
|---|---|---|---|---|
| Campbell, William | 1785 | Guysborough Township | 500 | |
| Campbell, William | 1790 | Guysborough (Not reg'd) | T. L. | |
| Campbell, William | 1790 | " " " | W. L. | |
| Canty, Terence | 1784 | Bay of St. Lewis | 300 | |
| Cappard, John | 1785 | Manchester Township | 100 | Duke Cumb.'s Reg't |
| Cappard, John | 1790 | Guysborough (Not reg'd) | T. L. | |
| Carey, William | 1785 | Manchester Township | 100 | Duke Cumb.'s Reg't |
| Carey, William | 1790 | Guysborough | T. L. | |
| Carey, William | 1790 | " (Not reg'd) | T. L. | |
| Carney, Abel | 1784 | Country Harbour, E. | 100 | S.C. Reg't |
| Carney, Cornelius | 1785 | Manchester Township | 100 | Duke Cumb.'s Reg't |
| Carney, Cornelius | 1790 | Guysborough (Not reg'd) | T. L. | |
| Carr, Robert | 1784 | Country Harbour, E. | 100 | R.N.C. Reg't |
| Carter, Joseph | 1785 | Manchester Township | 400 | St. Augustine |
| Cary, James | 1784 | Country Harbour, E. | 100 | R.N.C. Reg't |
| Caserty, Matthew | 1784 | " " " | 200 | Corp'l R.N.C. Reg't |
| Caswell, Thomas | 1790 | Guysborough (Not reg'd) | 5 | |
| Caulder, David | 1790 | " | T. L. | |
| Certerius, Valentine | 1790 | " (Not reg'd) | 5 | |
| Chapman, Amos | 1790 | " " " | T. L. | |
| Charly, William | 1784 | Bay of St. Lewis | 100 | |
| Christ, George | 1785 | Guysborough Township | 100 | |
| Christie, William | 1785 | " " | 100 | |
| Christie, William | 1790 | Guysborough | T. L. | |
| Christie, William | 1790 | " (Not reg'd) | W. L. | |
| Clark, Charles | 1784 | Country Harbour, E. | 100 | R.N.C. Reg't |
| Clark, John | 1785 | Guysborough Township | 500 | |
| Clark, John | 1790 | Guysborough (Not reg'd) | T. L. | |
| Clark, Lewis | 1785 | Manchester Township | 100 | Duke Cumb.'s Reg't |
| Clark, Lewis | 1790 | Guysborough (Not reg'd) | T. L. | |
| Clark, Pompey | 1787 | Tracadie | 40 | Negro |
| Clark, Thomas | 1784 | Bay of St. Lewis | 100 | |
| Clary, William | 1785 | Guysborough Township | 100 | |
| Clavel, Frederick | 1784 | Country Harbour, E. | 100 | S.C. Reg't |
| Clayton, John | 1784 | " " " | 200 | Corp'l R.N.C. Reg't |
| Cleary, William | 1790 | Guysborough (Not reg'd) | T. L. | |
| Clements, John | 1785 | Manchester Township | 100 | Duke Cumb.'s Reg't |
| Clements, John | 1790 | Guysborough (Not reg'd) | T. L. | |
| Clyburn, James | 1784 | Country Harbour, E. | 300 | K.C. Rangers |
| Cochran, Tobias | 1784 | " " " | 100 | S.C. Reg't |
| Coffee, Christopher | 1784 | Bay of St. Lewis | 100 | |
| Coffin, John | 1790 | Guysborough (Not reg'd) | 5 | |
| Coggill, Daniel | 1785 | Guysborough Township | 300 | |
| Coggill, Daniel | 1790 | Guysborough (Not reg'd) | 5 | |
| Coggill, John | 1790 | " " " | 5 | |
| Cogill, Daniel | 1790 | " | T. L. | |
| Cogill, Daniel | 1790 | " (Not reg'd) | W. L. | |
| Coleman, Daniel | 1784 | Country Harbour, E. | 100 | Dr. R.N.C. Reg't |
| Coleman, William | 1784 | " " " | 200 | Corp'l R.N.C. Reg't |
| Collins, Cage | 1784 | " " " | 100 | R.N.C. Reg't |
| Colt, Pompey | 1787 | Tracadie | 40 | Negro |
| Colts, Joseph | 1787 | " | 40 | " |
| Combs, Thomas | 1790 | Guysborough (Not reg'd) | T. L. | |
| Connell, Edmund | 1784 | Bay of St. Lewis | 100 | |
| Connell, William | 1784 | " " " " | 200 | |
| Connelly, Patrick | 1784 | Country Harbour, E. | 100 | R.N.C. Reg't |
| Connor, John | 1784 | " " " | 100 | K.C. Rangers |
| Connors, Nathaniel | 1790 | Guysborough (Not reg'd) | T. L. | |
| Conway, Robert | 1787 | Tracadie | 40 | Negro |
| Conyers, Nathan | 1785 | Manchester Township | 100 | Duke Cumb.'s Reg't |
| Cook, Benjamin | 1784 | Bay of St. Lewis | 100 | |
| Cook, David | 1784 | Country Harbour, E. | 100 | K.C. Rangers |
| Cook, John | 1790 | Guysborough (Not reg'd) | 5 | |
| Cook, Nathaniel | 1784 | Country Harbour, E. | 100 | R.N.C. Reg't |

# LOYALISTS AND LAND SETTLEMENT IN NOVA SCOTIA 123

| Name | Date | Situation | Acres | Origin or Rank |
|---|---|---|---|---|
| Cook, Ralph | 1785 | Manchester Township | 150 | St. Augustine |
| Coombs, Thomas | 1785 | Guysborough " | 150 | |
| Copeld, Thomas | 1784 | Country Harbour, E. | 850 | Lieut. R.N.C. Reg't |
| Corgen, Edward | 1790 | Guysborough (Not reg'd) | T. L. | |
| Corner, Alexander | 1790 | " " " | T. L. | |
| Corns, Francis | 1784 | Country Harbour, E. | 100 | K.C. Rangers |
| Cornwill, Daniel | 1784 | " " " | 600 | Lieut. S.C. Reg't |
| Costly, Prince | 1787 | Tracadie | 40 | Negro |
| Coward, Benjamin | 1785 | Guysborough Township | 200 | |
| Coward, Benjamin | 1790 | Guysborough (Not reg'd) | T. L. | |
| Coward, Benjamin | 1790 | " " " | W. L. | |
| Cowen, John | 1785 | Manchester Township | 200 | Corp'l, Duke Cumb.'s |
| Cowen, John | 1790 | Guysborough | T. L. | (Reg't |
| Cowen, John | 1790 | " (Not reg'd) | T. L. | |
| Cramer, Henry | 1785 | Guysborough Township | 150 | |
| Cramer, Henry | 1790 | Guysborough (Not reg'd) | 5 | |
| Cramer, Henry | 1790 | " " " | T. L. | |
| Cramer, Henry | 1790 | " " " | W. L. | |
| Creeson, John | 1790 | " " " | T. L. | |
| Creson, John | 1785 | Guysborough Township | 100 | |
| Creugar, Bartholomew | 1784 | Country Harbour, E. | 100 | K.C. Rangers |
| Critchet, Benjamin | 1790 | Guysborough | T. L. | |
| Critchett, Benjamin | 1785 | Manchester Township | 200 | Serg't, Duke Cumb.'s |
| Critchett, Benjamin | 1790 | Guysborough (Not reg'd) | T. L. | (Reg't |
| Crofts, Benjamin | 1785 | Guysborough Township | 100 | |
| Crofts, Benjamin | 1790 | Guysborough (Not reg'd) | T. L. | |
| Crofts, Benjamin | 1790 | " " " | W. L. | |
| Crosby, Richard | 1784 | Country Harbour, E. | 100 | S.C. Reg't |
| Crotty, Peter | 1784 | Bay of St. Lewis | 200 | |
| Crowder, David | 1785 | Guysborough Township | 100 | |
| Crowder, David | 1790 | Guysborough (Not reg'd) | T. L. | |
| Crowie, James | 1790 | Guysborough (Not reg'd) | 5 | |
| Crowie, W. | 1790 | " " " | 5 | |
| Crusine, John | 1790 | " " " | 5 | |
| Cuffman, Jacob | 1784 | Country Harbour, E. | 100 | S.C. Reg't |
| Cummin, Alexander | 1790 | Guysborough (Not reg'd) | T. L. | |
| Cummine, Alexander | 1790 | " " " | W. L. | |
| Cumming, Alexander | 1785 | Guysborough Township | 250 | |
| Cunningham, Ralph | 1785 | Manchester Township | 900 | Capt., Duke Cumb.'s |
| Cunningham, Ralph | 1790 | Guysborough (Not reg'd) | T. L. | (Reg't |
| Cunningham, Thomas | 1790 | " " " | 5 | |
| Cunningham, W. | 1790 | " " " | 5 | |
| Cunningham, W. P. | 1790 | " " " | 5 | |
| Curley, Owen | 1784 | Country Harbour, E. | 100 | S.C. Reg't |
| Curry, John | 1784 | " " " | 100 | R.N.C. Reg't |
| Curry, Neil | 1784 | " " " | 550 | Q. Master, R N.C. |
| Curtis, John | 1785 | Guysborough Township | 700 | (Reg't |
| Curtis, John | 1790 | Guysborough (Not reg'd) | T. L. | |
| Curvengen, James | 1784 | Bay of St. Lewis | 900 | |
| Cutlar, Robert M. | 1790 | Guysborough (Not reg'd) | T. L. | |
| Cutler, Robert M. | 1790 | " " " | 5 | |
| Cutler, Thomas | 1785 | Guysborough Township | 600 | |
| Cutler, Thomas | 1790 | Guysborough (Not reg'd) | 5 | |
| Cutler, Thomas | 1790 | " " " | T. L. | |
| Cutler, Thomas | 1790 | " " " | W. L. | |
| Cutler, Thomas | 1792 | Guysborough Township | 600 | |
| David, William | 1785 | " " | 100 | |
| David, William | 1790 | Guysborough | T. L. | |
| Davidson, James | 1785 | Guysborough Township | 100 | |
| Davis, John | 1784 | Country Harbour, E. | 100 | S.C. Reg't |
| Davis, John | 1785 | Guysborough Township | 300 | |
| Davis, John | 1785 | Manchester " | 100 | Duke Cumb.'s Reg't |
| Davis, John | 1790 | Guysborough (Not reg'd) | T. L. | |

| Name | Date | Situation | Acres | Origin or Rank |
|---|---|---|---|---|
| Davis, Thomas | 1784 | Country Harbour, E. | 100 | S.C. Reg't |
| Davis, Timothy | 1784 | " " " | 100 | R.N.C. Reg't |
| Davis, William | 1784 | Bay of St. Lewis | 100 | |
| Davis, William | 1785 | Guysborough Township | 150 | |
| Davis, William | 1790 | Guysborough | T. L. | |
| Davis, William | 1790 | " (Not reg'd) | W. L. | |
| Davis, Zachariah | 1790 | " | T. L. | |
| Davis, Zackeus | 1785 | Manchester Township | 100 | Duke Cumb.'s Reg't |
| Davison, James | 1790 | Guysborough | T. L. | |
| Dawkins, George | 1784 | Country Harbour, E. | 850 | Capt. S.C. Reg't |
| Dawton, Robert | 1787 | Tracadie | 40 | Negro |
| Dayly, Daniel | 1784 | Country Harbour, E. | 100 | R.N.C. Reg't |
| Deal, Joseph | 1785 | Guysborough Township | 100 | |
| Deckhoff, Herman | 1790 | Guysborough | T. L. | |
| Dee, James | 1785 | Guysborough Township | 100 | |
| Demas, John Conrad | 1785 | " " | 200 | |
| Demay, Stephen | 1784 | Country Harbour, E. | 100 | K.C. Rangers |
| Demmitt, John | 1784 | Bay of St. Lewis | 250 | |
| Denevish, George | 1785 | Manchester Township | 100 | Duke Cumb.'s Reg't |
| Derr, John | 1790 | Guysborough | T. L. | |
| Derr, Valentine | 1790 | " | T. L. | |
| Derry, Adam | 1785 | Guysborough Township | 100 | |
| Derry, Adam | 1790 | Guysborough (Not reg'd) | T. L. | |
| Desser, William | 1785 | Guysborough Township | 100 | |
| Desson, William | 1790 | Guysborough (Not reg'd) | T. L. | |
| Desson, William | 1790 | " " " | T. L. | |
| Devenish, Georgie | 1790 | " | T. L. | |
| Devoirs, Cornelius | 1784 | Country Harbour, E. | 100 | R.N.C. Reg't |
| Devos, John | 1787 | Tracadie | 40 | Negro |
| Dewhurst, John | 1785 | Guysborough Township | 250 | |
| Dickison, William | 1784 | Country Harbour, E. | 100 | R.N.C. Reg't |
| Dieckhoff, Herman | 1785 | Guysborough Township | 200 | |
| Dietrich, Adam | 1785 | " " | 300 | |
| Dismal, Samuel | 1787 | Tracadie | 40 | Negro |
| Disson, William | 1790 | Guysborough (Not reg'd) | 5 | |
| Dixon, Francis | 1785 | Guysborough Township | 300 | |
| Dixon, Francis | 1790 | Guysborough (Not reg'd) | T. L. | |
| Dixon, Francis | 1790 | " " " | W. L. | |
| Doerr [Doen] John | 1785 | Guysborough Township | 100 | |
| Dogget, Abner | 1790 | Guysborough (Not reg'd) | T. L. | |
| Dogherty, Jeremy | 1784 | Country Harbour, E. | 100 | R.N.C. Reg't |
| Dogherty, John | 1784 | " " " | 100 | K.C. Rangers |
| Dogherty, Michael | 1784 | " " " | 100 | R.N.C. Reg't |
| Domat, John Conrad | 1790 | Guysborough | T. L. | |
| Donally, Barney | 1790 | " (Not reg'd) | T. L. | |
| Donally, Barney | 1790 | " " " | W. L. | |
| Donely, Burney | 1785 | Guysborough Township | 100 | |
| Dorsey, George | 1785 | Manchester | 100 | St. Augustine |
| Dortt, Valentine | 1785 | Guysborough " | 200 | |
| Dotten, Robert | 1784 | Country Harbour, E. | 100 | Dr. R.N.C. Reg't |
| Douglass, Benjamin | 1784 | " " " | 650 | Ensign, K.C. Rangers |
| Douglass, Randal | 1790 | Guysborough | T. L. | |
| Doyle, Thomas | 1784 | Bay of St. Lewis | 100 | |
| Drasey, Thomas | 1785 | Guysborough Township | 100 | |
| Drasey, Thomas | 1790 | Guysborough | T. L. | |
| Driver, Henry | 1785 | Manchester Township | 100 | Duke Cumb.'s Reg't |
| Driver, Henry | 1790 | Guysborough | T. L. | |
| Drummond, Alexander | 1784 | Country Harbour, E. | 100 | R.N.C. Reg't |
| Dryden, Thomas | 1784 | Bay of St. Lewis | 100 | |
| Dryer, William | 1785 | Guysborough Township | 100 | |
| Dryer, William | 1790 | Guysborough (Not reg'd) | T. L. | |
| Drysdale, Dennis | 1785 | Guysborough Township | 100 | |
| Drysdale, Dennis | 1790 | Guysborough | T. L. | |
| Duffe, Peter | 1790 | " | T. L. | |

LOYALISTS AND LAND SETTLEMENT IN NOVA SCOTIA 125

| Name | Date | Situation | Acres | Origin or Rank |
|---|---|---|---|---|
| Duhurst, John | 1790 | Guysborough (Not reg'd) | T. L. | |
| Dunaway, John | 1790 | " | T. L. | |
| Dunbar, Alexander | 1785 | Guysborough Township | 100 | |
| Dunbar, Alexander | 1790 | Guysborough (Not reg'd) | T. L. | |
| Dunbar, William | 1785 | Guysborough Township | 200 | |
| Dunbar, William | 1790 | Guysborough (Not reg'd) | T. L. | |
| Dunfy, Dennis | 1784 | Bay of St. Lewis | 100 | |
| Dunn, William | 1784 | " " " " | 100 | |
| Dunnavon, Richard | 1784 | Country Harbour, E. | 100 | R.N.C. Reg't |
| Duriah, John | 1784 | " " " | 100 | S.C. Reg't |
| Dyer, Samuel | 1784 | " " " | 100 | R.N.C. Reg't |
| | | | | |
| Ehler, John | 1785 | Guysborough Township | 200 | |
| Elar, John | 1790 | Guysborough | T. L. | |
| Elliott, Benjamin | 1790 | " (Not reg'd) | T. L. | |
| Ellis, Daniel | 1784 | Country Harbour, E. | 650 | Lieut. K.C. Rangers |
| Ellis, John | 1785 | Guysborough Township | 100 | |
| Ellist, [Elliott] Benjamin | 1790 | Guysborough | 5 | |
| Elmer, Alexander | 1787 | Tracadie | 40 | Negro |
| Elmsby, Alexander | 1790 | Guysborough | T. L. | |
| Elmsley, Alexander | 1785 | Guysborough Township | 100 | |
| Emma, James | 1787 | Tracadie | 40 | Negro |
| Erbash, Godfrey | 1785 | Guysborough Township | 250 | |
| Ervin, Baccus | 1787 | Tracadie | 40 | Negro |
| Esbach, Godfrey | 1790 | Guysborough | T. L. | |
| Essex, David | 1785 | Manchester Township | 100 | Duke Cumb.'s Reg't |
| Evans, John | 1784 | Country Harbour, E. | 100 | S.C. Reg't |
| Evans, William | 1784 | " " " | 200 | Serg't S.C. Reg't |
| Everidge, Isaac | 1785 | Manchester Township | 100 | Drummer, Duke |
| Everidge, Isaac | 1790 | Guysborough | T. L. | (Cumb.'s Reg't |
| Everige, Isaac | 1790 | " (Not reg'd) | T. L. | |
| | | | | |
| Fagen, Samuel | 1784 | Country Harbour, E. | 200 | Corp'l S.C. Reg't |
| Farmer, John | 1787 | Tracadie | 40 | Negro |
| Farr, King | 1787 | " | 40 | " |
| Farr, William | 1785 | Guysborough Township | 100 | |
| Farrow, James | 1785 | Manchester " | 100 | Duke Cumb.'s Reg't |
| Fasso, John | 1784 | Country Harbour, E. | 100 | K.C. Rangers |
| Featherstone, Francis | 1790 | Guysborough | T. L. | |
| Featherstone, Francis | 1790 | " (Not reg'd) | W. L. | |
| Feltmitt, Frederick | 1784 | Country Harbour, E. | 100 | S.C. Reg't |
| Fenn, Thomas | 1790 | Guysborough (Not reg'd) | 5 | |
| Fenn, Thomas | 1790 | " " " | T. L. | |
| Fenney, John | 1784 | Country Harbour, E. | 100 | K.C. Rangers |
| Fenton, Jacob | 1784 | " " " | 250 | Serg't K.C. Rangers |
| Ferdinand, Ludivic | 1790 | Guysborough | T. L. | |
| Ferguson, Alexander | 1785 | Guysborough Township | 300 | |
| Ferguson, Alexander | 1790 | Guysborough (Not reg'd) | T. L. | |
| Ferguson, Alexander | 1790 | Guysborough (Not reg'd) | W. L. | |
| Ferser, Joseph | 1785 | Guysborough Township | 100 | |
| Fetherstone, Francis | 1785 | " " | 150 | |
| Field, Stephen | 1785 | " " | 350 | |
| Field, Stephen | 1790 | Guysborough | 100 | |
| Fielder, Charles | 1785 | Manchester Township | 100 | Duke Cumb.'s Reg't |
| Fielder, Charles | 1790 | Guysborough (Not reg'd) | T. L. | |
| Filce, Thomas | 1784 | Country Harbour, E. | 250 | Serg't K.C. Rangers |
| Finah, Aza | 1784 | . " " " | 100 | R.N.C. Reg't |
| Finer, Henry | 1784 | " " " | 100 | " " |
| Finlay, James | 1790 | Guysborough | T. L. | |
| Fitzgerald, James | 1784 | Bay of St. Lewis | 100 | |
| Fitzpatrick, John | 1785 | Guysborough Township | 250 | |
| Fitzpatrick, John | 1790 | Guysborough (Not reg'd) | 5 | |
| Fitzpatrick, John | 1790 | " " " | T. L. | |
| Fiva, Anthony | 1785 | Guysborough Township | 450 | |

| Name | Date | Situation | Acres | Origin or Rank |
|---|---|---|---|---|
| Fiva, Anthony | 1790 | Guysborough | | T. L. |
| Fleisher, Conrad | 1785 | Guysborough Township | 150 | |
| Fleisher, Conrad | 1790 | Guysborough (Not reg'd) | | T. L. |
| Fleming, John | 1784 | Country Harbour, E. | 100 | K.C. Rangers |
| Fletcher, William | 1785 | Guysborough Township | 200 | |
| Fletcher, William | 1790 | Guysborough | | T. L. |
| Fletcher, William | 1790 | " (Not reg'd) | | W. L. |
| Flick, John | 1785 | Manchester Township | 100 | Duke Cumb.'s Reg't |
| Flick, John | 1790 | Guysborough (Not reg'd) | | T. L. |
| Flieger, John H. | 1784 | Country Harbour, E. | 500 | Ensign. S.C. Reg't |
| Flinn, Michael | 1785 | Guysborough Township | 150 | |
| Follit, John | 1784 | Country Harbour, E. | 100 | S.C. Reg't |
| Forhill, Jasper | 1790 | Guysborough (Not reg'd) | | W. L. |
| Forkell, Jasper | 1785 | Guysborough Township | 200 | |
| Forkill, Jasper | 1790 | Guysborough | | T. L. |
| Forrest, William | 1785 | Guysborough Township | 100 | |
| Forst, Abraham | 1790 | Guysborough (Not reg'd) | | T. L. |
| Forster, William | 1785 | Guysborough Township | 250 | |
| Foster, William | 1790 | Guysborough | | T. L. |
| Fotheringham, George | 1785 | Guysborough Township | 100 | |
| Fotheringham, R. | 1790 | Guysborough (Not reg'd) | 5 | |
| Fouler, Daniel | 1784 | Country Harbour, E. | 100 | R.N.C. Reg't |
| Fox, John | 1785 | Guysborough Township | 300 | |
| Fox, John | 1790 | Guysborough | | T. L. |
| Fox, Thomas | 1785 | Manchester Township | 100 | St. Augustine |
| Francklin, Esom | 1790 | Guysborough (Not reg'd) | | T. L. (Reg't |
| Franklin, Esom | 1785 | Manchester Township | 200 | Corp'l Duke Cumb.'s |
| Franks, Joseph | 1784 | Country Harbour, E. | 100 | K.C. Rangers |
| Fraser, A. | 1790 | Guysborough (Not reg'd) | 5 | |
| Fraser, Charles | 1785 | Manchester Township | 100 | Duke Cumb.'s Reg't |
| Fraser, Charles | 1790 | Guysborough (Not reg'd) | | T. L. |
| Fraser, William | 1785 | Guysborough Township | 150 | |
| Fraser, William | 1790 | Guysborough | | T. I. |
| Frederic, Prince | 1787 | Tracadie | 40 | Negro |
| French, Peter | 1787 | " | 40 | " |
| Frend, Ulderick | 1785 | Manchester Township | 100 | Fifer Duke Cumb.'s |
| Fricke, Augustus | 1785 | Guysborough " | 600 | (Regt. |
| Frieke, Augustus | 1790 | Guysborough (Not reg'd) | | T. L. |
| Friend, Uldrick | 1790 | " " " | | T. L. |
| Frike, Aug't. | 1790 | " " " | 5 | |
| Fryer, William | 1785 | Manchester Township | 100 | Duke Cumb.'s Reg't |
| Fryer, William | 1790 | Guysborough (Not reg'd) | | T. L. |
| Fulsom, Nathaniel | 1784 | Bay of St. Lewis | 350 | |
| Furnay, James | 1784 | Country Harbour, E. | 100 | K.C. Rangers |
| Gaffard, Thomas | 1784 | " " " | 200 | Corp'l S.C. Reg't |
| Gaggar, Michael | 1784 | " " " | 100 | K.C. Rangers |
| Galihoo, John | 1784 | " " " | 100 | " " |
| Garlock, Michael | 1790 | Guysborough (Not reg'd) | | T. L. |
| Garrett, John | 1784 | Bay of St. Lewis | 100 | |
| Gass, John | 1784 | Country Harbour, E. | 100 | K.C. Rangers |
| Genovally, David | 1785 | Guysborough Township | 150 | |
| George, William | 1785 | Manchester " | 100 | St. Augustine |
| Gergon, Justel | 1790 | Guysborough | | T. L. |
| Gero, Benjamin | 1787 | Tracadie | 40 | Negro |
| Gibson, William | 1785 | Guysborough Township | 700 | |
| Gibson, William | 1790 | Guysborough (Not reg'd) | | T. L. |
| Gibson, William | 1790 | " " " | | W. L. |
| Glasco, Walter | 1785 | Manchester Township | 100 | Duke Cumb.'s Reg't |
| Gleigh, Martin | 1785 | Guysborough " | 100 | |
| Glen, James | 1784 | Country Harbour, E. | 100 | R.N.C. Reg't |
| Goldman, Christian | 1790 | Guysborough | | T. L. |
| Goldman, Christopher | 1785 | Guysborough Township | 200 | |
| Goltney, Isaac | 1785 | Manchester " | 100 | St. Augustine |

## LOYALISTS AND LAND SETTLEMENT IN NOVA SCOTIA 127

| Name | Date | Situation | Acres | Origin or Rank |
|---|---|---|---|---|
| Goodin, Edward | 1790 | Guysborough (Not reg'd) | T. L. | |
| Gooding, Edmund | 1790 | " " " | T. L. | |
| Goodman, William | 1785 | Guysborough Township | 100 | |
| Goodman, William | 1790 | Guysborough | T. L. | |
| Goodwin, Edward | 1785 | Manchester Township | 100 | Duke Cumb.'s Reg't |
| Gordon, Hugh McKay | 1785 | Aubushie. St. Lewis Bay | 700 | Major |
| Gordon, Robert | 1784 | Country Harbour, E. | 100 | K.C. Rangers |
| Gordon, William | 1787 | Tracadie | 40 | Negro |
| Grady, James | 1784 | Bay of St. Lewis | 150 | |
| Grady, Joseph | 1790 | Guysborough (Not reg'd) | 5 | |
| Graham, John | 1785 | Guysborough Township | 100 | |
| Graham, John | 1790 | Guysborough | T. L. | |
| Graham, William | 1784 | Country Harbour, E. | 100 | R.N.C. Reg't |
| Graham, William | 1790 | Guysborough | T. L. | |
| Graham, William | 1790 | " | T. L. | |
| Grant, John | 1785 | Guysborough Township | 900 | |
| Grant, John | 1790 | Guysborough (Not reg'd) | T. L. | |
| Grant, John | 1790 | " " " | W. L. | |
| Grant, Samuel | 1785 | Guysborough Township | 300 | |
| Grant, Samuel | 1790 | Guysborough (Not reg'd) | 5 | |
| Grant, Samuel | 1790 | " " " | T. L. | |
| Grant, W. | 1790 | " " " | 5 | |
| Grant, William | 1785 | Guysborough Township | 450 | |
| Grant, William | 1790 | Guysborough | T. L. | |
| Grasson, Samuel | 1790 | " (Not reg'd) | W. L. | |
| Gratto, James | 1784 | Bay of St. Lewis | 100 | |
| Gray, Archibald | 1785 | Guysborough Township | 200 | |
| Gray, Archibald | 1790 | Guysborough | T. L. | |
| Gray, Archibald | 1790 | " (Not reg'd) | W. L. | |
| Graysen, Samuel | 1785 | Guysborough Township | 100 | |
| Greason, Samuel | 1790 | Guysborough | T. L. | |
| Green, John | 1787 | Tracadie | 40 | Negro |
| Green, John, Jr. | 1787 | " | 40 | " |
| Greencorn, Adam | 1785 | Guysborough Township | 100 | |
| Greencorn, John | 1790 | Guysborough | T. L. | |
| Greencorn, Ludovic | 1785 | Guysborough Township | 300 | |
| Greencorn, Ludivic | 1790 | Guysborough | T. L. | |
| Greencorn, Nicholas | 1790 | " | T. L. | |
| Grierson, Samuel | 1787 | Tracadie | 40 | Negro |
| Griffin, James | 1785 | New Manchester Tp. | 500 | Lieut. Duke Cumb.'s |
| Griffin, James | 1790 | Guysborough (Not reg'd) | 5 | (Reg't |
| Griffin, James | 1790 | " " " | T. L. | |
| Griffin, John | 1785 | Guysborough Township | 100 | |
| Griffin, John | 1790 | Guysborough (Not reg'd) | T. L. | |
| Griffin, John | 1790 | " " " | W. L. | |
| Griffin, Joseph | 1784 | Country Harbour, E. | 100 | S.C. Reg't |
| Grigg, Matthew | 1784 | " " " | 500 | Q. Master S.C. Reg't |
| Grimes, Robert | 1785 | Guysborough Township | 100 | |
| Grimes, Robert | 1790 | Guysborough (Not reg'd) | T. L. | |
| Gunn, Alexander | 1785 | Guysborough Township | 100 | |
| Gunn, John | 1785 | " " | 300 | |
| Gunn, John | 1790 | Guysborough | T. L. | |
| Gurlash, Michael | 1785 | Guysborough Township | 100 | |
| Haddock, Jacob | 1790 | Guysborough (Not reg'd) | T. L. | |
| Haddox, John | 1785 | Manchester Township | 100 | Duke Cumb.'s Reg't |
| Haddox, John | 1790 | Guysborough | T. L. | |
| Hagan, James | 1784 | Country Harbour, E. | 100 | K.C. Rangers |
| Hall, Jesse | 1784 | " " " | 100 | " " |
| Hamilton, John | 1784 | " " " | 100 | " " |
| Hamilton, John | 1784 | " " " | 100 | S.C. Reg't |
| Hamilton, Robert | 1784 | " " " | 550 | Ensign. R.N.C. Reg't |
| Hamilton, Thomas | 1784 | " " " | 900 | Capt. R.N.C. Reg't |
| Hammand, John | 1790 | Guysborough (Not reg'd) | W. L. | |

| Name | Date | Situation | Acres | Origin or Rank |
|---|---|---|---|---|
| Hammond, John | 1785 | Guysborough Township | 100 | |
| Hammond, John | 1790 | Guysborough (Not reg'd) | T. L. | |
| Hamper, John | 1790 | Guysborough | T. L. | |
| Hannigan, Henry | 1790 | " (Not reg'd) | T. L. | |
| Hannigan, Patrick | 1785 | Manchester Township | 100 | Duke Cumb.'s Reg't |
| Hannigan, Patrick | 1790 | Guysborough | T. L. | |
| Hannigan, Patrick | 1790 | " (Not reg'd) | T. L. | |
| Hanning, John | 1790 | " | T. L. | |
| Hansell, Christopher | 1785 | Guysborough Township | 200 | |
| Hansell, Christopher | 1790 | Guysborough | T. L. | |
| Hansford, William | 1784 | Country Harbour, E. | 100 | R.N.C. Reg't |
| Hanshill, Christopher | 1790 | Guysborough (Not reg'd) | 5 | |
| Haragan, Jeremiah | 1790 | " " " | T. L. | |
| Harbourn, William | 1785 | Manchester Township | 350 | Music Master, Duke |
| Hardin, John | 1790 | Guysborough | T. L. | (Cumb.'s Reg't |
| Harding, John | 1785 | Manchester Township | 100 | Duke Cumb.'s Reg't |
| Hardy, John | 1784 | Bay of St. Lewis | 700 | |
| Harrell, Peter | 1785 | Manchester Township | 350 | Serg't Duke Cumb.'s |
| Harrell, Peter | 1790 | Guysborough (Not reg'd) | T. L. | (Reg't |
| Harrie, James | 1790 | " " " | T. L. | |
| Harrigan, Jeremiah | 1785 | Manchester Township | 100 | Duke Cumb.'s Reg't |
| Harris, George | 1784 | Country Harbour, E. | 100 | S.C. Reg't. (Reg't |
| Harris, James | 1785 | Manchester Township | 250 | Corp'l Duke Cumb.'s |
| Harris, James | 1785 | " " | 100 | Duke Cumb.'s Reg't |
| Harris, James | 1790 | Guysborough | T. L. | |
| Harris, Joseph | 1787 | Tracadie | 40 | Negro |
| Harris, Samuel | 1785 | Guysborough Township | 100 | |
| Harris, Samuel | 1790 | Guysborough (Not reg'd) | T. L. | |
| Harris, Samuel | 1790 | " " " | W. L. | |
| Harrison, Richard | 1784 | Country Harbour, E. | 150 | R.N.C. Reg't |
| Hart, Garret | 1787 | Tracadie | 40 | Negro |
| Hartman, Joseph | 1785 | Guysborough Township | 200 | |
| Hartman, Joseph | 1790 | Guysborough | T. L. | |
| Hase, John | 1784 | Bay of St. Lewis | 100 | |
| Hatton, Joseph | 1784 | Country Harbour, E. | 200 | Surgeon S.C. Reg't |
| Haunsheld, John | 1785 | Guysborough Township | 150 | |
| Havers, John | 1784 | Country Harbour, E. | 100 | S.C. Reg't |
| Hawkins, Samuel | 1787 | Tracadie | 40 | Negro |
| Hayman, William | 1784 | Country Harbour, E. | 100 | R.N.C. Reg't |
| Hays, Gabriel | 1784 | " " " | 100 | K.C. Rangers |
| Heath, Nicholas | 1784 | Bay of St. Lewis | 100 | |
| Heaton, Henry | 1784 | Country Harbour, E. | 100 | R.N.C. Reg't |
| Hefferman, Edmund | 1790 | Guysborough (Not reg'd) | T. L. | |
| Hefferman, Edward | 1785 | Manchester Township | 100 | Duke Cumb.'s Reg't |
| Henderick, Prince | 1787 | Tracadie | 40 | Negro |
| Henderson, Alexander | 1785 | Guysborough Township | 100 | |
| Henderson, Alexander | 1790 | Guysborough | T. L. | |
| Henderson, James | 1785 | Guysborough Township | 550 | |
| Henderson, James | 1790 | Guysborough (Not reg'd) | T. L. | |
| Henderson, James | 1790 | " " " | W. L. | |
| Henley, George | 1785 | Guysborough Township | 200 | |
| Henley, George | 1790 | Guysborough (Not reg'd) | 5 | |
| Henley, George | 1790 | " " " | T. L. | |
| Henley, George | 1790 | " " " | W. L. | |
| Henning, John | 1785 | Guysborough Township | 100 | |
| Henry, Edward | 1790 | Guysborough (Not reg'd) | T. L. | |
| Henry, Harry | 1785 | Manchester Township | 100 | Duke Cumb.'s Reg't |
| Henry, Martha | 1785 | Guysborough | 150 | |
| Hepburn, William | 1790 | " (Not reg'd) | T. L. | |
| Herring, Clause | 1787 | Tracadie | 40 | Negro |
| Herswell, George | 1790 | Guysborough (Not reg'd) | T. L. | |
| Hew, Frederick | 1784 | Country Harbour, E. | 100 | S.C. Reg't |
| Hewen, John | 1790 | Guysborough (Not reg'd) | T. L. | Reg't. |
| Hewin, John | 1785 | Manchester Township | 200 | Corp'l Duke Cumb's. |

## LOYALISTS AND LAND SETTLEMENT IN NOVA SCOTIA 129

| Name | Date | Situation | Acres | Origin or Rank |
|---|---|---|---|---|
| Hierlihy, James | 1784 | Bay of St. Lewis | 650 | |
| Hierlihy, John | 1784 | "   "   "   " | 650 | |
| Hierlihy, Timothy | 1784 | "   "   "   " | 1600 | Lt.-Col. |
| Hierlihy, Timothy Wm. | 1784 | "   "   "   " | 900 | |
| Hierlihy, William | 1785 | Antigonishe Harbour | 6 | Captain |
| Higgins, William | 1785 | Manchester Township | 350 | St. Augustine |
| Hildrith, Thomas | 1790 | Guysborough (Not reg'd) | 5 | |
| Hinds, George | 1790 | " | T. L. | (Reg't |
| Hines, George | 1785 | Manchester Township | 200 | Corp'l Duke Cumb.'s |
| Hines, George | 1790 | Guysborough (Not reg'd) | T. L. | |
| Hines, Peter | 1785 | Manchester Township | 100 | Duke Cumb.'s Reg't |
| Hines, Peter | 1790 | Guysborough (Not reg'd) | T. L. | |
| Hinis, Benjamin | 1784 | Country Harbour, E. | 100 | S.C. Reg't |
| Hogle, Stephen | 1784 | "   "   " | 200 | "   " |
| Holliday, John | 1784 | "   "   " | 100 | R.N.C. Reg't |
| Hollingsworth, Henry | 1785 | Guysborough Township | 200 | |
| Homan, Conrad | 1785 | "   " | 250 | |
| Homan, Conrad | 1785 | "   " | 100 | |
| Homan, Conrod | 1790 | Guysborough | T. L. | |
| Homan, Conrod, Jr. | 1790 | | T. L. | |
| Hoop, John | 1790 | "   (Not reg'd) | T. L. | |
| Hope, John | 1785 | Manchester Township | 100 | Duke Cumb.'s Reg't |
| Hopkins, John | 1785 | "   "   " | 100 | "   "   " |
| Hopkins, John | 1790 | Guysborough (Not reg'd) | T. L. | |
| Hopkins, William | 1784 | Country Harbour, E. | 300 | Serg't K.C. Rangers |
| Hopkinson, James | 1784 | "   "   " | 100 | K.C. Rangers |
| Horsewell, George | 1785 | Guysborough Township | 100 | |
| Horsford, James | 1785 | Manchester   " | 300 | Serg't Duke Cumb.'s |
| Horsford, James | 1790 | Guysborough | T. L. | (Reg't |
| Horsford, Jonas | 1790 | "   (Not reg'd) | T. L. | |
| Hounshill, John | 1790 | " | T. L. | |
| Hubbill, Nathan | 1785 | Guysborough Township | 700 | |
| Hubbill, Nathan | 1790 | Guysborough (Not reg'd) | 5 | |
| Hubbill, Nathan | 1790 | "   "   " | W. L. | |
| Hubbill, Nathaniel | 1790 | " | T. L. | |
| Hudson, Agan | 1784 | Country Harbour, E. | 200 | Serg't S.C. Reg't |
| Hudson, Joel | 1784 | "   "   " | 600 | Lieut. S.C. Reg't |
| Hugh, Hugh | 1785 | Guysborough Township | 750 | |
| Hugh, Hugh | 1790 | Guysborough (Not reg'd) | 5 | |
| Hugh, Hugh | 1790 | " | T. L. | |
| Hugh, Hugh | 1790 | "   (Not reg'd) | W. L. | |
| Hugh, John | 1790 | "   "   " | 5 | |
| Hughes, Owen | 1785 | Guysborough Township | 100 | |
| Hughes, Owen | 1790 | Guysborough (Not reg'd) | 5 | |
| Hughes, Owen | 1790 | "   "   " | T. L. | |
| Hughes, Owen | 1790 | | W. L. | |
| Hull, Henry | 1785 | Guysborough Township | 200 | |
| Hulme, W. B. | 1790 | Guysborough (Not reg'd) | 5 | |
| Hulme, William | 1790 | "   "   " | T. L. | |
| Hulsman, Lewis | 1790 | "   "   " | T. L. | |
| Hulssman, Ludovick | 1785 | Guysborough Township | 250 | |
| Hunt, Cornelius | 1787 | Tracadie | 40 | Negro |
| Hunt, Joseph | 1784 | Bay of St. Lewis | 100 | |
| Hunt, Madderson | 1785 | Manchester Township | 350 | St. Augustine |
| Hunt, Samuel | 1784 | Fisherman's Har. (Port Montague) | 200 | |
| Hunt, Samuel | 1790 | Guysborough | T. L. | |
| Hurley, Patrick | 1785 | Guysborough Township | 250 | |
| Hurly, P. | 1790 | Guysborough (Not reg'd) | 5 | |
| Hurly, Patrick | 1790 | "   "   " | T. L. | |
| Hurly, Patrick | 1790 | "   "   " | W. L. | |
| Hurst, Samuel | 1785 | Guysborough Township | 300 | |
| Hyde, James | 1790 | Guysborough (Not reg'd) | 5 | |

| Name | Date | Situation | Acres | Origin or Rank |
|---|---|---|---|---|
| Hyde, John | 1790 | Guysborough (Not reg'd) | T. L. | |
| Hylindagin, Christopher | 1784 | Country Harbour, E. | 100 | K.C. Rangers |
| Igler, Michael | 1784 | " " " | 100 | S.C. Reg't |
| Inglis, James | 1784 | " " " | 100 | Dr. R.N.C. Reg't |
| Inlay, James | 1790 | Guysborough (Not reg'd) | 5 | |
| Inlay, James | 1790 | " " " | W. L. | |
| Ireland, John | 1787 | Tracadie | 40 | Negro |
| Irvin, Francis | 1784 | Guysborough (Not reg'd) | T. L. | |
| Irvin, John | 1784 | Country Harbour, E. | 100 | R.N.C. Reg't |
| Irwine, Francis | 1785 | Guysborough Township | 250 | |
| Izard, Andrew | 1787 | Tracadie | 40 | Negro |
| Jackson, Ring'd | 1784 | Bay of St. Lewis | 200 | |
| James, Thomas | 1785 | Guysborough Township | 100 | |
| James, Thomas | 1790 | Guysborough | T. L. | |
| Jameson, John | 1785 | Guysborough Township | 300 | |
| Jameson, John | 1790 | Guysborough | T. L. | |
| Jappee, Lud. | 1790 | " (Not reg'd) | 5 | |
| Jarvas, Henry | 1790 | Guysborough (Not reg'd) | 5 | |
| Jarvis, Henry | 1785 | Guysborough Township | 150 | |
| Jarvis, Henry | 1790 | Guysborough (Not reg'd) | T. L. | |
| Jervis, Stephen | 1784 | Country Harbour, E. | 500 | Lieut. S.C. Reg't |
| Jessop, James | 1784 | " " " | 100 | K.C. Rangers |
| Jessop, Thomas | 1784 | " " " | 100 | " " |
| Jewell, Samuel | 1785 | Manchester Township | 100 | Duke Cumb.'s Reg't |
| Jewell, Samuel | 1790 | Guysborough (Not reg'd) | T. L. | |
| Johns, Henry | 1785 | Manchester Township | 250 | St. Augustine |
| Johnson, Barney | 1784 | Country Harbour, E. | 100 | R.N.C. Reg't |
| Johnson, John | 1784 | Bay of St. Lewis | 100 | |
| Johnson, John | 1790 | Guysborough | T. L. | |
| Johnson, Reuben | 1790 | " | T. L. | |
| Johnson, Ruben | 1790 | " | T. L. | |
| Johnson, Thomas | 1790 | " | T. L. | |
| Johnson, William | 1784 | Country Harbour, E. | 100 | S.C. Reg't |
| Johnston, David | 1784 | " " " | 350 | Serg't R.N.C. Reg't |
| Johnston, James | 1784 | " " " | 100 | S.C. Reg't |
| Johnston, John | 1785 | Guysborough Township | 100 | |
| Johnston, Joseph | 1784 | Country Harbour, E. | 100 | S.C. Reg't |
| Johnston, Reuben | 1785 | Manchester Township | 200 | Corp'l Duke Cumb.'s |
| Johnstone, David | 1785 | Guysborough " | 100 | (Reg't |
| Johnstone, David | 1790 | Guysborough | T. L. | |
| Jones, H. | 1790 | " (Not reg'd) | 5 | |
| Jones, Henry | 1785 | Guysborough Township | 250 | |
| Jones, Henry | 1790 | Guysborough (Not reg'd) | T. L. | |
| Jones, Henry | 1790 | " " " | W. L. | |
| Jones, John | 1784 | Country Harbour, E. | 100 | R.N.C. Reg't |
| Jones, Malachi | 1785 | Guysborough Township | 100 | |
| Jones, Malachi | 1790 | Guysborough (Not reg'd) | T. L. | |
| Jones, Stephen | 1785 | Manchester Township | 250 | Corp'l Duke Cumb.'s |
| Jones, Stephen | 1790 | Guysborough | T. L. | (Reg't |
| Jones, Stephen | 1790 | " (Not reg'd) | T. L. | |
| Jones, Thomas | 1785 | Manchester Township | 100 | Band. Duke Cumb.'s |
| Jones, Thomas | 1790 | Guysborough (Not reg'd) | T. L. | (Reg't |
| Joppy, Ludivic | 1790 | " | T. L. | |
| Joppy, Ludovic | 1785 | Guysborough Township | 250 | |
| Jordan, Cesar | 1787 | Tracadie | 40 | Negro |
| Jordan, John | 1784 | Country Harbour, E. | 100 | S.C. Reg't |
| Jordan, Richard | 1787 | Tracadie | 40 | Negro |
| Joyce, Mat. | 1790 | Guysborough (Not reg'd) | 5 | |
| Jurgen, Justus | 1785 | Guysborough Township | 100 | |
| Karr, Robert | 1790 | Guysborough (Not reg'd) | T. L. | |
| Kell, John | 1784 | Bay of St. Lewis | 250 | |

LOYALISTS AND LAND SETTLEMENT IN NOVA SCOTIA 131

| Name | Date | Situation | Acres | Origin or Rank |
|---|---|---|---|---|
| Kell, John, Jr. | 1784 | Bay of St. Lewis | 200 | |
| Kelly, James | 1784 | Country Harbour, E. | 100 | K.C. Rangers |
| Kelly, John | 1784 | Bay of St. Lewis | 100 | |
| Kelly, John | 1784 | Country Harbour, E. | 100 | K.C. Rangers |
| Kelly, Thomas | 1784 | " " " | 100 | R.N.C. Reg't |
| Kelly, Thomas | 1785 | Manchester Township | 100 | Duke Cumb.'s Reg't |
| Kelly, Thomas | 1790 | Guysborough (Not reg'd) | T. L. | |
| Kendrick, Thomas | 1784 | Bay of St. Lewis | 300 | |
| Kennedy, Isaac | 1785 | Manchester Township | 100 | Duke Cumb.'s Reg't |
| Kennedy, Isaac | 1790 | Guysborough | T. L. | |
| Kenselougt, Charles | 1790 | " (Not reg'd) | T. L. | |
| Kenslough, Charles | 1790 | " | T. L. | |
| Kent, William | 1785 | Guysborough Township | 100 | |
| Kent, William | 1790 | Guysborough (Not reg'd) | T. L. | |
| Kent, William | 1790 | " " " | W. L. | |
| Kergan, Edward | 1790 | " " " | 5 | |
| Kergun, John | 1785 | Guysborough Township | 100 | |
| Kerr, John | 1785 | " " | 100 | |
| Kerr, John | 1790 | Guysborough (Not reg'd) | T. L. | |
| Kerr, John | 1790 | " " " | W. L. | |
| Kerr, Robert | 1785 | Guysborough Township | 200 | |
| Kerr, William | 1784 | Country Harbour, E. | 100 | K.C. Rangers |
| Kervin, Thomas | 1784 | Bay of St. Lewis | 100 | |
| Key, James | 1785 | Guysborough Township | 400 | |
| Key, James | 1790 | Guysborough (Not reg'd) | 5 | |
| Key, James | 1790 | " " " | W. L. | |
| Kief, John | 1784 | Bay of St. Lewis | 100 | |
| Kief, William | 1784 | " " " " | 100 | |
| Kilby, Christopher | 1784 | " " " " | 650 | |
| King, Christopher | 1787 | Tracadie | 40 | Negro |
| King, George | 1785 | Manchester Township | 300 | St. Augustine |
| King, John | 1785 | " " | 100 | " " |
| King, Sterling | 1785 | " " | 100 | " " |
| Laffarts, Gilbert | 1787 | Tracadie | 40 | Negro |
| Lamb, Charles | 1787 | " | 40 | " |
| Lamb, John | 1784 | Bay of St. Lewis | 100 | |
| Land, James | 1785 | Manchester Township | 100 | Duke Cumb.'s Reg't |
| Lane, Thomas | 1784 | Country Harbour, E. | 500 | Ensign. S.C. Reg't |
| Lang, James | 1790 | Guysborough | T. L | |
| Lank, Edward | 1790 | " | T. L. | |
| Lawrence, John | 1784 | Country Harbour, E. | 100 | K.C. Rangers |
| Lawrie, Robert | 1785 | Guysborough Township | 200 | |
| Laws, Elijah | 1784 | Country Harbour, E. | 100 | S.C. Reg't |
| Lawson, David | 1785 | Guysborough Township | 100 | |
| Lawson, David | 1790 | Guysborough (Not reg'd) | T. L. | |
| Lawson, W. | 1790 | " " " | 5 | |
| Lawson, William | 1785 | Guysborough Township | 150 | |
| Lawson, William | 1790 | Guysborough (Not reg'd) | T. L. | |
| Leach, John | 1784 | Country Harbour, E. | 100 | R.N.C. Reg't |
| Lebeau, Jane | 1790 | Guysborough (Not reg'd) | T. L | |
| LeBeau, Jean | 1785 | Guysborough Township | 100 | |
| Legatt, John | 1784 | Country Harbour, E. | 1050 | Capt. R.N.C. Reg't |
| Legett, David | 1784 | " " " | 200 | Serg't R.N.C. Reg't |
| Leister, Abraham | 1784 | " " " | 100 | R.N.C. Reg't |
| Lenox, James | 1787 | Tracadie | 40 | Negro |
| Lewis, David | 1785 | Manchester Township | 100 | Band. Duke Cumb.'s |
| Lewis, David | 1790 | Guysborough | T. L. | (Reg't |
| Lewis, David | 1790 | " | T. L. | |
| Lewis, John | 1784 | Country Harbour, E. | 250 | Serg't S.C. Reg't |
| Lewis, Henry | 1784 | " " " | 100 | R.C. Reg't |
| Lewis, Richard | 1784 | " " " | 500 | Lieut. S.C. Reg't |
| Lewis, William | 1785 | Manchester Township | 100 | Duke Cumb.'s Reg't |
| Lewis, William | 1790 | Guysborough | T. L. | |

| Name | Date | Situation | Acres | Origin or Rank |
|---|---|---|---|---|
| Lewis, William | 1790 | Guysborough (Not reg'd) | T. L. | |
| Lieck, Charles | 1784 | Country Harbour, E. | 200 | Serg't S.C. Reg't |
| Lindsay, James | 1784 | " " " | 100 | K.C. Rangers |
| Lodge, James | 1790 | Guysborough (Not reg'd) | T. L. | |
| Lodge, John | 1790 | " | T. L. | |
| Lodge, Henry | 1790 | " " " | T. L. | |
| Lodge, Richard | 1790 | " " " | T. L. | |
| Lodge, William | 1790 | " " " | T. L. | |
| Lovell, Joseph | 1785 | Guysborough Township | 100 | |
| Lovell, Joseph | 1790 | Guysborough | T. L. | |
| Lovely, James | 1784 | Country Harbour, E. | 100 | R.N.C. Reg't |
| Low, James | 1784 | " " " | 100 | " " |
| Lowice, Robert | 1790 | Guysborough (Not reg'd) | W. L. | |
| Lowrey [Lowrie] James | 1785 | Guysborough Township | 300 | |
| Lowrie, Robert | 1790 | Guysborough | T. L. | |
| Lucast, James | 1790 | " | 5 | |
| Lumian, Dinnah | 1787 | Tracadie | 40 | Negro |
| Lyle, James | 1785 | Manchester Township | 250 | St. Augustine |
| Lynch, Daniel | 1784 | Bay of St. Lewis | 100 | |
| Lynch, Thomas | 1784 | " " " " | 100 | |
| Lyon, George | 1784 | Country Harbour, E. | 100 | R.N.C. Reg't |
| Lyons, Daniel | 1784 | Bay of St. Lewis | 100 | |
| Mabery, Benjamin | 1784 | Country Harbour, E. | 100 | R.N.C. Reg't |
| McAdams, Donald | 1784 | " " " | 100 | " " |
| McAlleman, John | 1784 | " " " | 100 | " " |
| McAllister, John | 1784 | " " " | 100 | " " |
| McAllum, M. | 1790 | Guysborough (Not reg'd) | 5 | |
| McAllum, Malcolm | 1790 | " | T. L. | |
| McAlpine, Donald | 1784 | Country Harbour, E. | 200 | Corp'l R.N.C. Reg't |
| McAlpine, John | 1784 | " " " | 100 | R.N.C. Reg't |
| McArthur, Samuel | 1785 | Guysborough Township | 200 | |
| McArthur, Samuel | 1790 | Guysborough | T. L. | |
| McArthur, Samuel | 1790 | " (Not reg'd) | W. L. | |
| McCaffrae, Edward | 1790 | Guysborough (Not reg'd) | 5 | |
| McCaffrae, Edward | 1790 | " | T. L. | |
| MacCaffray, Edward | 1785 | Manchester Township | 100 | Duke Cumb.'s Reg't |
| McCarter, Neil | 1784 | Country Harbour, E. | 1000 | Capt. R.N.C. Reg't |
| MacCarthy, Daniel | 1785 | Manchester Township | 200 | Fife Major. Duke Cumb.'s Reg't |
| MacCarthy, William | 1785 | " " | 100 | " " " |
| McCartney, Jeremiah | 1784 | Country Harbour, E. | 100 | S.C. Reg't |
| McCartney, John | 1784 | " " " | 200 | Serg't S.C. Reg't |
| McCarty, Daniel | 1790 | Guysborough | T. L. | |
| McCarty, Daniel | 1790 | " (Not reg'd) | T. L. | |
| McCarty, Duncan | 1784 | Country Harbour, E. | 100 | S.C. Reg't |
| McCarty, William | 1790 | Guysborough (Not reg'd) | T. L. | |
| McCaskel, Alexander | 1784 | Country Harbour, E. | 550 | Ensign. R.N.C. Reg't |
| McClam, John | 1784 | " " " | 100 | K.C. Rangers |
| McColla, John | 1784 | Bay of St. Lewis | 750 | |
| McCord, John | 1784 | Country Harbour, E. | 100 | S.C. Reg't |
| McCord, Martin | 1784 | " " " | 100 | " " |
| McCord, William | 1784 | " " " | 100 | " " |
| McCormick, Donald | 1784 | " " " | 100 | R.N.C. Reg't |
| MacCoy, William | 1785 | Manchester Township | 100 | Duke Cumb.'s Reg't |
| McCullen, Malcolm | 1785 | Guysborough " | 200 | |
| McDonald, Alexander | 1785 | " " | 100 | |
| MacDonald, Angus | 1785 | Manchester " | 600 | Lieut. Duke Cumb.'s (Reg't |
| McDonald, Angus | 1790 | Guysborough (Not reg'd) | 5 | |
| McDonald, Angus | 1790 | " | T. L. | Lieut. |
| McDonald, Angus | 1790 | " (Not reg'd) | T. L. | |
| MacDonald, Archibald | 1785 | Manchester Township | 250 | St. Augustine |
| McDonald, James | 1790 | Guysborough | T. L. | |
| McDonald, James | 1790 | " (Not reg'd) | T. L. | |

LOYALISTS AND LAND SETTLEMENT IN NOVA SCOTIA 133

| Name | Date | Situation | Acres | Origin or Rank |
|---|---|---|---|---|
| McDonald, James | 1790 | Guysborough (Not reg'd) | W. L. | |
| McDonald, James, Jr. | 1785 | Guysborough Township | 100 | |
| McDonald, James, Sr. | 1785 | " " | 100 | |
| McDonald, John | 1785 | " " | 100 | |
| *McDonald, John | 1785 | " " | 350 | |
| McDonald, John | 1790 | Guysborough | T. L. | |
| McDonald, John | 1790 | " (Not reg'd) | T. L. | |
| McDonald, Neel | 1790 | " " " | W. L. | |
| McDonald, Niel | 1785 | Guysborough Township | 450 | |
| McDonald, Niel | 1790 | Guysborough (Not reg'd) | T. L. | |
| McDonnald, John | 1784 | Country Harbour, E. | 800 | Capt. R.N.C. Reg't |
| McDonnald, John | 1784 | " " " | 100 | R.N.C. Reg't |
| McDonnald, John | 1784 | " " " | 200 | Corp'l R.N.C. Reg't |
| McDonnald, Thomas | 1784 | " " " | 550 | Ensign. " " |
| McDougal, Alexander | 1790 | Guysborough (Not reg'd) | 5 | |
| McDougal, Alexander | 1790 | " " " | T. L. | |
| McDougal, Alexander | 1790 | " " " | W. L. | |
| McDougald, Archibald | 1784 | Country Harbour, E. | 550 | Ensign. R.N.C. Reg't |
| McDugald, Alexander | 1785 | Guysborough Township | 200 | |
| McIntire, Malcolm | 1785 | " " | 200 | |
| McIntire, Malcolm | 1785 | " " | 100 | |
| McIntosh, Duncan | 1785 | " " | 100 | |
| McIntosh, Duncan | 1790 | Guysborough (Not reg'd) | T. L. | |
| McIntosh, William | 1785 | Guysborough Township | 100 | |
| McIntosh, William | 1790 | Guysborough (Not reg'd) | T. L. | |
| McIntyre, James | 1784 | Country Harbour, E. | 100 | K.C. Rangers |
| McIntyre, John | 1784 | " " " | 200 | Corp'l R.N.C. Reg't |
| McIntyre, Malcolm | 1790 | Guysborough (Not reg'd) | T. L. | |
| McIntyre, Malcolm | 1790 | " " " | T. L. | |
| McIntyre, Malcolm | 1790 | " " " | W. L. | |
| McEacherin, Archibald | 1784 | Country Harbour, E. | 600 | Ensign. R.N.C. Reg't |
| McEachren, Alexander | 1784 | " " " | 100 | R.N.C. Reg't |
| McElmon, James | 1784 | Bay of St. Lewis | 100 | |
| McFarley, John | 1784 | Country Harbour, E. | 100 | K.C. Rangers |
| MacGee, Oliver | 1785 | Manchester Township | 150 | Duke Cumb.'s Reg't |
| McGee, Oliver | 1790 | Guysborough (Not reg'd) | T. L. | |
| McGill, James | 1790 | " | T. L. | |
| McGregor, Peter | 1785 | Guysborough Township | 200 | |
| McGregor, Peter | 1790 | Guysborough (Not reg'd) | T. L. | |
| McKay, Alexander | 1785 | Guysborough Township | 100 | |
| McKay, Alexander | 1790 | Guysborough (Not reg'd) | 5 | |
| McKay, Alexander | 1790 | " | T. L. | |
| McKay, Alexander | 1790 | Guysborough (Not reg'd) | W. L. | |
| McKay, Angus | 1785 | Guysborough Township | 100 | |
| McKay, Donald | 1784 | Country Harbour, E. | 100 | R.N.C. Reg't |
| McKay, James | 1790 | Guysborough | T. L. | |
| McKay, John | 1785 | Guysborough Township | 200 | |
| McKay, John | 1785 | " " | 100 | |
| McKay, John | 1785 | " " | 100 | |
| McKay, John | 1790 | Guysborough (Not reg'd) | W. L. | |
| McKay, Robert | 1790 | " " " | 5 | |
| McKay, William | 1790 | " | T. L. | |
| McKeathen, Dougald | 1784 | Country Harbour, E. | 750 | Lieut. R.N.C. Reg't |
| MacKeel, Nathan | 1785 | Manchester Township | 100 | Duke Cumb.'s Reg't |
| McKeel, Nathaniel | 1790 | Guysborough (Not reg'd) | T. L. | |
| McKenley, Jacob | 1784 | Country Harbour, E. | 200 | Corp'l S.C. Reg't |
| McKenzie, Alexander | 1790 | Guysborough (Not reg'd) | T. L. | |
| McKenzie, Donald | 1785 | Guysborough Township | 100 | |
| McKenzie, Donald | 1790 | Guysborough (Not reg'd) | 5 | |
| McKenzie, Donald | 1790 | " " " | T. L. | |
| McKenzie, James | 1785 | Guysborough Township | 200 | |
| McKenzie, James | 1790 | Guysborough (Not reg'd) | 5 | |

\* Three hundred acres of this land were escheated in 1827. Since this was not in his lifetime it was not listed in tne regular eecheats.

134  PUBLIC ARCHIVES OF NOVA SCOTIA

| Name | Date | Situation | Acres | Origin or Rank |
|---|---|---|---|---|
| McKenzie, James | 1790 | Guysborough (Not reg'd) | T. L. | |
| McKenzie, John | 1784 | Country Harbour, E. | 100 | R.N.C. Reg't |
| McKenzie, Joseph | 1784 | " " " | 100 | S.C. Reg't |
| McKenzie, Mary | 1785 | Guysborough Township | 100 | |
| McKenzy, Alexander | 1785 | " " | 100 | |
| McKiel, Nathaniel | 1790 | Guysborough | T. L. | |
| McKnight, Alexander | 1785 | Manchester Township | 200 | St. Augustine |
| McKoy, Agnes | 1790 | Guysborough (Not reg'd) | T. L. | |
| McKoy, John | 1790 | " " " | T. L. | |
| MacLeese, John | 1785 | Manchester Township | 100 | Duke Cumb.'s Reg't |
| McLeesse, John | 1790 | Guysborough (Not reg'd) | T. L. | |
| McLeod, Alexander | 1785 | Guysborough Township | 100 | |
| McLeod, Alexander | 1790 | Guysborough | T. L. | |
| McLeod, Donald | 1785 | Guysborough Township | 100 | |
| McLeod, Donald | 1790 | Guysborough (Not reg'd) | 5 | |
| McLeod, Donald | 1790 | " | T. L. | |
| McLeod, John | 1784 | Country Harbour, E. | 100 | R.N.C. Reg't |
| McLeod, Murdock | 1784 | " " " | 800 | Surgeon R.N.C. Reg't |
| McLeod, Murdock | 1784 | " " " | 200 | Corp'l " " |
| McLunen, Donald | 1784 | " " " | 100 | R.N.C. Reg't |
| McMan, John | 1784 | " " " | 100 | S.C. Reg't |
| McMullan, Gilbert | 1784 | " " " | 100 | R.N.C. Reg't |
| McMullen, William | 1784 | Bay of St. Lewis | 350 | |
| McNair,— | 1790 | Guysborough (Not reg'd) | 5 | Colonel |
| Macnair, Colin | 1785 | Guysborough Township | 200 | |
| McNair, Colin | 1790 | Guysborough | T. L. | |
| Macnair, William | 1785 | Guysborough Township | 200 | |
| McNair, William | 1790 | Guysborough | T. L. | |
| McNamara, Patrick | 1784 | Bay of St. Lewis | 100 | |
| McNeal, Daniel | 1784 | Country Harbour, E. | 1250 | Capt. R.N.C. Reg't |
| McNeil, Andrew | 1790 | Guysborough | T. L. | |
| McNiel, Andrew | 1785 | Guysborough Township | 100 | |
| McPherson, Edward | 1785 | " " | 100 | |
| McPherson, John | 1784 | Country Harbour, E. | 200 | Serg't R.N.C. Reg't |
| MacPherson, John | 1785 | Manchester Township | 600 | Surg. Duke Cumb.'s |
| McPherson, John | 1790 | Guysborough (Not reg'd) | 5 | (Reg't |
| McPherson, John | 1790 | " | T. L. | |
| McPherson, John | 1790 | " (Not reg'd) | T. L. | Dr. |
| McPherson, Paul | 1785 | Guysborough Township | 200 | |
| McPherson, Paul | 1790 | Guysborough | T. L. | |
| McQuack, Malcolm | 1784 | Country Harbour, E. | 100 | R.N.C. Reg't |
| Magee, James | 1785 | Manchester Township | 100 | St. Augustine |
| Magill, James | 1785 | Guysborough " | 100 | |
| Magra, Samuel | 1787 | Tracadie | 40 | Negro |
| Mahony, Samuel | 1784 | Bay of St. Lewis | 250 | |
| Mains, Samuel | 1790 | Guysborough (Not reg'd) | T. L. | |
| Man, Thomas | 1784 | Country Harbour, E. | 100 | S.C. Reg't |
| Mann, John | 1785 | Guysborough Township | 100 | |
| Mann, John | 1790 | Guysborough | T. L. | |
| Mare, Patrick | 1784 | Country Harbour, E. | 150 | R.N.C. Reg't |
| Mare, Simeon | 1784 | " " " | 100 | " " |
| Mares, Robert | 1784 | " " " | 100 | " " |
| Markham, Robert | 1785 | Manchester Township | 100 | Duke Cumb.'s Reg't |
| Markham, Robert | 1790 | Guysborough | T. L. | |
| Markham, Robert | 1790 | Guysborough (Not reg'd) | T. L. | |
| Marshall, Joseph | 1784 | Country Harbour, E. | 1050 | Capt. K.C. Rangers |
| Martin, David | 1785 | Manchester Township | 100 | St. Augustine |
| Martin, John | 1784 | Country Harbour, E. | 1000 | Capt. R.N.C. Reg't |
| Martin, Gregory | 1785 | Guysborough Township | 100 | |
| Martin, Gregory | 1790 | Guysborough (Not reg'd) | 5 | |
| Martin, Gregory | 1790 | " " " | T. L. | |
| Martin, Martin | 1784 | Country Harbour, E. | 200 | Serg't R.N.C. Reg't |
| Martin, Norman | 1784 | " " " | 200 | " " " |
| Mason, Patrick | 1784 | Bay of St. Lewis | 100 | |

# LOYALISTS AND LAND SETTLEMENT IN NOVA SCOTIA 135

| Name | Date | Situation | Acres | Origin or Rank |
|---|---|---|---|---|
| Mason, William | 1784 | Bay of St. Lewis | 100 | |
| Mathis, Henry | 1784 | Country Harbour, E. | 100 | S.C. Reg't |
| Matterson, John | 1785 | Manchester Township | 150 | St. Augustine |
| Mattertal, George | 1784 | Bay of St. Lewis | 100 | |
| Matthews, Bryan | 1785 | Manchester Township | 100 | Duke Cumb.'s Reg't |
| Matthews, Ryan | 1790 | Guysborough (Not reg'd) | T. L. | |
| Mattison, Allen | 1784 | Country Harbour, E. | 100 | R.N C. Reg't |
| Matts, Thomas | 1784 | " " " | 100 | S.C. Reg't |
| Maxwell, Orlando | 1785 | Guysborough Township | 100 | |
| Maxwell, Orlando | 1790 | Guysborough (Not reg'd) | T. L. | |
| May, James | 1785 | Guysborough Township | 100 | |
| Mayes, William | 1785 | Manchester " | 400 | St. Augustine |
| Mead, Samuel | 1785 | Guysborough " | 100 | |
| Mead, Samuel | 1790 | Guysborough (Not reg'd) | T. L. | |
| Meighan, B. | 1790 | " " " | 5 | |
| Meighan, Bryan | 1785 | Manchester Township | 600 | Lieut. Duke Cumb.s |
| Meighan, Bryan | 1790 | Guysborough (Not reg'd) | T. L. | (Reg't |
| Meighan, Bryan | 1790 | " | T. L. | |
| Meyer, Charles | 1785 | Guysborough Township | 100 | |
| Meyer, Ferdinand | 1785 | " " | 100 | |
| Meyer, Ferdinand | 1790 | Guysborough | T. L. | |
| Meyer, George | 1785 | Guysborough Township | 100 | |
| Midcalf, James | 1784 | Country Harbour, E. | 200 | S.C. Reg't |
| Mikell, Roger | 1784 | " " " | 100 | R.N.C. Reg't |
| Miles [Mills] Thomas | 1785 | Manchester Township | 200 | Serg't Duke Cumb.'s |
| Miles, Thomas | 1790 | Guysborough | T. L. | (Reg't |
| Miles, Thomas | 1790 | " (Not reg'd) | T. L. | |
| Millar, John | 1790 | " | T. L. | |
| Miller, Christian | 1790 | " (Not reg'd) | T. L. | |
| *Miller, Christian | 1794 | Chedabucto Bay, S. | 500 | |
| Miller, Christopher | 1785 | Guysborough Township | 250 | |
| Miller, Christopher | 1790 | Guysborough (Not reg'd) | 5 | |
| Miller, David | 1784 | Country Harbour, E. | 100 | S.C. Reg't |
| Miller, John | 1785 | Guysborough Township | 100 | |
| Miller, Violet | 1787 | Tracadie | 40 | Negro |
| Mills, Armstead | 1784 | Country Harbour, E. | 300 | Serg't K.C. Reg't |
| Mills, Robert | 1785 | Guysborough Township | 250 | |
| Mills, Robert | 1790 | Guysborough (Not reg'd) | T. L. | |
| Mills, Robert | 1790 | " " " | W. L. | |
| Minton, Adam | 1787 | Tracadie | 40 | Negro |
| Minton, Samuel | 1787 | " | 40 | " |
| Mollison, William | 1790 | Guysborough (Not reg'd) | T. L. | |
| Mollison, William | 1797 | " | 1000 | |
| Molloy, Richard | 1784 | Country Harbour, E. | 100 | R.N.C. Reg't |
| Montague, Chas. (Heirs) | 1785 | Manchester Township | 1000 | |
| Montague, Chas. " | 1790 | Guysborough (Not reg'd) | T. L. | |
| Montgomery, John | 1784 | Country Harbour, E. | 100 | S.C. Reg't |
| Moon, James | 1790 | Guysborough (Not reg'd) | 5 | |
| Moore, James | 1784 | Country Harbour, E. | 300 | Serg't S.C. Reg't |
| Moore, James | 1785 | Guysborough Township | 150 | |
| Moore, James | 1790 | Guysborough (Not reg'd) | T. L. | |
| Moriam, El. | 1790 | " " " | 5 | |
| Morris, Anthony | 1787 | Tracadie | 40 | Negro |
| Morris, Edward I. | 1790 | Guysborough (Not reg'd) | T. L. | |
| Morris, Edward J. | 1790 | " " " | 5 | |
| Morris, Richard | 1785 | Guysborough Township | 800 | |
| Morris, Richard | 1790 | Guysborough (Not reg'd) | 5 | |
| Morris, Richard | 1790 | " " " | T. L. | |
| Morris, Richard | 1790 | " " " | W. L. | |
| Morris, Richard, Jr. | 1790 | Guysborough (Not reg'd) | 5 | |
| Morris, Richard, Jr. | 1790 | " " " | T. L. | |
| Morris, Thomas | 1790 | " " " | 5 | |

\* To replace 250 acres not accepted by Miller in Guysborough Township, 1785.

## PUBLIC ARCHIVES OF NOVA SCOTIA

| Name | Date | Situation | Acres | Origin or Rank |
|---|---|---|---|---|
| Morris, Thomas I. | 1790 | Guysborough (Not reg'd) | T. L. | |
| Morris, William | 1784 | Country Harbour, E. | 100 | K.C. Rangers |
| Morrison, John | 1784 | " " " | 100 | R.N.C. Reg't |
| Morton, James | 1785 | Guysborough Township | 200 | |
| Muir, George | 1790 | Guysborough | T. L. | |
| Mulcahy, Michael | 1784 | Bay of St. Lewis | 100 | |
| Munro, John | 1785 | Guysborough Township | 100 | |
| Munro, John | 1790 | Guysborough | T. L. | |
| Murdock, James | 1790 | " (Not reg'd) | T. L. | |
| Murdock, Jo. | 1790 | " " " | 5 | |
| Murkison, Murdock | 1784 | Country Harbour, E. | 100 | R.N.C. Reg't |
| Murphy, James | 1784 | Bay of St. Lewis | 950 | |
| Murphy, James | 1784 | Country Harbour, E. | 100 | R.N.C. Reg't |
| Murphy, John | 1784 | Bay of St. Lewis | 100 | |
| Murphy, John | 1785 | Manchester Township | 100 | Duke Cumb.'s Reg't |
| Murphy, John | 1790 | Guysborough | T. L. | |
| Murphy, John | 1790 | " (Not reg'd) | T. L. | |
| Murphy, Michael | 1785 | Guysborough Township | 150 | |
| Murphy, Michael | 1790 | Guysborough (Not reg'd) | T. L. | |
| Murphy, Miles | 1785 | Manchester Township | 100 | Duke Cumb.'s Reg't |
| Murphy, Miles | 1790 | Guysborough (Not reg'd) | T. L. | |
| Murphy, Timothy | 1784 | Country Harbour, E. | 100 | R.N.C. Reg't |
| Murphy, William | 1784 | Bay of St. Lewis | 100 | |
| Murray, Alexander | 1785 | Guysborough Township | 100 | |
| Murray, Alexander | 1790 | Guysborough (Not reg'd) | 5 | |
| Murray, Alexander | 1790 | " | T. L. | |
| Murray, James | 1784 | Country Harbour, E. | 200 | Corp'l R.N.C. Reg't |
| Myers, Jacob | 1784 | " " " | 100 | S.C. Reg't |
| Myers, John | 1784 | Bay of St. Lewis | 100 | |
| Nash, Ann | 1785 | Guysborough Township | 100 | |
| Nash, John | 1785 | " " | 450 | |
| Nash, John | 1790 | Guysborough (Not reg'd) | 5 | |
| Nash, John | 1790 | " " " | T. L. | |
| Nash, John | 1790 | " " " | W. L. | |
| Needham, John | 1784 | Country Harbour, E. | 200 | Corp'l R.N.C. Reg't |
| Neil, Henry | 1784 | " " " | 100 | " " " |
| Neilson, Jesse | 1785 | Manchester Township | 100 | Duke Cumb.'s Reg't |
| Nelson, Jesse | 1790 | Guysborough (Not reg'd) | T. L. | |
| Newton, John | 1784 | Country Harbour, E. | 100 | R.N.C. Reg't |
| Niblit, Levi | 1784 | " " " | 100 | S.C. Reg't |
| Nicholson, Ann | 1785 | Guysborough Township | 100 | |
| Norris, Patrick | 1784 | Bay of St. Lewis | 200 | |
| North, Thomas | 1785 | Manchester Township | 150 | St. Augustine |
| Nouse, Philip | 1785 | " " | 100 | Duke Cumb.'s Reg't |
| Nouse, Philip | 1790 | Guysborough (Not reg'd) | T. L. | |
| Nox, John | 1784 | Country Harbour, E. | 100 | S.C. Reg't |
| Nutt, Daniel | 1785 | Guysborough Township | 100 | |
| Nutt, Daniel | 1790 | Guysborough | T. L. | |
| Oat, Michael | 1785 | Guysborough Township | 100 | |
| O'Brien, James | 1784 | Bay of St. Lewis | 100 | |
| O'Brien, Michael | 1784 | " " " | 100 | |
| O'Brien, Patrick | 1784 | Country Harbour, E. | 100 | R.N.C. Reg't |
| Ogilvie, John | 1785 | Manchester Township | 100 | St. Augustine |
| Ogilvie, Peter | 1785 | " " | 100 | " " |
| Oldham, Isaac | 1784 | Country Harbour, E. | 100 | Band. S.C. Reg't |
| Oliver, Samuel | 1785 | Manchester Township | 100 | Duke Cumb.'s Reg't |
| Oliver, Samuel | 1790 | Guysborough (Not reg'd) | T. L. | |
| Orphenius, Wilhelm | 1785 | Guysborough Township | 100 | |
| Orpin, Edward | 1790 | Guysborough (Not reg'd) | T. L. | |
| Oxworth, Peter | 1784 | Country Harbour, E. | 100 | R.N.C. Reg't |
| Page, John | 1784 | " " " | 100 | Dr. R.N.C. Reg't |
| Page, Willis | 1787 | Tracadie | 40 | Negro |

## LOYALISTS AND LAND SETTLEMENT IN NOVA SCOTIA 137

| Name | Date | Situation | Acres | Origin or Rank |
|---|---|---|---|---|
| Panlon, Timothy | 1785 | Manchester Township | 150 | St. Augustine |
| Paris, Elijah | 1784 | Country Harbour, E. | 100 | S.C. Reg't |
| Parnell, Abraham | 1785 | Manchester Township | 100 | Duke Cumb.'s Reg't |
| Parnell, Abraham | 1790 | Guysborough (Not reg'd) | T. L. | |
| Parris, Eliakim | 1790 | Guysborough (Not reg'd) | 5 | |
| Parsons, David | 1784 | Country Harbour, E. | 100 | S.C. Reg't |
| Parsons, William | 1784 | " " " | 100 | " " |
| Parsons, William | 1785 | Manchester Township | 100 | Duke Cumb.'s Reg't |
| Parsons, William | 1790 | Guysborough | T. L. | |
| Patch, Frederick | 1785 | Guysborough Township | 200 | |
| Patch, Frederick | 1790 | Guysborough | T. L. | |
| Paton, Patrick | 1785 | Guysborough Township | 250 | |
| Patton, Patrick | 1790 | Guysborough (Not reg'd) | T. L. | |
| Patton, Patrick | 1790 | " " | W. L. | |
| Paylon, William | 1785 | Manchester Township | 200 | Corp'l Duke Cumb.'s |
| Paylor, William | 1790 | Guysborough | T. L. | (Reg't |
| Pearce, William | 1785 | Manchester Township | 100 | Band. Duke Cumb.'s |
| Pearson, Robert | 1785 | Guysborough " | 100 | (Reg't |
| Pearson, Robert | 1790 | Guysborough (Not reg'd) | 5 | |
| Pearson, Robert | 1790 | " " " | T. L. | |
| Pendleberry, Marmaduke | 1790 | " " " | T. L. | |
| Pendlebury, Marmaduke | 1785 | Manchester Township | 100 | Duke Cumb.'s Reg't |
| Penn, Richard | 1790 | Guysborough (Not reg'd) | T. L. | |
| Penn, Richard | 1790 | " " " | W. L. | |
| Penoice, [Penrice] Edwd. | 1790 | " " " | T. L. | |
| Penrice, Edmund | 1785 | Manchester Township | 100 | Duke Cumb.'s Reg't |
| Penrice, Edward | 1790 | Guysborough | T. L. | |
| Pentleberry, Marmaduke | 1790 | " | T. L. | |
| Phillips, Basil | 1785 | Manchester Township | 100 | Duke Cumb.'s Reg't |
| Pierce, William | 1790 | Guysborough (Not reg'd) | T. L. | |
| Pinkley, George | 1785 | Manchester Township | 100 | St. Augustine |
| Pites, Stephen | 1790 | Guysborough (Not reg'd) | T. L. | |
| Pope, Frederick | 1785 | Guysborough Township | 150 | |
| Pope, Frederick | 1790 | Guysborough | T. L. | |
| Pope, Humphry | 1784 | Country Harbour, E. | 100 | S.C. Reg't |
| Pope, Joseph | 1785 | Guysborough Township | 100 | |
| Porter, John | 1784 | Bay of St. Lewis | 100 | |
| Porter, John | 1785 | Manchester Township | 100 | Duke Cumb.'s Reg't |
| Porter, John | 1790 | Guysborough (Not reg'd) | T. L. | |
| Porter, Solomon | 1784 | Country Harbour, E. | 100 | R.N.C. Reg't |
| Pottle, Samuel | 1784 | " " " | 100 | " " |
| Powers, Thomas | 1784 | " " " | 100 | S.C. Reg't |
| Pratt, John | 1784 | Bay of St. Lewis | 100 | |
| Pringle, John | 1785 | Manchester Township | 200 | Corp'l Duke Cumb.'s |
| Pringle, John | 1790 | Guysborough | T. L. | (Reg't |
| Pringle, John | 1790 | " (Not reg'd) | T. L. | |
| Procter, James | 1784 | Country Harbour, E. | 100 | R.N.C. Reg't |
| Procter, John | 1784 | " " " | 100 | Dr. R.N.C. Reg't |
| Proctor, Benjamen | 1785 | Manchester Township | 150 | St. Augustine |
| Proctor, James | 1785 | " " | 150 | " " |
| Punch, Patrick | 1784 | Country Harbour, E. | 100 | R.N.C. Reg't |
| Pushee, Nathan | 1785 | Manchester Township | 200 | Serg't Duke Cumb.'s |
| Pushee, Nathaniel | 1790 | Guysborough (Not reg'd) | T. L. | (Reg't |
| Pyle, Stephen | 1785 | Guysborough Township | 100 | |
| Raburn, David | 1784 | Country Harbour, E. | 100 | S.C. Reg't |
| Raburn, George | 1784 | " " " | 100 | Dr. S.C. Reg't |
| Rain, Conrad | 1784 | " " " | 100 | S.C. Reg't |
| Raymer, William | 1784 | " " " | 100 | K.C. Rangers |
| Read, Edward | 1785 | Manchester Township | 100 | Duke Cumb.'s Reg't |
| Read, John | 1785 | " " | 100 | " " " |
| Read, Moses | 1784 | Country Harbour, E. | 100 | R.N.C. Reg't |
| Read, William | 1785 | Manchester Township | 300 | St. Augustine |
| Redding, William | 1784 | Country Harbour, E. | 100 | R.N.C. Reg't |

| Name | Date | Situation | Acres | Origin or Rank |
|---|---|---|---|---|
| Redman, John | 1784 | Country Harbour E. | 100 | K.C. Rangers |
| Redman, John | 1784 | " " " | 100 | R.N.C. Reg't |
| Redman, William | 1784 | " " " | 100 | K.C. Rangers |
| Redmond, Henry | 1784 | " " " | 100 | Dr. R.N.C. Reg't |
| Redwick, Moses | 1787 | Tracadie | 40 | Negro |
| Reed, Edward | 1790 | Guysborough (Not reg'd) | T. L. | |
| Reed, Thomas | 1785 | Guysborough Township | 100 | |
| Reed, William | 1790 | Guysborough (Not reg'd) | T. L. | |
| Reeves, James | 1785 | Manchester Township | 100 | St. Augustine |
| Reid, Alexander | 1785 | Guysborough " | 100 | |
| Reid, George | 1790 | Guysborough (Not reg'd) | 5 | |
| Reid, John | 1790 | " " | T. L. | |
| Reider, Henry | 1790 | " | T. L. | |
| Reidiker, Cutlip | 1790 | " | T. L. | |
| Reuter, Henry | 1785 | Guysborough Township | 300 | |
| Reynolds, Anne (Widow) | 1785 | Manchester Township | 350 | St. Augustine |
| Reynolds, Thomas | 1785 | " " | 100 | Duke Cumb.'s Reg't |
| Reynolds, Thomas | 1790 | Guysborough (Not reg'd) | T. L. | |
| Rheideker, Cutleip | 1790 | " | T. L. | |
| Rheinhold, Casper | 1785 | Guysborough Township | 300 | |
| Rhiedeker, Cutlick | 1785 | Manchester " | 100 | Duke Cumb.'s Reg't |
| Rhoeden, Moritz | 1785 | Guysborough " | 250 | |
| Rhoden, Moritz | 1790 | Guysborough | T. L. | |
| Rhodes, Matthew | 1785 | Manchester Township | 100 | Duke Cumb.'s Reg't |
| Rhodes, Matthew | 1790 | Guysborough (Not reg'd) | T. L. | |
| Rhoney, James | 1790 | " " " | T. L. | |
| Rice, Thomas | 1784 | Bay of St. Lewis | 100 | |
| Rice, Thomas | 1785 | Guysborough Township | 100 | |
| Rice, Thomas | 1790 | Guysborough (Not reg'd) | T. L. | |
| Richardson, John | 1785 | Guysborough Township | 100 | |
| Richardson, Thomas | 1787 | Tracadie | 40 | Negro |
| Riddock, John | 1790 | Guysborough | T. L. | |
| Rielly, Patrick | 1785 | Manchester Township | 100 | Duke Cumb.'s Reg't |
| Ring, William | 1784 | Country Harbour, E. | 200 | Corp'l R.N.C. Reg't |
| Ringwood, Charles | 1787 | Tracadie | 40 | Negro |
| Ringwood, Joseph | 1787 | " | 40 | " |
| Ritchie, Benjamin | 1784 | Country Harbour, E. | 100 | K.C. Rangers |
| Roach, John | 1784 | Bay of St. Lewis | 100 | |
| Roads, Thomas | 1784 | Country Harbour, E. | 100 | S C. Reg't |
| Roady, Anthony | 1784 | Bay of St. Lewis | 100 | |
| Roberts, John | 1785 | Manchester Township | 100 | Duke Cumb 's Reg't |
| Robertson, Andrew | 1785 | " " | 100 | " " " |
| Robertson, Andrew | 1790 | Guysborough | T. L. | |
| Robertson, Duncan | 1785 | Guysborough Township | 150 | |
| Robertson, Duncan | 1790 | Guysborough | T. L. | |
| Robertson, Joseph | 1784 | Country Harbour, E. | 100 | |
| Robertson, Neil | 1789 | Abushie Harbour | 500 | |
| Robertson, Robert | 1784 | Country Harbour, E. | 100 | K.C. Rangers |
| Robins, James | 1784 | " " " | 250 | Serg't K.C. Rangers |
| Robinson, Andrew | 1785 | Manchester Township | 100 | St. Augustine |
| Robinson, John | 1787 | Tracadie | 40 | Negro |
| Rochford, Thomas | 1790 | Guysborough | T. L. | |
| Rochforth, Thomas | 1785 | Guysborough Township | 100 | |
| Roe, William | 1784 | Country Harbour, E. | 300 | Serg't R.N.C. Reg't |
| Roemple, Wilhelm | 1785 | Guysborough Township | 250 | |
| Rogers, Eli | 1785 | Manchester " | 200 | Corp'l Duke Cumb.'s |
| Rogers, Eli | 1790 | Guysborough | T. L. | (Reg't |
| Rogers, Eli | 1790 | " (Not reg'd) | T. L. | |
| Rogers, Joseph | 1785 | Manchester Township | 450 | St. Augustine |
| Rogers, William | 1785 | " " | 100 | Duke Cumb.'s Reg't |
| Rogers, William | 1790 | Guysborough (Not reg'd) | T. L. | |
| Ross,— | 1790 | " " " | 5 | Dr. |
| Ross, Donald | 1785 | Guysborough Township | 100 | |
| Ross, Donald | 1790 | Guysborough | T. L. | |

LOYALISTS AND LAND SETTLEMENT IN NOVA SCOTIA 139

| Name | Date | Situation | Acres | Origin or Rank |
|---|---|---|---|---|
| Ross, George | 1785 | Guysborough Township | 200 | |
| Ross, George | 1790 | Guysborough | T. L. | |
| Ross, Jacob see Boss, Jacob | 1784 | | | |
| Rowland, John | 1784 | Country Harbour, E. | 100 | K.C. Rangers |
| Rowneg, James | 1785 | Guysborough Township | 100 | |
| Royale, David | 1784 | Country Harbour, E. | 100 | S.C. Reg't |
| Rush, Andrew | 1784 | " " " | 100 | " " |
| Russell,— | 1790 | Guysborough (Not reg'd) | T. L. | Major |
| Russell, Hugh | 1784 | Bay of St. Lewis | 100 | |
| Russell, Major | 1785 | Manchester Township | 200 | Corp'l Duke Cumb.'s |
| Russell, Thomas | 1784 | Bay of St. Lewis | 100 | (Reg't |
| Russell, William | 1784 | Country Harbour, E. | 100 | K.C. Rangers |
| Rutherford, Peter | 1785 | Guysborough Township | 100 | |
| Rutherford, Peter | 1790 | Guysborough | T. L. | |
| Rutherford, Peter | 1790 | " (Not reg'd) | W. L. | |
| Ryan, John | 1785 | Guysborough Township | 150 | |
| Ryan, William | 1784 | Bay of St. Lewis | 100 | |
| Ryley, John | 1784 | Country Harbour, E. | 200 | Serg't R.N.C. Reg't |
| Ryley, John | 1784 | " " " | 100 | R.N.C. Reg't |
| Sadler, John | 1784 | " " " | 100 | S.C. Reg't |
| St. George, George | 1784 | " " " | 200 | Serg't S.C. Reg't |
| Sales, Mary | 1785 | Guysborough Township | 100 | |
| Sales, Thomas | 1790 | Guysborough | T. L. | |
| Sampson, William | 1787 | Tracadie | 40 | Negro |
| Samwise, William | 1784 | Bay of St. Lewis | 250 | |
| Sangster, James | 1790 | Guysborough (Not reg'd) | 5 | |
| Sangster, James | 1790 | " " " | T. L. | |
| Sangster, John | 1790 | " " " | 5 | |
| Sangster, Joseph | 1785 | Guysborough Township | 300 | |
| Sangster, Joseph | 1790 | Guysborough (Not reg'd) | 5 | |
| Sarriet, Samuel | 1790 | " " " | T. L. | |
| Sartonius, Ludovic | 1785 | Guysborough Township | 100 | |
| Sartonius, Valentine | 1785 | " " | 200 | |
| Sartorius, Walter | 1790 | Guysborough | T. L. | |
| Saunders, David | 1784 | Country Harbour, E. | 100 | K.C. Rangers |
| Saunders, Stephen | 1784 | " " " | 100 | R.N.C. Reg't |
| Sawyer, George | 1790 | Guysborough (Not reg'd) | 5 | |
| Saxton, Matthew | 1784 | Country Harbour, E. | 100 | K.C. Rangers |
| Schlaughman, Jeremiah | 1785 | Guysborough Township | 100 | |
| Scott, John | 1784 | Country Harbour, E. | 100 | R.N.C. Reg't |
| Scott, Samuel | 1785 | Manchester Township | 300 | St. Augustine |
| Selick, Charles | 1790 | Guysborough (Not reg'd) | T. L. | |
| Sellars, Daniel | 1790 | " " " | T. L. | |
| Sellers, Daniel | 1785 | Manchester Township | 100 | Duke Cumb.'s Reg't |
| Sellers, Robert | 1784 | Country Harbour, E. | 100 | R.N.C. Reg't |
| Senator, Anthony | 1784 | Bay of St. Lewis | 100 | |
| Serratt, Samuel | 1785 | Manchester Township | 100 | Duke Cumb.'s Reg't |
| Shaffer, John | 1790 | Guysborough (Not reg'd) | T. L. | |
| Shanks, John | 1785 | Manchester Township | 100 | Duke Cumb.'s Reg't |
| Shanks, John | 1790 | Guysborough (Not reg'd) | T. L. | |
| Shaper, John | 1785 | Guysborough Township | 200 | |
| Sharp, Alexander | 1784 | Country Harbour, E. | 100 | R.N.C. Reg't |
| Shaw, Alexander | 1790 | Guysborough (Not reg'd) | 5 | |
| Shaw, Edward | 1785 | Guysborough Township | 250 | |
| Shaw, Evan | 1790 | Guysborough (Not reg'd) | 5 | |
| Shaw, Even | 1790 | " | T. L. | |
| Shaw, John | 1790 | " (Not reg'd) | 5 | |
| Shaw, John | 1790 | " " " | T. L. | |
| Shaw, Robert | 1784 | Country Harbour, E. | 100 | R.N.C. Reg't |
| Shaw, William | 1790 | Guysborough (Not reg'd) | T. L. | |
| Shaw, William | 1790 | " " " | W. L. | |
| Shearing, William | 1790 | " | T. L. | |

# 140    PUBLIC ARCHIVES OF NOVA SCOTIA

| Name | Date | Situation | Acres | Origin or Rank |
|---|---|---|---|---|
| Sheerin, William | 1790 | Guysborough(Not reg'd) | T. L. | |
| Shehan, Patrick | 1784 | Bay of St. Lewis | 100 | |
| Shelling, John William | 1784 | " " " " | 100 | |
| Shellnut, George | 1784 | Country Harbour, E. | 200 | Corp'l S.C. Reg't |
| Shephard, Quart | 1787 | Tracadie | 40 | Negro         (Reg't |
| Sherrin, William | 1785 | Manchester Township | 100 | Band. Duke Cumb.'s |
| Shippard, John | 1784 | Country Harbour, E. | 100 | S.C. Reg't |
| Shneider, Christopher | 1785 | Guysborough Township | 200 | |
| Shneider, John, Jr. | 1785 | " " | 100 | |
| Shneider, John, Sr. | 1785 | " " | 100 | |
| Shoenaweis, John | 1785 | " " | 100 | |
| Shoenwise, John | 1790 | Guysborough | T. L. | |
| Shores, Thomas | 1785 | Manchester Township | 100 | Duke Cumb.'s Reg't |
| Shores, Thomas | 1790 | Guysborough | T. L. | |
| Showen, Thomas | 1790 | " | T. L. | |
| Sidney, John | 1784 | Country Harbour, E. | 100 | K.C. Rangers |
| Sillock, Charles | 1785 | Guysborough Township | 200 | |
| Simonds, Gideon | 1790 | Guysborough (Not reg'd) | T. L. | |
| Simpson, James | 1790 | " | T. L. | |
| Simpson, William | 1785 | Guysborough Township | 100 | |
| Simpson, William | 1790 | Guysborough | T. L. | |
| Sims, James | 1785 | Guysborough Township | 100 | |
| Skelly, John | 1787 | Tracadie | 40 | Negro |
| Skiles, Henry | 1785 | Guysborough Township | 100 | |
| Skiles, Henry | 1790 | Guysborough | T. L. | |
| Slaughter, John | 1787 | Tracadie | 40 | Negro |
| Sline, Thomas | 1784 | Country Harbour, E. | 100 | K.C. Rangers |
| Sloane, Robert | 1785 | Manchester Township | 100 | St. Augustine |
| Sloughman, Jeremiah | 1790 | Guysborough (Not reg'd) | T. L. | |
| Smaltz, Ernest | 1785 | Guysborough Township | 200 | |
| Smith, Charles | 1784 | Country Harbour, E. | 100 | K.C. Rangers |
| Smith, Frederick | 1785 | Manchester Township | 100 | Duke Cumb.'s Reg't |
| Smith, Frederick | 1790 | Guysborough | T. L. | |
| Smith, Frederick | 1790 | "       (Not reg'd) | T. L. | |
| Smith, George | 1784 | Country Harbour, E. | 150 | K.C. Rangers |
| Smith, Hammond | 1790 | Guysborough | T. L. | |
| Smith, Hammond | 1790 | "    (Not reg'd) | W. L. | |
| Smith, Hayman | 1785 | Guysborough Township | 100 | |
| Smith, James | 1784 | Country Harbour, E. | 100 | R.N.C. Reg't |
| Smith, John | 1784 | " " " | 200 | Corp'l S.C. Reg't |
| Smith, John | 1785 | Guysborough Township | 200 | |
| Smith, John | 1790 | Guysborough (Not reg'd) | T. L. | |
| Smith, Jonathan | 1784 | Country Harbour, E. | 100 | K.C. Rangers |
| Smith, Joseph | 1784 | " " " | 100 | |
| Smith, Samuel | 1785 | Manchester Township | 100 | St. Augustine |
| Smith, Samuel | 1787 | Tracadie | 40 | Negro |
| Smith, William | 1784 | Bay of St. Lewis | 200 | |
| Smydick, William | 1784 | Country Harbour, E. | 300 | Serg't R.N.C. Reg't |
| Smyth, Thomas | 1785 | Manchester Township | 100 | St. Augustine |
| Snarlock, Thomas | 1785 | " " | 100 | " " |
| Sneider, Christopher | 1790 | Guysborough | T. L. | |
| Sneider, John | 1790 | " | T. L. | |
| Sneider, John | 1790 | "    (Not reg'd) | T. L. | |
| Snum, John | 1784 | Country Harbour, E. | 100 | S.C. Reg't |
| Spain, William | 1785 | Manchester Township | 100 | Band. Duke Cumb.'s |
| Spain, William | 1790 | Guysborough | T. L. | (Reg't |
| Spain, William | 1790 | "    (Not reg'd) | T. L. | |
| Spangs, George | 1785 | Manchester Township | 100 | St. Augustine |
| Spank, George | 1785 | Guysborough " | 100 | |
| Spank, George | 1790 | Guysborough (Not reg'd) | 5 | |
| Spank, George | 1790 | " " " | T. L. | |
| Sparks, Richard | 1785 | Guysborough Township | 100 | |
| Sparks, Richard | 1790 | Guysborough (Not reg'd) | T. L. | |
| Squints, William | 1784 | Country Harbour, E. | 100 | S.C. Reg't |

# LOYALISTS AND LAND SETTLEMENT IN NOVA SCOTIA 141

| Name | Date | Situation | Acres | Origin or Rank |
|---|---|---|---|---|
| Stafford, Oliver | 1790 | Guysborough (Not reg'd) | T. L. | |
| Stampar, John | 1790 | " " " | W. L. | |
| Stamper, John | 1790 | " " " | 5 | |
| Stanagin, Henry | 1785 | Manchester Township | 100 | Duke Cumb.'s Reg't |
| Stanton, James | 1790 | Guysborough | T. L. | |
| Stanton, James | 1790 | " (Not reg'd) | T. L. | |
| Stapleton, Thomas | 1784 | Bay of St. Lewis | 100 | |
| Stark, P. | 1790 | Guysborough (Not reg'd) | 5 | |
| Stark, Peter | 1785 | Guysborough Township | 600 | |
| Stark, Peter | 1790 | Guysborough (Not reg'd) | W. L. | |
| Starks, Peter | 1790 | " " " | T. L. | |
| Staunton, James | 1785 | Manchester Township | 100 | Duke Cumb.'s Reg't |
| Stepleton, John | 1784 | Country Harbour, E. | 100 | K.C. Rangers |
| Stevens, Thomas | 1784 | " " " | 200 | Serg't R.N.C. Reg't |
| Stevenson, James | 1784 | " " " | 600 | Adjutant R.N.C. Reg't |
| Stevenson, Samuel | 1784 | " " " | 200 | Serg't S.C. Reg't |
| Stewart, James | 1784 | " " " | 100 | K.C. Rangers |
| Stewart, James | 1790 | Guysborough (Not reg'd) | T. L. | |
| Stewart, John | 1790 | ' | T. L. | |
| Stewart, John | 1790 | " (Not reg'd) | T. L. | |
| Stewart, John | 1790 | " " " | W. L. | |
| Stewart, William | 1784 | Country Harbour, E. | 100 | S.C. Reg't |
| Stewart, William | 1790 | Guysborough (Not reg'd) | 5 | |
| Stewart, William | 1790 | " | T. L. | |
| Stinson, David | 1784 | Country Harbour, E. | 200 | Corp'l R.N.C. Reg't |
| Stockwell, Joseph | 1784 | " " " | 100 | Dr. S.C. Reg't |
| Stoker, John | 1785 | Guysborough Township | 100 | |
| Stoker, John | 1790 | Guysborough (Not reg'd) | T. L. | |
| Stone, Charles | 1784 | Country Harbour, E. | 100 | K.C. Rangers |
| Storey, James | 1790 | Guysborough | T. L. | |
| Story, James | 1785 | Guysborough Township | 100 | |
| Stout, John | 1785 | " " | 100 | |
| Stowart, J. | 1790 | Guysborough (Not reg'd) | 5 | |
| Stowart, Ja. | 1790 | " " " | 5 | |
| Stowart, James | 1787 | Salmon River | 500 | Ass't Commissary to |
| Stowart, James | 1790 | Guysborough (Not reg'd) | T. L. | (the Br. Army in Amer. |
| Stowart, William | 1790 | " " " | T. L. | |
| Strahan, George | 1785 | Guysborough Township | 350 | |
| Strahan, George | 1790 | Guysborough (Not reg'd) | T. L. | |
| Strahan, George | 1790 | Guysborough (Not reg'd) | W. L. | |
| Strahen, George | 1790 | " " " | 5 | |
| Strople, George | 1785 | Guysborough Township | 300 | |
| Strople, George | 1790 | Guysborough (Not reg'd) | 5 | |
| Strople, George | 1790 | " " " | T. L. | |
| Stuart, John | 1785 | Guysborough Township | 550 | |
| Stuart, John | 1785 | " " | 650 | |
| Stuart, John | 1790 | Guysborough (Not reg'd) | 5 | |
| Stuart, John | 1790 | " " " | 5 | |
| Studevin, Barnabas | 1785 | Manchester Township | 100 | Band. Duke Cumb.'s |
| Studhaven, Barnabas | 1790 | Guysborough | T. L. | (Reg't |
| Stumper, John | 1785 | Guysborough Township | 150 | |
| Sutherland, William | 1790 | Guysborough (Not reg'd) | T. L. | |
| Swan, William Nesbitt | 1784 | Bay of St. Lewis | 650 | |
| Sweeney, Charles | 1787 | Tracadie | 40 | Negro |
| Swinney, John | 1784 | Country Harbour, E. | 100 | K.C. Rangers |
| Symonds, Gideon | 1785 | Manchester Township | 150 | Duke Cumb.'s Reg't |
| Symonds, John | 1784 | Country Harbour, E. | 100 | R.N.C. Reg't |
| Syms, John | 1784 | " " " | 200 | Serg't R.N.C. Reg't |
| Tankard, Thomas | 1784 | Bay of St. Lewis | 100 | |
| Tanks, Johannes | 1785 | Guysborough Township | 100 | |
| Tanner, Isaac | 1790 | Guysborough (Not reg'd) | T. L. | |
| Tanner, Isaac | 1790 | " " " | W. L. | |
| Tarrel, Hugh | 1784 | Bay of St. Lewis | 100 | |

| Name | Date | Situation | Acres | Origin or Rank |
|---|---|---|---|---|
| Taylor, James | 1785 | Manchester Township | 100 | Duke Cumb.'s Reg't |
| Taylor, James | 1790 | Guysborough (Not reg'd) | T. L. | |
| Taylor, John | 1785 | Guysborough Township | 100 | |
| Taylor, John | 1790 | Guysborough (Not reg'd) | T. L. | |
| Taylor, John | 1790 | " " " | W. L. | |
| Taylor, Joseph | 1785 | Guysborough Township | 250 | |
| Taylor, Joseph | 1790 | Guysborough (Not reg'd) | 5 | |
| Taylor, Joseph | 1790 | " | T. L. | |
| Telford, James | 1790 | " (Not reg'd) | T. L. | |
| Tennes, Isaac | 1785 | Guysborough Township | 400 | |
| Terrymouth, Adam | 1785 | Manchester " | 250 | St. Augustine |
| Thomas, George | 1784 | Bay of St. Lewis | 150 | |
| Thomas, James | 1787 | Tracadie | 40 | Negro |
| Thomas, Nathaniel Ray | 1784 | Plaister Cove | 1000 | Massachusetts Bay |
| Thompson, George | 1784 | Country Harbour, E. | 100 | R.N.C. Reg't |
| Thompson, John | 1784 | " " " | 100 | K.C. Rangers |
| Thompson, John | 1784 | " " " | 100 | S.C. Reg't |
| Thompson, Philip | 1787 | Tracadie | 40 | Negro |
| Thomspon, Samuel | 1785 | Manchester Township | 100 | Duke Cumb.'s Reg't |
| Thompson, Samuel | 1790 | Guysborough | T. L. | |
| Thompson, William | 1790 | " (Not reg'd) | T. L. | |
| Thomson, Samuel | 1785 | Guysborough Township | 100 | |
| Thorogood, Lovett | 1784 | Country Harbour, E. | 100 | K.C. Rangers |
| Thorogroog, John | 1784 | " " " | 100 | " " |
| Thurston, Jo. | 1790 | Guysborough (Not reg'd) | 5 | |
| Thurston, Joseph | 1785 | Guysborough Township | 150 | |
| Thurston, Joseph | 1790 | Guysborough | T. L. | |
| Till, Robert | 1790 | " (Not reg'd) | 5 | |
| Tillay, L. | 1790 | " " " | 5 | |
| Tilley, Lewis | 1785 | Manchester Township | 100 | Duke Cumb.'s Reg't |
| Tilley, Lewis | 1790 | Guysborough (Not reg'd) | T. L. | |
| Tillford, James | 1785 | Guysborough Township | 150 | |
| Todd, John | 1785 | Manchester " | 450 | St. Augustine |
| Todd, John | 1788 | New Manchester | 200 | |
| Tool, Charles | 1784 | Country Harbour, E. | 200 | Corp'l R.N.C. Reg't |
| Townsend, William | 1784 | " " " | 300 | Serg't S.C. Reg't |
| Townshend, Mina | 1787 | Tracadie | 40 | Negro |
| Tree, George | 1785 | Guysborough Township | 150 | |
| Tree, George | 1790 | Guysborough (Not reg'd) | 5 | |
| Tree, George | 1790 | " " " | T. L. | |
| Tucker, William | 1785 | Manchester Township | 100 | St. Augustine |
| Tullock, Alexander | 1785 | Guysborough " | 200 | |
| Tullock, Alexander | 1790 | Guysborough | T. L.. | |
| Ule, John | 1790 | Guysborough | T. L. | |
| Ulith, Adam | 1790 | Guysborough (Not reg'd) | T. L. | |
| Uloth, Adam | 1785 | Guysborough Township | 300 | |
| Upnal, Abraham | 1784 | Country Harbour, E. | 100 | K.C. Rangers |
| Upton, John | 1785 | Manchester Township | 100 | Duke Cumb.'s Reg't |
| Upton, John | 1790 | Guysborough | T. L. | |
| Upton, John | 1790 | " (Not reg'd) | T. L. | |
| Vanbright, John | 1787 | Tracadie | 40 | Negro |
| Veal, Joseph | 1785 | Guysborough Township | 100 | |
| Waggoner, Simeon | 1790 | Guysborough (Not reg'd) | T. L. | |
| Waggoner, Simon | 1785 | Guysborough Township | 100 | |
| Wagner, Simeon | 1790 | Guysborough (Not reg'd) | 5 | |
| Walbreight, William | 1785 | Guysborough Township | 200 | |
| Walbretch, William | 1790 | Guysborough | T. L. | |
| Walbright, W. | 1790 | " (Not reg'd) | 5 | |
| Walden, James | 1784 | Country Harbour, E. | 100 | R.N.C. Reg't |
| Waldron, Liffard | 1784 | " " " | 700 | Ensign. K.C. Rangers |
| Walling, John | 1785 | Guysborough Township | 100 | |
| Wallman, John | 1784 | Country Harbour, E. | 100 | K.C. Reg't |

# LOYALISTS AND LAND SETTLEMENT IN NOVA SCOTIA 143

| Name | Date | Situation | Acres | Origin or Rank |
|---|---|---|---|---|
| Walpole, Joseph | 1784 | Bay of St. Lewis | 200 | |
| Wantlow, Andrew | 1785 | Guysborough Township | 100 | |
| Wardlow, Andrew | 1790 | Guysborough (Not reg'd) | T. L. | |
| Wardlow, William | 1785 | Guysborough Township | 200 | |
| Wardlow, William | 1790 | Guysborough | T. L. | |
| Warrington, Henry | 1785 | Guysborough Township | 100 | |
| Warrington, Henry | 1790 | Guysborough | T. L. | |
| Waters, Leven | 1787 | Tracadie | 40 | Negro |
| Watkins, Shaduck | 1785 | Manchester Township | 100 | Duke Cumb.'s Reg't |
| Watson, Charles | 1784 | Country Harbour, E. | 100 | K.C. Rangers |
| Watson, Thomas | 1784 | " " " | 100 | S.C. Reg't |
| Watters, John | 1784 | " " " | 100 | R.N.C. Reg't |
| Weatherford, John | 1790 | Guysborough | T. L. | |
| Weatherford, John | 1790 | " (Not reg'd) | T. L. | |
| Webb, Michael | 1784 | Bay of St. Lewis | 200 | |
| Weeks, George | 1784 | Country Harbour, E. | 100 | Dr. S.C. Reg't |
| Weeks, John | 1784 | " " " | 550 | Ensign. R.N.C. Reg't |
| Weetman, William | 1790 | Guysborough (Not reg'd) | W. L. | |
| Weight, John | 1785 | Guysborough Township | 100 | |
| Welch, David | 1785 | Manchester " | 100 | St. Augustine |
| Weld, Matthew | 1790 | Guysborough (Not reg'd) | T. L. | |
| Weller, Philip | 1785 | Manchester Township | 100 | Duke Cumb.'s Reg't |
| Welsh, Mat. | 1790 | Guysborough (Not reg'd) | 5 | |
| Wendel, Christopher | 1785 | Guysborough Township | 250 | |
| Wendel, Peter | 1785 | " " | 200 | |
| Wetherford, John | 1785 | Manchester Township | 200 | Corp'l Duke Cumb.'s |
| Wetmore, George | 1784 | Bay of St. Lewis | 800 | (Reg't |
| Wheaton, Caleb | 1784 | " " " " | 650 | |
| Wheeler, William | 1785 | Manchester Township | 100 | Duke Cumb.'s Reg't |
| Wheeler, William | 1790 | Guysborough (Not reg'd) | T. L. | |
| Whelan, John | 1790 | " " " | T. L. | |
| White, Gideon | 1785 | Manchester Township | 850 | Capt. Duke Cumb.'s |
| White, Gideon | 1790 | Guysborough (Not reg'd) | T. L. | (Reg't |
| White, Isom | 1790 | " | T. L. | |
| White, Thomas | 1785 | Guysborough Township | 100 | |
| White, Thomas | 1790 | Guysborough (Not reg'd) | T. L. | |
| White, Thomas | 1790 | " " " | W. L. | |
| Whitehead, Andrew | 1787 | Tracadie | 40 | Negro |
| Whitman, George | 1785 | Manchester Township | 100 | Duke Cumb.'s Reg't |
| Whitman, George | 1790 | Guysborough | T. L. | |
| Whitman, George | 1790 | " (Not reg'd) | T. L. | |
| Whitt [White] Isom | 1785 | Manchester Township | 100 | Duke Cumb.'s Reg't |
| Whitt, Isom | 1790 | Guysborough | T. L. | |
| Whitt, John | 1785 | Manchester Township | 100 | Duke Cumb.'s Reg't |
| Whitt, John | 1790 | Guysborough (Not reg'd) | T. L. | |
| Whittendale, Christopher | 1790 | " " " | 5 | |
| Whittendale, Christopher | 1790 | " | T. L. | |
| Wich, Henry | 1790 | " | T. L. | |
| Wick, Henry | 1785 | Guysborough Township | 250 | |
| Wicks, Andrew | 1785 | " " | 100 | |
| Wilkie, Abraham | 1785 | Manchester " | 100 | St. Augustine |
| Willaughby, David | 1790 | Guysborough | T. L. | (Reg't |
| Williams, Daniel | 1785 | Manchester Township | 100 | Drum. Duke Cumb.'s |
| Williams, Daniel | 1790 | Guysborough (Not reg'd) | T. L. | |
| Williams, James | 1785 | Guysborough Township | 100 | |
| Williams, James | 1790 | Guysborough (Not reg'd) | T. L. | |
| Williams, John | 1784 | Country Harbour, E. | 100 | S.C. Reg't |
| Williams, Philip | 1785 | Guysborough Township | 100 | |
| Williams, Philip | 1790 | Guysborough (Not reg'd) | T. L. | |
| Williams, Zephaniel | 1790 | " " " | T. L. | |
| Williams, Zepheon | 1785 | Manchester Township | 100 | Duke Cumb.'s Reg't |
| Willis, George | 1784 | Country Harbour, E. | 100 | S.C. Reg't |
| Willis, Samuel | 1787 | Tracadie | 40 | Negro |
| Willoughby, David | 1785 | Manchester Township | 100 | Duke Cumb.'s Reg't |

PUBLIC ARCHIVES OF NOVA SCOTIA

| Name | Date | Situation | Acres | Origin or Rank |
|---|---|---|---|---|
| Wilson, Francis | 1790 | Guysborough (Not reg'd) | T. L. | |
| Wilson, James | 1784 | Country Harbour, E. | 100 | S.C. Reg't |
| Wilson, John | 1785 | Guysborough Township | 100 | |
| Wilson, John | 1785 | Manchester " | 100 | Duke Cumb.'s Reg't |
| Wilson, John | 1785 | " " | 100 | St. Augustine |
| Wilson, John | 1790 | Guysborough | T. L. | |
| Wilson, John | 1790 | " (Not reg'd) | T. L. | |
| Wilson, Lawrence | 1785 | Guysborough Township | 100 | |
| Wilson, Lawrence | 1790 | Guysborough (Not reg'd) | T. L. | |
| Wilson, Samuel | 1785 | Guysborough Township | 150 | |
| Wilson, Samuel | 1790 | Guysborough (Not reg'd) | 5 | |
| Wilson, Samuel | 1790 | " | T. L. | |
| Wilson, William | 1784 | Country Harbour, E. | 100 | R.N.C. Reg't |
| Win, William | 1784 | " " " | 100 | S.C. Reg't |
| Windell, Peter | 1790 | Guysborough | T. L. | |
| Wingate, Thomas | 1784 | Country Harbour, E. | 100 | S.C. Reg't |
| Wishart, James | 1785 | Manchester Township | 100 | Duke Cumb.'s Reg't |
| Wishart, James | 1790 | Guysborough | T. L. | |
| Wishart, James | 1790 | " (Not reg'd) | T. L. | |
| Wistoff, Jacob | 1787 | Tracadie | 40 | Negro |
| Wood, Henry | 1784 | Country Harbour, E. | 250 | Corp'l R.N.C. Reg't |
| Wooley, John | 1785 | Guysborough Township | 100 | |
| Wooley, John | 1790 | Guysborough (Not reg'd) | T. L. | |
| Wright, James | 1784 | Country Harbour, E. | 1150 | Major K.C. Rangers |
| Wyatt, James | 1785 | Guysborough Township | 800 | |
| Wyatt, James | 1790 | Guysborough (Not reg'd) | 5 | |
| Wyatt, James | 1790 | Guysborough | T. L. | |
| Wyatt, John | 1784 | Country Harbour, E. | 300 | Serg't K.C. Rangers |
| Yallow, Gilbert | 1784 | " " " | 100 | K.C. Rangers |
| Young, William | 1784 | " " " | 100 | " " |

## Sydney County

### WARRANTS

| Name | Date | Situation | Acres | Origin or Rank |
|---|---|---|---|---|
| Armstrong, William | 1788 | Gut of Canso, W. | 700 | Captain 71st. Reg't |
| Chapman, Amos | 1786 | Aubushie Harbour | 500 | |
| Cunningham, Richard | 1785 | Antigonish | 1000 | |
| Dawkins, George | 1786 | Fisherman's Harbour | 500 | |
| Forst, Abraham | 1786 | Next to Jonathan Binney's Land | 300 | |
| Graham, William | 1790 | Milford Haven River | 226 | Captain |
| Graham, William | 1790 | Tracadie | 576 | " |
| Hodgson [Hudson] Thos. | 1786 | Fisherman's Harbour | 700 | " |
| McCalla, Mary (Mrs) | 1785 | Antigonish | 500 | |
| McNeil, Daniel | 1786 | Fisherman's Harbour | 500 | |
| Sickles, John | 1786 | Antigonish | 100 | Qt. Master H.M.S. (Union |

## Sydney County
### ESCHEATS

| Name | Date | Situation | Acres | Esch'd | Origin or Rank |
|---|---|---|---|---|---|
| Brownrigg, Richard Fleetwood | 1785 | Manchester Township | 850 | 1817 | Captain Duke Cumb.'s Reg't |
| Dunnaway, John* | 1785 | " " | 250 | 1820 | Serj't Duke Cumb.'s Reg't |
| McDonald, John | 1785 | Guysborough Township | 300 | 1827 | |
| Osborne, Joseph | 1784 | Bay of St. Lewis | 1000 | 1810 | |
| Peeples [Peebles] John | 1785 | Manchester Township | 500 | 1827 | |
| Stewart, George | 1787 | Guysborough Township Salmon River, S. | 500 | 1812 | Capt. 33rd. Reg't (of Foot |
| Wilson, John | 1785 | Manchester Township | 500 | 1805 | |
| Wyatt, James | 1787 | Salmon River | 500 | 1810 | |

\* There were three other grants escheated with Dunnaway's, but these were not held by original grantees, so are not listed. (See escheat No. 236,).

# APPENDIX A

New York July 22nd 1783

Sir –

Your Excellency's kind attention and offers of your Support to us, demand our warmest Thanks which we beg the Favor of you to Accept –

The unhappy Termination of the War obliges us, who have ever been steady in our Duty as Loyal Subjects to leave our Homes, And being desirous of continuing to enjoy the Benefits of the British Constitution we mean to seek an Asylum in the Province of Nova Scotia –

Considering our several Characters, and our former Situations in Life we trust, you will perceive, that our Circumstances will probably be the Contrast to what they have been heretofore especially as from our respective Occupations we shall be unable personally to obtain the Means of a tollerably decent Support unless Your Excellency shall be pleased to Countenance us, by Your Recommendations, in the following Proposals which are with the utmost Deference submitted for Your Excellency's Consideration –

*First* –That a Tract, or Tracts of land free from disputed Titles be laid out for us, in Nova Scotia, in such Part of that Province as one or more Gentlemen whom we propose to [act] as Agents for that Purpose, being first approved of by Your Excellency shall pitch upon for us –

*Second,* That this Tract or Tracts be sufficient to put us on the same Footing with Field officers in His Majesty's Army with respect to the Number of Acres –

*Third,* That if possible these Lands may be exonerated of Quit-Rents –

*Fourth,* That they be surveyed and divided at the Expence of Government and the Deeds delivered to us, as soon as possible, remitting the Fees of Office –

*Fifth,* That while we make this Application to Your Excellency – we wish not to be understood as Soliciting a compensation for the Losses we have Sustained during the War –Because, we are humbly of opinion, that the Settling such a Number of Loyalists, of the most respectable Characters, who have Constantly had great Influence in His Majesty's American Dominions –will be highly Advantageous in diffusing and supporting a Spirit of Attachment to the British Constitution as well as To, His Majesty's Royal Person and Family –

We have only to add, our earnest Request of Your Excellency's, Aid and Support, in Carrying this Matter into Execution, as soon as it Shall comport with Your Leisure, and to assure Your Excellency, that we are with great Respect

Your Excellency's
Most Humble
And Most Obedient Servants –

| | | |
|---|---|---|
| John Watson | T. Knox | Jos Taylor |
| David Seabury | Ward Chipman | John LeC Roome |
| Andrew Bell | Isaac Wilkins | George Panton |
| Nathl Chandler | Philip J Livingston | Hugh Henderson |
| Rufus Chandler | John Bowden | Samuel Goldsbury |
| A Willard | James Fairlie | Aaron Cortelyon |
| William Wanton | E G Lutwyche | John Smyth |
| Benjn Seaman | Isaac Longworth | William Taylor |
| Richard Seaman | Abijah Willard | Colin Campbell |
| Charles Inglis | John Sayre | Benja Davis |
| Nat Coffin | Anthony Stewart | Wm Campbell |
| George Taylor | Jno Potts | Thomas Horsfield |
| James Anderson | Christopher Billopp | Colborn Barrell |
| Walter Chaloner | Wm Taylor | James Sayre |
| Abia [ther] Camp | James Peters | Harry Peters |
| Bartholomew Crannell | Saml Donaldson | John Mawdsley |
| James Clarke | Thomas Blane | Thomas Banister |
| Joseph Taylor | H Addison | John Moore |
| Stephen Skinner | | |

His Excellency General Sir Guy Carleton
&c &c &c
P.A.N.S. Vol. 369, doc. 135.

To his Excellency Sir Guy Carleton Knight of the most honorable Order of the Bath General and Commander in Chief &ca &ca &ca
The Memorial of the Subscribers

Humbly Sheweth

That your Memorialists having been deprived of very valuable Landed Estates and considerable Personal Propertys without the Lines and being also obliged to abandon their possessions in this City on Account of their Loyalty to their Sovereign and Attachment to the British Constitution and seeing no prospect of their being reinstated –had determined to remove with their Families and settle in His Majesty's Province of Nova Scotia on the Terms which they understood were held out equally to all his Majesty's persecuted Subjects.

That your Memorialists are much alarmed at an application which they are informed Fifty Five Persons have joined in to your Excellency solliciting a recommendation for Tracts of Land in that Province amounting together to Two Hundred and Seventy Five Thousand Acres and that they have dispatched forward Agents to survey the unlocated Lands and select the most fertile Spots and desirable situations.

That chagrined as your Memorialists are at the manner in which the late Contest has been terminated and disappointed as they find themselves in being left to the lenity of their Enemys on the dubious recommendation of their Leaders they yet hoped to find an Assylum under British Protection little suspecting there could be found amongst their Fellow sufferers Persons ungenerous enough to attempt ingrossing to themselves so disproportionate a Share of what Government has allotted for their common benefit –and so different from the original proposals

That your Memorialists apprehend some misrepresentations have been used to procure such extraordinary recommendations the applications for which have been most studiously concealed until now that they boast its being too late to prevent the effect –Nor does it lessen your Memorialists surprise to observe that the Persons concerned (several of whom are said to be going to Britain) are most of them in easy Circumstances and with some Exceptions more distinguished by the repeated favors of Government than by either the greatness of their sufferings or the importance of their Services.

That your Memorialists cannot but regard the Grants in Question if carried into Effect as amounting nearly to a total exclusion of themselves and Familys who if they become Setlers must either content themselves with barren or remote Lands Or –submit to be Tenants to those most of whom they consider as their superiors in nothing but deeper Art and keener Policy –thus Circumstanced

Your Memorialists humbly implore redress from your Excellency and that enquiry may be made into their respective Losses Services Situations and Sufferings and If your Memorialists shall be found equally intitled to the favor and protection of Government with the former applicants – that they may be all put on an equal footing –But should those who first applied be found on a fair and candid inquiry more deserving than your Memorialists –then your Memorialists humbly request that the locating those extensive Grants may at least be postponed untill your Memorialists have taken up such small Portions as may be allotted to them.

And Your Memorialists as in Duty bound shall ever pray &c.

| | | |
|---|---|---|
| Christopher Benson | Peter Tullock | Jas. Birmingham |
| Thos. Farrer | Quinten Robinson | Dinnis Murphy |
| Lancelot Farrer | Isaac Bonnet | Israel Goell [?] |
| George Davies | John Johnston | Humphrey Wady |
| Richd. Horton | Lewis Grant | Christopher Putts |
| Charles McDonald | John Hutchings | William Lewis |
| Robert Cleghorn | William Devenport | Bilious Ward |
| John Watson | Thos. Curren | |

Jno McQueen
Robert McCargor
Joseph Hains
Peter Hauthorn
William Black
Joseph West
Thomson J Reid
his
Abraham x Vantassel¹
mark
David Wilson
Jos Zarighan
James Stewart
John Hislop
James Scott
Ralph Brankston
Andre Eastman
John Currie
Andw Watson
John Kerr
Scott L Clark
Stephen Hayden
S. Coops
Danl Ketcham
Jas Ketchum
Peter Gyre
Andrew Bennetts
John Harrison
James Rogers
Daniel James Brooke
Hugh Kelly, B. Master
  Brooklyn
John Parr
John Huggeford
Jacob C-----[?]
Robert Bell
Henry Graham
George Wilson
James Skean
Alexander Boyn
James Wilmot
Michael Schooley
Christopher Hennegar
Adam Hannegar
Michael Henegar
Edward Mooney
William Mooney
John Mooney
Jacob Hoffman
Saml. Pell
Samuel Stillwell
David Braymer
Charles Kingsland

John Gordan
John Van Emburgh
John Davis
Philip Eley
Caleb White
John Barron
Benjamin Graves
James Tillot
William Peters
John Yeamons
Malank Thorn
Samuel Peters
Moses Beal
Danl Pine
Gilbert Forbes
Quintin Millen
Hugh Millen
Lockard Backstcr
Solomon Baxter
Enock Mulnix
Gideon Baxter
John Baker
Jarvis Coles
Charles Ackermann
William Sinsebaugh
James Clubb
John Booth
Andrew Durand
Isaac Redman
Timothy Cain
Laurence Fegan
Richard Chambers
Benjn Head
Josiah Davis
Joseph Paxton
Hugh Dreake
Fredke Wiser [Hisen]
his
Andrew x Lintner
mark
John Bond
Thomas Potts
his
John x Anderson
mark
his
William x Hodges
mark
Benjamin Brown
John Wiggins
Alexander Simpson
Amos Dillon
Edwd Johnston

Thomas flunrelling [sic]
Thomas Ireland
Hugh Ellis
William Buiota
his
Abraham x Lockwood
mark
his
Joseph x Fluell
mark
Alexr Cowon
Arthur B. Nugent
William Style
Thos Chadwick
Thomas Bird
John Warnock
Michl Hutchinson
John Fitzpatrick
Luke Bird
Hugh Mcdonll
Joseph Thomas
Joseph Botner
Sam Street
John Gomez
John Marsh
Sam[u]el aiken [sic]
Owen Hughes
Cornelius Helling [Flelling]
Amos Rooke
Rouillin McQuilin
John Jones
Frederick Bender
Benjn Harrison
his
William x Bethell
mark
his
John x Burns
mark
Abraham Barrey
William Williams
George Ensor
John groff [sic]
Daniel Hugunien
James Nicholls
James Goff
James Cuthbert
his
Willm x Molleneaux
mark
Davis Haltridge
Louhn McLean
Mikel McDonel

James Maine
John Bain
Thos Cotton
Thos. Treadwell Smith
Albt. V. Norstrand
Stephen x Baxter
    his mark
Samuel Baker
Philip Lenzi
John Clark
Willm Muckelvain
George Conoly
Elijah Sandford
John Ferrel
John Lawson
Nathaniel Lcofbourrow
Archd Herly
Wm Farrer
Thomas Clapp
Dionys. O'Reily
Joshua Pell
Jonathin Pell
James Mitchell
Jas. Stivens
William Bathgate
Patrick McL: Way
Geo. Shaw
Robt. McGinnis
Geo. Linkleter
John Humes
David Mallows Junr
David H Mallows
Samuel Magkee
Christopher Hanigar
John Maghee
Adam Hanigar
Jacob Mellows
Wm. Russell
John Huggéford
Jacob Jeroleman
Dennis Kennedy
John Bicker
Wm Caldwell
Adam Graves
Nichs Andrews
Jno. Geo Graves
Anovy Offhoner
Christian Weynan
Conrad Andrews
Geo Ryme
Jacob Shaw
Robt. Robertson

John Collin
Robert Fenton
Rich. McGinnis
Jacob Likeson
Charles Anno
John Slone
Abm. Rhyhart
John Forrester
John McGinnis
Alexr. Hakkett
John Patterson
James Smith
John Holmes
Henry Humphrey
Alexr. McGraugham
Henry Dawson
Elijah Fowler
John Dougherty
James McNeil
Thomas Henning
Jas Dickinson
James Trinder
Isaa gedney [sic]
Ezekil Bramon
William green [sic]
John Robinson
Thomas Houston
Samuel Barns
Benjamin Birdsill
Isaac Devenport
Thomas Devenport
Andres Bohaker
Andres Bohaker Junr
Wm Caldwell
Wm Musse:ls ⎫
John Hendersons ⎬ Pillots
Robert Beenath ⎭ [sic]
Thos Edwards
S Waterbury
John Oman S Peters
Thos De St. Croix
Anthony Closson
Christian Brenan
Samuel Street
Jasper Drake
John Kennedy
John Cottrell
William Johnson
John Monan
Thomas Bowden
Micll Nugent
John Mortal

    his
Jacob x Brower
    mark
Thomas Semple
Samuel Washburn
Thomas Spragg
Reuben Finch
Daniel odell [sic]
andrew brundige [sic]
John C. Baxter [sic]
Joseph Dowers
Jehunder hill [sic]
Janeihesen [sic]
johannes mejer [sic]
Gilbert Purdy
Thomas Purdy
Lancelot Smith
Richard Deleney
    his
John x Bates
    mark
    his
Jeremiah x Gans
    mark
John Faulkner
Thomas Faulkner
    his
George x Woolf
    mark
William Woderspoon
James McLean
Robert Hill
Jeremiah Rushton
William Totten
Thos. Barker
Thomas Wotton
John P Smith
Samuel Totten
Aaron Fowler
Joseph Prichard
    his
John x Howell
    mark
Peter Farrah
    his
Jonan x Worden
    mark
Cornelius Steger
John Burns
Abrm Cunard
Amos Lockwood
Edward Pryor
John Houseman
Thomas Barker

Ebenr Street
Thomas Goudge
Dennis Cronin
Henry Gower
Abraham Golding
his
Josiah x Fowler
mark
Abram Tilley
James Barron
his
Peter x Wood
mark
Edward Dawkins
William muir [sic]
his
John x Clark
mark
Peter Totten
Matthew Mangan
Saml Marshall
Andrew Brown
Thos Cunningham
his
Thomas x Lowrie
mark
Patrick MaCay
John makay [sic]
Joseph mckeel sic]
Thoms Merritt
Abraham Iredell [Tredell]
Jno Hackett
Isaac Atken
Andw Snodgrass
Ezekiel youmans [sic]
his
James x Ramsey
mark
James Hamilton
John Ritchie
Joseph Galbreath
John Hardwick
David Peterkin
David Smith
Alexr Munro
James Rose
John McQueen
John Ure
Johallen [sic]
his
John x Allen
mark

his
John x Parker
mark
John Ryan Junior
John Ryan [Senior] Seijnor
Thomas Florantine
his
Abraham x Florantine
mark
Nathl. Dowdney
James fergus [sic]
Gilbert Bush
Zefaniah hubbs [sic]
Joseph Hubbs
John Martin
John Haines
Thos Robblee
Jeremiah mabee [sic]
Andrew fowler [sic]
Ben., Hunts C 5
of Vr. Cl. Mil
Will: Branthwaite
Jno Cameron
Gorge Carskadon
Daniel Hammill
Titus Babb
John A Hardenbrook
Alexander Carskaden
Thomas Carskadon
John Driver
Michl. McDonnell
Abel Hardenbrook
Robt. Cannell
Edward Lockwood
Thomas H Wagstaffe
James V: Buren
George Davis
Robert Fenton Junr.
John Smith
his
Jacob x Brill
mark
Robart Thorn
Thomas Pearsall
Abel Southan
Ebenr Spicer
Charles Cann
his
Henry x Pearsall
mark
his
Jonathan x Mott
mark
Elias Glover

Danl. Baldwin
Wm King
Richard Bonsall
Nehet. Clarke
Nicholas A Hardenbrook
Peter Roome
Robt. Wood
Gideon Palmer
James x Mullennex
Jeremiah Fowler
Jeremiah Fowler Junr
Amous Fowler
Abijah Miller
Isaac Baxter
Milkington Lockwood
Ambrose Haight
Wilet Carpenter
Cales Carpenter
Daniel Lyon
Henry Watkeys
Joseph Robinson
Jonathan Fowler
his
Tunis x D'Ferger
mark
Weden fowler [sic]
Matthew Buckley
Stephen Embree
James Irwin
Thomas Seaman
Jose Ishbadd
O Jono Haines
Jotham Willson
Nathanel T Taylor
Jeremiah Andeson
Daniel Tuttle
James Seacord
Joseph Prescott
John Miller
James Chadwick
Ephm Sanford
Joseph Smith
Fagann Rab
Joseph Smith
his
William x Burnse
mark
his
Abraham x Bazeley
mark
Isaac Hamman
John Shoemaker
Wm. Williams

Edmund Ward
Joshua T. De St. Croix
John Blair
Henry Ackerman
James Totten
Wm. Maxey
John Willson
Benjn. Daggetts
Peres Gilbert
Ambrose Cleavland
Robt. Colefax
Isaac Livesay
Hezekiah Smith
Robt. Henley
Solomon Hains
his
Barrey x Waldron
mark
Cornelius Ackerman
James Rankin
Wm. White
John Stevenson
Duncan Ferguson
Christr. Carter
Frederick Davoue
Jacob Muss
Simon Bantal
Ferk. Hickey
John Deforest
Thomas Hunter
his
James x Morehouse
mark
his
Noah x Morehouse
mark
his
Hezekiah x Smith
mark
Henry Dusinberry
Fitch Rogers
Jared Bell
Henry Woolley
Stephen Thorne
John Fegan
Alexr Murray Pilot
Hough Hamilton
John Cameron
James Blaike
Philip Phende [?]
Beniamen Lewis
John Evins

Joseph Burchell
Jarvis Roebuck
Uriah Pearsall
James Brebner
William Gordon
Wm Cook
Robert moor [sic]
his
Jacob x Staman
mark
his
Jacob x Senbech
mark
Jesse Evans
Robert Samson
Thomas Gillespie
Danl Fraser
Samuel Hake
Daniel Wright
John Hinshull
Samuel Jarvis
Abel Hardenbrook Junr
Robt Leonard
J Leonard
Danl Leonard
Lawrence Hortwick
John Casey
Daniel Dunscomb
Adam Watson
Frs Conihane
Samuel Devenport
James Robertson
Mamon Jarvis
Isaac Bell
David Roberts
Thomas Hanlord
Joseph Thorne
John McKee
Samuel Dickinson
John Miller
his
John x Hahan
mark

Samuel X Clark

John McMahon
John Perrot
John Welsh
Thos. Berry
William Holmes
David Wright

Moses Smith
his
William x Thorne
mark
Roger Shannon
Thomas Nickeson
Archelaus Carpenter
William Cunningham
Thomas North
Richard Mathews

Daniel X Campbell

William Snyder
Lawrence Van Buskirk
John Crabb
Richard Collier
John Reeves
James Wall

Thompson X Harwood

Matthew Partelon
Thos Woolley
Jas Leonard

Benj X Archard

Caleb Morgan
James Inglis
Stephen Marchant
James Hearn
Geo: Dennison
John G. Van Norden
theunis Blauvelt [sic]

James X Beasley

James Jordan
Nicholas Conehein
Wm Demayne
John Hockenhull
Jos: Rd De Peyster
William Doty
Jesse Bunnels
Israel Rogers
Elias Botner
William Blisard
John McGie
Isaac Reed
Edward Arvin /Irvin]
Jacob Philips

James Carskadon      George Fasdo              Samuel Dea
Wm Carskadon         Wm Gillas                 Thos Austin
Benjn Brooks         Danl Elliot               Will Slant
   his               John Bridgson             James Hariss [?]
Robert x B Barber    Isaac Swayze              Leggett Lawrence
   mark              Alexr. McDonald           David Harper
Robert Mills         Joseph Fox                Luke Owens
Edwd Agar            John Burket [Burker]      James Banner
Joseph Cowan         Nathaniel Taylor          Andrew Murray
John Wallace         Leonard Tarrant           Alexdr. Watson
John Smith           Edward Taylor             Thomas Lawrence
James Jerimiah Rice  Joseph Pence              Samuel Parr [?]
John Tancay [?]      Benja. Farrar             Daniel Southick
Ths. Mahan           Thos. Mounsey             Jameson Cox
John Eager           John Brecken              Wm McMeetnie [?]
James Van Emburgh    James Sproull             John Vanlan
George Fisher        William Sproull           John Hornor
John Tolley          John Sproull              Andrew Laul
Richard ackerman [sic]  Jehiel Partelon        Thomas King
Adoniah Van Emburgh  Francis King              Edward Jones
Jer: Connor

# Appendix B

Douglass 1st Jany 1815

To the Honorable Speaker & the Honourable House of Assembly – –

Gentlemen,

  The Pettition of your Subscribers Most respectfully Sheweth – – That Whereas in the year of our Lord 1783, on the Proclamation of Peace between Great Britain & the United States of AMERICA, his Majestys late 84th. regiment was discharged with a Promise of a certaine proportion of Lands to Officers Non commisd officers & privates, free of any charges from his Majestys Government as a compensation for their Serviseses during the late contest with america, to such as would actually Settle & become Inhabitants: In consequence of which Colo. Small the commandant of sd. regt. Procured a Grant in trust for sd. regt.; upon the Strength of which a number of sd. regt. Settled in the wilderness where they encountered many difiquelties Namely up cannetcook, five mile & Nine Mile Rivers, now called the Township of Douglass and because the Major part of sd. regimt. did abscond & abandon their Lands, and a number of other persons (trying to avail themselves of the same Priviledge the

Soldiers had Promised) Settled in among us who were actually Soldiers, and on acct: of Colo. Smalls Grant not being fully Complied with according to Government wish, it became Escheated with that reserve, that those disbanded Soldiers whom had actually Settled Should be established in their former Promise; and the same lands, altho long ago Settled, is still Lying under the same escheet, & neither of your Petitioners, have any title to our farmes  We therefore pray the Lajislative body will represent our Situation to his Majestys Council & to the Goverour, expressing our wish to obtain a Genel. Grant to the undersigned who were actually Soldiers as it was originally intended of their then Promised Locations for themselves & families, Previous to their new applications Since whereof a true return will be laid before you with the names of the occupiors of the above description at present residing in the above Township, and your Petitioners will ever pray —

Lewis Ettinger
Thomas Laffen
Christian Heniger
Archd Carr
Widdow Carr
Finley Murdock
Wm Gill
John P. McDonald
James Dalrymple
Widdow McDougall
Donald McDonald
John McDonald Senr
John McDonald
Thomas Welch

Donald Grant
Alexander Scott
John McNeil
James McPhee
Donald McDougall, Senr.
Alexander McPhee Senr
Even McPhee
Donald McPhee
Alexr. McDonald
Alexr. Ferguson
Dond. McDonald
John Grant
Peter Grant

Donald McDougall
Dun: McKinzie
Malcolm McKenzie
Donald McKinzie
Alexr. Ferguson
John Ferguson
Donald Thompson
James Thompson
Alexr. Thompson
Neal Frasers Widdow & her son Donald Fraser
Stephen Taggard
John Rafter